teach yourself...

dBASE IV

CHARLES SIEGEL

A Subsidiary of
Henry Holt and Co., Inc.

Copyright © 1993 by Management Information Source, Inc.
a subsidiary of Henry Holt and Company, Inc.
115 West 18th Street
New York, New York 10011

All rights reserved. Reproduction or use of editorial or pictorial content in any manner is prohibited without express permission. No patent liability is assumed with respect to the use of the information contained herein. While every precaution has been taken in the preparation of this book, the publisher assumes no responsibility for errors or omissions. Neither is any liability assumed for damages resulting from the use of the information contained herein.

Throughout this book, trademarked names are used. Rather than put a trademark symbol after every occurrence of a trademarked name, we used the names in an editorial fashion only, and to the benefit of the trademark owner, with no intention of infringement of the trademark. Where such designations appear in this book, they have been printed with initial caps.

First Edition—1991

ISBN 1-55828-263-7

Printed in the United States of America.

10 9 8 7 6 5 4 3 2 1

MIS:Press books are available at special discounts for bulk purchases for sales promotions, premiums, fund-raising, or educational use. Special editions or book excerpts can also be created to specification.

For details contact: Special Sales Director
MIS:Press
a subsidiary of Henry Holt and Company, Inc.
115 West 18th Street
New York, New York 10011

Trademarks:
Epson is a trademark of Seiko Epson Corporation
FoxBASE and FoxPro are trademarks of Fox Software, Inc.
Hewlett-Packard is a trademark of Hewlett-Packard Company
LaserWriter is a trademark of Apple Computer
MS-DOS is a trademark of Microsoft Corporation
WordStar is a trademark of Wordstar International, Inc.
dBASE is a trademark of Ashton-Tate Corporation

*To Bernie and Helen Navasky
of Phillipsburg, Mystic Pointe and Malibu*

Acknowledgements

It is impossible to thank everyone who works on a book, but I would like to give special thanks to the following people: Dawn Erdos for her excellent job of editing and technical review, Patricia Wallenburg for her layout and production work, Cary Weinberger for bringing it all together, and finally thanks to Steve Berkowitz.

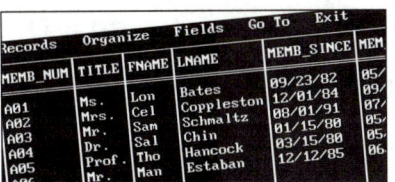

Contents

Introduction 1

    Is This Book for You? 2

PART 1 ◆ UP AND RUNNING

Chapter 1: Introducing dBASE IV 7

A Quick Tour of dBASE IV 8

    Using dBASE IV 8

    dBASE IV Catalogs 10

    The Control Center 10

    Pull-Down Menus 17

    A Note on Indexes 23

    The Help System 24

    Summary 26

Chapter 2: Creating a Database File 27

Fields and Records 28
Data Types 28
Analyzing the Database 30
    Breaking Down the Data 31
One-to-One Relationships 32
    The Fields of the Sample Database 34
Working with Catalogs 36
    Creating a New Catalog 36
    Other Operations with Catalogs 38
Creating a Database File 41
Using a Database 49
Modifying the Structure of a File 50
Summary 52

Chapter 3: Entering, Editing, and Viewing Data 53

Edit and Browse Modes 54
The Editing Keys 56
The Browse and Edit Menu Systems 58
    The Records Menu 58
    Marking and Deleting Records 59
    The Go To Menu 61
    The Exit Menu 61
Memo Fields 62
    The dBASE IV Word Processor 63

Editing Memo Fields 64

Automatic Indent.. 65

Saving Changes in the Word Processor 66

Working with Sample Data 66

The Fields Menu.. 72

Moving Around the Database... 76

Adding Groups of Records from Other Files...................................... 78

Summary 80

Chapter 4: Indexing and Sorting.. 81

The Differences Between Indexing and Sorting 82

Should You Index or Sort?... 82

The Advantages of Indexing 83

The Disadvantages of Indexing.. 83

Types of Index Files... 84

Indexing Your Database 85

Creating a Simple Index 85

Indexing on Multiple Fields 88

Using Indexes.. 89

Modifying or Removing an Index 92

Sorting 93

Summary 95

Chapter 5: Queries... 97

Searches and Queries 98

Searching for a Single Record... 98
    Unindexed Searches 99
    Indexed Searches 100
Queries... 102
    The Basics of the File and View Skeleton 105
    Altering the View Skeleton 109
    Using Delimiters 111
    Using Operators 112
    The $ Operator 115
    Queries Using LIKE and SOUNDS LIKE 116
    Queries with AND and OR 117
    Finding a Single Record 122
    Speeding Up Queries 123
    Other Features of Queries 124
Summary 133

Chapter 6: Quick Reports, Advanced Queries, and Mailing Labels 135

The Print Menu 137
Quick Reports 138
    Printing a Quick Report 139
    Editing Column Headings 139
    A Sample Quick Report 140
Advanced Queries 144
    Calculated Fields 144
    Summary Queries 148

Mailing Labels 152

    Designing a Label Form 153

    Modifying the Label Form 160

    Printing Labels 161

    Sample Labels 162

Summary 166

Chapter 7: Formatted Reports 167

The Basics of Report Design 168

    Report Bands 169

    Quick Layouts 173

    Field Display Attributes 176

    Other Features of the Report Generator 186

A Sample Report 192

Grouping the Records in Reports 198

    Modifying or Removing a Group 200

    A Sample Report with Groups 201

Summary 205

PART 2 ◆ ADDING POWER

Chapter 8: Forms and Quick Applications 209

About Custom Forms and Applications 210

Forms 210

The Menu System of the Forms Design Screen 211
The Display Attributes Menu 214
A Sample Form 223
Quick Applications 231
Summary 236

Chapter 9: Utilities 237

The Word Processor 238
Editing Keys 239
The Words Menu 241
The Go To Menu 246
The Print Menu 248
The Basics 249
Print Forms 250
Controlling Printing 251
Controlling the Printer 253
The Tools Menu 257
Macros 257
Import/Export 260
DOS Utilities 262
Protect Data 269
Settings 269
Summary 273

Chapter 10: Relational Databases 275

About Relational Databases 276

Normalizing Data 277
    The One-to-Many Relationship 277
    The Many-to-Many Relationship 279
    More Complex Data 280
    The Key Field 282

Creating the Database 283

Creating a Query to Join Related Files 286

Including All Records 289

Working with a Relational Database 291
    Viewing and Editing Data 291
    Finding Specific Records 291
    Sorting the Data 296
    Reports 298

More Complex Data 301

Summary 305

PART 3 ◆ THE dBASE LANGUAGE

Chapter 11: dBASE Expressions 309

Why Learn Expressions and Commands 310

Using the Dot Prompt 310

Expressions 313
    Literals 314
    Memory Variables 316

Functions 318

Operators 328

Logical Expressions 331

The Expression Builder... 336

Summary 337

Chapter 12: dBASE Commands 339

About Commands 340

The Database File 341

Adding, Editing, and Viewing Data................................ 342

Using the Browse and Edit Screens 343

Other Commands for Editing and

Viewing Data 343

Deleting Records 345

Moving the Pointer.. 345

Indexed and Unindexed Searches........................... 346

Indexes 346

Using Other Objects.. 347

Using Label and Report Forms 348

Using Queries and Data Entry Forms 348

Creating and Using Applications and

Programs 348

SET Commands 349

Settings that Toggle ON and OFF............................ 349

Settings Using TO 350

Contents ◆ **xiii**

    Sending Output to the Printer or a File 350

    Scope, Fields, FOR, and WHILE Clauses 351

    Specifying the Scope of a Command 351

    Specifying a Field List 353

    FOR and WHILE Clauses 354

    Quick Reports Using LIST 356

Relational Databases 358

    Using Multiple Files at the Same Time 358

    Setting a Relation 360

Indispensable Utilities 362

Summary 362

Chapter 13: An Introduction to Programming 363

Programming Basics 364

The Mechanics of Creating a Program 364

    A Sample Program 367

    Errors 369

    The Esc Key 371

Simple Input/Output 372

Structured Programming 377

    Selection 378

    IF ... ELSE ... ENDIF 378

    The IF ... ELSE Ladder 381

    DO CASE ... ENDCASE 382

    Looping 384

    Modular Program Design 389

Formatted Input/Output 397

    A Sample Program 398

    Format Files 401

Summary 406

Chapter 14: Programming an Application 407

Analysis 408

    Structuring the Program 409

    Other Basic Issues 410

The Main Menu 411

    Setting Environment Variables 414

    Adding the Main Loop 415

    Restoring the Environment 416

Stub Testing 416

The View Submenu 420

The PRNTCHK Module 425

The Modify Submenu 426

The Report Submenu 434

The Label Submenu 439

Summary 442

Appendix A

Installing dBASE IV 445

Installation 445

A Note on Configuring dBASE IV 447

Introduction

dBASE has been the industry standard database management system ever since IBM introduced its first personal computers. Its users range from people without specialized computer training—who use it for simple tasks such as managing mailing lists—to software developers, who use it as a programming language to create complex, specialized data management applications.

When the IBM PC first appeared, dBASE II, which had already been popular on earlier computers, quickly established itself as the most widely used program for managing lists of names and addresses and other similar business data. Like many other programs on early PC's—MS-DOS, for example—it required the user to learn commands and enter them at a prompt.

As an extra feature, dBASE II let users put lists of commands in program files, so you could simply run the program instead of typing in an entire list of commands at the prompt every time. It also included a few commands that could not be used at the prompt, which were designed specifically to make programs a bit more powerful. This simple programming facility was enough to attract a group of people who thought of dBASE as a programming language and who stretched it until it did things its designers had never dreamed of.

dBASE III and dBASE III PLUS added features to dBASE II for both users and programmers. The ASSIST mode made the program easier for users by letting them work from menus rather than memorizing and entering commands. Extensions to the dBASE language gave it almost all of the features of most ordinary programming languages, in addition to the special features it had that made it easy to use to manage data.

dBASE IV goes much further.

The user interface has been completely redesigned for ease of use. The Control Center makes it easy to see at a glance exactly what you can do. Query By Example (QBE) makes it easy to find records that you need without having to learn complex programming expressions. The band-oriented reports design screen gives you a simple but very powerful way to create formatted reports.

Later versions of dBASE IV add some new features to the ones included in versions 1.0 and 1.1. Version 1.5 adds mouse support, makes it easier to edit relational databases, improves the performance of queries, and includes many extensions of the dBASE language for advanced programmers. Version 2.0 also includes extensions of the language for advanced programmers, but its most important difference from earlier versions, as far as the average user is concerned, is that it takes advantage of the more powerful hardware that many users now have to speed up performance. Earlier versions of dBASE IV can run using 640 kilobytes of RAM; version 2.0 requires 4 megabytes of RAM, and it uses all of this extra memory to make the program run more quickly.

The dBASE language now has all of the features of ordinary programming languages and much more. For example, it not only has arrays and user-defined functions but also includes commands that make it easy to create windows and pop-up menus.

Both beginners and advanced programmers will find that dBASE now is more powerful than ever.

Is This Book for You?

This book takes you from the basics of using the dBASE IV menu-driven Control Center all the way to programming a complete application. It is designed so that it can be used in several different ways.

Part 1, *Up and Running*, gives you the most direct introduction possible to the essentials of using dBASE IV, to allow you get to work as quickly as possible. This part of the book introduces you to the dBASE IV user interface and teaches you to create a database file, add, edit, and delete data, use indexes to put the data in the order you want, use Query By Example to find the data you want, and create mailing labels and reports—all you need to know for many ordinary applications.

Part 1 of this book serves as a quick introduction to dBASE IV for people who want to get right down to work. Unlike most tutorials, Part 1 does not make beginners spend time on more advanced features of the program, such as dBASE *expressions*, which they might never use. As its name indicates, it is the most direct way to get "up and running" with the program. Part 1 is enough to make you a competent dBASE IV user. You can read it and get right to work and, if you want, you can come back and read more of the book later.

Part 2 is for people who want to move beyond the basics and become dBASE IV power users. It introduces you to all of the features of the dBASE IV interface. For example, you learn about *macros,* which save you work by letting you execute a series of commands with a single keystroke. You learn about *custom data entry forms*, which let you set up the screen so it is easy for a novice to enter data and use templates to validate the data that is entered. And you learn to use *relational databases*, to analyze your data and break it up into several files—something that is sometimes necessary to avoid duplication of stored data and increase the efficient operation of your database.

Part 2 of this book teaches you everything you need to know about dBASE IV if you do not want to learn a programming language. If you want to get the most from dBASE IV by using its menu-driven interface—without having to make the effort to learn dBASE commands and expressions—then you should read this book through Part 2.

Finally, Part 3 of this book is a tutorial on the dBASE language and on programming. First, it introduces dBASE expressions and commands, which can be useful to dBASE users as well as to programmers. Then it uses dBASE to introduce you to the basic principles of computer programming with an emphasis on structured programming techniques. Finally, Part 3 guides you through the process of writing a complete program of the sort that a dBASE programmer might actually write to set up a menu-driven system for a specific application that would allow users who know nothing about using dBASE to manage data simply by making choices from the menus.

dBASE is an extremely rich programming language and it has more features than can be covered in any one book. Part 3 of this book introduces you to the fundamental principles of dBASE programming. Once you have learned the basics, you can go on to study books on advanced dBASE programming or you can learn more about programming by browsing through reference books of dBASE commands and functions, such as the *dBASE IV Language Reference* that comes with the program or through one of the many dBASE IV programmer's references that are available at book stores. This book will not make you an expert dBASE programmer, but it gives you a thorough grounding in the basics. What you learn is good preparation to go on to study advanced dBASE programming, and how to set up simple, menu-driven applications for other dBASE users.

This book uses graphic icons to note specific warnings, time-saving tips or suggestions that you may find helpful. They include:

Proceed with caution. Data may be lost if procedure is not followed closely.

Suggestions to keep in mind when using dBASE IV.

Time-saving shortcuts or tips for ease in using the dBASE program.

Part 1

UP AND RUNNING

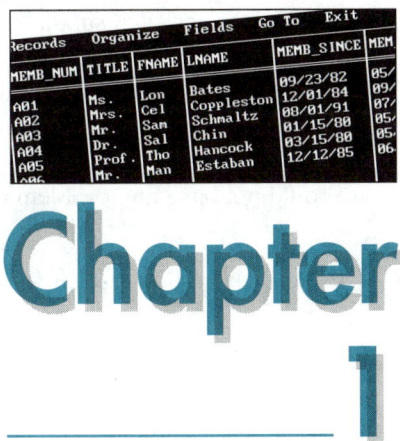

Chapter 1

Introducing dBASE IV

This chapter teaches you the basics of dBASE IV, including how to use the dBASE menu-driven Control Center interface and the context-sensitive Help System.

In this chapter you learn:

- ◆ How to start dBASE IV from DOS
- ◆ The basics of the Control Center interface
- ◆ How to navigate in the Control Center
- ◆ How to use the pull-down menus
- ◆ How to return to the Control Center from dBASE IV dot prompt
- ◆ How to use the on-line Help System
- ◆ How to exit dBASE IV

This book also uses DOS subdirectories to help you organize your work, and the exercises in this book assume that you are using the DOS PATH command to let you run dBASE IV from any subdirectory. The dBASE installation program automatically alters the PATH command in your AUTOEXEC.BAT file in this way when the program is installed according to the directions in the appendix, so you should not have any problem running it from any subdirectory.

A Quick Tour of dBASE IV

Before you go on to learn the details of how to use dBASE IV, you should take a look at its interface to see, in general, the sorts of things that it lets you do. The interface is so simple to understand that you should have no trouble getting a general idea of how to use dBASE IV just by looking at its main screen, which is called the *Control Center*.

For now, you might find it easiest to think of dBASE simply as a tool for managing lists—such as the lists of names, addresses, and telephone numbers that are kept in an address book or on Rolodex cards. In Part 1 of this book, you will learn to use dBASE to keep simple lists of this sort. In Part 2 of this book, you will see that dBASE also allows you to manage data in complex ways by creating *relational databases*.

Of course, when you are keeping these lists on a computer, you can use them in much more powerful way than you could when you were keeping them on paper. You can print out reports or mailing labels as simply as pressing a button. You can use your data in different orders for different purposes; for example, you can print your mailing labels in zip code order and print your reports in alphabetical order by name. You can instantly find the name that you want, rather than flipping through card after card to search for it. And you can use data that meets certain criteria: For example, you could print mailing labels only for people who live in California.

Using dBASE IV

Before you can use dBASE IV, it must be installed on your computer. If you still have dBASE in the package and have not installed it yet, see Appendix A of this book for instructions on installation.

Once dBASE IV is installed on your computer, you are ready to create a working subdirectory and to start the program: You may want to name this working directory LEARNDB, since you are using it to learn dBASE. Before you start the exercise, make sure you are at the DOS prompt in the disk drive that you want to use for the exercises. For example, if you want to use drive C (the usual designation for the hard drive) for the exercises, and you are not sure whether you are in the right drive, enter the command *C:* before beginning.

1. To create a subdirectory to hold the exercises in this book, type *md \learndb* and press **Enter**.
2. To make this subdirectory the current directory, type *cd \learndb* and press **Enter.**
3. To start dBASE IV, type *dbase* and press **Enter**.

If you have used dBASE IV on your computer previously, some of the results may not match exactly those described in this book.

N O T E

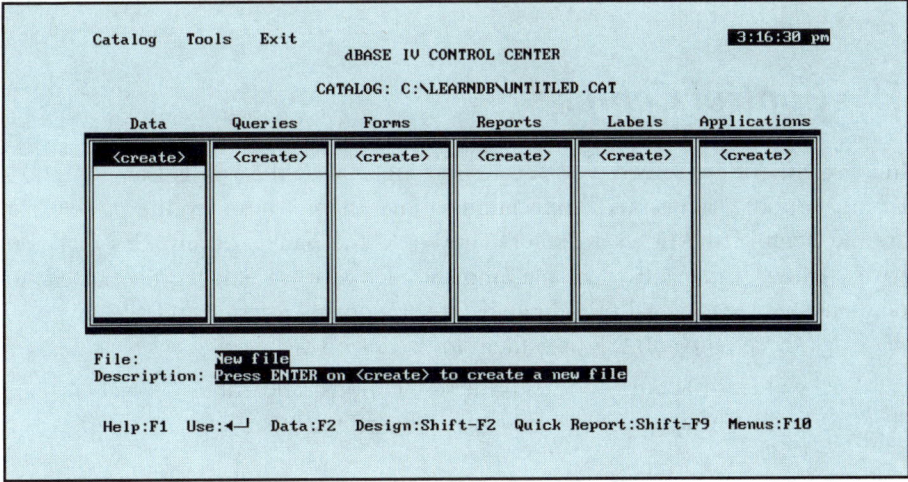

Figure 1.1 *The dBASE IV Control Center.*

The dBASE IV Control Center is shown in Figure 1.1. (For instructional purposes, some illustrations in this chapter include the MEMBERS file that you will create in Chapter 2.) The Control Center is the heart of the dBASE IV interface, and you can understand a great deal about how the program works simply by looking at it carefully.

dBASE IV Catalogs

At the center of the screen, near the top, you see the words dBASE IV CONTROL CENTER. Immediately underneath are the words: CATALOG: C:\LEARNDB\UNTITLED.CAT, the name of the current catalog and the subdirectory it is in.

In older versions of dBASE, you had to rely on your memory to keep track of all of the files you created to hold data, mailing labels, reports, and so on—and, needless to say, it was often a strain to remember the names of the files for each application you used.

A dBASE IV catalog is simply a collection of related files. dBASE IV catalogs give you an easier way of keeping track of your files. The names of all of the files you have created for a single application are displayed when you use the catalog you created for that application.

When you begin, dBASE IV displays a catalog named UNTITLED.CAT. (All catalogs have the extension CAT following their name.) In a moment, you will see how to use the menu system to name a catalog or to use a catalog that you created earlier.

The Control Center

In the center of the screen, you see six rectangles with the words Data, Queries, Forms, Reports, Labels, and Applications above them. These are the *panels* that are the heart of the Control Center. They hold the names of any files that you have created to manage your data, and they let you use existing files or create new ones very easily. All of the panels are sometimes referred to collectively as the *work space*, since dBASE uses them to organize your work.

You will learn about the Data, Queries, Reports, and Labels panels in Part 1 of this book. These panels are basic to using dBASE IV.

- **Data**: contains the names of database files that you have created. These are the actual files that hold your data: they contain lists of names and addresses or similar lists.
- **Reports**: contains the names of *report formats* (often called *report forms* for short). To create one of these files, you design a printed report: the dBASE reports design screen lets you choose what data is included in the report and how it is arranged, and lets you add other features to the

report. Reports are discussed in greater detail in Chapters 6 and 7 of this book. Once you have created a report format, you can save it and use it any time to print a report.

- **Labels**: contains the name of label formats (or label forms), which are similar to report formats. When you create one, you use a special screen that lets you specify how you want the data to appear on the label, the size of your labels, and so on. Once you have created a label format, you can use it to print out mailing labels for all of the names and addresses (or any other data) currently in your database. You will learn to create label forms in Chapter 6.

- **Queries**: contains the names of queries, which are among the most powerful features of dBASE IV. Among other things, queries let you specify which data will be used. If you want to print mailing labels only for addresses in California, for example, you can do this by using a query that includes only those in which the address is in California, and then using the Label form. To create a query, you use a special Query By Example screen, which makes it very easy to design even sophisticated queries. Once they have been created, queries can be used at any time with the data currently in the database file, like reports and labels.

When you create a report form or label form, dBASE IV generates a program that it uses to print the report or labels that you designed. If you are a programmer, you can modify these generated dBASE programs to add other features to the reports or labels. However, you do not have to know anything about programming to be able to use the report and label features.

As you can see, the Control Center also includes panels for Forms and Applications. These are more advanced features of dBASE IV that are used primarily to set up the program for novices. Forms lets you create custom data entry forms and Applications lets you create programs. These features of dBASE will be covered in Parts 2 and 3 of this book.

If you have a mouse, versions 1.5 and later of dBASE IV display a solid block that moves when you move the mouse. This is called the *mouse pointer*. You can move it to any location on the screen and use it in three ways:

- **Click**: press the mouse button for an instant and release it.
- **Double-click**: press the mouse button and release it twice in rapid succession.

- **Drag (or Click and Drag)**: press the mouse button and hold it down, move the mouse to relocate the pointer, and release the button when the pointer is in a new location.

In any case, if your mouse has more than one button, you must use its left button: other buttons have no effect. Later sections of this book tell you when to use the mouse in these ways.

Notice that when you first begin, the word <create> in the Data panel is highlighted. Try moving this highlight among the panels by using your computer's right and left arrow keys or by clicking the word in other panels. Once you have created files, their names also are listed in the appropriate panels. You can move the highlight among the files listed in each panel by using the Up and Down Arrow keys or by clicking a file's name with the mouse.

You create a new database, query, report, or label file simply by highlighting the word <create> in the appropriate panel and pressing **Enter**, or by double-clicking the word <create> with the mouse. dBASE then transfers you from the Control Center to a special design screen. There are different design screens for databases, queries, reports, and labels. When you finish designing the file, save it, and return to the Control Center, the name you gave that file is added to the list of file names in that panel.

Notice that immediately under the panels are lines labeled File and Description. As you use the Arrow keys to move around the panels, these lines will display the name and the description of the file that is currently highlighted. You can enter this description while you are designing the file. Because file names must be no more than eight characters long, a longer description is often helpful to remind you what that file is used for.

To remove a file from the catalog or to delete it completely, simply highlight its name in the Control Center and press **Del**. dBASE first asks for confirmation that you want to remove it from the catalog and then asks if you want to delete it from the disk. If you just remove it from the catalog, you can add it again at any time by using the Catalog menu, which is discussed later in this chapter. If you delete it from the disk, though, it is gone forever. You can never recover it unless you use some sophisticated DOS utility that recovers deleted files.

You can use a file or modify its design in any one of these ways:

- Highlight its name in the Control Center and press **Data:F2** or **Design:Shift-F2**.

- Highlight its name in the Control Center and press **Enter** or click the already highlighted name with the mouse. dBASE displays a prompt box that gives you the options of using the file or modifying the file's design.

Instructions in this book use the form "press **Data:F2**" or "press **Design:Shift-F2**", because including the word that describes the key makes the text easier to follow. Of course, these instructions just mean to press **F2** or to press **Shift-F2**. As you will see, you can also use the mouse to make these selections.

dBASE IV comes with two templates in the package that list the uses of all of the function keys, one for keyboards that have the function keys at their left and one for keyboards that have the function keys at the top. Some people find these templates useful, but others find it confusing to look at a list of all of the function keys, including those that do not apply to the current screen and prefer looking at the *navigation line*, which lists only the function keys for the current screen. Though the navigation line sometimes omits some active keys because of lack of space, it includes the most important, and it is not difficult to remember the few keys that it omits. You might want to try using one of the templates to see if you find it helpful, and remove it if you find that you prefer using just the navigation line.

When you do these things, you will want to use two other features of the dBASE IV interface: the navigation line and *prompt boxes*, which are discussed below.

The Navigation Line

At the bottom of most screens in dBASE IV, there is a *navigation line* that tells you the most important keys to use. Of course, the keys differ in different screens. For example, you use different keys when you are designing a report than when you are working from the Control Center. Glancing down at the bottom of the screen always gives you a reminder of the keys that you might need to use in the current situation.

Look at the navigation line at the bottom of the Control Center. The two keys that are most important are the two that were just mentioned:

- **Data:F2** shows you the data in the object that is currently highlighted in the Control Center panels.
- **Design:Shift-F2** lets you redesign the object that is currently highlighted in the Control Center panels.

NOTE

Remember that **Shift-F2** means that you hold down the **Shift** key and press the function key **F2** simultaneously.

An example makes the use of these keys clear. If the name of a query is highlighted, pressing the function key **F2** shows you the data that that query lets you use, for example, the actual names and addresses of all of the people in the database who live in California. If the name of a query is highlighted and you press **Shift-F2**, you can change the design of the query. You might want to change it, for example, so it shows the names of people who live in Oregon as well as those who live in California.

Also on the navigation line of the Control Center are:

- **Menu:F10**, which lets you use pull-down menus, covered later in this chapter.
- **Quick Report:Shift-F9**, which lets you print out reports on queries or on the entire database, covered in Chapter 6.

If you are using a mouse, you can simply click the navigation line rather than using the function keys. When you move the pointer to any location on the words **Data:F2** on the navigation line, for example, these words are highlighted, and you can click to select them. The effect is the same as pressing **F2**. Again, for the sake of brevity, instructions in this book simply say something like "Press **Data:F2**"—but, if the option is available on the navigation line, you can click it instead of pressing the function key.

Prompt Boxes

The bent arrow next to the word Use in the navigation line refers to the Enter key. As an alternative to using the Data:F2 and Design:Shift-F2 keys, you can simply press **Enter** when the highlight is on the appropriate object (or click the highlighted object with the mouse).

Figure 1.2 shows the prompt box that appears when you highlight a file in the Data panel and press **Enter**; similar prompt boxes are used with the other panels. Two of the options on this prompt box do the same thing as you can do by pressing **Data:F2** or **Design:Shift-F2**. You can make selections from a prompt box in either of three ways:

- Press the first letter of the option you want
- Use the Right and Left Arrow keys to move the highlight to the option you want and then press **Enter.**
- Click the option that you want with the mouse.

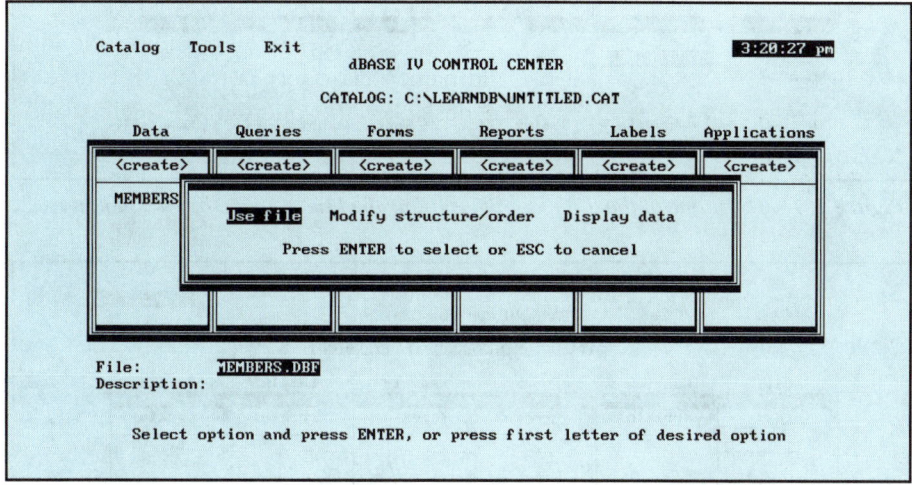

Figure 1.2 *The prompt box that appears when you use a database file.*

dBASE IV uses prompt boxes for many different purposes, and options can always be chosen in the same ways. To avoid repetition, instructions in this book simply tell you to select **<option name>**, and you can select the option that is specified in any way.

Using a Database File

It is necessary to use a database before you can create a Query, Report, or any other object that is connected with that database. When you select **Use File** from the prompt box that was just illustrated, the line in the Data panel moves below the file name to indicate that it is in use. Notice that in Figure 1.3, the name of the MEMBERS file is below the line. But in Figure 1.4, MEMBERS is displayed above the line to show that that file is in use and that you can now create queries or other objects for it.

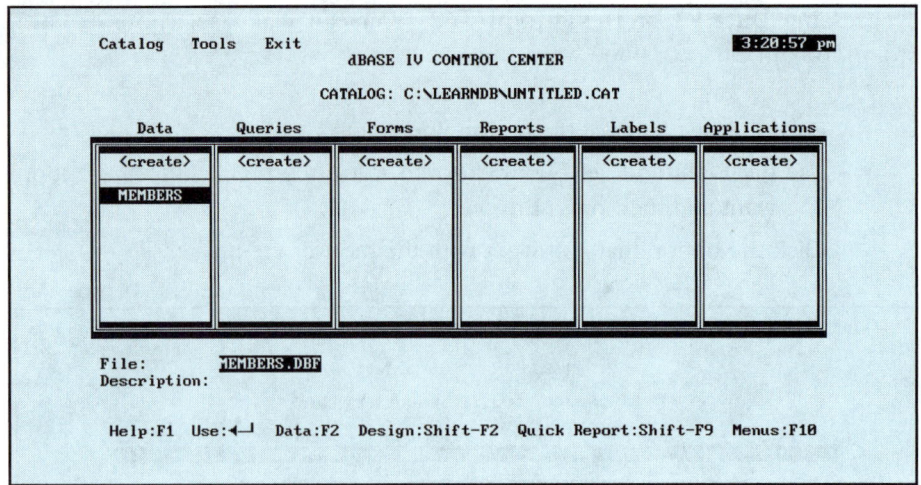

Figure 1.3   *The name of the database file is below the line to show that it is not in use.*

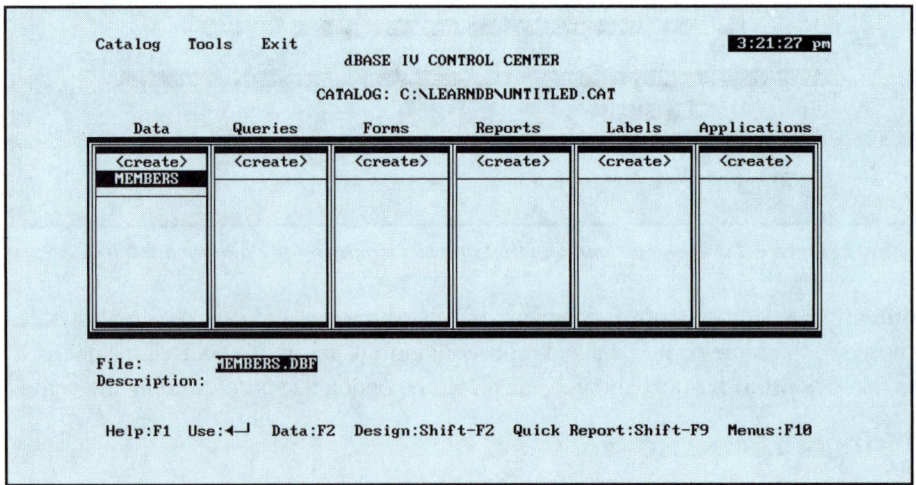

Figure 1.4   *The name of the database file is above the line to show that it is in use.*

After you have created other objects, you will see that when you use a database file all of the objects that are based on it are moved above the line in their panels at the same time as the database file is moved above the line in the Data panel.

As you will see in Chapter 5, you can also use a query rather than using a database file, in order to perform operations with only the records that are included in the query.

Pull-Down Menus

The menu bar is on the upper-left of the Control Center screen: it includes the menus Catalog, Tools, and Exit. By selecting one of these, you pull down a menu, which appears below the menu name.

You can use these pull-down menus in either of two ways:

- Press **F10:** The last menu that you used is pulled down. If you did not use a menu previously, the left-most menu on the screen (for example, the Catalog menu of the Control Center) is pulled down. Then you can use the Left and Right Arrow keys to move among the pull-down menus to use the one that you want.
- Hold down the **Alt** key and press the key that is the first letter of the menu that you want, and it is pulled down immediately. For example, press **Alt-T** to pull down the Tools menu. (Remember that this means to press **T** while you are holding down the **Alt** key.)

Click an option on the menu bar to pull down its menu. Click an option on the menu to select it.

When the menu appears, some of the options on it are dimmed. This indicates that those particular options are not active, because they cannot be used in the current situation.

Once you have the menu you want, you can use the Up and Down Arrow keys to move the highlight to the option that you want to use and press **Enter** to select that option.

There are other keys that you can use as shortcuts to select options more quickly:

- **PgDn** or **End**: moves the cursor immediately to the option at the bottom of the current menu.

- **PgUp** or **Home**: moves the cursor immediately to the option at the top of the current menu.
- **First letter of an option**: immediately selects that option.

At first, you will find it easiest to use the Up and Down Arrow keys to select options. After you become accustomed to using dBASE IV, though, you will probably find it easiest to press the first letter of the option you want to use.

Some options have an arrowhead on the left. This means that, if you select them, you either select an option (such as a file name) from a picklist, or you pull-down a submenu—another menu with more options to choose from.

Press the **Esc** key at any time to leave the current menu. If you are using a picklist or a submenu, it disappears and you return to the last menu level. If you are using one of the main menus, pressing **Esc** returns you to the Control Center.

A Look at the Menu System

You will find that other screens in dBASE IV, such as the screens that you use to design databases and queries, also have menu bars that let you pull down menus. It is generally a good idea to look through the menu system of a screen before you start to use it, to see what options it offers.

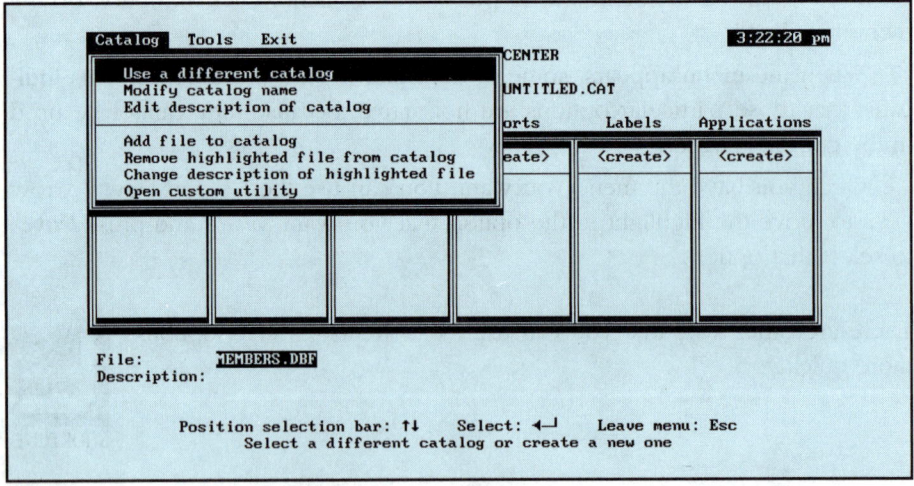

Figure 1.5   The Catalog menu.

Glance at the Control Center's menu system. You will get some experience using pull-down menus, and you will also see what sorts of things the menus let you do:

1. Press **Alt-C** to pull down the Catalog menu, shown in Figure 1.5. (Remember to hold down the **Alt** key and then press **C**.) Alternatively, click Catalog with the mouse. You can see that the Catalog menu lets you do things that you obviously need to do when you work with catalogs, such as using a different catalog or change the name or description of the catalog.

2. Press the **Right Arrow** key to pull down the Tools menu. You can see that it is a sort of a Swiss army knife of the dBASE world—it contains utilities that are handy in various situations, though they are not fundamental to using dBASE IV. These tools are covered in Part 2 of this book.

3. Notice that many of the options on the Tools menu have an arrowhead to the left. Many of the utilities found in the Tools menu are complex enough that they require submenus. Select **Macros** to look at the Macros submenu, shown in Figure 1.6.

4. Press **Esc** to leave this submenu and return to the main Tools menu.

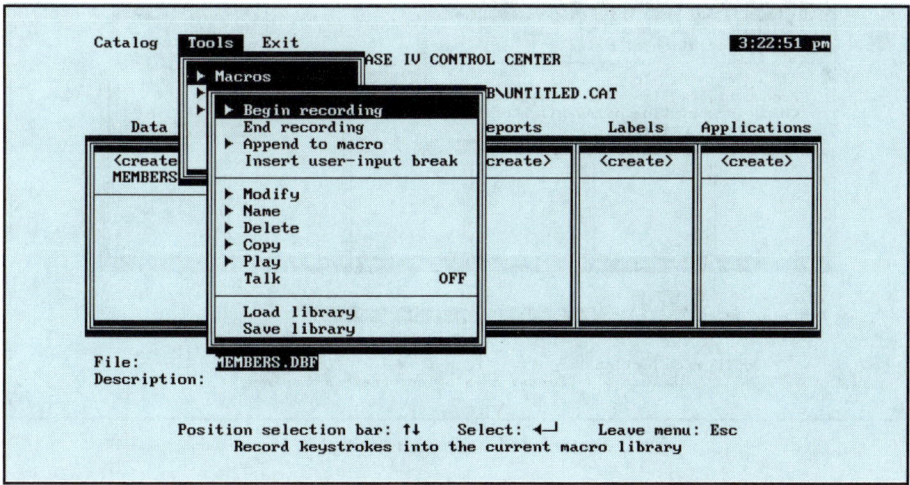

Figure 1.6 Using a submenu.

The menu system is so easy to use that this brief exercise should be enough to make you comfortable with it.

NOTE In the future, to avoid repetition, instructions in this book simply says Select **<option>** from the <menu name> menu. When you see this instruction, use any method of pulling down the menu and selecting the option that is specified.

Picklists

Some of menu options with arrows to the left let you use a *picklist* rather than a submenu.

For example, if you select **Use a different catalog** from the Catalog menu, you use the picklist shown in Figure 1.7 to select the catalog you want from among all the catalogs that are available. (Figure 1.7 includes catalogs that you create later in this book.) The picklist lets you choose among catalogs in the current directory. Many picklists also let you choose **<parent>** (the root directory) or choose the names of child directories (subdirectories) of the current directory in order to move through the directory tree.

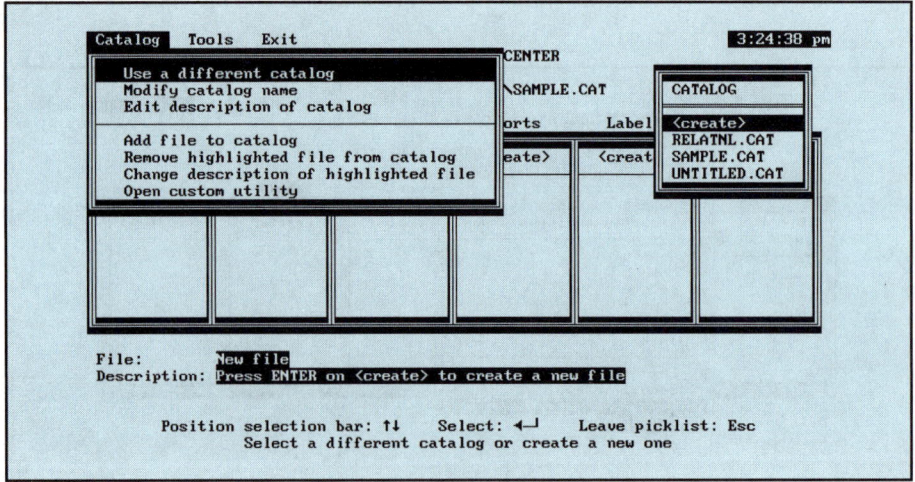

Figure 1.7 *Using a picklist.*

With the keyboard, use the Up and Down Arrow keys to move the highlight to an item in the list, and then press **Enter** to select it. Some lists are too long to fit in the box that holds them, and you can use either the Up and Down Arrow keys or PgUp and PgDn to scroll through the list.

With the mouse, you generally can simply double-click an item to select it. If you just want to move the highlight, you can click any item to highlight it. You can also click the top or bottom border of the box to move the highlight up or down a line: this is equivalent to pressing the Up or Down Arrow. And, if the list is too long to fit in the box, you can double-click the top or bottom border to move the highlight up or down a page: this is equivalent to pressing PgUp or PgDn.

The Dot Prompt

The Exit pull-down menu lets you end your session with dBASE IV and return to your computer's operating system.

It also includes an option to Exit to the dot prompt, which keeps you in dBASE IV but lets you run dBASE by entering commands rather than by using the Control Center.

If you exit to the dot prompt, you can use dBASE IV as people used earlier versions of dBASE. In dBASE, the prompt at which you enter dBASE commands is simply a dot. dBASE IV includes all of the commands that were offered in dBASE III and dBASE III PLUS, in addition to many new commands. People who are accustomed to using these older dBASE programs by entering commands can move to dBASE IV and work from the dot prompt without any added learning time.

Chapter 12 of this book covers important dBASE commands that you can use from the dot prompt. Beginners need to know about the dot prompt only because there is a danger that they will select this menu option by mistake. (You can also exit to the dot prompt by pressing **Esc** and then pressing **Y** from some locations within dBASE IV, increasing the chance that you will find yourself there by error.)

Unlike the Control Center, the dot prompt gives you no clues about what to do next: you have to know the command, or you are stuck. If you find that you have exited to the dot prompt by mistake, you must know the command ASSIST to return to the Control Center. (In dBASE III, the menus were known as the *assist mode*, and the command ASSIST is retained in dBASE IV to let you use the menu system.)

You should try returning from the dot prompt to the Control Center, so you will know what to do if you exit to the dot prompt by mistake:

1. If you still have the Tools menu pulled down, press the **Right Arrow** key to pull down the Exit menu. If you have returned to the Control Center, press **Alt-E** to pull down the Exit menu (or click **Exit** with the mouse).
2. Press **E** to select the option Exit to the dot prompt (or move the highlight to that option and press **Enter** or click that option with the mouse). You see the screen shown in Figure 1.8.
3. Type *assist* and press **Enter** to return to the Control Center.

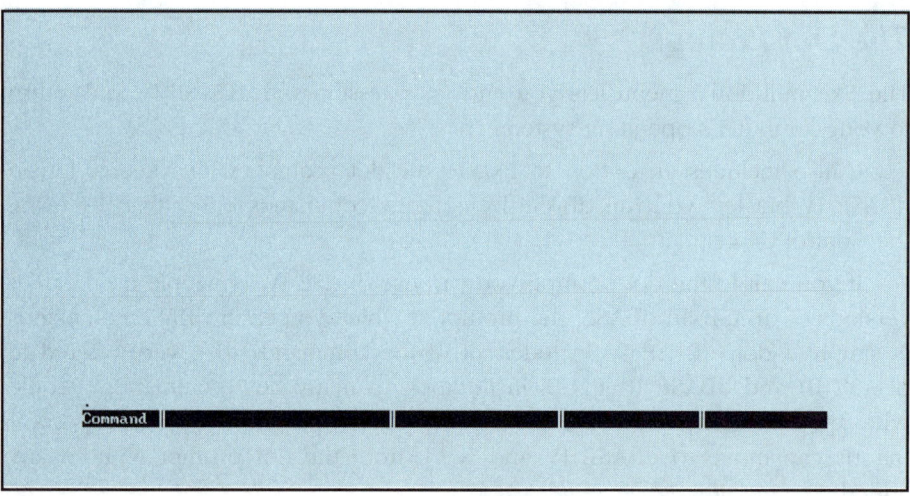

Figure 1.8 *The dot prompt.*

You can see that screen with the dot prompt is totally mystifying unless you are prepared for it in advance, so remember the command ASSIST.

Alternatively, you can just press the **F2** function key to return from the dot prompt to the Control Center, but this is may be more difficult to remember for some.

The Status Bar

While you were using the dot prompt, you also had a chance to look at the *status bar*, the highlighted bar near the bottom of the screen. The status bar is used in many dBASE IV screens, and it often has important information on it. For example, if you are editing a database file, the status bar would include the name of the file, the number of the record that you are currently editing, the total number of records in the file, the word Ins (if you are editing in insert mode), and more information. The status bars for the different dBASE IV screens are described when necessary: You should also keep your eye on the status bar whenever it is displayed and see what information it contains.

Exiting from dBASE IV

The other option on the Exit menu, Quit to DOS, ends your session with dBASE IV and returns you to your operating system. (If you used dBASE from some DOS shell, it returns you to wherever you were when you started dBASE IV.)

dBASE consultants sometimes run into users who complain that names and addresses are disappearing from their files. The most common cause of this complaint is that the user forgets what to do next and becomes frustrated enough to end the session by turning off the computer. If you value your data, remember these unhappy users and always quit dBASE IV before turning off your computer.

You must always quit dBASE IV when you are done with your work. If you do not, you can lose data.

WARNING

A Note on Indexes

Apart from Database, Query, Report, and Label files, which have their own panels in the Control Center, there is one other type of file that is fundamental to using dBASE IV that you learn about in Part 1 of this book: the *index file*, which determines the order in which records are displayed. In this book, for example, you use data both in zip code order and in alphabetical order by name, so you need to create two indexes.

Because an index can be associated only with a single database file, index files are created and used through a special Organize menu that is included in the screens you use to design or view that database file, rather than on a Control Center panel of their own. You will look at the menu in Chapter 2, when you design a database file, and use it to create indexes in Chapter 3.

You now have an overview of the basic files that you use when you are working with dBASE IV and what these files do:

- **Database files** store information
- **Indexes** determine the order in which the information is used
- **Queries** pull out specific data
- **Report** and **label** formats produce printed reports and mailing labels

In Part 2 of this book, as a more advanced user, you also use forms to create custom data-entry screens and applications to set up a system for a novice.

The Help System

The navigation line also includes the key **Help:F1**. F1 can be used from anywhere in dBASE IV—not just from the Control Center—to give you context-sensitive help. That is, it gives you help with whatever you are doing at the moment.

For example, since the highlight is on <create> in the Data panel when you start dBASE IV, pressing **Help:F1** displays a screen with help on creating files, shown in Figure 1.9. Notice that the navigation line says <MORE F4>, telling you which function key to press to read more screens with help on the current topic.

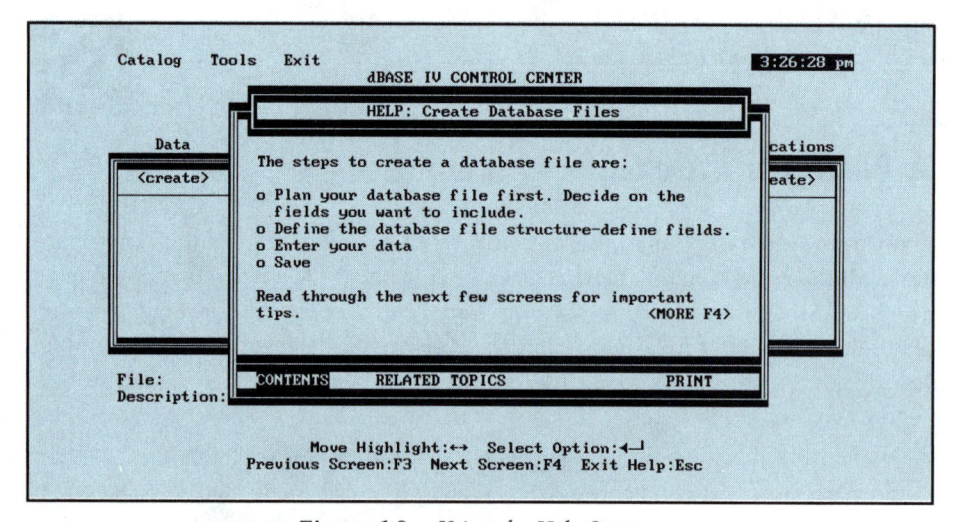

Figure 1.9 Using the Help System.

After you have entered the Help system, you can get help on any topic by selecting **Contents** and then selecting any item from the table of contents that dBASE IV displays. You can change the table of contents that is listed by pressing the keys indicated in the navigation line: press **F3** for more general topics or to go back to the previous screen and **F4** for more specific topics or to move forward to the next screen. To move to an unrelated topic, press **F3** to back up and select the general area of interest you want or press **C** to access the Help table of contents.

The options on the Help menu are:

- **Contents:** displays a general table of contents with current topic highlighted.
- **Related Topics:** displays a table of contents that only includes topics related to the current topic.
- **Backup:** moves back to the previous screen.
- **Print:** prints the current help screen.

To leave the Help System and return to the Control Center, just press **Esc**.

1. With <create> highlighted in the Data panel, press **F1**. The Help table of contents is displayed containing information on creating databases, the topic that was highlighted when you pressed the F1 key.
2. To move forward one screen and get more specific information, press **F4**, or click **Next Screen:F4**.
3. To back up to more general topics, press **F3**, or click **Previous Screen:F3**.
4. Use the Right Arrow key to move the highlight off Contents to Related Topics and press **Enter** or click **Related Topics** with the mouse. A picklist of related topics is displayed from which you can use the Up and Down Arrow keys and **Enter** to select another topic or double-click the topic to select it. Press **Esc** to return to the Help table of contents.
5. Press **Esc** again to return to the Control Center.

Now, if you would like to take a break before going on with the next chapter of this book, select **Quit to DOS** from the Exit menu. Even though you do not yet have data to lose, you should get in the habit of always quitting dBASE IV at the end of a session. You have been warned about possible loss of data, and the rest of this book assumes that you know enough to quit dBASE IV at the end of each chapter if you want to take a break.

Summary

This chapter introduced you to the basics of dBASE IV, including starting the program from DOS, getting around the Control Center and using the menus, and using the extensive dBASE IV on-line Help System to get help on your current location in the program or on many other topics. In the next chapter, you begin to put some of what you learned into practice when you design and create a dBASE IV database.

Chapter 2

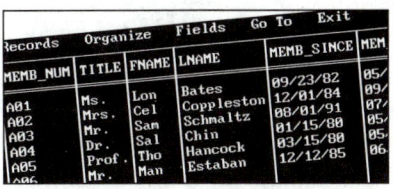

Creating a Database File

This chapter teaches you how to design and create a simple dBASE IV database to begin to organize and manage your data. In addition to general information about databases and dBASE IV, you will learn:

- ◆ The meaning of commonly used database terms such as *fields*, *records*, and *data types*
- ◆ The difference between one-to-one relationships and one-to-many relationships in a database
- ◆ How to design a simple database
- ◆ How to create and modify catalogs in the dBASE IV Control Center
- ◆ How to create a dBASE IV database and define its structure
- ◆ How to modify a database's structure
- ◆ How to save a database structure

Fields and Records

A simple database, you have learned, is like a rolodex file or like a file folder filled with printed forms. Each card or form has spaces for name, address, and phone number—or for whatever information the file holds.

No doubt you are familiar with this sort of simple database or list even if you have never used a computer before. However, there are a couple of special terms used to describe this sort of list when discussing computer databases:

- **Field**: each of the "spaces" on a paper form that would be used to hold a specific piece of information is called a *field* when you are working with computers. For example, a database file might have one field for name, a second field for address, and so on.
- **Record**: all of the information that would be kept on a single rolodex card or form is called a *record*. For example, a record could hold the name, address, and phone number of one person.

When you create a database file, what you are doing is similar to designing a paper form—deciding what fields it should have and what information each field will hold. This is called defining the *structure* of the database.

As you will see, you have to be more precise when you define the structure of a computerized database than you are when you design a paper form. For one thing, computerized databases have a variety of different *data types*, and you must specify in advance whether a field will contain characters, numbers, or some other type of data. For another, in order to take advantage of all of the capabilities of your database management program, you must think carefully about how to break down the data into separate fields and about what fields to include. If you do not organize the fields and carefully define the database's structure before you begin, your database will not be as useful as it could be because you will not be able to perform all the tasks you might want to do.

Data Types

When you define the structure of a database field, you must specify the *data type* of each field.

Beyond letting you define fields to store characters and numbers, dBASE IV has a variety of other data types that give you extra power. *Date fields* let you perform calculations to find the number of days between two dates. *Logical fields* can contain only the values True or False (or Yes or No) and do not let the user enter other data. *Memo fields* can hold text of variable length.

dBASE IV's data types are:

- **Character**: holds letters, numbers, or special characters (such as & or #) up to a total of 256 characters.
- **Numeric**: holds numbers on which you want to perform calculations. (A field that is made up of numbers but that is not used in calculations, such as zip code, should be defined as a character field.)
- **Float**: is similar to a numeric field, but the computer can perform calculations on it with more precision to avoid rounding errors. This data type is meant for scientific and advanced statistical data and is not important for most dBASE users.
- **Date**: holds dates and lets the user enter only valid dates. For example, dBASE IV does not let you enter 02/30/91 in a date field, because February does not have thirty days.
- **Logical**: holds only the value T or F and lets the user enter only T, F, Y, or N (for True, False, Yes, or No).
- **Memo**: holds variable lengths of text. This type is useful for fields that hold text with more than the 256 characters (for example, long descriptions of products) or for fields that might have long entries in some places and short entries or no entries in others (for example, general notes about employees).

When you create a character, numeric, or float field, you must specify its width. For example, you would specify a field to hold the name of a state as two characters long because abbreviations for state names are always two characters.

dBASE IV stores the number of characters that you specify as the field's width, even if there are fewer characters in the actual entry. For example, if you define the field that holds the first name so that it is twenty characters long, and you later add a record to the database with the name **SAM** in that field, dBASE stores the letters SAM followed by seventeen blank spaces, to add up to the total of twenty characters.

There is a trade-off involved when you define the width of a character field. If you make it too short, it will not be able to hold some of the names in your database. If you make it too long, it takes up extra space on your hard disk with blank spaces and slows down performance at times when dBASE has to read through these blank spaces in large files in order to find the data you need.

When you create a numeric or float field, you must specify both its total width and the number of decimal places that it displays. The one tricky thing about these fields is that the decimal point and the leading minus sign, if they are needed, count as part of the total width. For example, if you wanted a field to hold amounts of money less than $100, you would have to make it five spaces wide: two spaces for a dollar amount, one space for the decimal point, and two spaces for the cents amount (up to 99.99). If you wanted this field to display negative amounts also, you would have to add another space for the minus sign, making it six spaces wide.

When you create date, logical, or memo fields, you do not specify their width. A date is automatically eight spaces to hold MM/DD/YY (that is, two digits for the month, two for the day, and two for the year, separated by slashes). A logical field is automatically one space to hold T or F. A memo field has a width of ten spaces, but it does not actually hold the text that you type into the memo: instead, the memo field holds a pointer that tells dBASE IV where the text is stored in another file.

If you are copying your data from one computer to another, it is important for you to understand that memo fields are stored in a separate file from the rest of the database. If you create a file named EMPLS to hold a list of your employees, for example, and if you include a memo field in that file, then dBASE IV uses a file named EMPLS.DBF to hold the database and a file named EMPLS.DBT to hold the memo fields of that database. The .DBF stands for "database file" and the .DBT stands for "database text." If you are copying your data, you must be sure to copy both of these files.

If your database file does not include a memo field, then dBASE IV holds it all in one file with a .DBF extension.

Analyzing the Database

When you are creating a database, the saying goes, the first thing you should do is turn off your computer. If you take a bit of time to think about what fields should be in the file—how the data must be broken down into fields to let you use it most effectively—before you start banging on your computer keyboard, you will save yourself no end of trouble in the long run.

In this book, you create a sample database to keep track of the members of an organization. The database must store members' names and addresses to produce mailing labels, form letters, and the like. In addition, the database must keep track of when membership expires to send letters asking members to renew.

Let's imagine that this particular organization also has people who volunteer to do work for the group, perhaps to write letters, so that the database also needs a field to indicate whether or not a member is a volunteer. It also sends special requests for donations to people who have been members for several years and to people who have given donations in the past, so that it must have fields to indicate the date when a member first joined and any donations made. Members can pay dues ranging from $15 for low-income membership to $100 for sustaining membership, so there should be a field to indicate which level of membership each person has.

An actual dBASE database might also include telephone numbers, Social Security numbers, a field for country name, enough space for foreign zip codes if there are members from other countries, and perhaps other data on each member. Leave these items out of the sample database in order to save time.

Breaking Down the Data

As a general rule, it is best to break down the data into as many separate fields as possible.

Consider an error that inexperienced people often make. A person computerizing a mailing list for the first time may create a single field for city, state, and zip, because these were previously written on a single line on the index cards used to keep records. Then, a data-entry person spends a couple of weeks copying the data from thousands of index cards into the computer. But when it's time to do the first mass mailing and produce mailing labels sorted in order of zip code, everyone realizes for the first time that the database can't be sorted in this way, because a sort must be based on data that is in a field of its own (or that is at the beginning of a field). To produce labels in zip code order, the structure of the database must be modified and the city, state, and zip of everyone on the list must be reentered.

If you will ever want to use the data in zip code order or to find the people who live in certain zip codes, then you should put the zip code in a separate field. Also, if you ever want to use the names in alphabetical order or to look people up by last name, then you must put the last names in a separate field from the first name.

On the other hand, it is fairly common to keep the middle initial in the same field as the first name. However, you may want to produce form letters that address people by first name, then you should create a separate field for the middle initial so that your letter will say "Dear John" instead of "Dear John Q." But if you will never need to use the first name by itself, then you could combine it with the middle initial in a single field.

The important point here is to think about how you will want to use the data and what information the database should contain before data entry is begun.

You will make data entry a bit easier if you keep data in one field rather than breaking it up into several. If you are in doubt, though, the prudent course is to break down the data into *more* rather than *fewer* fields.

With our sample database file, let's imagine that you want to produce form letters addressed to "Dear Mr. Smith" rather than to "Dear John," and that you will not have any other occasion to use the first name alone. In this case you can combine first name and middle initial in a single field, but you also need another field to hold Mr., Ms., Dr., Prof., or whatever other title you combine with the last name when you address the person.

One-to-One Relationships

Apart from breaking down the data into enough separate fields, the one other thing you need to check very carefully when you are designing a database file is the *one-to-one relationship* among the data in all the fields.

In the sample database that you will create to manage a membership organization, for example, each person has one name, one address, and one date of joining the organization. On the other hand, one person can make many donations to the organization. Donations are not in a one-to-one relation with the other data.

What would happen if you included a field for donations in the database file? As long as everyone had given no more than one donation, there would be no problem. When someone gave a second donation, though, the data-entry person would see that the donation field for that person was already filled and might try to solve the problem by entering the person's name and address a second time, along with the second donation. Then, when you produced mailing labels, you would have two labels for that person. If this went on for very long, the database file would no longer be usable.

Donations are an example of a *one-to-many relationship*, since *one* person can make *many* donations. To handle data that includes this sort of relationship, you should use a *relational database*. Relational databases are discussed at length in Chapter 10 of this book.

Also notice that the fields that hold the amount of dues paid and the date membership expires could also create a problem with one-to-many relationships. Each member pays dues and has a new expiration date every year. As long as you are using a simple (rather than a relational) database, you can keep track of only one-to-one relationships. So, in a simple database, you can keep records only for members' *current* expiration date and of the amount of their *most recent* dues payment, for example, in a simple database, when a member pays dues, you replace the old expiration date with a new one, and (if necessary) you replace the old amount of dues paid with a new amount. This is an adequate way of keeping track of dues payments, and many organizations actually do this sort of thing.

Similarly, to keep a record of donations in your sample database that you will use in Part 1, you can keep a record only of the date of the most recent donation by each member, and you can send letters asking for more help only to members who have recent dates in the donation field. Needless to say, real organizations keep track of the dates and amounts of all donations. In Part 2 of this book, you set up a relational database to do just that.

For now, and for as long as you are only working with simple databases, you just need to remember to look for one-to-many relationships when you are designing database files and to realize that there are some sorts of data that you cannot handle with a simple database, so that you do not make errors.

In most actual applications, a member number, customer number, or similar key field is used only if the database is relational: as you will see, the key is used to relate data in separate files. A simple database does not need a key field, though there are some occasions where one is useful. The sample database you create in this chapter includes a member number, however, for instructional purposes: the member numbers are also handy in Part 2, when you convert this file to a relational database.

The Fields of the Sample Database

The fields that should be included in your sample database and their data types are in Table 2.1

Table 2.1 Sample database fields and their data types.

Member number	character
Title	character
First name	character
Last name	character
Address 1	character
Address 2	character
City	character
State	character
Zip	character
Member since	date
Membership expires	date
Last dues payment	numeric
Last donation	date
Volunteer	logical
Notes	memo

It is generally a good idea to include two lines (Address 1 and Address 2) for the address in any database, since you often must include an organization name or the name of a building complex, in addition to the actual street address.

The field Volunteer is logical data type It indicates whether or not this member has volunteered to do extra work, so it can only be true or false.

Notes is a memo field, since it will hold extra remarks about members, which could vary in length from nothing to several paragraphs. Member since, Membership expires, and Last Donation are date fields. Last dues payment is a numeric field because it represents an amount of money on which you might want to perform calculations—for example, you might want to add all dues payments for the organization or determine the average dues payment for all members.

All of the other fields are character data types. Novices are often tempted to make a field such as zip code numeric, because zip codes are all numbers, but it is a temptation that you should resist for several reasons. For one thing, zip codes for foreign countries include letters as well as numbers, and extended zip codes in the United States include a hyphen in the middle. In addition, dBASE IV generally suppresses the leading zeroes of numeric fields; you would have trouble with a zip code such as 09567 if you made the field numeric, but not if you made it a character field. As you will see in later chapters, you would also have more trouble combining the zip code with the City and State if it were numeric and they were character fields.

Making the zip field numeric rather than character is not necessary and could only cause problems in an actual case. There are ways around these problems, but it is easier not to create them in the first place. As a general rule, it is best to use the character data type unless you have good reason to make a field numeric.

With this background, you will find the actual mechanics of creating a database file extremely easy. As you know from the quick tour of dBASE IV in Chapter 1, you simply select **<create>** from the database panel of the Control Center to create a new file. Once you have done this, dBASE IV displays virtually all of the information you need to create the file.

In Chapter 1, you created a subdirectory titled LEARNDB designed to hold all of the exercises you do in this book.

To use the subdirectory for the work in this book, you should have allowed dBASE to alter the DOS search path when you installed dBASE IV; if you followed the instructions in the Appendix when you installed dBASE, you did this. If dBASE IV has already been installed on your computer and you do not know what the search path is, try typing *dbase* and pressing **Enter** when you are in any subdirectory except the DBASE subdirectory in which the program is installed. If the program starts, then the search path does include dBASE and you can use the special directory that is created in this section. If dBASE does not start, use any text editor to add the name of the directory to the PATH command in your AUTOEXEC.BAT file. See your operating system manual for more information.

As you use this book, before you start dBASE IV, always enter the command *cd \learndb* to enter this subdirectory. Then all of the files you create when you do the exercises from this book will be in this subdirectory.

When you have finished all the exercises in this book, you can enter the command *del \learndb*.** to delete all the files that you created. Finally, enter the command *rd \learndb* to remove this subdirectory. You can see how much easier it is to deal with groups of files when you keep them in a separate subdirectory.

Working with Catalogs

You should create a new catalog to hold the files that you are creating in this book. The menu-driven methods that you use to work with catalogs are so simple that you can learn them all "on the fly," simply by looking through the Catalog menu as you create the new catalog.

Creating a New Catalog

When you start dBASE IV, dBASE automatically creates a catalog named UNTITLED.CAT if there is no other catalog available for it to use. All catalogs are in files with this .CAT extension. The catalog name itself can have up to eight letters, like the name of any DOS file.

There are two ways to create a new catalog. You can use the most direct:

1. First, start dBASE IV, if you have not already done so. Remember that, before starting dBASE, you should always enter the command *cd \learndb* at the DOS prompt to get into the special subdirectory you have created. Then enter *dbase* to use the Control Center .

2. Select **Use a different catalog** from the Catalog menu. (Remember that this means to pull down the Catalog menu pop-up and then select the option **Use a different catalog** from that pop-up, as you learned in Chapter 1.) When you do this a picklist appears, as you can see in Figure 2.1, with <create> as its first option and the names of other catalogs following it. As the navigation line says, you can use the Up and Down Arrows to move through this list, press **Enter** to select an item from this list, or press **Esc** to leave the list and return to the Catalog menu. Using the mouse, click an item to highlight it, or double-click it to select it.

3. Press **Enter** to select <create>. dBASE IV prompts you to enter the name for the new catalog. You can simply type the name of the new catalog here. (Note that the navigation line says that you can press **Enter** to accept the name you have typed, press **Esc** to cancel (that is,

to reject what you have typed, stop naming the catalog, and return to the menu) or press **F9** to Zoom.)

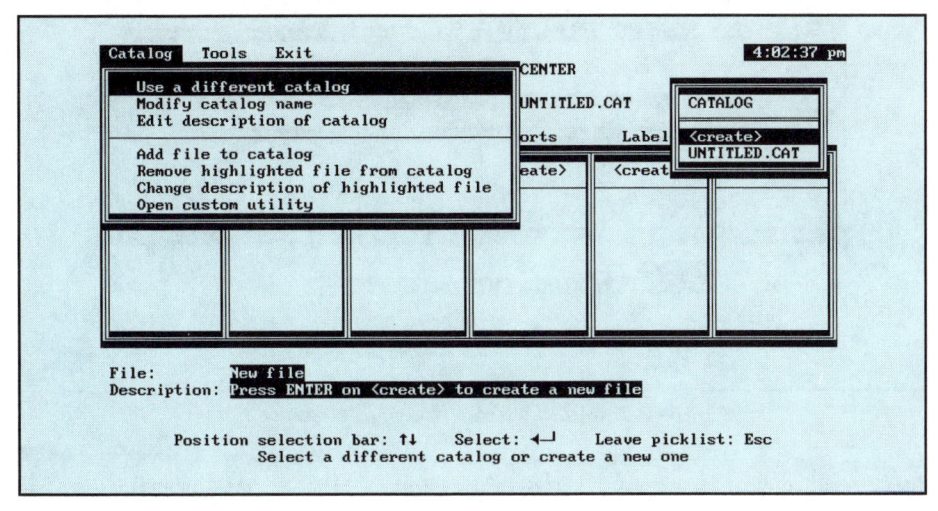

```
Catalog  Tools  Exit                                    4:02:37 pm
┌─────────────────────────────────┐CENTER
│ Use a different catalog         │
│ Modify catalog name             │UNTITLED.CAT    ┌─CATALOG──┐
│ Edit description of catalog     │                │ <create> │
├─────────────────────────────────┤orts     Label  │UNTITLED.CAT
│ Add file to catalog             │
│ Remove highlighted file from catalog  eate>   <creat
│ Change description of highlighted file
│ Open custom utility             │
└─────────────────────────────────┘

File:        New file
Description: Press ENTER on <create> to create a new file

      Position selection bar: ↑↓   Select: ←┘   Leave picklist: Esc
              Select a different catalog or create a new one
```

Figure 2.1   *A picklist lets you create a new catalog.*

4. Press **F9** to try Zoom, though it is not really necessary here. You can see that a much longer data entry area appears near the bottom of the screen, just above the navigation line. Zoom is useful when you have more to enter than you can fit in the original data entry area and does not really apply to a catalog name, but you can use it now as an exercise.

5. Type *sample* as the name of the catalog and press **Enter**. dBASE IV returns you to the Control Center, the line near the top of the screen that tells you what catalog you are using reads CATALOG: C:\LEARNDB\SAMPLE.CAT.

6. Now you should give the catalog a description. Select **Edit description of catalog** from the Catalog menu. dBASE IV prompts you to edit the description of the current catalog file, as you can see in Figure 2.2. Since you have not entered any description previously, the field you are editing is blank. If you had entered a description earlier, you would be able to edit the description using the usual editing keys.

7. Type *Sample data used with the book Teach Yourself dBASE IV* as the description and then press **Enter**.

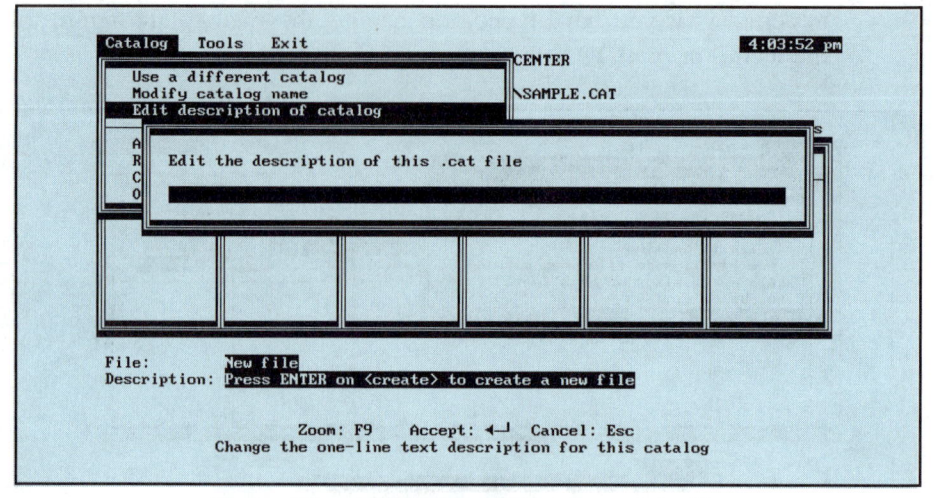

Figure 2.2 *Adding a description to a catalog file.*

In general, if you have not created other catalogs, dBASE IV automatically displays all of the files in this SAMPLE catalog when you start it. If dBASE IV does not display this catalog when you begin (for example, because you have created other catalogs), just select **Use a different catalog** from the Catalog menu and select **SAMPLE** from the picklist of catalog names to use this catalog.

Other Operations with Catalogs

The other options on the Catalog menu are generally self-explanatory. Try out the various options in order to become accustomed to working with dBASE IV catalogs.

1. Select **Use a different catalog** from the Catalog menu, and the picklist appears as before, except that it now includes SAMPLE.CAT as well as UNTITLED.CAT and <create>.

2. Press the **Down Arrow** key once or drag with the mouse (but do not release the button) to move the highlight to SAMPLE.CAT. The description of the catalog that you just entered is displayed in a window, as in Figure 2.3.

3. Press the **Down Arrow** again to move to UNTITLED.CAT and press **Enter**, to make UNTITLED the current catalog once again or continue

dragging with the mouse to move the highlight to UNTITLED.CAT, and then release the button to make it the current catalog.

```
Catalog   Tools   Exit                                    4:05:00 pm
 ┌─────────────────────────────────┐ CENTER
 │ Use a different catalog         │
 │ Modify catalog name             │ \SAMPLE.CAT    ┌─ CATALOG ────┐
 │ Edit description of catalog     │                │ <create>     │
 ├─────────────────────────────────┤ rts     Label  │ SAMPLE.CAT   │
 │ Add file to catalog             │                │ UNTITLED.CAT │
 │ Remove highlighted file from catalog  eate>  <creat└──────────────┘
 │ Change description of highlighted file│
 │ Open custom utility             │
 └─────────────────────────────────┘

              ┌─────────────────────────────────────────┐
              │Sample data used with the book Teach Yourself│
              │dBASE IV                                  │
              └─────────────────────────────────────────┘
    File:
    Description: Press ENTER on <create> to create a new file

              Position selection bar: ↑↓   Select: ↵   Leave picklist: Esc
                    Select a different catalog or create a new one
```

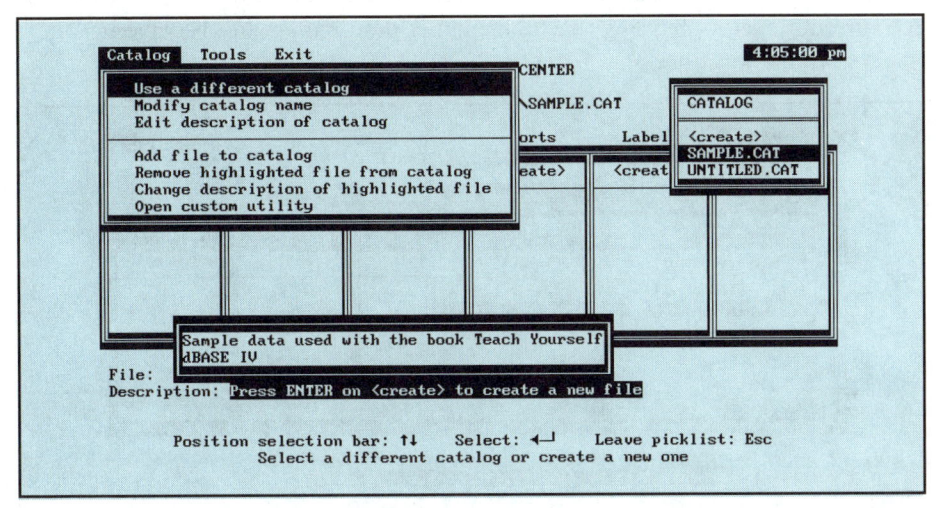

Figure 2.3   *The description of the catalog is displayed.*

4. Select **Modify catalog name** from the Catalog menu. dBASE IV lets you enter a new name for the catalog, as you can see in Figure 2.4. This is also another way of creating a new catalog. For example, if you had wanted to create the SAMPLE catalog in this way, you could have deleted the name UNTITLED.CAT, typed in SAMPLE.CAT, and then added a description as you did above. You can also rename a catalog that already has objects in it by using this menu option.

5. Press **Esc** to cancel renaming and return to the Catalog menu pop-up, since you just tried this option as an exercise and do not actually want to rename the UNTITLED catalog.

6. Select **Use a different catalog** from the Catalog menu. Select **SAMPLE.CAT** from the picklist that is displayed to make SAMPLE the current catalog once again.

If you select **Add file to catalog** from the Catalog menu, dBASE IV displays a picklist, shown in Figure 2.5, to let you select files from various directories. The name of the current directory is at the top of the list. Immediately below it is <C:>, the current drive. If you select this, dBASE IV displays a list of drives, and you can select any one to display a list of files and subdirectories in that drive.

Likewise, selecting **<parent>** displays a picklist with the files and subdirectories of the directory immediately above the current directory. By going through parent directories and subdirectories, you can move to any directory on a disk. If the current directory has any dBASE files in it, their names are displayed.

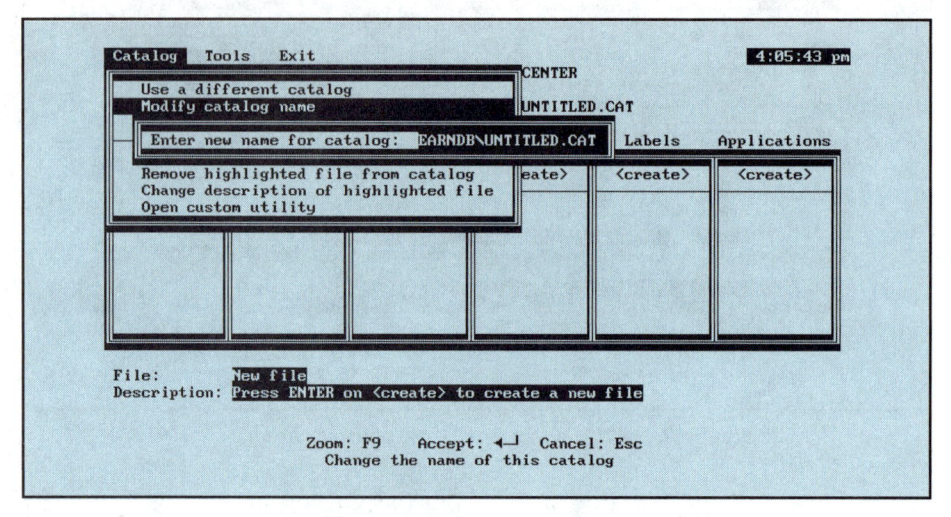

Figure 2.4   *Modifying a catalog name.*

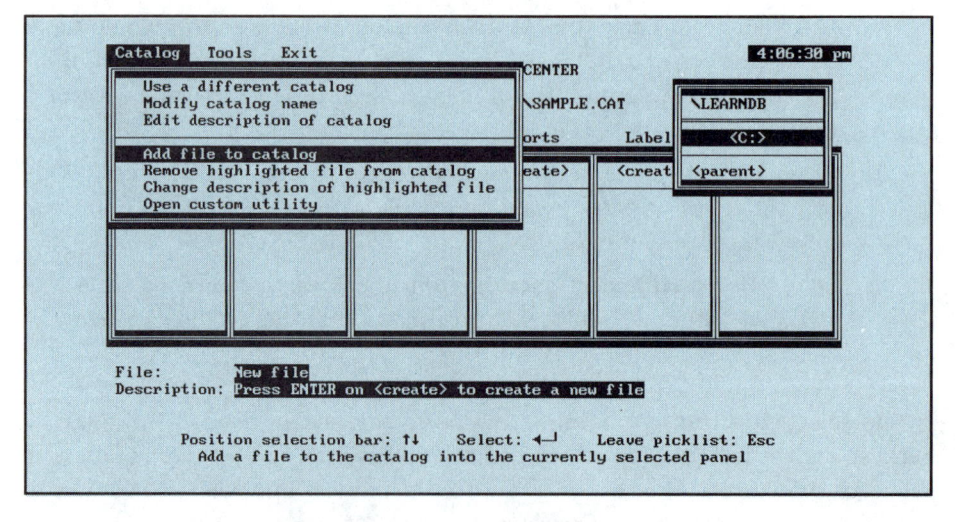

Figure 2.5   *The picklist to select files and directories.*

You can add a file to the currently selected panel of the Control Center by selecting it from the picklist. Remember to select the panel you want before you make this menu selection.

This menu option is useful because you often want to use files in more than one catalog. For example, you might use the same label forms for mailings to two different membership organizations. You need to create only one copy of the label form, which is stored on your hard disk, and the catalogs organize this label form together with the other files that you use with each membership organization.

If you select **Remove highlighted file from catalog** from the Catalog menu, it lets you remove files from the catalog. After you confirm that you want to remove the file from the catalog, it also asks if you want to erase it from the disk. If you think you may ever want that file, do not erase it from the disk. Instead of selecting this option, you could highlight the file name and press **Del**. dBASE IV removes the file from the catalog and deletes it from the disk after asking you for confirmation.

Finally, you can select **Change description of highlighted file** from the Catalog menu to edit the description of a file. If no file is highlighted, these last two options are dimmed and unavailable.

Creating a Database File

Now that you have created a catalog, you can create the database file with the fields listed earlier. After selecting **<create>** from the Data panel of the Control Center, use the database design screen to define the structure the database file. This screen is shown in Figure 2.6.

As you can see, you simply enter the name and data type of each field in the spaces provided. If you enter Character as the data type, dBASE IV requires you to also enter a field width; if you enter Numeric or Float, it requires you to enter both a field width and a number of decimal places, but it skips these spaces if you do not need to use them.

This screen also has a column that lets you create an index for certain data types simply by entering a **Y** in the Index column. This book covers indexes in Chapter 4. For now, leave an **N** in the index column for all the fields.

The navigation line at the bottom of the database design screen gives you most of the information that you need to define the structure of the database.

Notice in Figure 2.6 that when the cursor is located in the Field Name column, the navigation line tells you that field names must begin with a letter and may contain letters, digits, and underscores. Because field names may not contain spaces, the underscore is sometimes used to break up a field name into separate words, making it easier to read.

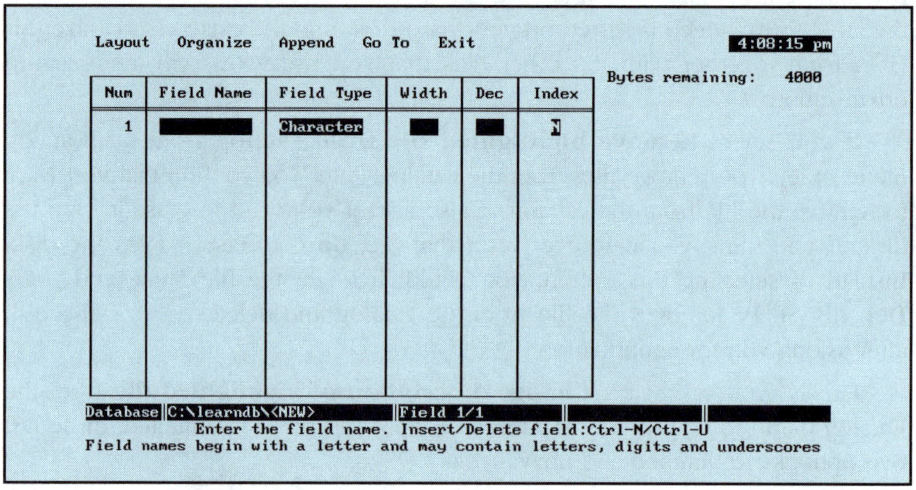

Figure 2.6 *Defining the structure of a database file.*

When you move to the Field Type column, the navigation line tells you to press the **spacebar** to choose among field types. Using the mouse, you may click the **Field Type** repeatedly rather than pressing the spacebar to cycle among the available options. You may also enter a data type by typing its first letter—easier if you know the names of the data types.

When you move to the Width column, the navigation line tells you the widths that are allowed for that data type.

Notice that the navigation line for the Field Name column also tells you that you can insert or delete a field by pressing **Ctrl-N** or **Ctrl-U**. Pressing **Ctrl-N** opens a blank line above the line where the cursor is, so you can enter a new field. **Ctrl-U** deletes the line where the cursor is. Generally, you use these when you are modifying the structure of a database, though you might also change your mind when you are creating it. You use them in the next section to modify the structure that you create in this section.

The only other things that you need to know that the navigation line does not mention is that you can press either **Tab** and **Shift-Tab** or **Next:F4** and

Prev:F3 to move right and left through the columns. You can also press **Home** to move to the left column and **End** to move to the right column. Use the **Up** and **Down Arrow** keys and **PgUp** and **PgDn** to move up and down through the rows that you have already filled in. Using the mouse, simply click any location to move the cursor there. To edit existing entries, you can type over them; but you can also press **Ins** to toggle between type-over and insert mode for editing. Type-over mode is the default. You cannot use any of these methods to move beyond the current column, however, unless you have already entered a valid value in it.

You can also use the Go To menu, shown in Figure 2.7, to move quickly among the fields: it lets you select **Top field**, **Last field**, or **Field number**. In general, though, it is easier to use **Up Arrow**, **Down Arrow**, **PgUp** and **PgDn** to move through the file, unless the database file has an extraordinary number of fields.

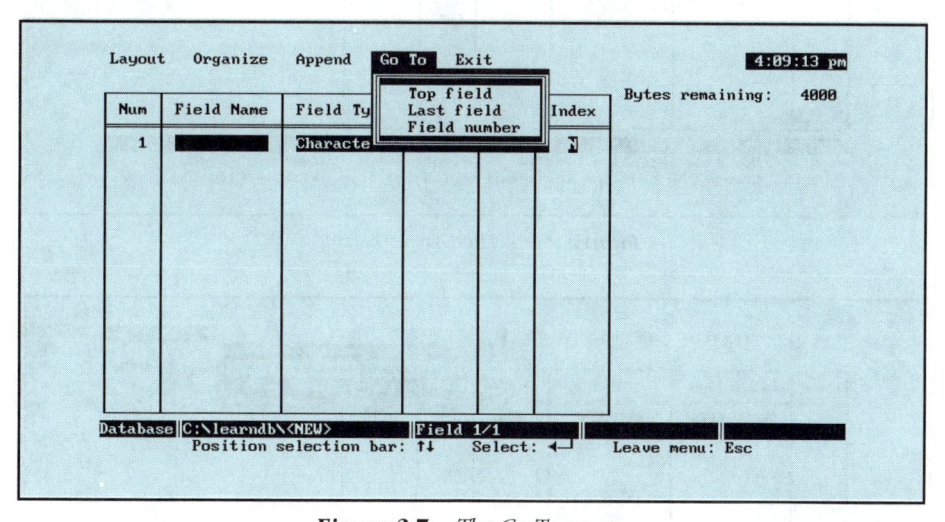

Figure 2.7 The Go To menu.

As far as other the menus for the database design screen are concerned, you only need to use the Layout menu, shown in Figure 2.8, and the Exit menu, shown in Figure 2.9, when you are defining the structure of a database. These two menus are used (with slight variations) in many dBASE IV screens and are fundamental to using dBASE IV.

The Layout menu has an option to Edit database description, used much in the same way to edit the description of of a database file as the option to Edit catalog description on the Catalog menu, is used to edit the description of a catalog. Notice that the Layout menu also has an option to Save this database file structure. This is useful if you want to stop work for a while before finishing defining the structure of the database file. If you save the changes you have made, then you will not lose your work up to that point in case the electricity fails or your computer is turned off for some other reason.

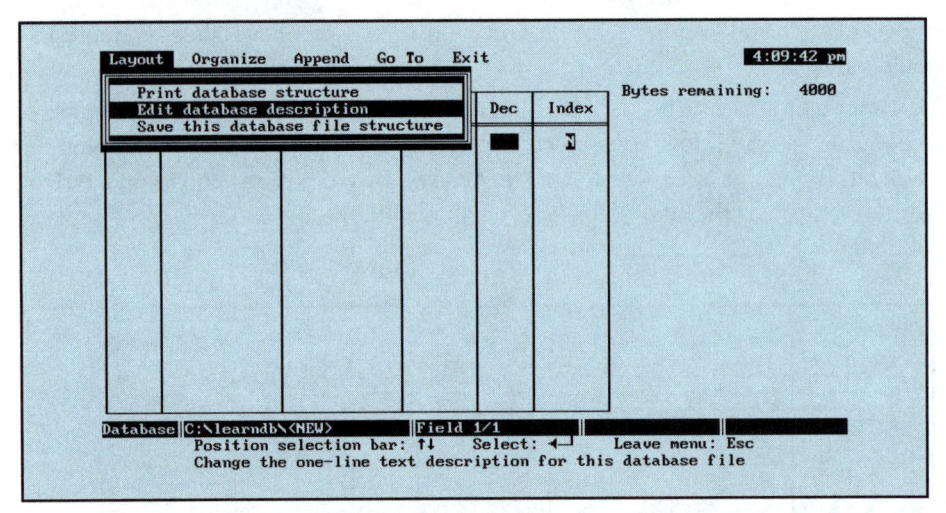

Figure 2.8 *The Layout menu.*

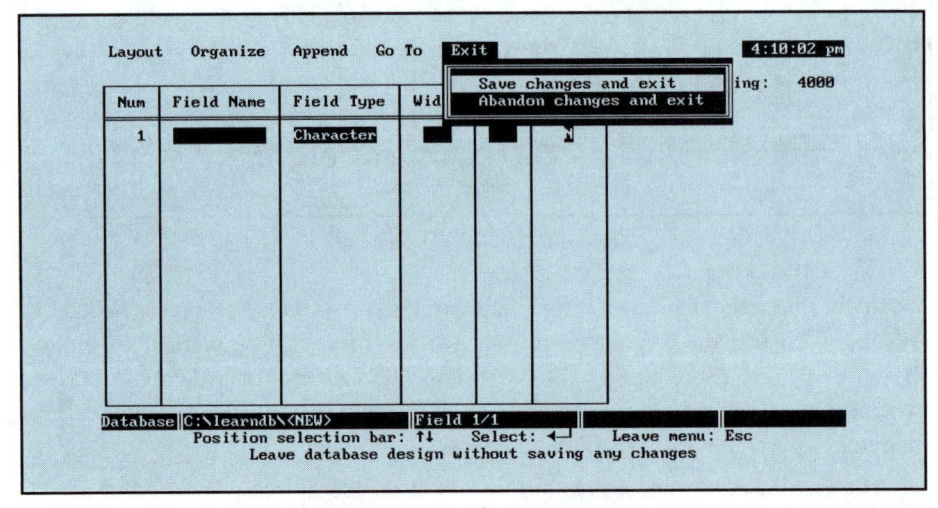

Figure 2.9 *The Exit menu.*

When you select this option, dBASE IV prompts you to enter the name you wish to save as. It gives you the current name of the file as a default, which you can use simply by pressing **Enter**. But you can also edit this default and save the file with a different name, so you do not overwrite the original file. Sometimes, the easiest way to create a new database file is to modify the structure of an existing file and to use this option to save it under a new name. You keep the original file, with its original name and also create a new file with the new name. (As you will see, the Layout menu on many other screens lets you do the same thing—for example, when you are working with reports or mailing labels.)

The option on the Layout menu to Print database structure is useful if you are modifying the structure of an existing database and there are too many fields to fit on one screen, or if you are programming and want a printed copy of the database structure for reference.

There are shortcuts that substitute for the two options on the Exit menu. Instead of selecting **Save changes and exit** from this menu, you can simply press **Ctrl-End** to save your work and return to the Control Center and save your work. Instead of selecting **Abandon changes and exit**, you can press **Esc** to abandon the operation. In either case, dBASE IV asks for confirmation before discarding your work and returning you to the Control Center. Press **Esc** if you have made such a mess of things, either creating a new database or modifying the structure of an existing one, that you want to start all over.

SHORTCUT

You will find that there is an Exit menu like this one on many dBASE IV screens. The menu is there to make the program easier for beginners to use. Once you become used to it, you will save time by pressing **Ctrl-End** or **Esc** instead.

If you have not yet entered a name for the file when you select **Save changes and exit** from the Exit menu or press **Ctrl-End**, dBASE IV prompts you for a file name. This is the easy way to name a database file and return to the Control Center in one step. (It also works for Queries, Labels, Reports, and other objects.)

The Organize menu is used to index or sort, and you will learn about it in Chapter 4. The Append menu is used to add data to a file and you will learn about it in Chapter 3. You do not need to worry about them for now.

You should already be using the SAMPLE catalog that you just created. If you are not, use it as you learned to do in the previous section. Then define the structure of the new database, as it was described earlier in this chapter:

1. Select **<create>** from the Data panel and dBASE IV displays the database design screen.

2. As the Field Name for the first field, type *memb_num*. Notice that the letters are automatically capitalized, though you do have to press the **Shift** key to type the underscore. As dBASE does not distinguish on the basis of capitalization in the names of fields, it capitalizes all of their letters. Notice also that dBASE IV does not let you type an invalid character—if you try to type + or *, for example, it just beeps.

3. Press **Enter** to move to the Field Type column. Press **Enter** again to accept Character as the Field Type and move to the Width column.

4. Notice that the message line tells you that the Character field can be any width from one to 254 spaces wide. Try pressing **Enter** without typing a value first. dBASE beeps and displays a message saying that is an illegal field width. Press any key to continue. Then Type *3* in the width column and press **Enter**. The cursor moves to the index column.

5. Press **Enter** to confirm that dBASE IV should not create an index based on this field and to move to the description of field number 2.

6. For field 2, enter *title* in the Field Name column. Then enter *5* in the Width column, and press **Enter** to accept the N in the Index column and move to the next field.

7. For field 3, enter *fname* in the Field Name column. Then enter *15* in the Width column, and press **Enter** to accept the N in the Index column and move to the next field.

8. For field 4, enter *lname* in the Field Name column. Then enter *20* in the Width column, and press **Enter** to accept the N in the Index column and move to the next field.

9. For field 5, enter *address1* in the Field Name column. Then enter *35* in the Width column, and press **Enter** to accept the N in the Index column and move to the next field.

10. For field 6, enter *address2* in the Field Name column. Then enter *35* in the Width column, and press **Enter** to accept the N in the Index column and move to the next field.

11. For field 7, enter *city* in the Field Name column. Then enter *20* in the Width column, and press **Enter** to accept the N in the Index column and move to the next field.

12. For field 8, enter *state* in the Field Name column. Then enter *2* in the Width column, and press **Enter** to accept the N in the Index column and move to the next field.

13. For field 9, enter *zip* in the Field Name column. Then enter *5* in the Width column, and press **Enter** to accept the N in the Index column and move to the next field.

14. For field 10, type *memb_since.* for the Field Name. Notice that, since this name fills the entire space, dBASE IV beeps and automatically moves to the next column without your pressing **Enter**. You can see that ten characters is the maximum length for field names. Since this is a date field, press the **Spacebar** (or click it with the mouse) three times to cycle through the available choices, until Date appears in the field type column: notice that 8 automatically appears in the width column. Press **Enter** and the cursor skips the width column, as dates are fixed width, and moves to the Index column. Press **Enter** to move to the next row.

15. For field 11, type *mem_expirs* as the Field Name. dBASE IV beeps and moves to the Field Type column. This time, just type *d* for Date. dBASE enters the date data type and the width of 8 and skips to the Index column. Press **Enter** to move to the next row.

16. For field 12, type *last_dues* as the Field Name. Press **Enter** to move to the Field Type column and press *n* for Numeric. The cursor moves to the width column.

17. You need a width of three spaces for the dollar amount plus one space for the decimal point plus two spaces for the cents amount—a total width of 6. Enter 6 in this column, then Enter *2* in the Dec column, then press **Enter** to go the next row.

18. For field 13, type *last_donat* as the Field Name, *d* as the Field Type, and press **Enter** to move to the next row.

19. For field 14, enter *volunteer* as the Field name. Type *l* for the Logical Field Type. dBASE IV automatically enters a Width of 1 and, since you cannot index on a logical field, moves you to the next row.

20. For field 15, enter *notes* as the field name. Type *m* for Memo as the Field Type. dBASE IV automatically enters the width of 10 and, since you can not index on a memo field, moves to the next row.

21. That is all of the fields of your database file. Your screen should look like Figure 2.10. Before saving your work, select **Edit database**

description from the Layout menu. As the description of the file, type *List of members of the organization*, as in Figure 2.11, and press **Enter**.

Figure 2.10   *The structure of the database.*

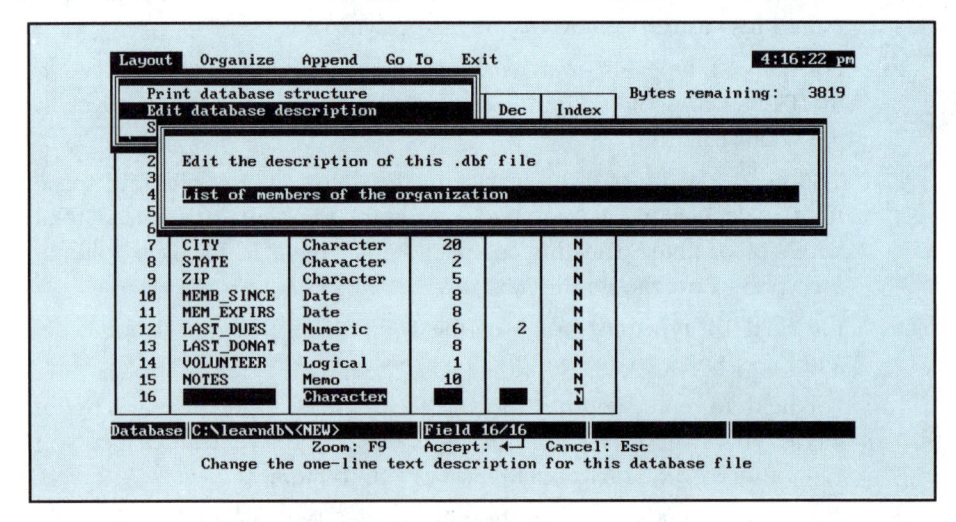

Figure 2.11   *Adding the description of the database.*

22. Press **Ctrl-End** or select **Save changes and exit** from the Exit menu.
23. dBASE IV asks you to enter a name for the new file. Type *members* and press **Enter**. When dBASE IV displays the prompt Input data records

now? (Y/N), press *n* to return to the Control Center, as you do not want to add records to this file now.

Using a Database

Now that you have returned to the Control Center, notice that the name of the MEMBERS database file that you just created has appeared in the data panel above the line. This file name is highlighted, and the file name (with the .DBF extension used for database files) and the description you entered are displayed below the panels.

The fact that the file name is above the line means that it is in use. You must *use* a file before you can perform certain operations with it; for example, before you create mailing labels, a database file must be in use, so dBASE IV knows what fields can go on the label.

The navigation line says that you can press **Enter** to use the highlighted file. As you will see, you can also press **Enter** to close the file if it is in use:

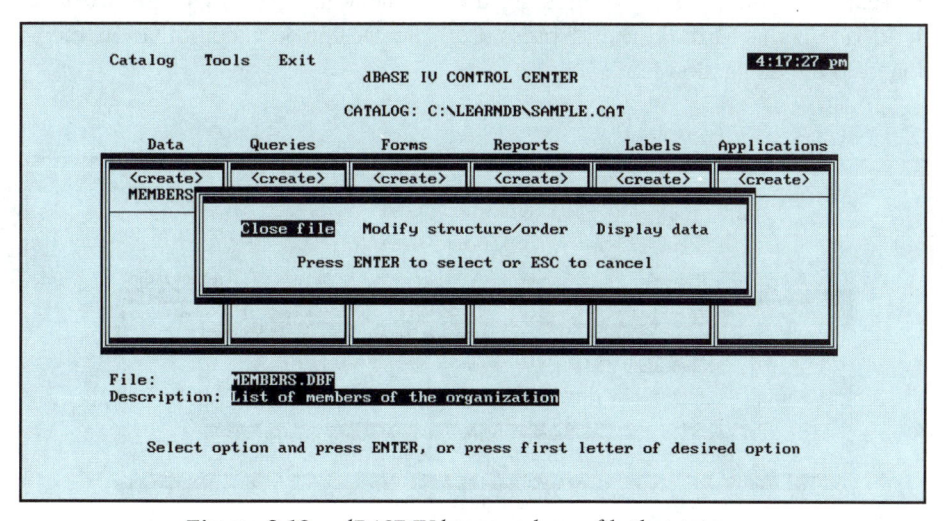

Figure 2.12 *dBASE IV lets you close a file that is in use.*

1. Press **Enter**. dBASE IV displays a prompt box that gives you the choice of closing the file, modifying the file's structure or order, or displaying the data in the file as shown in Figure 2.12.

2. Press **Enter** to select Close file. dBASE IV returns you to the Control Center. The MEMBERS file is now below the line in the data panel, showing that it is no longer in use.
3. Select **MEMBERS** from the Data panel. dBASE IV now lets you use the file, as shown in Figure 2.13. Press **Enter** to use the file again, and note that it is now above the line when you return to the Control Center.

If you have multiple database files, the one that is in use is closed automatically when you use another one.

Modifying the Structure of a File

Modifying the structure of an existing file is very similar to defining the structure of a new file.

You have just seen that, when you press **Enter** to use a file, dBASE IV gives you the option to Modify structure/order, and you can select this option. Alternatively, you can simply highlight the file name and press **Design:Shift-F2** (hold down the **Shift** key and press **F2**), the Design key combination mentioned in the navigation line.

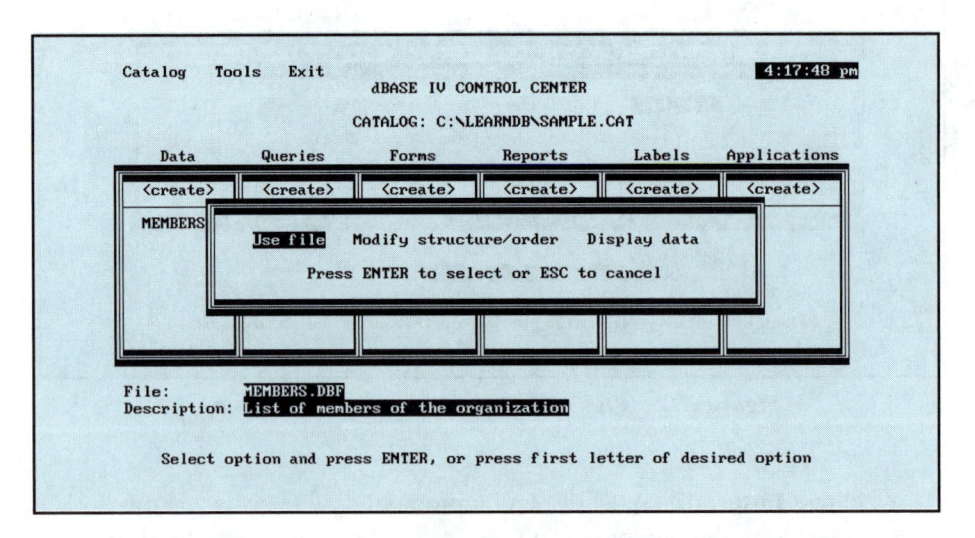

Figure 2.13 *dBASE IV lets you use a file that is closed.*

Either one returns you to the database design screen, where you can edit the structure, using the same editing keys that were available when you defined it:

1. **MEMBERS** should be highlighted. Press **Shift-F2**. Since this method is used to create indexes, the Organize menu appears automatically when the database design screen is displayed. Press **Esc** to remove this menu.
2. Move the highlight to field 4, the LNAME field. Press **Ctrl-N** to insert a new field (as the navigation line says). A new space appears above the LNAME field, and all of the fields that follow move down one.
3. Type *mname* and press **Enter**. Press **Enter** to confirm that it is a Character field. Enter a width of 15.
4. Imagine that you decide to change the name and width of this new field. Move the cursor back to the width column, and to the 5. Press **0** to overwrite the 5, changing 15 to 10. dBASE beeps and moves to the index column.
5. Move to the field name column, and to the letter N. Press **Ins** to toggle to insert mode. Type *id_* to change the field name to *mid_name*.
6. Now imagine that you realize that you do not need a middle name field after all. Press **Ctrl-U** to delete the field. It disappears and the following fields all move up.
7. Press **PgDn** to move to the bottom of the list of fields, press the **Up Arrow** key a few times to move up the list, and press **PgUp** to move to the top of the list.
8. If you have a mouse, move the cursor by clicking the location you want to move it to.
9. Now that you have gotten the basic idea of how the editing keys work, press **Ctrl-End** or select **Save changes and exit** from the Exit menu. dBASE IV asks you to press **Enter** to confirm that the changes you have made are correct or to press any other key to return to the database design screen and continue making changes. Press **Enter** to return to the Control Center.

dBASE IV asks you for confirmation because there is a danger of losing data when you modify the structure of a database file that already has data entered in it.

WARNING

One way you can lose data is if you make the width of a Character or Numeric field smaller, so that it can no longer hold some of the data that you have already entered in to it.

There is also danger of losing data if you change both the name of a field and the width of a field (not necessarily of the same field) when you are modifying the structure of a database file. If you must change the name and/or width of fields, do it in two steps: change the name first and save the change, and then change the width.

There is also some danger of data loss if your computer shuts off—for example, because of power failure—while you are modifying the structure of a file. You can help prevent some data loss due to power failure by saving your work frequently. To save your work and continue, you can select **Save this database file structure** from the Layout menu.

For these reasons, dBASE IV automatically backs up your data when you modify the structure of a database file. It creates a backup with the extension DBK for the database file and one with the extension .TBK for the memo file. If you find that you have lost data after modifying the structure of a file, you can recover it by using a DOS command like *copy <file name>.dbk <file name>.dbf* to use the backup file as the main database file again; you might also need a command like *copy <file name>.tbk <file name>.dbt* to recover the memo file. Remember that these are commands that you enter at the DOS prompt.

You probably feel like taking a break by now. Get into the habit of always quitting dBASE IV before turning off your computer.

1. To exit dBASE IV, select **Quit to DOS** from the Exit menu.
2. When the DOS prompt appears, you can safely turn off your computer.

Summary

This chapter instructed you in the basics of database design and organization. In addition, you created and saved the structure of the MEMBERS database that you will be using throughout this book In the next chapter, you earn how to enter data and edit and browse records in the database you just created.

Chapter 3

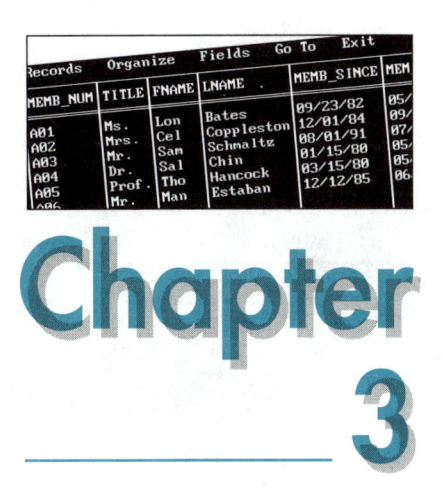

Entering, Editing, and Viewing Data

Now that you have created a database file, you are ready to begin to use it to enter and edit your data. In this chapter, you enter some sample data into the MEMBERS database and you learn how to edit and view the data you have entered. In addition, you learn about:

- The Browse screen
- The Edit screen
- Database editing and navigation keys
- The Browse and Edit menu systems
- Deleting records
- Memo fields and the dBASE IV word processor
- Other ways to move around the database using options from the Go To menu
- Adding records to an existing database

Edit and Browse Modes

When you enter, edit, or view data, the database can be displayed in one of two ways. You can use the Edit screen, shown in Figure 3.1, or the Browse screen, shown in Figure 3.2.

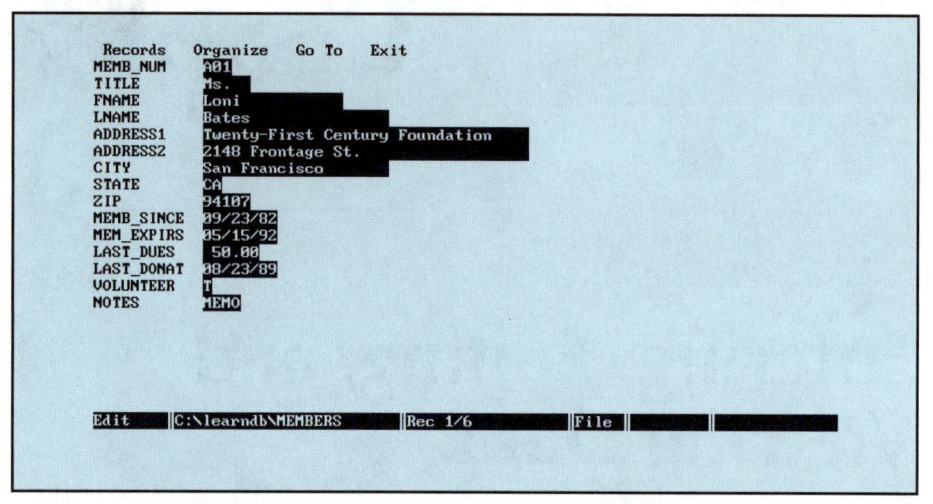

Figure 3.1   *The Edit screen.*

Figure 3.2   *The Browse screen.*

As you can see in the illustrations, the Edit screen displays the fields of a single record, one field on each line. The Browse screen displays the database in table form, with the fields next to each other so that there is one record on each line.

The Edit screen is record-oriented. That is, it lets you see as much of the data in a single record as will fit on a single screen. In most cases, you can see the entire record, though some databases have so many fields that an entire record does not fit on a single screen. This way of looking at the data is useful if you are editing it, accounting for the screen's name, but it is equally useful when you are entering new data or looking up specific records.

The Browse screen, just as obviously, is useful if you want to "browse" through all the records of a database. This screen is database-oriented. You can see many records at a time, though you cannot see all of the fields in any record.

The Browse and Edit screens can both be used for the same purposes. Despite their names, the Browse screen can also be used for editing and the Edit screen can be used to browse the database, one record at a time. You can choose whichever screen you find more convenient.

To use the Browse or Edit screen, highlight the name of the file in the Data panel of the Control Center and then press **Data:F2**. You can also use these screens by selecting the file in the Data panel. As you have seen, this displays a prompt box that includes the option **Display Data**, and you can select this option to use the Browse or Edit screen.

By default, whenever there are records in a database, dBASE IV begins by using the Browse screen. You can switch to the Edit screen by pressing **Data:F2**, which toggles you back and forth between the Edit and the Browse screens. When you return to the Control Center, dBASE IV remembers whether you were using the Browse or the Edit screen. The next time that you display the data, dBASE IV uses whichever screen you were using last.

When there are no records in a database, however, dBASE IV uses the Edit screen by default and does not allow you toggle to the Browse screen. If there are no records to browse through, there is no reason to use the Browse screen.

NOTE

dBASE IV also remembers the record that you were using when you returned to the Control Center, and when you Browse or Edit the database again, that record is still the current record. dBASE IV uses what is called the *pointer* to keep track of the current record.

Of course, the pointer also remains in the same place when you toggle between Browse and Edit screen. The same current record in the Browse screen is displayed on the entire screen when you switch to the Edit screen.

The Editing Keys

In general, you use the standard editing keys when you are entering new data or editing an existing record using either the Browse or the Edit screen, and there are a few added keys that you can use as shortcuts.

When you are editing non-memo fields, the effects of some of the editing keys differ slightly, depending on whether you are using the Edit or the Browse screens. As you will see, the reasons for these differences are obvious. (Memo fields are edited differently and are discussed later in this chapter.)

The Right and Left Arrow keys move the cursor one character to the right or left within a field. The Up and Down Arrow keys move the cursor up or down one line. When you are using the Edit screen, moving up one line moves you to the *previous field*. When you are using the Browse screen, moving up a line moves you to the *previous record*.

The PgUp and PgDn keys move up or down one screen. If you are using the Edit screen, PgDn generally moves you to the next record. (However, if the database file has so many fields that they cannot fit on one Edit screen, it takes you through each record one screen at a time, before moving to the next record.) If you are using the Browse screen, PgDn replaces the entire screen of records with the next screen of records.

The Home key moves you to the far left and the End key to the far right of the current line. In the Edit screen, Home or End moves the cursor to the first or last character of the current field. In the Browse screen, Home or End moves the cursor to the first field or last field in the record.

As usual, Ins toggles you from insert to type-over mode, Del deletes the character on which the cursor is located, and Backspace deletes the character to the left of the cursor. Pressing Enter confirms the entry in the current field and moves you to the next field.

Tab and Shift-Tab move you to the next or previous field, respectively. You can also use the Prev:Shift-F3 and Next:Shift-F4 keys to move to the previous or next field: This might be easier for people who rely heavily on their templates, but most people find it easier to use Tab and Shift-Tab.

You can use Ctrl-Y to delete all of the characters to the right of the cursor and Ditto:Shift-F8 to repeat the data that is in the same field of the previous record.

When you are done, you can use the familiar keys Ctrl-End to save your work and return to the Control Center, or Esc to discard changes in the current record and return to the Control Center.

Esc discards only changes that you made in the current record (including changes to the memo field of the current record). It does not discard any changes that you made to other records earlier in the editing session.

The uses of these editing keys are summarized in Table 3.1

Table 3.1 *Editing keys for the Browse and Edit screens.*

Enter	Confirm entry and move to next field
Right, Left Arrow	Move right or left one character
Up, Down Arrow	Move up or down one line
PgUp, PgDn	Move up or down one screen
Home, End	Move to the far left or far right of the current line
Ins	Toggle between insert and type-over mode
Del	Delete the character the cursor is on
Backspace	Delete the character left of the cursor
Tab, Shift-Tab	Move to the next or previous field
Next:F4, Prev:F3	Move to the next or previous field
Ctrl-Y	Delete characters to the right of the cursor
Shift-F8	Repeat data in same field of previous record
Ctrl-End	Return to Control Center and save work
Esc	Return to Control Center and discard work on current record

Using the mouse, you can simply click any field to move the highlight to it. Click any location in the field to move the cursor there. To move the highlight one field to the left or right, click the left or right border of the table, and to move the highlight to the first or last field, double-click the left or right border of the table. Likewise, to move the highlight up or down one line, click the upper or lower border of the table, and to move the highlight up or down one page, double-click the upper or lower border of the table.

The Browse and Edit Menu Systems

As you saw in the illustrations of the Browse and Edit screens at the beginning of this chapter, both have similar menus, except that the Browse screen has a Fields menu in addition to the Records, Organize, Go To, and Exit menus that it shares with the Edit screen.

The main use of the Fields menu is to let you rearrange and resize fields so you can more easily view the data in all the records that you are browsing. This feature is not needed on the Edit screen because you can generally see all the fields on that screen. Later in this chapter, after you have entered sample data in the database, you will see how to use the Fields menu to view that data.

The Records Menu

The Records menu, shown in Figure 3.3, is the most important menu for both the Browse and the Edit screen.

It has a useful and important option to Undo change to record, which you can use if you have edited a record incorrectly and want to start over. Remember that this option exists in case you make a mistake while you are entering or editing data.

The option to Add new records adds a blank record at the end of the database in which you can enter data, and continues to add new records as you finish making an entry in the current one. (You can also add a new record at the end of a database, if the cursor is on the last record, by pressing the **Down Arrow** key in Browse or the **PgDn** key in Edit. dBASE IV asks for confirmation before adding new records.)

The next option on the Record menu, Mark record for deletion, is part of a two-step deletion process and is covered in detail in the next section of this chapter.

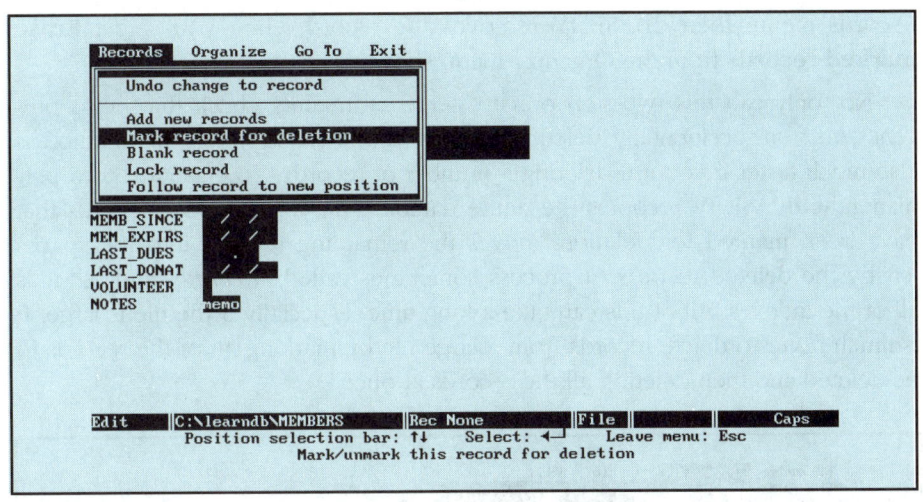

Figure 3.3   The Records menu.

The option Blank record removes all of the data in the current record. This option does not eliminate the record or mark it for deletion. It simply leaves it in the database as a blank record, and it is useful if you have to change the data in the record so completely that you want to start from scratch.

The option Lock record is used only on networks and is permanently dimmed if you are working on a stand-alone computer. If you are on a network and another user is accessing the same record that you are, dBASE IV automatically displays the message "Record may have been changed" to let you know that the record may have been changed since the time that you displayed it. If you select **Lock record**, then no other user may change the record while you are looking at it. A record is automatically locked while you are editing it.

The option Follow record to new position is used to keep the pointer on the current record when you are using indexes to change the order of records. Indexes are discussed in Chapter 4.

Marking and Deleting Records

The Records menu is used in combination with the Organize menu to delete unwanted records from the file.

dBASE IV uses a two-step process for deleting a record: first you designate the record by selecting the **Mark the record for deletion** option from the

Records menu; then dBASE IV removes the record when you select **Erase marked records** from the Organize menu shown in Figure 3.4.

Not only can this two-step process serve as a safety check that helps prevent you from accidentally deleting records you want to keep, this method is also much faster if you are deleting a number of records. To erase a record permanently, dBASE IV recopies the entire database file except those records that have been marked for deletion, moves the remaining records into the spaces left by the deleted records (a process sometimes called *packing*), and rebuilds all of the indexes. All of this can take a long time, especially if the file is large. It is much faster to delete records from a large file by marking all of the records to be deleted and then deleting all the records at once.

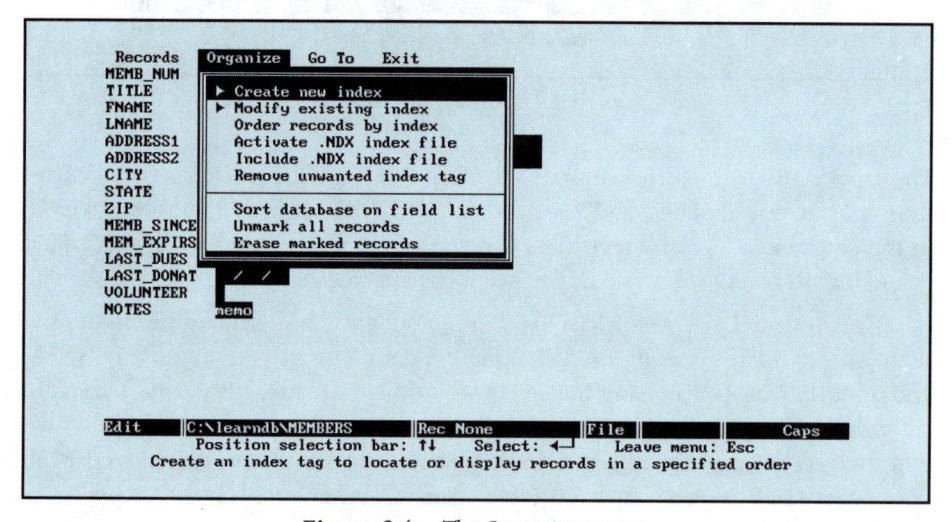

Figure 3.4 The Organize menu.

If the current record is already marked for deletion, Mark record for deletion changes to Clear deletion mark. You can also tell if the current record is marked for deletion by looking at the status bar at the bottom of the screen. The designation Del appears at the far right if the highlighted record is marked for deletion.

SHORTCUT

You can also press **Ctrl-U** to toggle the current record between marked and unmarked.

Erase marked records permanently removes from the database all records that have been marked for deletion. However, dBASE IV asks for confirmation before deleting the marked records. Once you have selected this option, the deleted data can no longer be recovered.

The Unmark all records option of the Organize menu removes the deletion mark from all marked records in a database. Again, however, dBASE IV asks for confirmation before actually unmarking all the marked records in a database. This option could potentially destroy hours of your work if it is used inadvertently.

It is important to remember that dBASE IV continues to display records that are marked for deletion and includes them in all reports, mailing labels, and so on until they are permanently erased from the file.

In Chapter 9, you will learn that, if you select Settings from the Tools menu of the Control Center, you can select Deleted from the Options submenu to toggle this feature On and Off. By default, the Deleted setting is Off, and marked records are included in the Browse screen, mailing labels, reports, and so on. If you toggle this setting On, though, you can make dBASE ignore marked records. This has the effect of "hiding" the records without actually deleting them.

For a beginner, though, rather than using this setting, it is advisable to select **Erase marked records** from the Organize menu before doing anything that should not include records marked for deletion, such as producing mailing labels or reports.

The Go To Menu

The Go To menu is used to move quickly around the database. It is discussed in more detail later in this chapter, after you have actually entered data.

The Exit Menu

The Exit menu of the Browse/Edit screens, shown in Figure 3.5, is a bit like the Exit menu you saw in the previous chapter, except that it has the options Exit and Transfer to query design. The query design screen is covered in Chapter 5; it is often convenient to create a query while editing.

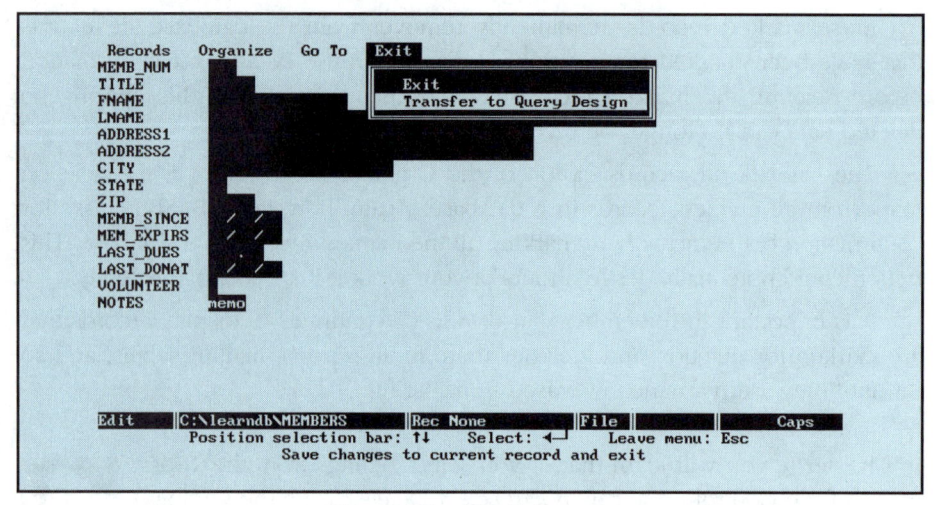

Figure 3.5 *The Exit menu.*

Though the Exit option may be useful for dBASE beginners, it is easier to return to the Control Center by pressing **Ctrl-End** to save your work or pressing **Esc** to discard work on the current record. Note again that pressing **Esc** does not discard changes you made to other records earlier in the current editing session; it only discards changes to the current record.

Memo Fields

Because they vary in size, the contents of a memo field are not displayed as part of the ordinary Edit or Browse screens. Instead, the screen displays a small field with the word *MEMO* in it as a marker.

If the word *MEMO* is capitalized, that means text has been entered in the memo field. If *memo* is in lower case, it means that there is no text in the memo field.

To add text to a memo field or to edit or view the contents already in a memo field, you can:

- Press **Ctrl-Home** when the cursor is on that field
- Press **Zoom:F9** when the cursor is on that field

- Move the cursor to that field using the **Next:F3** or **Prev:F4** keys, and the memo screen is displayed automatically when you reach the field.
- Using the mouse, double-click on the field.

The dBASE IV Word Processor

Any of these options lets you use the dBASE IV word processor, shown in Figure 3.6, to view or edit the contents of the memo field.

As you can see from Figure 3.6, the word processor is rather complex. It includes a complete menu system of its own and a ruler on the top, which lets you set tab stops and margins. The word processor is included in many dBASE screens—for example, it is used to lay out reports and form letters and to write dBASE programs, as well as for editing memo fields (though it is slightly different in different applications). Unlike most screens that use the word processor, the memo editing screen includes word wrap; that is, when you reach the end of the line, the text automatically continues on the next line.

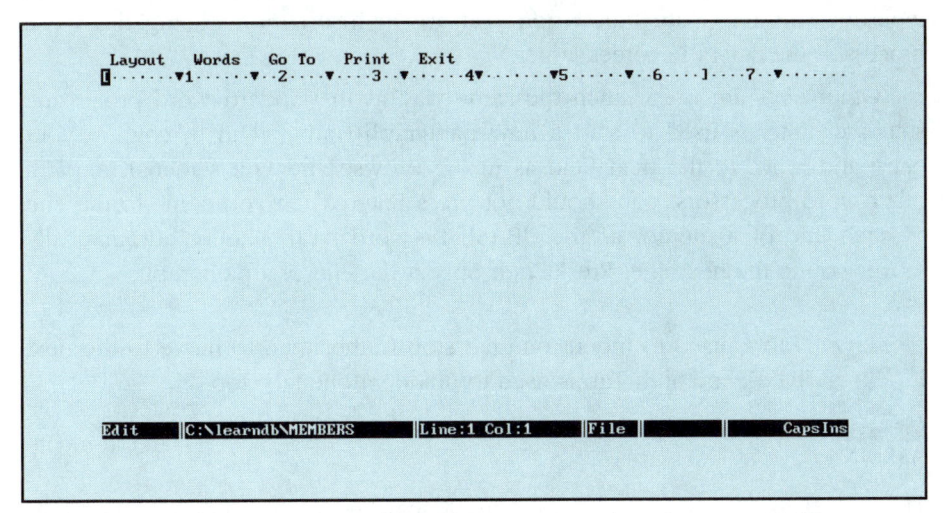

Figure 3.6 *The dBASE IV word processor used to edit a memo field.*

In some applications, you may actually use all of the power of the word processor when you are working with memos. For example, you might use dBASE IV to record bibliographic references, with a book's name, author, and key-word references displayed on the Browse screen and a complete summary or review of the book, which might be several pages long, kept in the memo fields. You would want a full-power word processor to edit this sort of memo.

In most cases, however, you do not need all this power. Most people just jot down notes in the memo field, rather than using them to work with entire documents.

Because many dBASE users rarely need all of the features of the word processor, it is discussed in greater detail in Chapter 9. Rather than spending time on it now, you should move ahead to learn the basics of dBASE IV.

Editing Memo Fields

For editing most memo fields, you can use the standard editing keys that you already have learned about.

Most are used just as they are when you are editing fields. The arrow keys move right or left one space or up and down one line. Home and End move the cursor to the left or right edge of the current line. Del deletes the letter the cursor is on; Backspace deletes the letter to the left; Ins toggles from insert to type-over mode. (Note that when you are in insert mode using the word processor, the cursor becomes larger.)

Other keys are used much the same way as in standard word processing software. Enter is used to start a new paragraph (rather than to confirm your entry and move to the next field as in the Browse and Edit screens). As with other word processors, you should not press Enter when you come to the end of each line of a memo, as the dBASE IV word wrap feature automatically moves you to the next line. Press Enter only at the end of a paragraph.

WARNING Tab is used to indent one tab stop (rather than to move to the next field), and Shift-Tab is used to unindent one tab stop.

The use of the Tab key in memo fields is a bit tricky. Though it is not commonly used, you might find yourself using tabs if you enter memos that are more than a paragraph long, and so you should know the possible pitfalls.

If you are using a mouse, you can position the cursor in any location simply by clicking that location. You can select (highlight) text by clicking and dragging the mouse over that text, and you can deselect text that is already selected by clicking in any other location or by using any cursor movement key. If text is selected, anything you type replaces the selected text, and pressing Del or Backspace deletes the selected text.

Automatic Indent

The Words menu of the word processor includes an Enable automatic indent option, shown in Figure 3.7. If automatic indent is on, the word *Yes* is included at the far right of this option; if not, the word *No* is included at the far right. The option is a toggle, so that if automatic indent is on, selecting it turns it off, and vice versa.

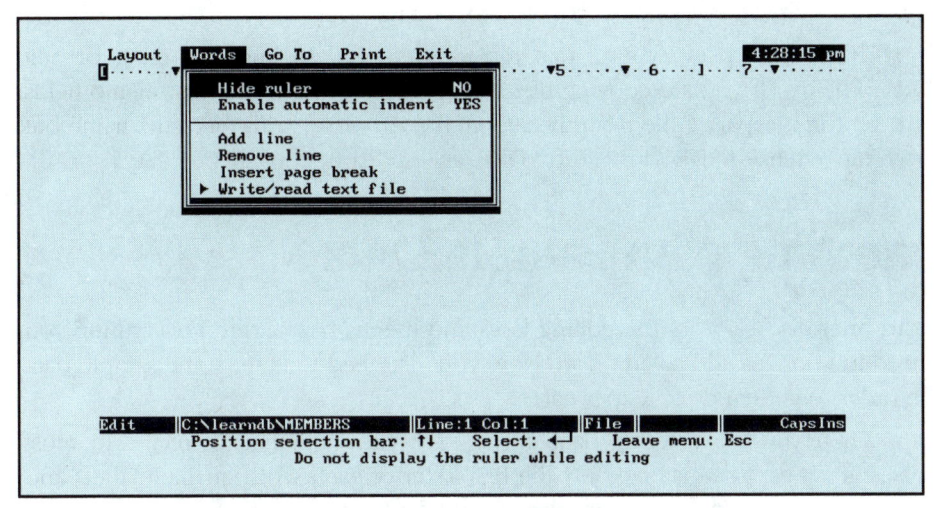

Figure 3.7 *The Words menu with automatic indent on.*

If automatic indent is on and you are in insert mode, then if you press Tab at the beginning of a paragraph, the word processor automatically changes the margin to indent the lines that follow, so that they line up under the line that you indented using Tab. You can unindent them using Shift-Tab. This feature is useful when you are writing programs, but it can be a nuisance when you are entering a memo. You might want to avoid the problem by double spacing between paragraphs of memos rather than indenting, by working in type-over rather than insert mode, or by pressing Shift-Tab to unindent after the first line of each paragraph. If automatic indent gives you any trouble, however, simply select **Enable automatic indent** from the Words menu to turn it off.

Saving Changes in the Word Processor

Automatic indent is the only potentially tricky feature of the word processor. Apart from it, using the word processor for entering and editing a typical memo is simple and intuitive.

When you are done editing the memo, you can press **Ctrl-End** to save your work and return to the browse/edit screen, or you can select **Save changes and exit** from the Exit menu of the word processor. You can also press **Prev:F3** or **Next:F4**, to save your work, return to the browse or edit screens, and move to the previous or next field.

To discard the work you have done on the memo, press **Esc** or select **Abandon changes and exit** from the Exit menu.

That sums up everything that most users need to know to enter or edit memo fields. (If you are copying files, you must also remember that memo fields are kept in a separate file from the rest of the database, with the same name but with the extension .DBT instead of .DBF, as you learned in Chapter 1.)

Working with Sample Data

This brief discussion of the editing keys and menus has covered everything you need to know to add or edit data. Now you just need to enter some sample data in order to get hands-on experience.

When you are entering data, make sure you capitalize correctly. In most cases, it is best to capitalize only the first letter of each word: mailing labels and reports look best, the names can be used in form letters, and so on.

1. If necessary start dBASE IV. First, enter *cd \learndb* at the DOS prompt to get into the LEARNDB subdirectory. Then enter *dbase*. When it starts up, dBASE IV should be using the SAMPLE catalog that you created earlier, but if it is not (for example, because you created other catalogs on your own), use the Catalog menu to select the SAMPLE catalog.

2. Select **MEMBERS** from the Data panel. Select **Display Data** from the prompt box that is displayed. Because no data has been entered, dBASE IV displays a blank edit screen.

3. Type *A01* in the MEMB_NUM field: there is no need to press Enter, because it fills the entire field, so that dBASE beeps and moves to the

next field. Now fill in the rest of the fields, pressing **Enter** after each entry is complete. Be careful to capitalize correctly.

4. Type *Ms.* in the TITLE field.
5. Type *Loni* in the FNAME field.
6. Type *Bates* in the LNAME field.
7. Type *Twenty-First Century Foundation* in ADDRESS1 and *2148 Frontage St.* in ADDRESS2.
8. Type *San Francisco* in CITY.
9. Type *CA* in STATE; dBASE beeps and moves to the next field.
10. Type *94107* in ZIP.
11. Type *09 23 82* in MEMB_SINCE, and type *05 15 92* in MEM_EXPIRS. Note that in these date fields, you only have to type the numbers: the slashes are already there.
12. Enter *50* in LAST_DUES: just type the amount beginning at the left edge of the field, and when you press **Enter**, 50 is moved right one space to leave the hundreds column blank and two zeros are added after the decimal point so that the entry reads *50.00*.
13. Type *08 23 89* in LAST_DONAT.
14. Type *t* in VOLUNTEER.
15. Now that you are in the NOTES field, press **Ctrl-Home** to use the Memo screen. Type *Executive director of the Twenty-First Century Foundation. Working on getting a grant for our organization.* and then press **Ctrl-End** to save the work and return to the Edit screen. Notice that the word MEMO is now capitalized to indicate that you have entered text in the NOTES field, as shown in Figure 3.8.
16. Your cursor should be on the NOTES field. To continue adding data, press **Enter**. If dBASE IV asks you to confirm that you want to add more records, press *Y* to move to a blank record.
17. Ordinarily, you would probably want to continue using the Edit screen as you add records. As an exercise, though, press **F2** to switch to the Browse screen. If the cursor is still on the blank record, press the **Up Arrow** key so that you can see the first record, and press **Down Arrow** to move back to the second record. Now you can see your entry in the Browse screen, as shown in Figure 3.9.

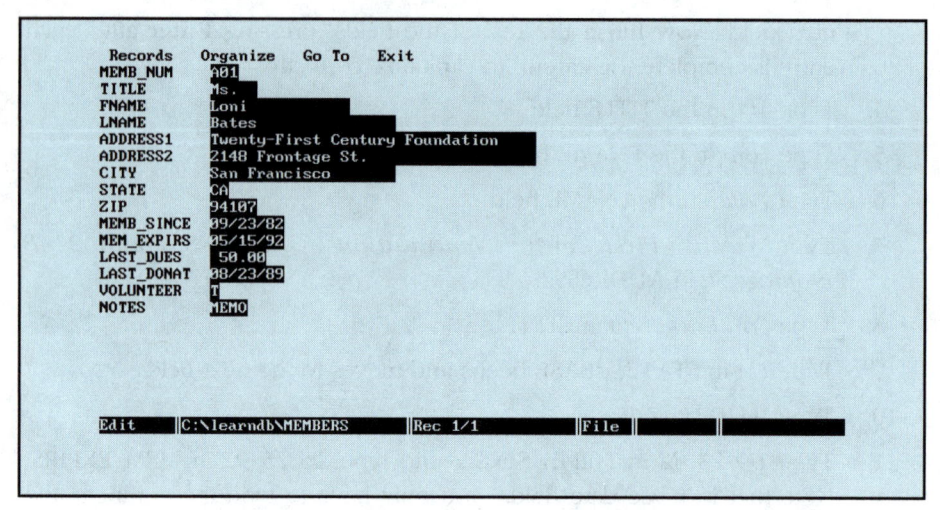

```
        Records    Organize   Go To    Exit
        MEMB_NUM   A01
        TITLE      Ms.
        FNAME      Loni
        LNAME      Bates
        ADDRESS1   Twenty-First Century Foundation
        ADDRESS2   2148 Frontage St.
        CITY       San Francisco
        STATE      CA
        ZIP        94107
        MEMB_SINCE 09/23/82
        MEM_EXPIRS 05/15/92
        LAST_DUES    50.00
        LAST_DONAT 08/23/89
        VOLUNTEER  T
        NOTES      MEMO




     Edit    C:\learndb\MEMBERS      Rec 1/1        File
```

Figure 3.8   *The first record in the Edit screen.*

Entering the first record has shown you a couple of tricks of data entry, such as entering numbers without worrying about their justification or the zeros following the decimal point. Now, you should have no trouble entering a few more sample records on your own. You might want to switch back and forth between Browse and Edit as you enter these records, to get experience with both.

```
     Records    Organize   Fields   Go To    Exit
    ┌─────────┬──────┬──────────┬─────────────┬──────────────────────────┐
    │MEMB_NUM │TITLE │FNAME     │LNAME        │ADDRESS1                  │
    ├─────────┼──────┼──────────┼─────────────┼──────────────────────────┤
    │A01      │Ms.   │Loni      │Bates        │Twenty-First Century Found│
    │         │      │          │             │                          │
    │         │      │          │             │                          │
    │         │      │          │             │                          │
    │         │      │          │             │                          │
    │         │      │          │             │                          │
    │         │      │          │             │                          │
    │         │      │          │             │                          │
    │         │      │          │             │                          │
    └─────────┴──────┴──────────┴─────────────┴──────────────────────────┘
     Browse   C:\learndb\MEMBERS      Rec EOF/1      File
                        Add new records
```

Figure 3.9   *The first record in the Browse screen.*

Just a few sample records follow, and they are used in all of the exercises in later chapters to represent the much larger number of records that you would have in an ordinary database. Using the steps you learned in the previous exercise, enter the following records into the MEMBERS database.

1. MEMB_NUM: A02
   TITLE: Mrs.
   FNAME: Celia
   LNAME: Copplestone
   ADDRESS1: 2031 Kenmore Terrace
   ADDRESS2: (none)
   CITY: St. Louis
   STATE: MO
   ZIP: 63114
   MEMB_SINCE: 12/01/84
   MEM_EXPIRS: 09/19/93
   LAST_DUES: 100.00
   LAST_DONAT: (none)
   VOLUNTEER: F
   NOTES: (none)

2. MEMB_NUM: A03
   TITLE: Mr.
   FNAME: Samuel
   LNAME: Schmaltz
   ADDRESS1: 1701 Albemarle Rd.
   ADDRESS2: (none)
   CITY: Brooklyn
   STATE: NY
   ZIP: 11226
   MEMB_SINCE: 08/01/91
   MEM_EXPIRS: 07/31/92

LAST_DUES: 15
LAST_DONAT: (none)
VOLUNTEER: F
NOTES: (none)

3. MEMB_NUM: A04
TITLE: Dr.
FNAME: Sally E.
LNAME: Chin
ADDRESS1: 1 Alvarado Plaza — Ste. 43
ADDRESS2: 10952 Pico Blvd.
CITY: Los Angeles
STATE: CA
ZIP: 90064
MEMB_SINCE: 01/15/80
MEM_EXPIRS: 05/12/92
LAST_DUES: 25
LAST_DONAT: 01/15/81
VOLUNTEER: T
NOTES: Very active as volunteer. Not only writes letters herself but also organizes letter writing meetings.

4. MEMB_NUM: A05
TITLE: Prof.
FNAME: Thomas
NAME: Hancock
ADDRESS1: National Research Laboratories
ADDRESS2: 1 Linear Accelerator Ave
CITY: Berkeley
STATE: CA
ZIP: 94720

MEMB_SINCE: 03/15/80

MEM_EXPIRS: 05/05/92

LAST_DUES: 50

LAST_DONAT: (none)

VOLUNTEER: F

NOTES: (none)

5. MEMB_NUM: A06

TITLE: Mr.

FNAME: Manuel

LNAME: Estaban

ADDRESS1: 476 Partridge Hill Rd.

ADDRESS2: (none)

CITY: Boston

STATE: MA

ZIP: 02165

MEMB_SINCE: 12/12/85

MEM_EXPIRS: 06/01/92

LAST_DUES: 100

LAST_DONAT: 12/29/89

VOLUNTEER: T

NOTES: A specialist in writing grant proposals. Is willing to review our proposals.

After you have finished entering all of these records, you should try out the editing techniques described earlier in this chapter. Try typing over a name, for example, or deleting some of its letters, and then selecting **Undo change** from the Records menu (or just editing the name again) so that it is what it should be. Try marking a record for deletion and then unmarking it. It should only take you a few minutes of practice to become comfortable using of the editing keys and the necessary features of the Edit/Browse menus.

When you are done, press **Ctrl-End** or select **Exit** from the Exit menu to save your work and return to the Control Center.

The Fields Menu

As you learned earlier, the Browse screen has one menu that the Edit screen does not have, the Fields menu, shown in Figure 3.10.

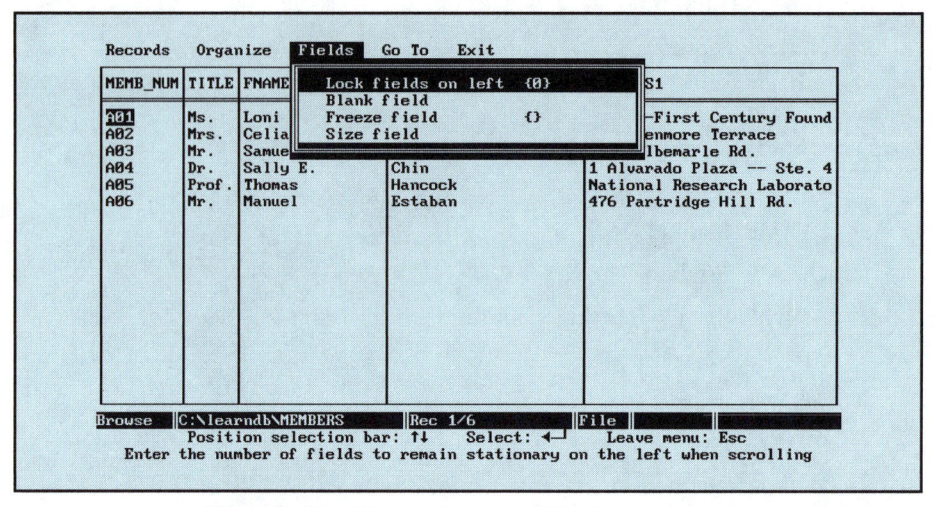

Figure 3.10 The Fields menu of the Browse screen.

The most common use of this menu is to allow you view the fields that you need to use while you are browsing through the database.

If you select the **Lock fields on left** option, dBASE IV asks you to specify the number of fields that you want to lock. When you view the fields to the right, these fields will not scroll off the screen. This feature is commonly used to keep people's names on the screen while you scroll to the right to see some other data (such as the telephone numbers) that you would want to use in combination with the names.

If you select the **Size fields** option, dBASE IV prompts you to use the Left and Right Arrow keys to change the width of the column where the field is displayed. These keys move the right edge of the column, so that the Left Arrow makes it narrower and the Right Arrow makes it wider. For example, you might want to make fields narrower, so that you can see more fields at once. Since fields are large enough for the longest entries, you can make them shorter and still see all the data in most records.

dBASE IV does not actually make a column narrower than the title at the top, though it displays fewer characters of data if you continue to press the **Left Arrow** key to make the field narrower. It also lets you press the **Right Arrow** key until the column is wider than the field itself: to avoid wasting space by making columns wider than necessary, look at the highlighted data entry area and do not make the column wider than it is.

Using a mouse, simply click the gridline to the right of a field, hold down the mouse button, and drag left or right to make the field smaller or larger.

These options are so often useful that you should try them out:

1. Select **MEMBERS** from the Data panel and select **Display Data** from the prompt box. If you are using the Edit screen, press **Data:F2** to toggle to the Browse screen.

2. Press **PgUp** and **Home** to move to the first field of the first record of the database. Your screen should look like Figure 3.11.

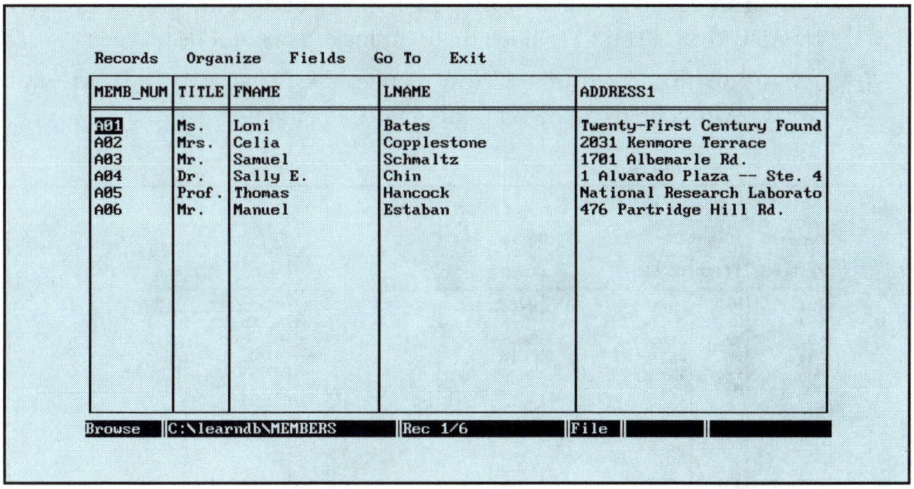

```
  Records    Organize    Fields    Go To    Exit
  MEMB_NUM TITLE FNAME           LNAME           ADDRESS1
  A01      Ms.   Loni            Bates           Twenty-First Century Found
  A02      Mrs.  Celia           Copplestone     2031 Kenmore Terrace
  A03      Mr.   Samuel          Schmaltz        1701 Albemarle Rd.
  A04      Dr.   Sally E.        Chin            1 Alvarado Plaza -- Ste. 4
  A05      Prof. Thomas          Hancock         National Research Laborato
  A06      Mr.   Manuel          Estaban         476 Partridge Hill Rd.




  Browse   C:\learndb\MEMBERS      Rec 1/6        File
```

Figure 3.11 *The default Browse screen.*

3. Select **Lock fields on left** from the **Fields** menu. dBASE IV prompts you to enter the number of fields that you want to remain stationary, as in Figure 3.12. Type *4* to lock the MEMB_NUM, TITLE, FNAME, and LNAME fields.

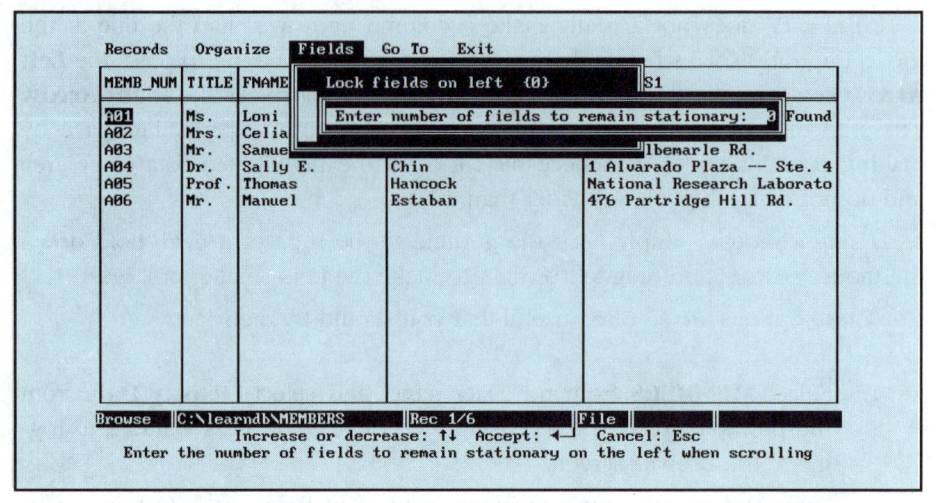

Figure 3.12   Specifying the number of fields to lock.

4. dBASE IV returns you to the Browse screen. Now, move to ADDRESS1. Press **Tab** again. Notice that only ADDRESS1 disappears and is replaced by ADDRESS2. The four fields that you locked are still displayed.

5. Press **Tab** five more times. Now you can see the MEMB_SINCE and MEM_EXPIRS fields along with the name, as in Figure 3.13.

Figure 3.13   Viewing the names and membership dates.

Chapter 3: Entering, Editing, and Viewing Data ◆ 75

6. Suppose you want to view even more data. Try narrowing the FNAME and LNAME fields. Press **Shift-Tab** seven times to move back to the LNAME field.

7. Select **Size field** from the Fields menu. dBASE IV prompts you to use the Left or Right Arrow key to change the current column width. Press **Enter** when you are done. Press the **Left Arrow** key ten times: you should still be able to read all of the last names, though the final letter is cut off of one of them. Press **Enter** to end sizing.

8. Press **Shift-Tab** to move back to the FNAME field. Select **Size field** from the Fields menu again. Press the **Left Arrow** key twelve times. Note that the last two times you press it, the names continue to get narrower but the column stays the same width, so that it can continue to display FNAME at the top. Press **Enter.**

9. Press **Tab** eleven times to scroll to the right. Now you can see the name and five columns of membership data, as shown in Figure 3.14.

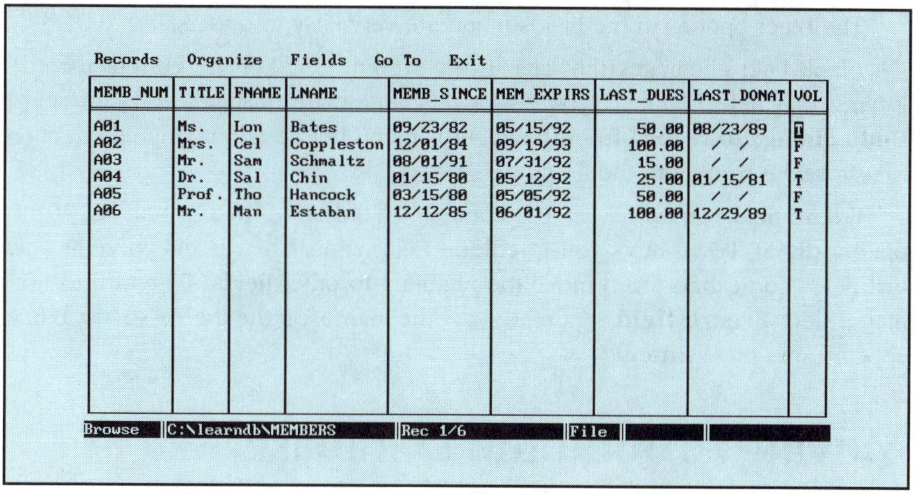

```
  Records    Organize    Fields    Go To    Exit
 MEMB_NUM TITLE FNAME LNAME     MEMB_SINCE MEM_EXPIRS LAST_DUES LAST_DONAT VOL
 A01      Ms.   Lon   Bates      09/23/82   05/15/92     50.00  08/23/89   T
 A02      Mrs.  Cel   Coppleston 12/01/84   09/19/93    100.00   /  /     F
 A03      Mr.   Sam   Schmaltz   08/01/91   07/31/92     15.00   /  /     F
 A04      Dr.   Sal   Chin       01/15/80   05/12/92     25.00  01/15/81   T
 A05      Prof. Tho   Hancock    03/15/80   05/05/92     50.00   /  /     F
 A06      Mr.   Man   Estaban    12/12/85   06/01/92    100.00  12/29/89   T




 Browse   C:\learndb\MEMBERS        Rec 1/6          File
```

Figure 3.14   *Narrowing the name columns to see more data.*

10. To return the Browse screen to normal, select **Lock fields on left** from the Fields menu. dBASE IV asks for the number of fields to remain stationary, and displays 4.

11. Press **Del** so no number is displayed. Then press **Enter**. Since fields are no longer locked, the ADDRESS1 field is displayed immediately to the right of the name fields once again.

12. Move to the LNAME field. Select **Size field** from the Fields menu. Press the **Right Arrow** key eleven times to make the field wider. Notice that the first ten times you press it, the highlight fills up the column entirely, but the eleventh time, there is a blank space to the right of the highlight, indicating that you have made the column wider than it needs to be.
13. Press the **Left Arrow** key once to make it the proper width, and press **Enter** to end sizing.
14. Press **Shift-Tab** to move to the FNAME field, select **Size field** from the Fields menu, and press the **Right Arrow** key ten times to make it the ordinary width. Press **Enter** to end sizing.
15. If you have a mouse, try clicking and dragging the vertical gridlines to resize the fields. When you are done, return the fields to their original size.

These options give a quick and easy way of controlling which fields you view in the Browse screen. You can get even more control by using queries, which you learn about in Chapter 5.

The other options in the Fields menu are very easy to understand.

Blank field eliminates the data in the current field (of the current record), leaving that field blank. If you select this option by mistake, you can select **Undo change to record** from the Records menu before taking any other action to restore the content to the field.

Freeze field is used to edit the contents of only one field. If you select this option, dBASE IV prompts you to enter a field name. Then it lets you edit only that field. You cannot even move the highlight to other fields. To return to normal, select **Freeze field** again, delete the name of the field, so no name appears, and press **Enter**.

Moving Around the Database

Working in either the Browse or the Edit screen, you can use the Go To menu, shown in Figure 3.15, to move through the database file.

The options above the line on this menu are virtually self-explanatory. Select **Top record** or **Last record** to move to the first or last record of the database file. If you select **Record number**, dBASE IV asks you the number of the record to which you want to move: you may not use this option often, as you do not usually know the number of the record that you need to use.

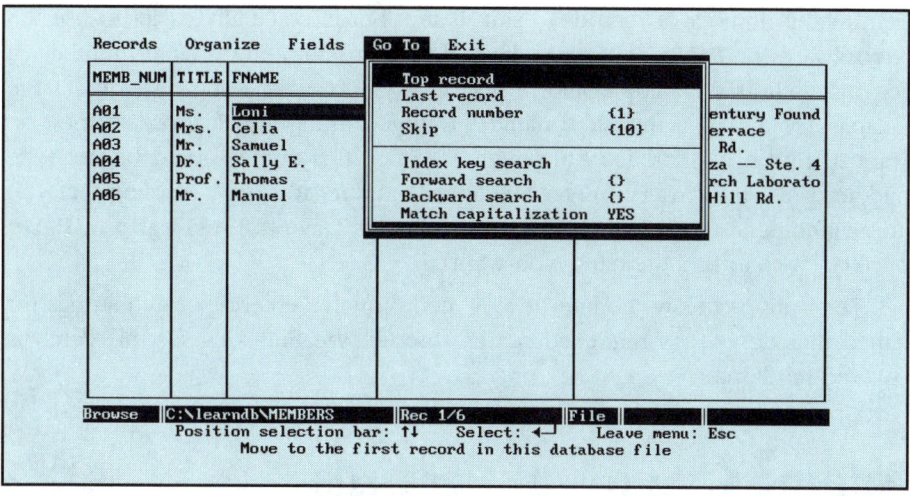

Figure 3.15   The Go To menu.

If you select **Skip,** dBASE IV prompts you to enter the number of records you want to skip. If you enter *1*, the highlight moves to the next record, enter *10*, the highlight moves down ten records; and so on. This menu option just moves the pointer once. It does not make dBASE IV skip records if you press **Down Arrow** or **PgDn** to move the highlight afterwards. As you can see in Figure 3.16, the message line tells you that you can also enter a negative number to Skip backward.

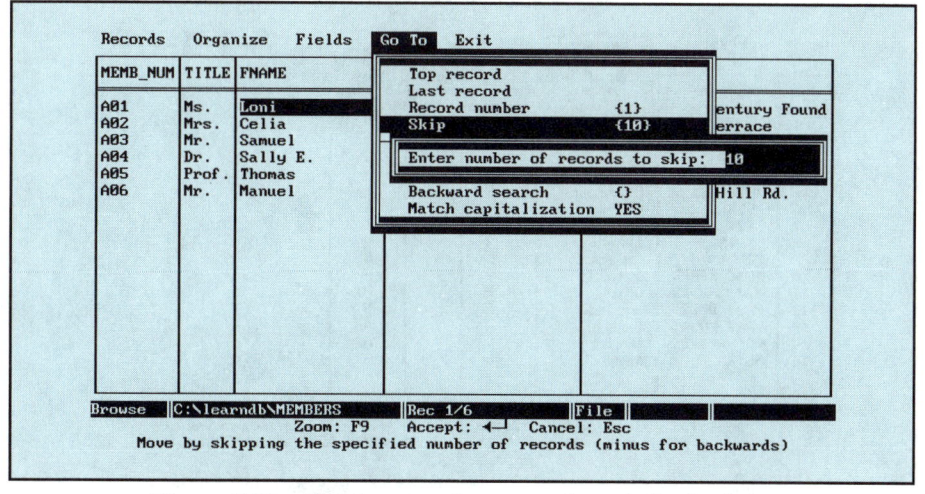

Figure 3.16   Skipping records to move through the database.

The default number of records to skip is ten, but it is actually easier to use the **Arrow** keys or **PgUp** and **PgDn** keys if you are skipping a small number of records such as this. Skip could be useful if you are browsing through a large database with, say, a thousand names, arranged in alphabetical order, and you want to find a name that begins with M. Since this name should be near the middle of the file, you can enter 500 as the number to skip (assuming that you are beginning at the top of the file), then you just have to press **PgUp** or **PgDn** once or twice to find the name you want.

The options below the line on this menu involve entering search strings for either an indexed or unindexed search through the file. This sort of search is covered in Chapter 5.

Adding Groups of Records from Other Files

This chapter has focused on the Browse and Edit screens, which let you add records to the database file one at a time.

You can also add records or groups of records imported from other files, by using the Append menu of the Database Design screen, shown in Figure 3.17.

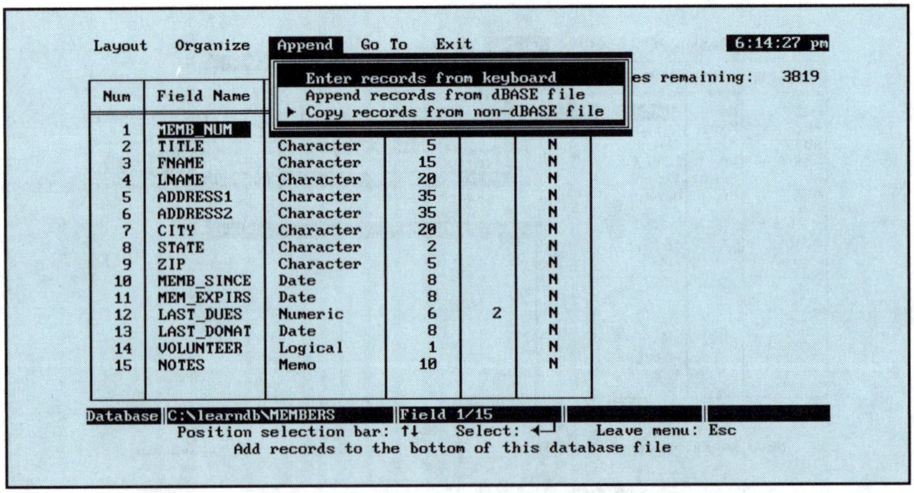

Figure 3.17   *The Append menu of the Database Design screen.*

Before appending records to your database from another file, be sure to save all changes that you have made to the structure of the database. This menu is part of the database design screen because the structure of the database is crucial when you are importing records.

The option Enter records from keyboard simply lets you use the Edit screen. If you use this option, then you return to the database design screen when you press **Ctrl-End** or **Esc**. The other two options of this menu let you append multiple records to the database file.

If you select **Append records from dBASE file**, dBASE IV displays a picklist with the names of database files in the current catalog. Using this option, you can append only records from a dBASE file in the current catalog. If the file is not already in the catalog, you must first use the Catalog menu of the Control Center to add it to the catalog. After you select a file from the picklist, dBASE IV appends any fields that have the same name as in the database file in use. (If the field names are not the same and you do not want to change them, you may add records from another dBASE file using the Update menu of the Query screen, covered in Chapter 5.)

Files created by dBASE II, III, III PLUS, and IV all are given the extension .DBF. Only dBASE III, III PLUS, and IV have compatible files, however, so that you can use files that you created with dBASE III and III PLUS directly with dBASE IV, or you can import them using the Append records from dBASE file option discussed above.

If you select **Copy records from non-dBASE file**, dBASE IV displays a list of programs whose files it can import and the extensions that these files must have for dBASE IV to use them, including dBASE II files, as shown in Figure 3.18. If you select one of these, dBASE IV displays a picklist of files with the extension that is specified. If you select **SYLK-Multiplan**, the picklist displays files that have no extension. If you select either **Text fixed-length fields**, **Blank delimited**, or **Character delimited**, the picklist displays all files with the extension .TXT: you must make sure that the files are in the correct format.

Notice that dBASE II files must have the extension .DB2 before they can be appended to dBASE IV. dBASE II files have a different format, and you must change their extension from .DBF to .DB2 in order to import them using this option so you can use them with dBASE IV.

For details on the structures of these source files, see the entry on the command Append From in the *dBASE IV Language Reference* manual distributed with the program.

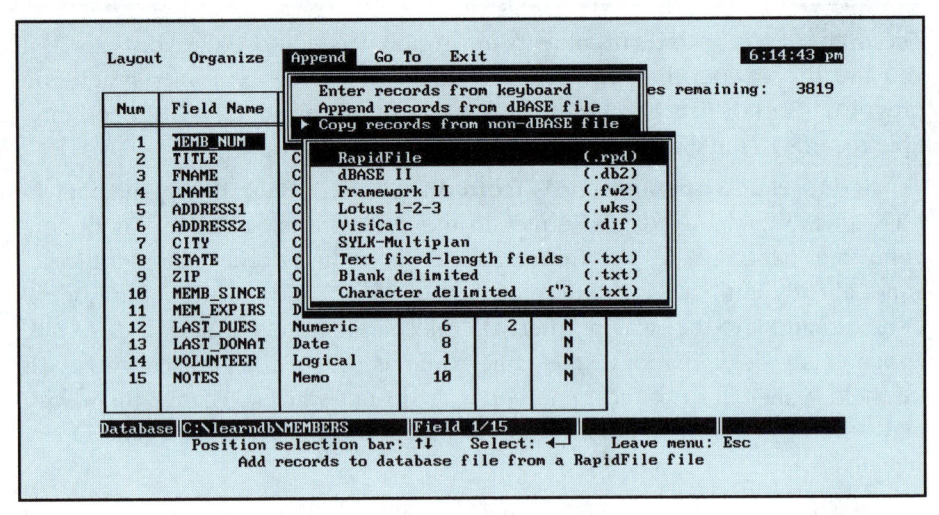

Figure 3.18 *File formats that dBASE can import.*

Summary

In this chapter, you learned to enter, edit, and view data in a dBASE IV database. In the next chapter, you will begin to see some of the power of dBASE IV when you learn how to organize and reorganize the data in your sample database rapidly by using indexing and sorting.

Chapter 4

Indexing and Sorting

This chapter teaches you how to get the most out of your database by using the data in any order you wish. You can quickly organize your data in alphabetical order by last name, for example, or zip code order to make bulk mailings easier. dBASE IV gives you two different ways to order your data: indexing and sorting.

In this chapter you learn:

- The differences between *indexing* and *sorting*
- The advantages and disadvantages of indexing
- How to create an index based on a single field
- How to create an index based on multiple fields
- How to use indexes to control the order of records
- How to modify or remove an index
- How to sort a database file

The Differences Between Indexing and Sorting

If you *sort* your data, dBASE IV actually creates a new database file with your data sorted in the order that you specified.

If you *index* your data, dBASE does not rewrite the data or create a new database. It leaves the data unchanged in the original database file, and it creates a separate index file, which lets it access the records in the order that you want.

This index file works a bit like the index of a book. It would take a long time to read through the entire book to find a certain topic in it. But it takes very little time to look up the topic in the index, where it is listed alphabetically, and then to go to the page to which the index refers. Likewise, the dBASE index file is an ordered listing that tells dBASE IV the location in the database file of each record. dBASE can find a specific record much more quickly by looking it up in the index file and going right to the proper place in the original file than it can by reading through an entire long database file looking for the specified record.

dBASE IV can also display the records in a database in index order. You can browse the database, for example, as if the records were actually arranged in alphabetical order or in zip code order. Though the order of the records in the original database file has not really been changed, you might think the records were sorted if you judged merely by looking at the Browse screen.

Should You Index or Sort?

Indexing has many advantages over sorting in terms of speed and power. Because dBASE IV does not create a separate database file, indexing uses less disk space than sorting. As a result sorting is rarely used in dBASE IV. Indexes are the method of choice, and they are covered at length in this chapter.

On the other hand, sorting does have some advantages over indexing in terms of ease-of-use for beginners, because you must use fairly complex dBASE *expressions* to get certain results when you are indexing—results that you could obtain more easily when you are sorting.

The Advantages of Indexing

dBASE IV can update indexes automatically, as you make new entries or edit existing records in your database. The index is always up-to-date, though it remains in the background and you cannot tell it is there until you want to use it.

You can maintain several indexes simultaneously without taking up a great deal of disk space, as you would if you sorted a database several times. In this chapter you create indexes that let you use the database file in both alphabetical and zip code order. You simply have to make a menu selection to use the data in either order.

Sorting a dBASE IV database creates an entirely new copy of the file with a new file name that you provide. The new database contains all of the same information sorted in the specified order. Because sorting is also slow, particularly when you have a large database, the advantages of indexing are generally decisive.

The Disadvantages of Indexing

The primary disadvantage of indexing, however, is that indexes are based on dBASE expressions, and you sometimes must use complex expressions to get the result you want.

This chapter covers only a few simple expressions that you as a beginner can pick up with no trouble. Chapter 11 of this book covers more complex expressions, and you will be more prepared to learn about expressions at that point.

The very simple expressions that you learn in this chapter are enough for most practical purposes, but they do have some limitations.

This chapter does not cover indexes that are based on fields of different data types. For example, if you wanted your file arranged in order of the amount of dues paid with the names of people who paid each amount of dues arranged in alphabetical order by last and first names, you would have to use a complex expression. You would have to use the LAST_DUES field plus the two name fields as the basis of the index, and these fields are different data types, numeric, and character. You are not likely to face this sort of problem, as it is rarely necessary to index a database on mixed data types. There is no reason to slow down your study of dBASE IV by learning to do this now.

In addition, this chapter does not include the expressions that you need to get around errors in capitalization of your data. By default, indexes on character fields arrange the data in ASCII order. (ASCII stands for the American Standard

Code for Information Interchange. It includes a code number for all of the letters and other characters that your computer uses.) In ASCII order, all of the capital letters come before all of the small letters. Thus, if you enter some names in all capitals and some in capital and small letters, they will not be indexed in proper alphabetical order: for example, SMITH would come before Sidney because capital M comes before small i in ASCII. Part 3 of this book discusses expressions you can use to solve the problem of inconsistent capitalization.

The sort screen, on the other hand, does have options that make it easy to sort in alphabetical, or dictionary order, rather than ASCII order and to base the sort order on fields of mixed data types. Despite the extra time it takes, this ease of use sometimes makes sorting worthwhile for beginners.

Types of Index Files

In previous versions of dBASE, each index was kept in a separate file. The user specified the index file's name, and dBASE automatically gave it the extension .NDX. The user also had to use each index explicitly before editing the database to make sure that it was automatically updated when data was added or edited. If you forgot to use the index, any records you added would seem to have disappeared at a later session, when you used the database with the index.

dBASE IV made indexing easier by adding a new type of index file, the .MDX or *multiple index file*.

When you index your database from the Control Center, dBASE IV automatically creates what is called a *production index file*, a file with the same name as the database file but with an .MDX file extension. All of the indexes you create can be included in the production index (.MDX) file. Whenever you use the database file, the production index file is automatically used along with it. It remains in the background and does not affect the order of the records unless you make it do so, but it is always updated.

Since these indexes are all kept in a single file, each one is called an *index tag* rather than an index file. One .MDX file can include up to forty-seven index tags, probably more than you will ever need in most actual applications.

.NDX files need to be mentioned here only because dBASE IV's menu lets you use them. This feature was included to make dBASE IV compatible with earlier versions of dBASE. You can still use applications with .NDX files that you created with dBASE III. When you work with indexes, you will notice that the menu includes two options to work with .NDX files: Include .NDX index file and Activate .NDX index file. The first of these lets you include an existing .NDX file in the current catalog. The second lets you use .NDX files that are in the current catalog. Unlike an .MDX file, which is updated automatically, an .NDX file must be activated with this second option before you add data to make sure it is updated properly. This option does not make the file you select into the controlling index that determines the order of the records, something which you can do by selecting Order records by index from the Organize menu.

.MDX files are so obviously superior to .NDX files that they replace them almost entirely, though there are cases in programming where you might prefer to use an .NDX index. .NDX files cannot be created from the Control Center. They must be created from the dot prompt. See the discussion of the INDEX ON command in your *Language Reference* manual. Except for rare cases, you can generally use an .MDX file for your indexes.

Indexing Your Database

In this section, you create several sample indexes for your database. The simplest index is based on a single field. For example, you index on the ZIP field to print mailing labels in zip code order. You also create a more complex index based on both LNAME and FNAME fields, used to browse records or produce reports in alphabetical order. This second index uses a simple dBASE expression, which is very easy for you to learn. Indexes can also be used more powerfully after you learn about more complex expressions in Chapter 11.

Creating a Simple Index

The actual mechanics of creating an index are so easy to understand that you should be able to pick them up simply by looking at the menu used to create indexes. In the exercise, you use the Organize menu of the database design screen to create the indexes. You could create an index using the Organize menu of the Browse or Edit screen.

1. If you have taken a break since the last chapter, enter *cd \learndb* to use the LEARNDB directory and then enter *dbase* to start dBASE IV, before beginning this exercise. You should be at the Control Center using the SAMPLE.CAT catalog when you begin.

2. Select **MEMBERS** from the Data panel.

3. Select **Modify structure/order** from the prompt box. dBASE IV displays the database design screen with the Organize menu already pulled down.

4. Select **Create new index**. dBASE IV displays the submenu shown in Figure 4.1, which lets you define the index.

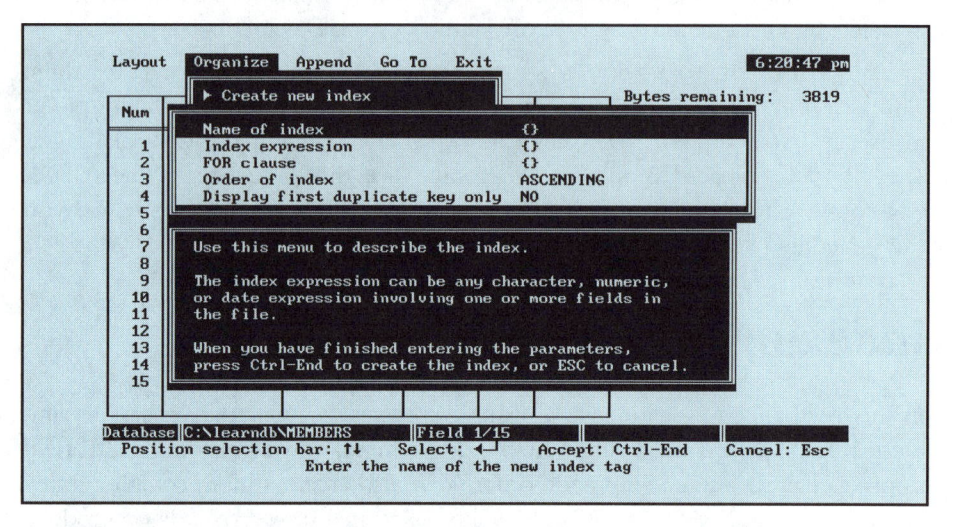

```
Layout   Organize   Append   Go To   Exit                    6:20:47 pm
         ▶ Create new index                    Bytes remaining:   3819
 Num     Name of index              {}
  1      Index expression           {}
  2      FOR clause                 {}
  3      Order of index             ASCENDING
  4      Display first duplicate key only   NO
  5
  6
  7      Use this menu to describe the index.
  8
  9      The index expression can be any character, numeric,
 10      or date expression involving one or more fields in
 11      the file.
 12
 13      When you have finished entering the parameters,
 14      press Ctrl-End to create the index, or ESC to cancel.
 15

Database C:\learndb\MEMBERS        Field 1/15
Position selection bar: ↑↓    Select: ↵    Accept: Ctrl-End    Cancel: Esc
                  Enter the name of the new index tag
```

Figure 4.1   Creating an index.

This submenu is virtually self-explanatory, and the message line at the bottom of the screen gives you additional prompts as you move from option to option.

To make an entry in any of the curly brackets, you must select that menu option; the curly brackets are then be replaced by a cursor, so you can type in the entry. Press **Enter** when you are done, and the entry appears between the curly brackets. To change the default selection of the last two lines, just press **Enter**.

You must enter a name for the index and an index expression. The name is for the index tag you are now defining. Tag names have the same restrictions as field names. If you enter an invalid tag name, dBASE IV displays an error message. If you try to enter a tag name with more than the maximum ten characters, dBASE IV beeps when you reach that length.

If an index with the same name that you have entered already exists, dBASE displays a warning, and you have the option to overwrite the existing index (to eliminate it and replace it with the index you just created) or to cancel.

The simplest index expression is a single field name. Later in this chapter, you also create expressions using multiple field names.

Rather than typing in the expression, you can select this option and then press **Pick:Shift-F1** to use the expression builder picklist, but using the expression builder may actually be more difficult than typing in the simple expressions used in this chapter, so it is not covered here. It is mentioned in Chapter 11.

SHORTCUT

The FOR clause option in this menu is a very powerful feature of dBASE IV that lets you add conditions to an index. However, indexes with FOR clauses should be avoided by beginners who are working from the Control Center. They are covered in more detail in Chapter 11.

By default, indexes are in *ascending order*. Numbers are arranged from the smallest to the largest, and dates from the earliest to the latest. As you have learned, character fields are arranged in ASCII order—assuming that capitalization is correct, this generally means alphabetical order from A to Z. You can select **Order of index** from the menu, though, to toggle from Ascending to Descending order. If you create the index in descending order, fields are arranged from the largest to the smallest.

By default, indexes display all records, even if they have the same key. By selecting Display first duplicate key only, you can create an index that displays only the first record with any given value as the index key. This option is occasionally useful. In many cases, though, it can lead to confusion because records are hidden, and so it should generally be avoided.

1. To index on zip code, select **Name of index**; then type *zips* and press **Enter**.
2. Select **Index expression**. Because the index is based solely on the zip code field, type the field name *zip* and press **Enter**. If you do not remember all the field names, you can press **Pick:Shift-F1**, and select the field name from the expression builder picklist that appears. That is all you need for this index.
3. Press **Ctrl-End** to save the index.
4. Now press **Data:F2** until you return to the Browse Screen. The data is now organized in order by zip code.

As another simple index, try indexing in order of last contribution, with the most recent contribution coming first: this involves descending order.

1. Select **Create new index** from the *Organize* menu.
2. Select **Name of index**, type *last_donat*, and press **Enter**.
3. Select **Index expression**, type *last_donat* and press **Ente**r. Select **Order of index** to toggle to DESCENDING. The menu should look like Figure 4.2.
4. Press **Ctrl-End** to create this index.
5. If necessary, press **Data:F2** to return to the Browse screen. The database now appears in chronological descending order by the date of the last donation.

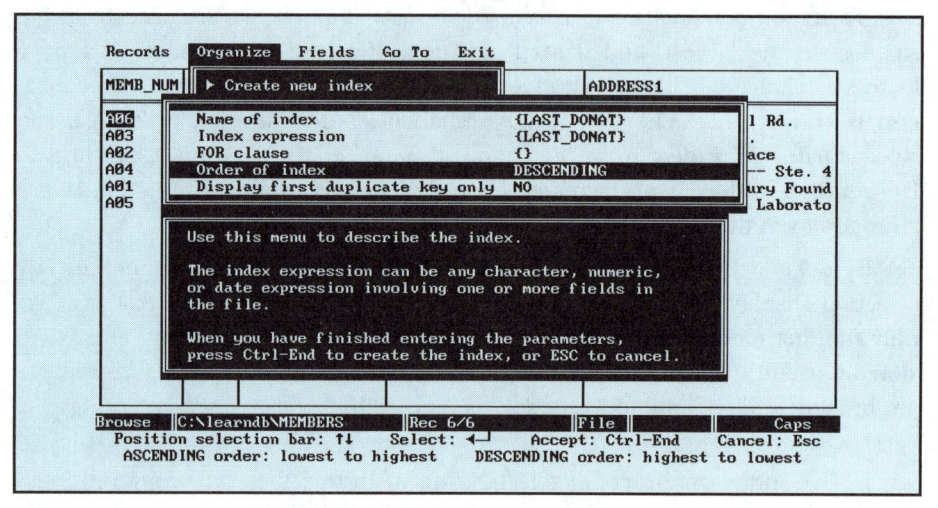

Figure 4.2   *Creating a simple index.*

That's about all there is to creating simple indexes. There are a few other details, but dBASE IV pretty much takes care of them for you.

Indexing on Multiple Fields

It is not much more difficult to create an index based on multiple fields. You simply have to enter an expression that includes the field names with + between them.

To arrange the database alphabetically by name you must create an index on multiple fields, LNAME + FNAME. If you just indexed on LNAME, then dBASE would not take the member's first name into account when it used the records; for example it might list Xavier Smith before Aaron Smith.

So, to order the database alphabetically by name, use the index expression LNAME + FNAME. Then, if last names are the same, dBASE IV uses the first name as a tiebreaker to determine which record comes first. (If you also had a field for middle initial, you could use an expression such as LNAME + FNAME + MID_INIT to index.)

You can use the + sign to combine as many fields as you want, but remember that the fields must all be the character data type. You cannot combine a character and numeric field, for example, simply by using **+**.

1. Select **Create new index** from the *Organize* menu.
2. Select **Name of index**, type *names* and press **Enter**.
3. Select **Index expression**, type *lname + fname* and press **Enter**.
4. Press **Ctrl-End** to save the index.

That's all you need to know to create most indexes.

Using Indexes

When you are done creating a new index, dBASE IV uses it as the controlling index that determines in which order the records are used.

When you first use a database file, records are in *natural order*, that is, in the order in which they were entered.

You may make an index the *controlling index* by selecting **Order records by index** from the Organize menu. As you have seen, the Browse and Edit screens also include an Organize menu identical to the Organize menu of the Database Design screen, which you used to create the index. It is most common to want to order records when you are browsing or editing them.

Try it out while browsing the records, so you can see how the indexes work.

1. Press **Esc** to return to the Control Center and if necessary *Y* to confirm. The highlight should be on the MEMBERS file. Press **Data:F2** to view

the data using the Browse screen. (If dBASE displays the Edit screen, press **Data:F2** again to toggle to the Browse screen.) Since you just created the NAMES index, the records are displayed in alphabetical order by name, as you can see in Figure 4.3.

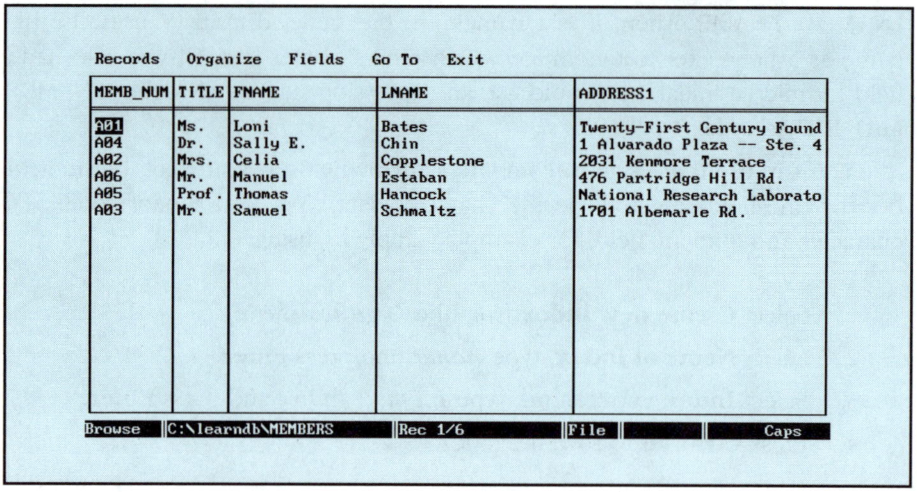

```
  Records   Organize   Fields   Go To   Exit
 ┌─────────┬─────┬────────┬───────────┬──────────────────────────────┐
 │MEMB_NUM │TITLE│FNAME   │LNAME      │ADDRESS1                      │
 ├─────────┼─────┼────────┼───────────┼──────────────────────────────┤
 │A01      │Ms.  │Loni    │Bates      │Twenty-First Century Found    │
 │A04      │Dr.  │Sally E.│Chin       │1 Alvarado Plaza -- Ste. 4    │
 │A02      │Mrs. │Celia   │Copplestone│2031 Kenmore Terrace          │
 │A06      │Mr.  │Manuel  │Estaban    │476 Partridge Hill Rd.        │
 │A05      │Prof.│Thomas  │Hancock    │National Research Laborato    │
 │A03      │Mr.  │Samuel  │Schmaltz   │1701 Albemarle Rd.            │
 └─────────┴─────┴────────┴───────────┴──────────────────────────────┘
  Browse   C:\learndb\MEMBERS      Rec 1/6       File         Caps
```

Figure 4.3 *The Data with the NAMES index as the controlling index.*

2. Select **Order records by index** from the Organize menu to call up the picklist that lets you choose among the indexes you have created, shown in Figure 4.4.

3. Select **Natural Order**. If necessary, press **PgUp** to see the entire screen. You can tell the records are in the order in which you originally entered them because all of the member numbers are in numeric order.

4. Select **Order records by index** from the Organize menu. Select **ZIPS** from the picklist. Notice that, as you scroll through the picklist, the expression that is the basis of the index is displayed to its left, as shown in Figure 4.5.

5. Press **Tab** until you can see the ZIP field, as in Figure 4.6, note that the records are in zip code order, and then press **Home**.

Remember that, if you want the pointer to stay on the same record when you change the controlling index, you can select the option **Follow record to new position** from the Records menu.

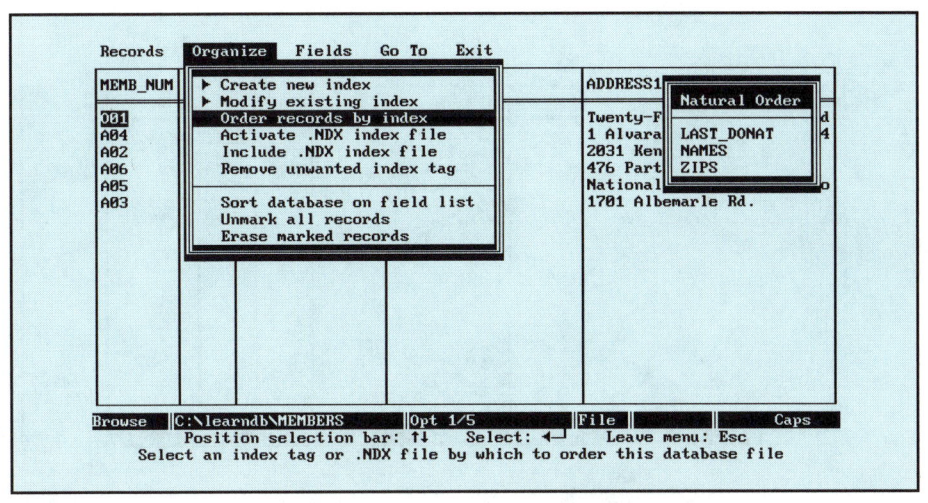

Figure 4.4   *Choosing the index order.*

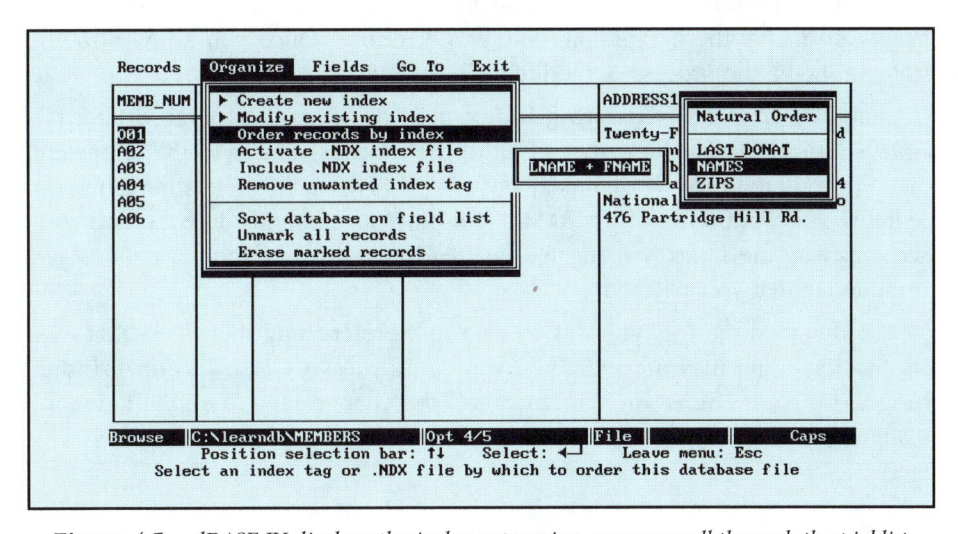

Figure 4.5   *dBASE IV displays the index expression as you scroll through the picklist.*

```
      Records   Organize   Fields   Go To   Exit
     ┌─────────────────────────┬──────────────────┬───────┬──────┬──────────┐
     │ADDRESS2                 │CITY              │STATE │ZIP   │MEMB_SINC │
     ├─────────────────────────┼──────────────────┼───────┼──────┼──────────┤
     │                         │Boston            │MA    │02165 │12/12/85  │
     │                         │Brooklyn          │NY    │11226 │08/01/91  │
     │                         │St. Louis         │MO    │63114 │12/01/84  │
     │10952 Pico Blvd.         │Los Angeles       │CA    │90064 │01/15/80  │
     │2148 Frontage St.        │San Francisco     │CA    │94107 │09/23/82  │
     │1 Linear Accelerator Ave.│Berkeley          │CA    │94720 │03/15/80  │
```

Figure 4.6 Using the ZIPS index as the controlling index.

Modifying or Removing an Index

After you have created an index, you may sometimes want to modify it to change the name, the expression, or the FOR clause. Once you know how to create an index, the process of modifying an index is easy.

Simply select **Modify existing index** from the Organize menu. dBASE IV displays a picklist with the names of all of the indexes, similar to the one used when you ordered records by index, as shown in Figure 4.7. Select the name of the index you want to modify. dBASE IV displays a screen just like the one you used to create the index, except that is already filled in with the specifications for the index that you selected.

Use this menu just as you did when you were creating the index. Edit the specifications until they are what you want, and press **Ctrl-End** to finalize the changes. Or press **Esc** at any time to cancel the changes and keep the index in its original form.

⊘ **WARNING** To remove an index completely, select **Remove unwanted index tag** from the Organize menu. Once again, dBASE IV displays a picklist with the names of all of the index tags you created. When you make a selection from this picklist, dBASE IV does not ask for confirmation before permanently removing the index you selected, so use it with caution.

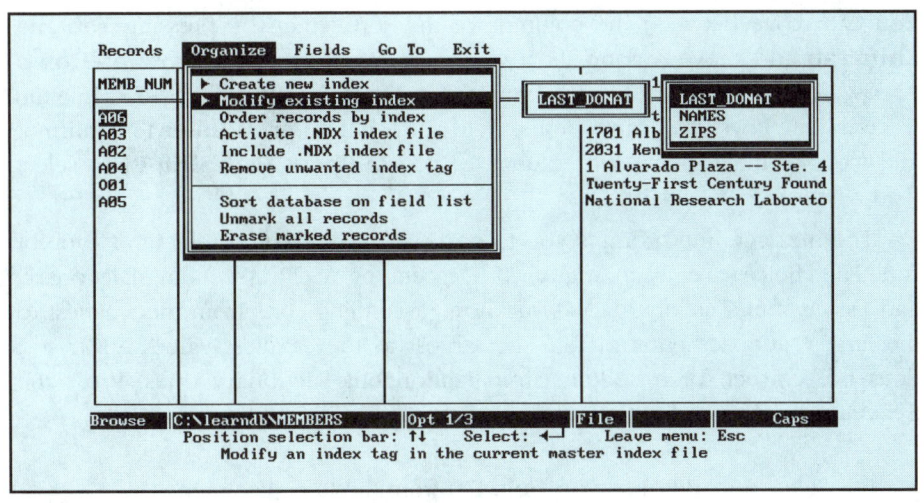

Figure 4.7   Selecting an index to modify.

Sorting

To sort a database, select **Sort database on field list** from the Organize menu to display the sort screen shown in Figure 4.8. Simply list all of the fields on which you want the sort to be based and whether each one should be in ascending or descending ASCII or Dictionary order.

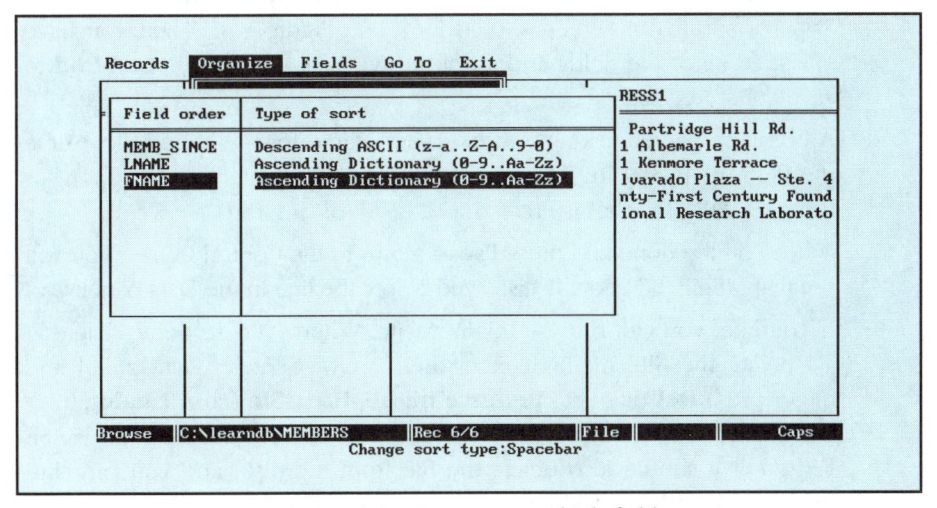

Figure 4.8   Sorting on multiple fields.

You can move between the columns of the sort screen by pressing **Tab** and **Shift-Tab** and move among its rows by pressing the **Up Arrow** or **Down Arrow** keys or clicking a location with the mouse to move directly to it. Use the usual editing keys. You can type the field name in and press **Enter** to confirm it and move to the Type of sort column, or you can press **Pick:Shift-F1** to select field names from a picklist.

The message line prompts you to press the **Spacebar** to select the Type of sort. The choices are Ascending ASCII, Descending ASCII, Ascending Dictionary, and Descending Dictionary. As you know, ascending sorts from the smallest to the largest and descending from the largest to the smallest value. ASCII sort does not correct for mistaken capitalization but Dictionary does. Press the **Spacebar** until you have the option you want for each field.

1. Select **Sort database on field list** from the Organize menu.

2. If you order the records by the date that the member first joined in descending order, the most recent members are listed first. Press **Pick:Shift-F1** to get the picklist of field names and select **MEMB_SINCE**. Select **Descending ASCII** as the Type of sort. Press **Enter**.

3. To sort the database by member's names so that, among those who joined on the same date, the names will be listed in alphabetical order, enter *lname* in the Field order column and select **Ascending Dictionary** as the Type of sort; press **Enter**. Then enter *fname* in the Field order column and again select **Ascending Dictionary** as the Type of sort. Your screen should look like Figure 4.8. When you have specified all of the fields and all of the types of sorts, press **Ctrl-End** to save the sorted file.

4. A box is displayed asking you to enter a name for the sorted file. Name the file MEMB_SIN. In the box that is displayed, enter a description for the new .DBF file that is created as a result of this sort.

5. When you are done and press **Esc** to return to the Control Center, you will see that MEMB_SIN now is displayed below the line in the Data panel.

6. If you like, you can browse this new file. When you are done, delete it. To delete the file, highlight it in the Control Center's Data panel and either press **Del** or select **Remove highlighted file from catalog** from the Catalog menu. After it has removed the file from the catalog, dBASE IV asks if it should also delete the file from the disk, and you can simply press *Y* to delete the file.

After you are done working with the sorted records, you should delete this new file. You can delete the original file immediately and work with the sorted one from then on. The newly created file should be deleted so that future screens match the book illustrations.

It is not a good idea to keep two files with the same data. Eventually, someone will add new records to the wrong one, and then you will not have all your data in a single file.

Again, indexing is almost always preferable to sorting because of the time it saves and the ability to maintain multiple indexes simultaneously, though the sort screen is easier for beginners to use. As a rule, you should always index unless you have some special reason to sort instead.

Summary

In this chapter you learned how to organize information in a database file by indexing and sorting using only the pull-down menu system. In the next chapter, you will see how to search for and extract specific information easily from your database to make it even more useful with the advanced dBASE IV Query By Example features.

Chapter 5

Queries

This chapter introduces you to two different ways to search for data in a database: searches and queries. A search lets you move the pointer to a simple record. A query in dBASE IV displays records in a database that meet specific criteria. You can also use a query to help you organize your data, make changes to a database file, and much more. Older database management systems require you to enter elaborate commands in order to create queries. In dBASE IV, you create a query by selecting fields from a screen form called the queries design screen. When you create a query in this way, it is called *query by example*. For all of its power, the dBASE IV Query by Example feature is easy to learn and use.

In this chapter, you learn how to:

- ◆ Search for single records using options of the Go To menu
- ◆ Create queries in the Queries Design screen
- ◆ Perform more sophisticated searches using queries containing operators, and indexes
- ◆ Create a new database file based on the filtered data contained in a query
- ◆ Make broad changes to the data in a database file with an update query

Searches and Queries

There are two fundamentally different ways that you might want to search for data in your database.

You might want to find a single record, for example, to look up a member's address. To do this, move the pointer to that record using the Go To menu of the Browse/Edit screen.

You might want to find a group of records—for example, all of the members who live in California or who paid more than $50 in dues. To do this, you can use the queries design screen, which creates a *filter*, so that dBASE uses only the records that meet the conditions that you used in the query. Then, when you Browse the database—or when you produce mailing labels or reports—only those records are included.

The queries design screen is very versatile. In addition to setting a filter that lets you use only certain specified records, it also lets you use only certain fields of each record. A query gives you what is called a *view* of the data, which may be a partial picture of the data that includes only some fields and some records.

Using a view is the easiest way to produce a quick report—for example, to print names and addresses of people who paid more than $50 in dues without printing all of the other fields. In fact, the queries design screen also lets you add calculated fields, do summary and group queries, and even update groups of records.

Views are fundamental to dBASE IV: whenever you are working with dBASE IV, you can either use a database, as you have been doing up to now, or you can use a view. Either the name of a data file or the name of a query may be above the line in its panel of the Control Center.

In Chapters 6 and 7 you see that you can use a view and then print mailing labels or reports, using only the records included in the view. In Chapter 10, you learn that you can easily work with relational databases by using views that include fields from more than one database file. The query screen is that powerful.

Searching for a Single Record

You have already seen how to use the options of the Go To menu of the Browse/Edit screen to move the record to the top or bottom of a file or to skip records. It is no more difficult to use the Go To menu to search for a specific name, address, or other specific data.

For small database files, you can use an ordinary forward or backward search, which does not use an index. For large databases, however, these searches can be slow and an indexed search is preferable.

Unindexed Searches

You can do an unindexed search for data in any field of the database.

First, you have to move the highlight of the Browse/Edit screen to the field that contains the data to be searched for. Then select **Forward search** or **Backward search** from the Go To menu. dBASE IV prompts you to enter what it calls the *search string*. Enter the value that you want it to find in that field.

There might be more than one record with the same value in that field—for example, if you enter *Smith* as the search string, dBASE might move the pointer to John Smith's record, when you were looking for Sam Smith's. You can move to the next record in the file that matches the search string by pressing **Find Next:Shift-F4**, and you can move backward to find the previous record that matches by pressing **Find Prev:Shift-F3**.

Though it is simple, this sort of search is something that you will do frequently in your work with dBASE IV. You should try it out. Begin from the Control Center with \LEARNDB\SAMPLE.CAT as the current catalog.

1. Select **MEMBERS** from the Data panel. Select **Display Data** from the prompt box to use the Browse screen. (If the Browse/Edit screen is in Edit mode when you use it, press **Data:F2** to shift to Browse mode.)
2. Move the highlight to the LNAME field.
3. Select **Forward search** from the Go To menu. dBASE IV prompts you to enter a search string. Type *Hancock*, as in Figure 5.1, and press **Enter**. dBASE IV immediately moves to the record of Thomas Hancock. Press **Find next:Shift-F4**. The highlight blinks but does not move, indicating that dBASE IV has not found another Hancock in the file.

Notice that this menu includes an option to Match capitalization with Yes displayed to its right when you begin. This means that you must capitalize the search string exactly as it is capitalized in the database file, or else dBASE IV does not consider it a match. Select this option to toggle it to No if you want dBASE IV to find records with the same letters as the search string even if they are not capitalized in the same way.

You can also do searches using two wildcard characters:

- **?**   matches any single character
- *****   matches any group of characters

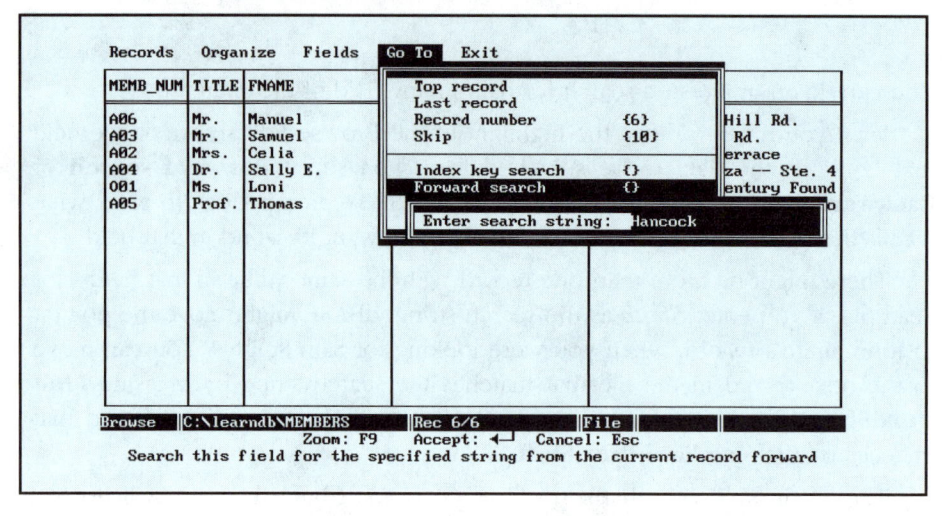

Figure 5.1   *A forward search.*

For example, if you are not sure whether Mr. Smith spells his name with an i or a y, you can use the search string i, which would match with both. If you want to find someone who lives in Manhattan, where zip codes begin with 100, you can use the search string *100** in the zip field.

If you do not use wildcards, the search string must match the data exactly (apart from capitalization, as you have seen). For example, if you search for *Sally* in the FNAME field, dBASE does not find Sally E. (It will not even find that name if you omit the period after the E from the search string.) However, because the * wildcard may stand for any group of characters or for no character at all, you could use the search string *Sally** to find Sally or Sally E.

Indexed Searches

If you have a database file with more than a few thousand records, you will find that ordinary forward and backward searches can be very slow. If you are looking up one name after another, you will feel like you are spending most of your life waiting.

That is because, when dBASE IV does an ordinary forward search, it begins at the current record and reads every record until it finds the one you want. When you do an indexed search, on the other hand, dBASE IV uses the index order to find the record you want almost immediately—just as you can find a name in a book much more quickly by looking it up in the index. No matter how large your database, even if it contains hundreds of thousands of records, dBASE IV should take only a few seconds to find the record you want if you do an indexed search.

Before you do an indexed search, you must use the appropriate index as the controlling index that determines the order of the records. Remember, you can make an index the controlling index by selecting **Order records by index** from the Organize menu. You may have noticed that the option Index key search is dimmed on your Go To menu, assuming that you have not used any index as the controlling index since you started this session with dBASE.

Since the search string must match the index key, you do not need to move the highlight to the field where the data is located before beginning the search. dBASE IV automatically looks in the field (or fields) on which the index key is based.

Unlike forward and backward searches, index key searches do not need to match exactly. In the exercise, you use the NAMES index, based on LNAME + FNAME, but you do not have to enter both the last name and the first name to get a match. You do not even need to enter the entire last name. dBASE finds a match as long as the initial letters of the record match the search string.

> If you do want to enter both the last and first name, you must remember that dBASE pads out each field with blanks in order to fill the entire field length. For example, if you want to use both names to find Celia Copplestone, you must use a search string made up of Copplestone followed by nine blanks followed by Celia. dBASE IV allows partial matches with indexed searches because it is difficult to enter the full match for complex indexes such as this one.
>
> **N O T E**

Indexed searches do not allow wildcard characters and they must match capitalization, but the fact that they allow partial matches makes them very powerful nevertheless.

1. Select **Order records by index** from the Organize menu. Select **NAMES** from the picklist of indexes.
2. Move the highlight to the MEMB_NUM column, so you can see that it does not have to be in the column that you are searching through. Press **PgDn** to move to the last record.
3. Select **Index key search** from the Go To menu. dBASE IV prompts you to enter the search string and, as you can see in Figure 5.2, it also displays the expression on which the current index is based, that the string must match. Enter *Han* and dBASE IV goes directly to the record for Thomas Hancock.

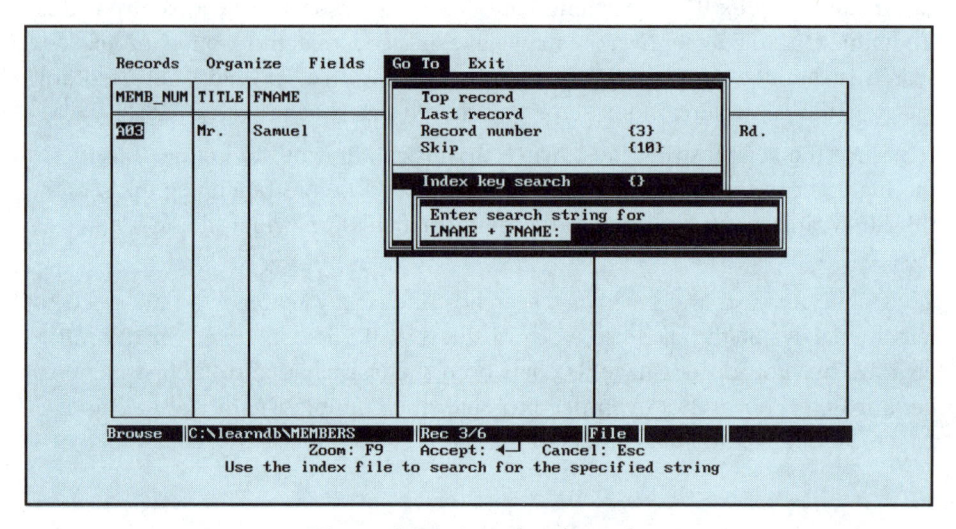

Figure 5.2   An indexed search.

This example shows that an indexed search, unlike an ordinary forward or backward search, has nothing to do with the current position of the highlight. The highlight was in the wrong column and in the last record of the database file, but that does not matter because this sort of search does not read through the database file to find the record you are searching for. It uses the index.

Queries

If you want to select multiple records to work with, rather than just moving the pointer to look up a single record, use the queries design screen.

Before you create a query, the database it is based on should be in use. If it is not already above the line in the Data panel, you can select it and then select **Use file** from the prompt box. When the appropriate database is in use, select **<create>** from the Queries panel to use the Queries Design screen, shown in Figure 5.3.

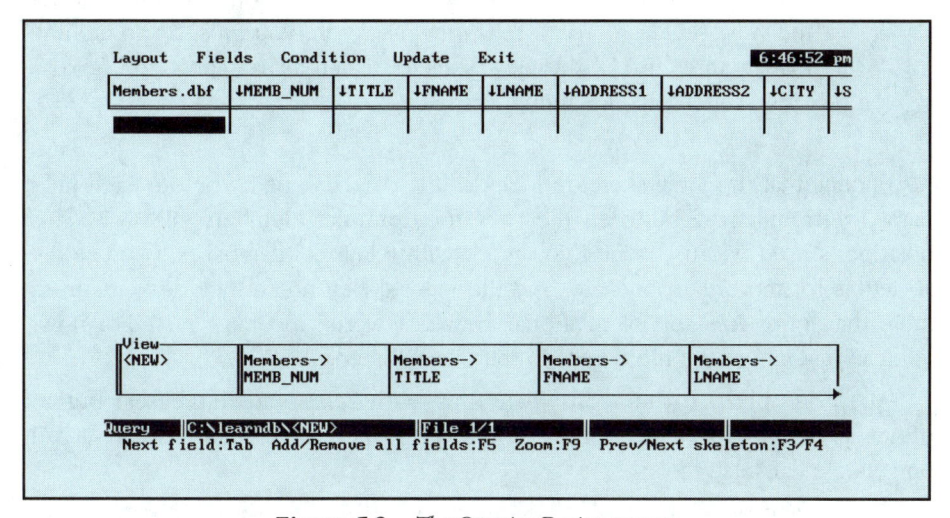

Figure 5.3   *The Queries Design screen.*

As you can see from the illustration, the Queries Design screen includes two lists of field names, one that goes across the top of the screen and another that goes across the bottom.

The list at the top is called the *file skeleton*. You use this list to determine which records are included in the result of the query, by filling in the criteria of the query under the field names.

The list at the bottom is called the *view skeleton*. You use this list to choose which fields are displayed. When you work with it, you will see that the small arrows appear at the right or left of the view skeleton to indicate that it includes other fields beyond the edge of the screen: note the arrow at the right of the view skeleton in the illustration.

When the view skeleton is first created from a database file that is in use, the view skeleton contains all of the fields that the database contained. You will decide which fields to keep in the new view. As you will see, you can press **Field:F5** to add fields to or remove fields from the view skeleton. Using the mouse, you can simply double-click the field name in the file skeleton to add it to or remove it from the view skeleton.

NOTE: If you do not have a database file in use when you begin to create a query, dBASE IV cannot display a field or view skeleton, but it does take you to the queries design screen with the Layout menu pulled down, so you can select Add file to query and specify the file you want to use. This option just adds the file skeleton, though, and not the view skeleton. To add the view skeleton, you must do something that requires use of the view skeleton, such as selecting Add field to view from the Fields menu.

Also notice that the view skeleton includes the database name before each field name, with an arrow between the two, for example, Members->FNAME. This notation is used because, when you work with relational databases, you use file skeletons for more than one file, and the view skeleton can include fields from more than one. This sort of relational view is covered in Chapter 10. For now, you can just ignore the file names in the view skeleton.

Many people use the word *view* only with relational databases, but in dBASE IV terminology, the result of a query is called a view even if it is based on a single database file.

Older database management systems required you to enter elaborate commands to create queries. When you create a query by filling in a form such as the Queries Design screen to show the sort of data that you want, it is called *Query by Example*. dBASE IV saves queries in files with the extension .QBE.

After you have created and saved a query, you can use it at any time. To see the data as it is filtered through that view, just highlight the name of the file in the Queries panel and press **Data:F2** to view your data as it is filtered through that query. Alternately, select the query name and select **Display data** from the prompt box. By default, the data is displayed in a browse screen, but you can toggle between the browse and edit screen (as usual) by pressing **Data:F2**.

To change the design of a query, highlight its name and press **Design:Shift-F2**, or press **Enter** (or click the highlighted file) and choose **Modify query** from the prompt box. You can also toggle back and forth between the queries design screen and the screen that displays the data by pressing **Data:F2** and **Design:Shift-F2**.

There are also many cases where you want to use the view without displaying the data or modifying the design of the query—for example, to produce mailing labels that include only some records. To use the view in this way, press **Enter** and choose **Use view** from the prompt box.

After you have used a view in any of these ways, the view is in use and its name is displayed above the line of the Queries panel, and the name of the database file is no longer above the line in the Data panel. You can use either a database file or a view, but not both. You learned in Chapter 2 that, when you use a database file, all the objects (such as reports and labels) that are based on it are listed above the line in their panels, just as the database file is above the line in the Data panel. The same is true when you use a query. All the other objects based on that query are listed above the line in their panels for as long as the query is in use.

The filter that you created when you designed the query remains in effect as long as the view is in use, and you can produce labels or reports that include only the records in the query. You can use these labels or reports even if they were based on the database file rather than the query, and even though they are not above the line, as long as the query includes all the fields that they use. When you do this, dBASE IV displays a prompt box asking whether you want them to be based on the database file or on the current view, and you can select **Current view** to produce filtered reports or labels.

To get rid of this filter and use all of the records in the database file again, select the name of the database file. It moves above the line in the Data panel and, at the same time, the query name no longer is above the line in the Queries panel.

You can also close the view without using the database file, by selecting the query name from the Queries panel. When the view is in use, the option Use view in the prompt box toggles to Close view, just as the option Use file toggles to Close file when a database file is in use.

It takes some time to use a view: to show you what it is doing while you wait, dBASE IV displays the command SET VIEW TO followed by the name of the query. If you have a large database, queries can also be slow to process records. In some cases, advanced dBASE users may want to gain extra speed by using an index with a FOR clause (covered in Chapter 11) or a command with a WHILE clause (covered in Chapter 12) instead of a query.

The Basics of the File and View Skeleton

It is easy to learn the basics of the file skeleton, view skeleton and other features of the query screen by creating a simple query.

In this section, you create a query that lets you look at just the names and membership data of members who live in California.

Including only the records from California involves entering a very simple criterion in the file skeleton. You will also use the simplest method of altering the view skeleton. You will learn more sophisticated methods of altering the view skeleton in the next section; you will learn to use more complex criteria in the file skeleton later in this chapter. This exercise gives you an overview of how the entire query screen works before you look at the parts of it in detail.

Begin the exercise from the Control Center, with C:\LEARNDB\SAMPLE.CAT as the current catalog:

1. To use the database file, select **MEMBERS** from the Data panel; then select **Use file** from the prompt box. The file name is now above the line in the panel.
2. To use the Queries design screen, select **<create>** from the Queries panel.

As you can see, on the queries design screen, the view skeleton has the word <NEW> displayed at the left when you first create a query. The actual name of the view you define is displayed there after you have named the query.

Using the keyboard, you can move among the columns of the field skeleton or of the view skeleton in the familiar ways: press **Tab** or **Shift-Tab** to move right or left one column, or press **Home** or **End** to move to the far left or far right.

As the navigation line at the bottom of the screen indicates, you can move between the two skeletons by pressing **Prev:F3** or **Next:F4**. (Which one of these you press matters only if you are working with a relational database with multiple file skeletons displayed. With only two skeletons from which to choose, either **F3** or **F4** moves you to the other one.)

Using the mouse, you can simply click any field in the file skeleton to move to it. You can also click **Tab** or **Shift-Tab** on the Navigation line to move one column right or left in the file skeleton. To move the highlight to any field in the view skeleton, click the top border of that field. To move one column right or left in the field skeleton, click the right or left arrowhead at the ends of the skeleton. Or to move to the far left or right of the field skeleton, double-click these arrowheads.

To design a query, you type criteria in the columns under the field names listed in the field skeleton. (To enter a longer criterion, you can press **Zoom:F9** or double-click the field for a larger entry area, or just keep typing in the area under the field skeleton. The column automatically expands to accommodate everything you type.)

The simplest way to determine which fields are displayed is to notice that the field names in the file skeleton have arrows pointing downward to their left if they are included in the view skeleton, and that the arrows disappear when fields are removed from the view skeleton. This lets you know at a glance whether or not a field is included in the view.

Use the Layout menu and the Exit menu in the familiar ways to save, name, and, enter the description of a query. To view the results of the query, press **Data:F2** from the queries design screen. To return from the results back to the queries design screen, press **Design:Shift-F2**.

You should still be using the queries design screen, which you called up in the last exercise:

1. Move the cursor to the STATE column. Type *"CA"* in that column; do not forget to include the quotation marks.

2. Move the highlight to the MEMB_NUM field of the view skeleton, and press **Field:F5** to remove it or simply double-click it in the view skeleton to remove it.

3. Press **Field:F5** again to remove the TITLE field.

4. Move to the ADDRESS1 field of the view skeleton, and press **Field:F5** to remove that field from the view or simply double-click it in the view skeleton to remove it.

5. In the same way, remove the ADDRESS2, CITY, STATE, and ZIP fields from the view.

6. Then press **End** to move to the NOTES field and press Field:F5 to remove it from the view.

7. Select **Edit description of query** from the Layout menu. dBASE IV displays the prompt Edit the description of this .qbe file. Type *Names and membership data for California members* and press **Enter**. (It is important to enter the description of the query *before* saving it Otherwise, the description will be lost.)

8. Select **Save this query** from the Layout menu. dBASE IV displays the prompt Save as. Enter the name *cal_data*, and note that this name is now displayed at the left of the view skeleton.

9. Now, you are done creating the query, which is shown in Figure 5.4. Press **Data:F2**, and, after taking a moment to process the query, dBASE IV displays the result shown in Figure 5.5.

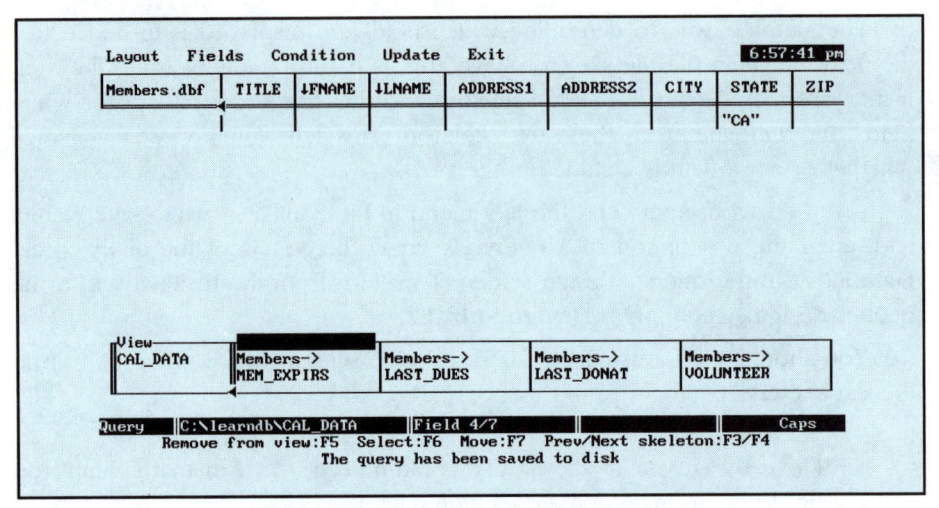

Figure 5.4 *The queries design in final form.*

Notice that the field where the criterion is entered does not have to be included in the view. This view includes only members from California, but the STATE field itself is not part of the view.

Figure 5.5 *The results of this query.*

Altering the View Skeleton

In the last section, you altered the view skeleton in the simplest way possible, by highlighting a field and pressing **Field:F5** to delete it. This is usually adequate, but there are also more powerful and sophisticated ways of using the view skeleton:

- When the highlight is under the name of a field in the file skeleton, press **Field:F5** to add that field to the view skeleton or to remove it from the view skeleton. If the field is added, it becomes the last field of the view skeleton.
- When the highlight is under the name of the file in the file skeleton, press **Field:F5** to add all of the fields in that file to the view skeleton or to remove them all from the view skeleton, as the navigation line says.
- When the highlight is on the name of a field in the view skeleton, you can rearrange the order in which the field appears in the view skeleton by pressing **Move:F7** to move that field, as the navigation line says. dBASE IV outlines the field name with a wide border, and the navigation line prompts you to press **Tab** or **Shift-Tab** to move it and press **Return** (that is, **Enter**) to end.

In addition, you can work with groups of fields. The navigation line just hints what you have to do by mentioning **Select:F6**. To use this feature, first place the highlight in the view skeleton on the name of a field that is at the far right or the far left of the group you want to work with. Then, press **Select:F6**. dBASE IV outlines the field name with a large border, and the navigation line prompts you to press **Tab** or **Shift-Tab** to select fields. As you do so, the border expands to surround a group of fields. Once you have selected the group you want, you can press **Field:F5** to delete the entire group from the view skeleton or press **Move:F7** to move the entire group. (You can also press **Select:F6** to unselect that group and begin selecting again from scratch.)

Now, you can see that, in the exercise above, there were actually two different shortcuts that would have been easier than removing fields from the view one at a time:

- You could have used **Select:F6** to select the ADDRESS1, ADDRESS2, CITY, STATE, and ZIP fields in the view skeleton and then have pressed **Field:F5** to remove them all at once.
- You could have pressed **Field:F5** when the highlight was under the file name in the file skeleton, to remove all the fields from the skeleton. Then you could have moved the highlight in the field skeleton to the fields you wanted and pressed **Field:F5** to move each to the view skeleton.

If you use the queries design screen frequently, you will find which way of using it is most convenient for you.

For now, you can try using **Move:F7** to change the design of your query a bit. Imagine that, after you pressed **Data:F2** to see the result of the query, you realized that it was not displayed in the way you wanted. When you look at the data, you need to know immediately whether the person is a volunteer or not, but now you can see that the VOLUNTEER field is beyond the right edge of the screen. You could alter the Browse screen to fix this, by making the fields narrower (as you learned to do in Chapter 3), but as an exercise, try altering the query instead:

1. Press **Design:Shift-F2** to return to the queries design screen.
2. Move the highlight to the VOLUNTEER field of the view skeleton.

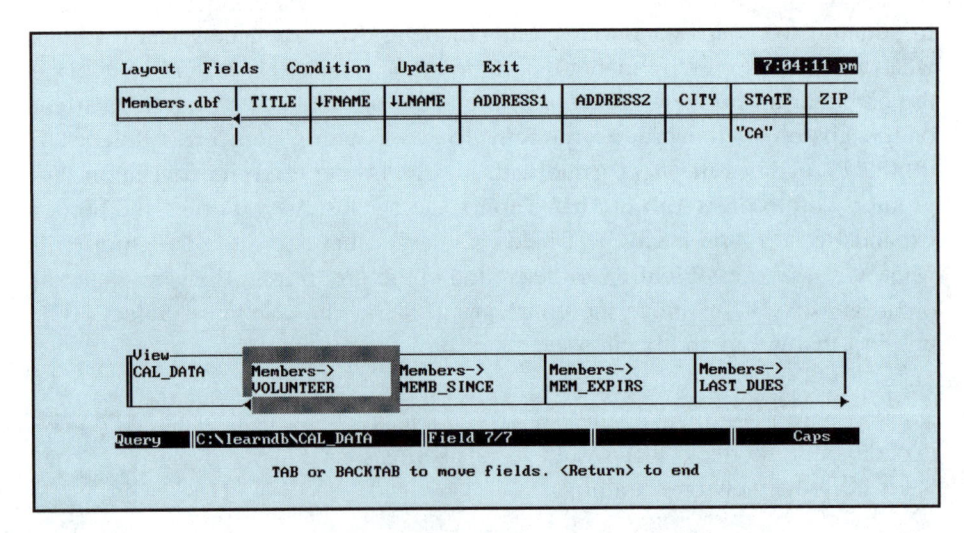

Figure 5.6 *Moving a field in the view skeleton.*

3. Press **Move:F7.** The field is surrounded by a wide border. Press **Shift-Tab** four times to move the field so that it is to the left of the other membership data, as in Figure 5.6, and then press **Enter**.
4. Press **Data:F2** to see the result of the query, shown in Figure 5.7.

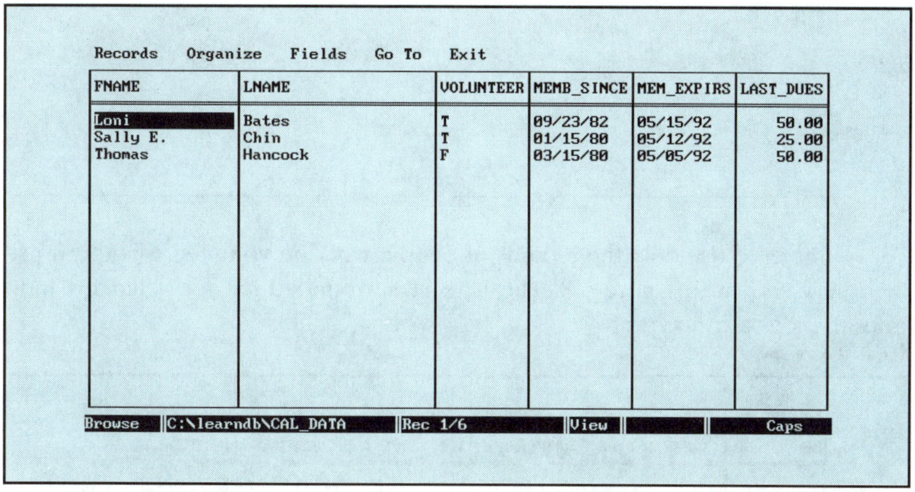

Figure 5.7   *The result of the query after the field is moved.*

In an earlier chapter, you learned to use the Fields menu of the Browse screen to view more fields. Now, you see that you can do much more by using a query to determine which fields you see: you can display whichever fields you want in whatever order you want.

Using Delimiters

In the example, you used quotation marks as the delimiter around CA, because this is a character field. *Delimiters* identify the beginning and the end of a character string. There are different delimiters for different data types, and these delimiters are used in many other places in dBASE, as well as in queries.

Though double quotation marks (" ") are most common, you can also use single quotation marks (' ') or square brackets ([ ]) as delimiters around character fields, if you find them more convenient. You must use curly brackets ({ })as delimiters if a field is the date type. Use dots (. .) as delimiters if the field is the logical type. Use a number without delimiters if the field is the numeric type.

The data entered under any field of the file skeleton must have the proper delimiter for the data type of that field. These delimiters are summarized in Table 5.1:

Table 5.1 *Delimiters used with queries.*

" " or ' ' or [ ]	character
{ }	date
. .	logical
(no delimiter)	number

For example, to use only the records of people who are volunteers, you can use the query shown in Figure 5.8. The letter T surrounded by dot delimiters indicates the logical value true.

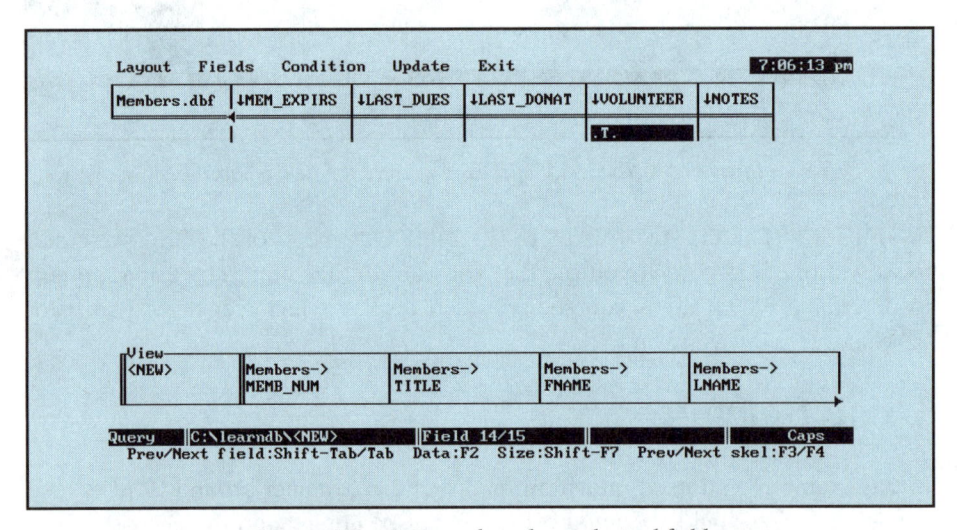

Figure 5.8 *A Query based on a logical field.*

Using Operators

The example was based on an exact match, but you can also use operators to make queries based on different sorts of matches. All of these operators are summarized in Table 5.2, and they are explained in the following sections.

Table 5.2 Operators used in queries.

=	equals
>	greater than
<	less than
>=	greater than or equal to
<=	less than or equal to
<> or #	not equal to
$	includes
LIKE	(allows use of wildcard characters)
SOUNDS LIKE	(allows an inexact match)

Notice that the = sign can be left out of queries. Typing *"CA"* under state, as you did in the earlier example, actually means that the contents of the field is equal to *"CA"*. If you insist on being strictly logical, you can create the query by typing =*"CA"* under the STATE field—omitting the = sign is just a way of saving time.

The Relational Operators

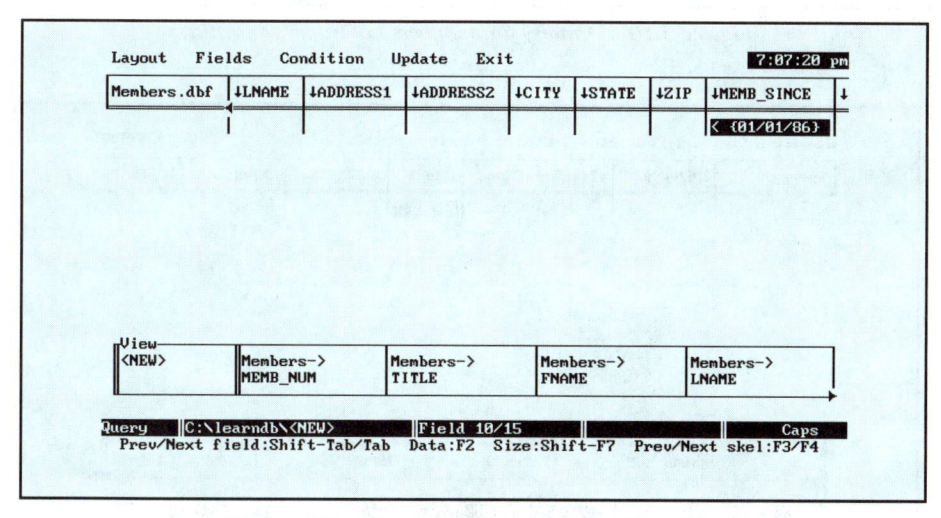

Figure 5.9 *A comparison based on a date field.*

Sometimes, all of these operators are referred to as *relational operators* but sometimes that term is used more strictly to refer only to the first six lines in the table, the operators that involve a relation of equality or inequality. Most people find these operators easy to use, because they are familiar with them from arithmetic.

For example, to find the records of people who have been members since 1985, use the query in Figure 5.9, and to find the records of all the members who are not from California, use the query in Figure 5.10.

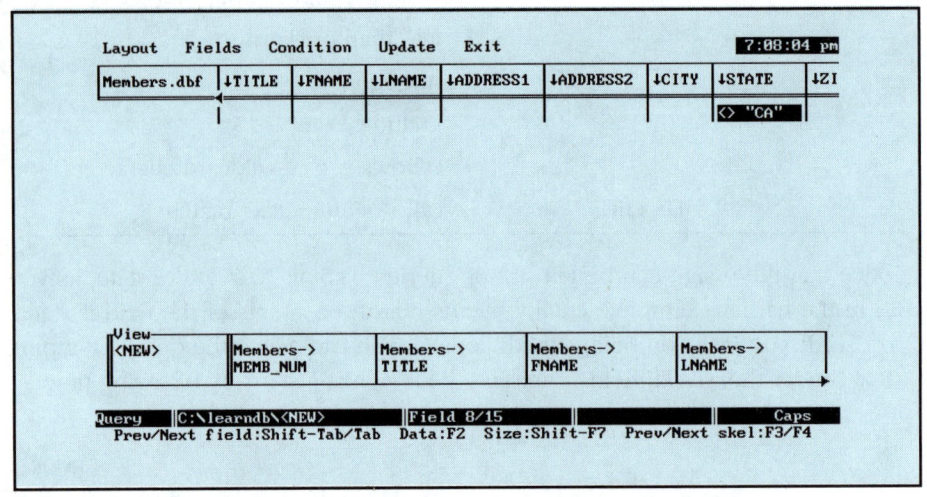

Figure 5.10 *A query for members not from California.*

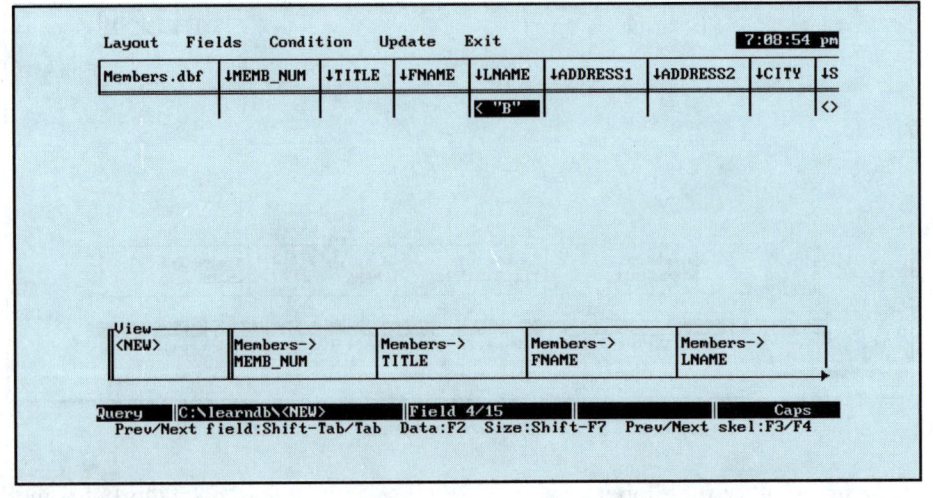

Figure 5.11 *A comparison based on a character field.*

In addition to their obvious use with dates and numbers, the >, <, >=, and <= operators can also be used with character fields. For example, if you wanted to find only the members whose last names begin with *A*, you could use the query shown in Figure 5.11.

The $ Operator

You can query only character fields with the inclusion operator, $, which can be read as "includes." This operator is used to find records where character fields include some substring.

For example, you can find everyone who lives on Shady Lane, regardless of their number on that street, by filling in the query form with *$ "Shady Lane"* under ADDRESS1, as shown in Figure 5.12. If you want people not only from Shady Lane but also from Shady Ave. and Shady Blvd., you can simply use **$** *"Shady"*.

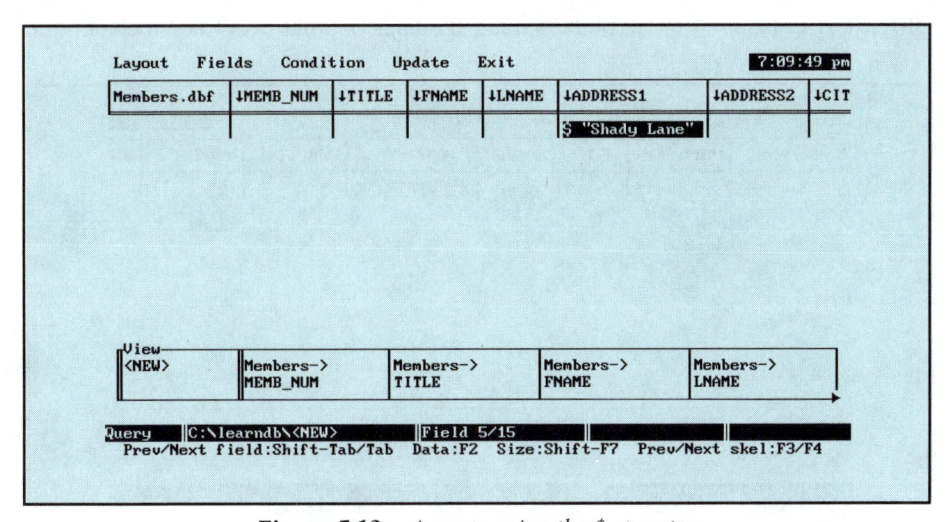

Figure 5.12   *A query using the $ operator.*

Unfortunately, the inclusion operator cannot be used to query memo fields for a substring. To do this, you must add a condition box to the query with a similar operator in a dBASE expression. This is covered in Chapter 11.

Queries Using LIKE and SOUNDS LIKE

LIKE and SOUNDS LIKE both let you make inexact searches, but you must not confuse the two.

LIKE lets you use the same wildcard characters you used when you did an unindexed search for a single record earlier in this chapter: **?** stands for any single character, and ***** stands for any group of characters. When you use the LIKE operator, you must allow for all of the possible spellings of a word, and you must explicitly include the wildcard character where spelling might differ.

SOUNDS LIKE does this thinking for you. dBASE automatically queries for words that sound like the criterion you entered.

SOUNDS LIKE is generally easier to use. For example, if you were looking for someone named Smith but forgot how to spell his name, you might try using the LIKE query shown in Figure 5.13, but this query would omit Mr. Smythe, even though it would include Smith and Smyth. On the other hand, if you used the SOUNDS LIKE query in Figure 5.14, all of the variant spellings of Smith would be included.

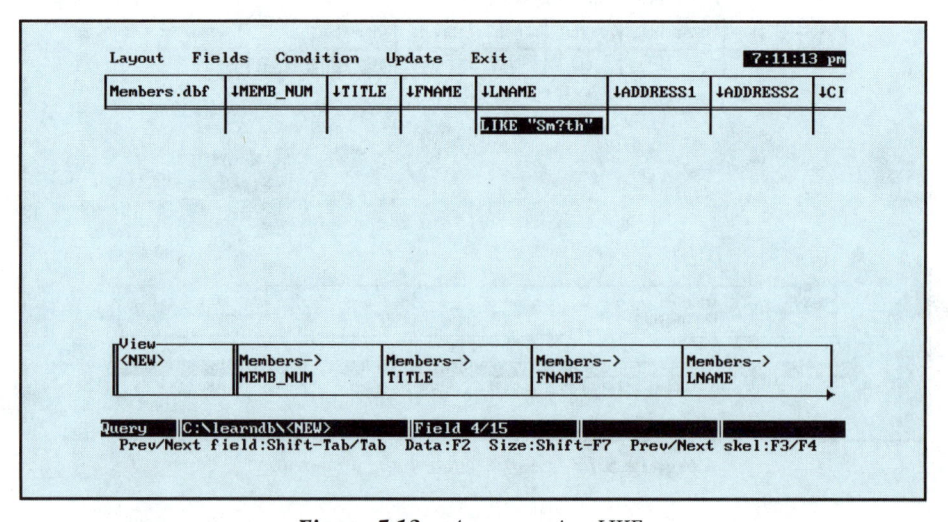

Figure 5.13   *A query using LIKE.*

LIKE is useful for character data if you know exactly what you want. It is also indispensable when you are querying for data that is not actually text but is kept in character fields—for example, to search for all the members from Manhattan, you can use the criterion LIKE **"100*"**, in the ZIP file, but obviously you can not use SOUNDS LIKE in this case.

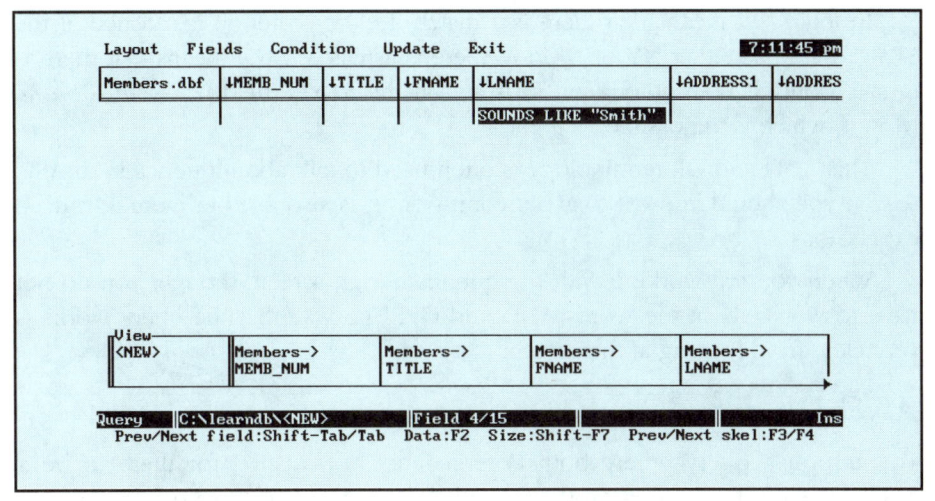

Figure 5.14 *A query using SOUNDS LIKE.*

Queries with AND and OR

So far, you have looked only at queries that use a single criterion. You can also use more that one criterion in a query.

There are two ways that you might want to use multiple criteria:

- To find a match only when the record meets both criteria: for example, to find every member who is from California and also is a volunteer.
- To find a match when the record meets either one of the criteria: for example, to find every member who is either from New York or from New Jersey.

The first of these is called a logical AND and the second is called a logical OR.

The words AND and OR are used more strictly in logic than in ordinary speech, and you should take a second to think about the difference to avoid confusion. If you wanted every member from New York and New Jersey, for example, in ordinary speech you might ask for members from New York and New Jersey. However, since no member can live in both New York AND New Jersey, a query constructed this way would return no records in answer to your question. In the stricter sense of the words used in logic, you must say New York OR New Jersey to get the correct result.

In logic, OR means that there is a match if either criterion is satisfied; if the STATE field has either NY or NJ in it, there is a match. AND means that there is a match only if both criteria are satisfied—if the STATE field has *both* NY *and* NJ in it, which is impossible.

This AND and OR terminology is often used to talk about queries in dBASE, so that you should know it to avoid confusion. It is also used in more advanced expressions.

When you are working with the queries design screen, though, you do not have to worry about the words AND and OR. The way that the query works is very clear from looking at the screen.

AND Queries

To perform a query where both criteria must be satisfied for there to be a match, just put the criteria on the same line. For example, Figure 5.15 shows a query to find members who are from California AND who have become members since 1986. Both conditions must be met for there to be a match.

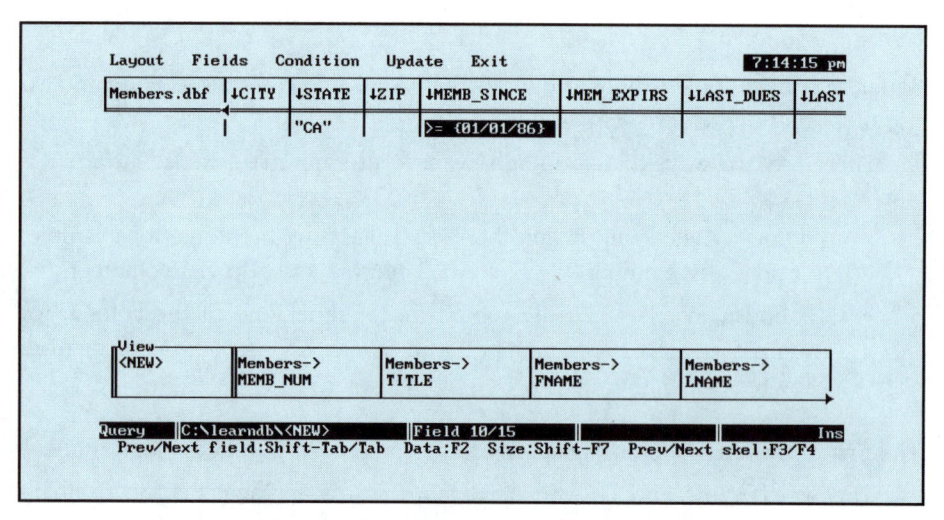

Figure 5.15 *A query using logical AND.*

If you want more than one criterion in a single field, type both criteria there with a comma between the two. This method is used most commonly to find a range of values. For example, if you want all the members who pay between $25 and $75 in dues, you can query for those with LAST_DUES greater or equal to 25 AND less than or equal to 75, as in Figure 5.16.

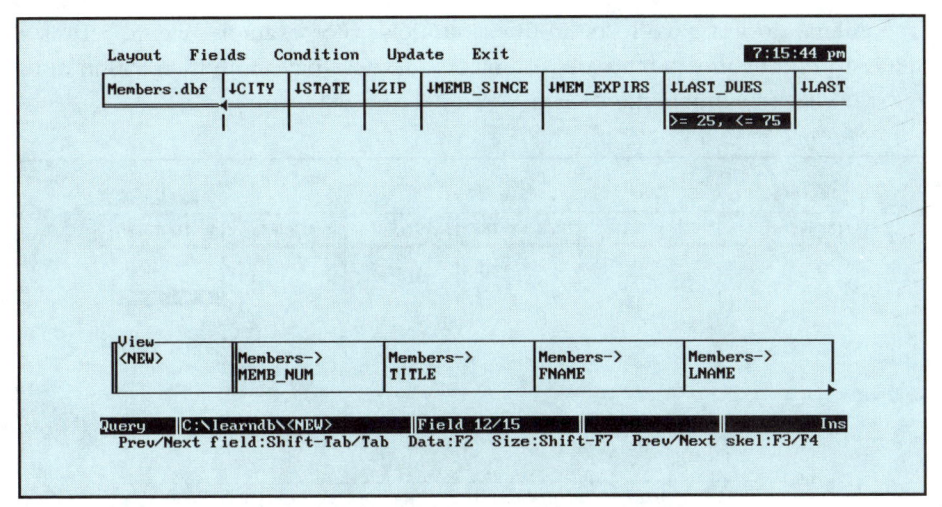

Figure 5.16 *A query for a range of values.*

OR Queries

To perform a query where either criterion may be satisfied for there to be a match, put the second criterion on a second line. You can just press the **Down Arrow** to move the cursor downward and add more lines to the file skeleton. dBASE finds a match if the record matches the criteria on any line. For example, Figure 5.17 shows a query to find members who are from New York OR from New Jersey OR from Connecticut.

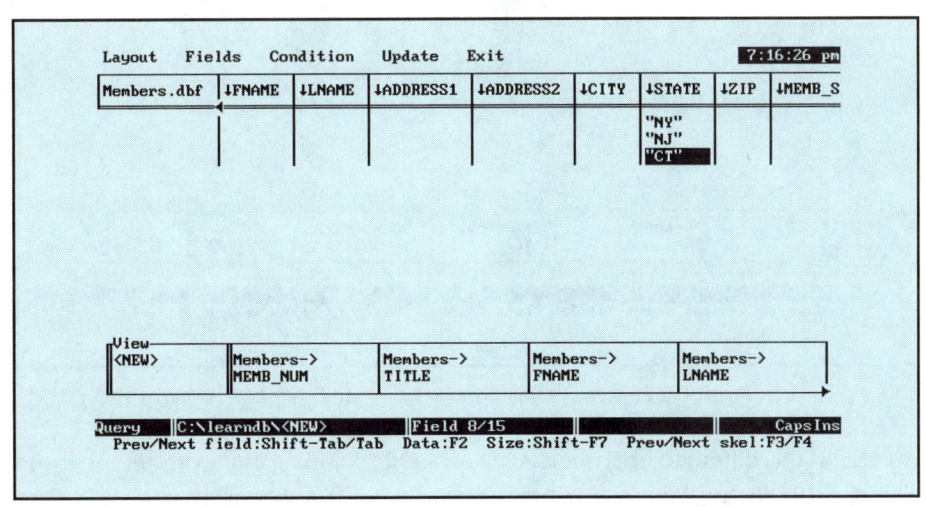

Figure 5.17 *A query using logical OR.*

The criteria do not have to be in the same fields. For example, Figure 5.18 is a query to find members who are Volunteers OR who pay more than $50 in dues OR who have been members since 1985.

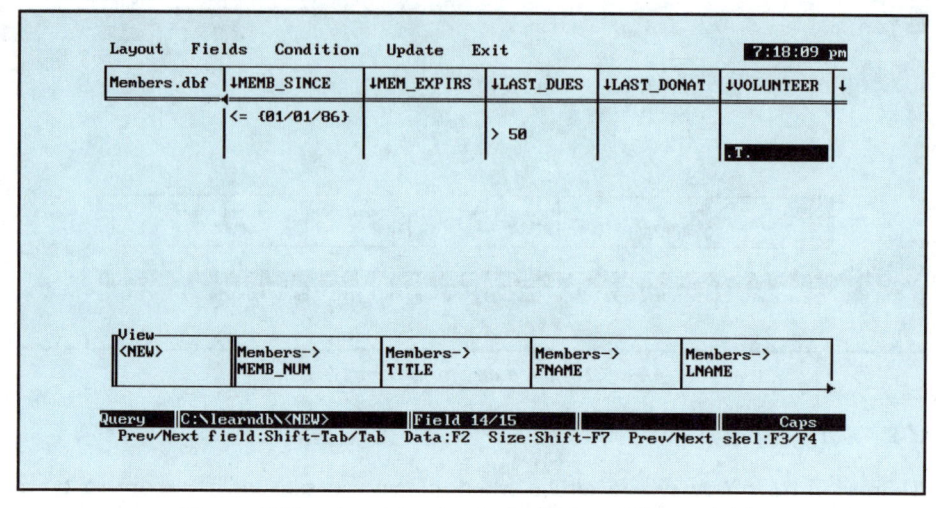

Figure 5.18   *A query using logical OR in different fields.*

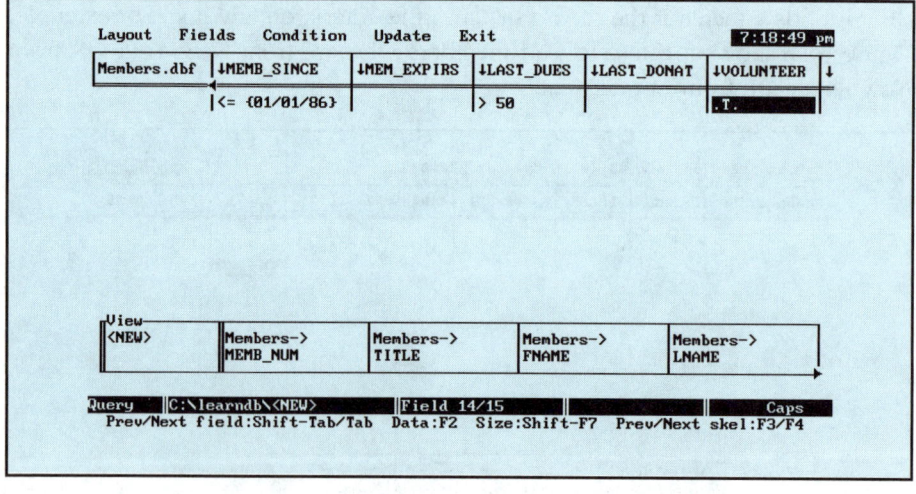

Figure 5.19   *The same criteria in an AND relationship.*

To clarify the difference between AND and OR, compare this with the query in Figure 5.19, where the same criteria are in an AND relationship. Notice that in

Figure 5.18, the OR query, the criteria are on different lines in the file skeleton, while in Figure 5.19, the AND query, the criteria are on the same line. Very few members would match the conditions of the AND query, where all of the criteria must be satisfied. Far more would match the OR query, where any one of the criteria may be satisfied. AND is exclusive, OR is inclusive.

Queries Combining AND and OR

To create a query combining AND and OR, just remember what you have already learned. dBASE IV reads across each line and finds a match only if all of the criteria on that line are satisfied: The criteria on each line are in an AND relationship. dBASE reads all of the lines and finds a match if the criteria on any one are satisfied: The lines are in an OR relationship.

Thus, Figure 5.20 shows a query that combines AND and OR to find all of the records where the member is from California AND has been a member since 1985 OR is from New York AND has been a member since 1985.

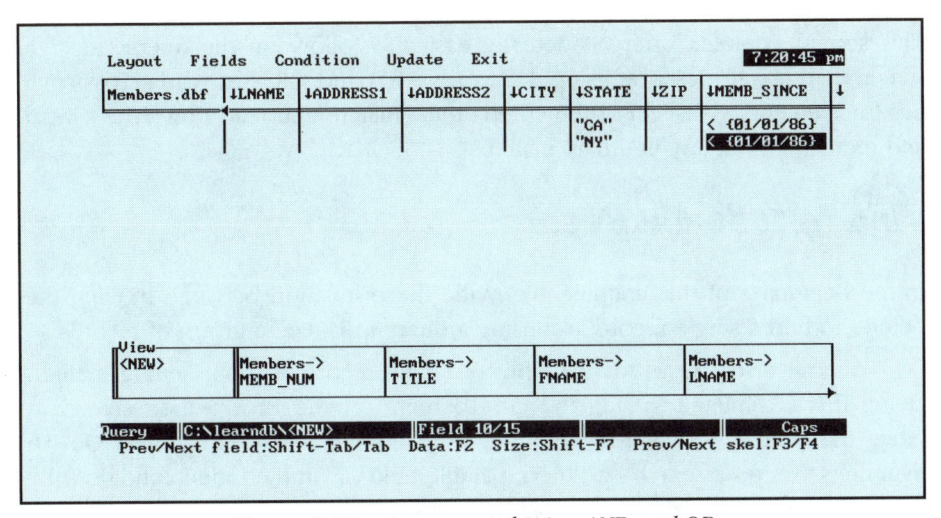

Figure 5.20 *A query combining AND and OR.*

This sort of complex query is often used in this way, with criteria in the same fields of each line. It may also be used with criteria in different fields, however, as in Figure 5.21, which finds records where the member is a volunteer OR is both a member since 1985 AND pays dues of $50 or more. (You could use this sort of query to find the most committed members, for example.)

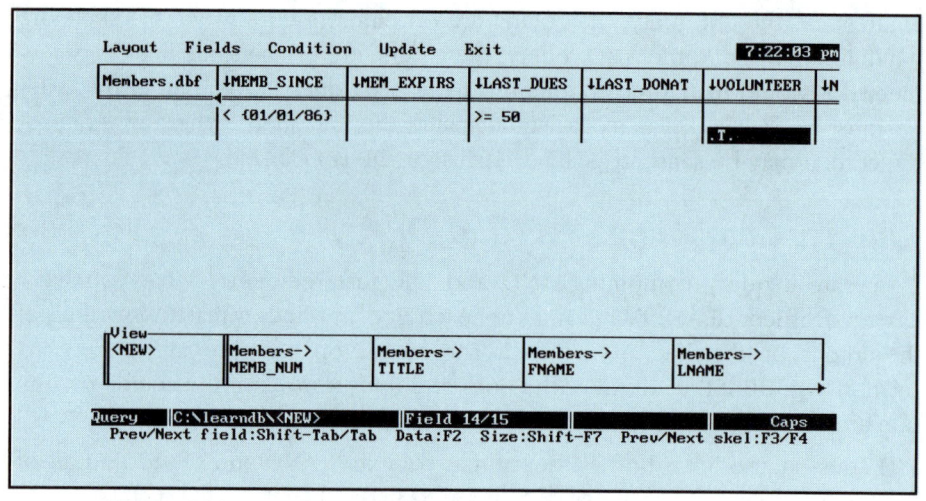

```
Layout    Fields   Condition   Update   Exit                    7:22:03 pm
Members.dbf |↓MEMB_SINCE |↓MEM_EXPIRS |↓LAST_DUES |↓LAST_DONAT |↓VOLUNTEER |↓N
            | < {01/01/86}|            | >= 50     |            |            |
            |            |            |           |            | .T.        |



View
<NEW>   |Members-> |Members-> |Members-> |Members->
        |MEMB_NUM  |TITLE     |FNAME     |LNAME

Query    C:\learndb\<NEW>      Field 14/15                        Caps
         Prev/Next field:Shift-Tab/Tab  Data:F2  Size:Shift-F7  Prev/Next skel:F3/F4
```

Figure 5.21 *Combining AND and OR, with criteria in different fields.*

This sort of complex query is actually easier to follow on the queries design screen than it is to describe using the words AND and OR. Just read across each line and remember that *all* of the criteria must match; and read down the screen and remember that any line may match.

Finding a Single Record

In the beginning of this chapter, we made the distinction between moving the pointer to find a single record and using a query to isolate a group of records.

You can also use a query to find a single record without setting a filter. Doing this is similar to using the Go To menu of the Browse/Edit screen to move the pointer, but it lets you use more complex conditions. The Go To menu lets you do a search based on a single field or on the index condition. By using the query screen, you can do a search based on any conditions in any number of fields. Now that you have seen the sort of complex criteria that you can use in queries, you can appreciate that there are times when they have a tremendous advantage over the Go To menu, even for finding a single record.

To find a single record, type the word *find* under the file name in the file skeleton. Then, when you press **Data:F2**, dBASE IV displays the Browse screen with the pointer on the record that meets the criteria in the query, and with all of the other records visible whether or not they meed the condition.

For example, imagine that your group has a dozen people who are named Mary Johnson as members, and that you want to find the one who lives on Shady Lane. You could use the query shown in Figure 5.22.

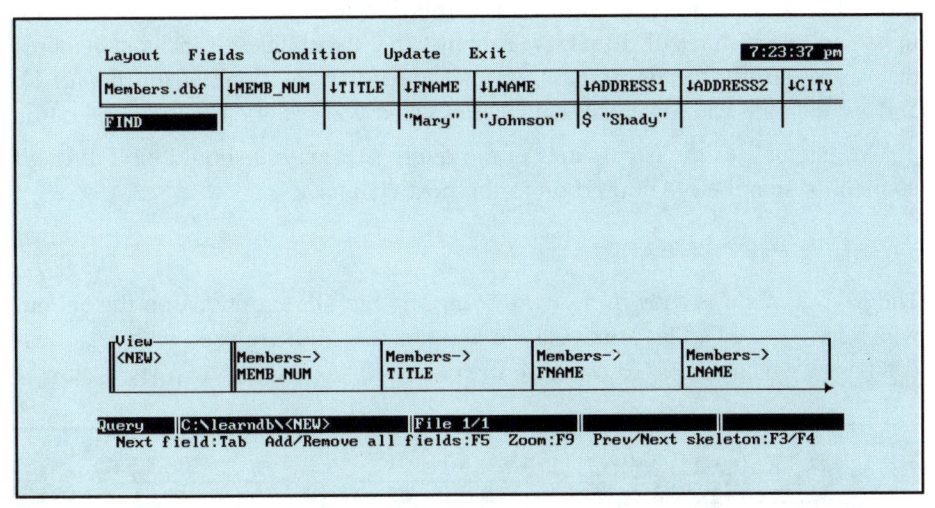

Figure 5.22 *A query using FIND.*

Speeding Up Queries

In dBASE IV versions 1.5 and later, the Fields menu of the query screen includes an option that can let you speed up subsequent executions of a query.

When you execute a query, dBASE creates temporary indexes to help it locate the records in the file. These are similar to the indexes discussed in Chapter 4.

By default, dBASE does not save these indexes. It creates them again from scratch each time you execute the query. When you use the same query repeatedly, however, it is faster to update the index created earlier than it is to create the new one. If you select **Keep Speedup Indexes** from the Fields menu, dBASE keeps and updates these temporary indexes rather than recreating them each time you execute the query.

This option is a toggle. By default, it has NO to its right to indicate that indexes are not saved. Select it repeatedly to toggle between YES and NO.

The only disadvantage of saving these indexes is that they take up disk space. If you are very short of disk space, keep this option on NO.

Other Features of Queries

You have learned all you need to know to use the query screen for its basic purpose of finding records that you want to use. But the query screen is one of the most versatile features of dBASE IV. Among other capabilities, it includes features that are useful for creating quick reports (which you will look at in Chapter 6), and for working with relational databases (which you will look at in Chapter 10).

To get an idea the capabilities of the query screen, you should look through its menu system before you go on to the next chapter.

The Layout Menu

The Layout menu is shown in Figure 5.23. The first three options on this menu, which let you add a file, remove a file and create a link, are used with relational databases, which are based on more than one file.

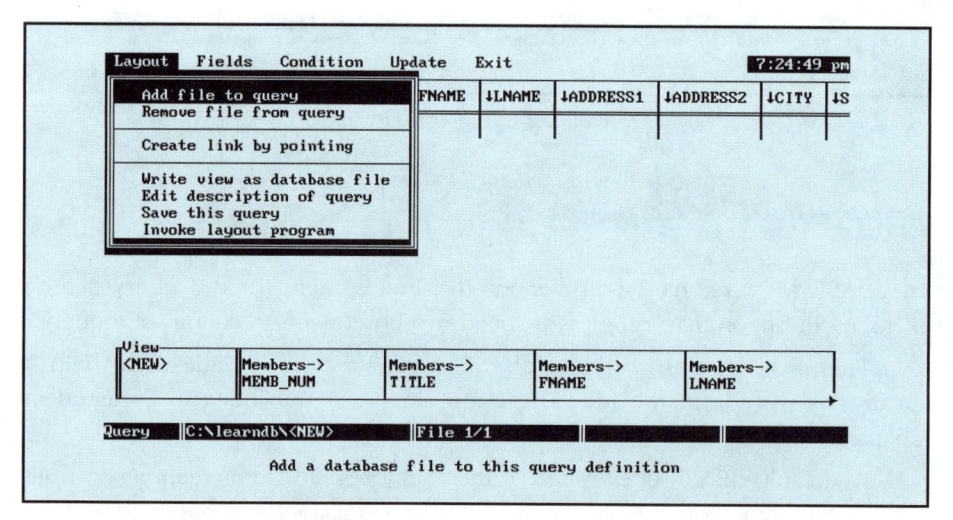

Figure 5.23   *The layout menu.*

WARNING   The option to Write view as a database file lets you create a new database file containing only the fields and records that are included in the view. If you select this option, dBASE IV prompts you to enter the name of the file. As you can see in Figure 5.24, it suggests that you use the name of the view as the name of this database file, but you can edit its suggestion to change the name and directory. You should always avoid keeping more than one copy of the same data, however, because of the extra time it takes to update multiple copies of the data and because of the inevitable errors that arise. Thus, for your own use, it is much better to use several views of the same database file than it is to keep a view in its own database file. This option is useful, though, if you want to give selected data to somebody else in the form of a .DBF file, which they could easily use with their own copy of dBASE IV.

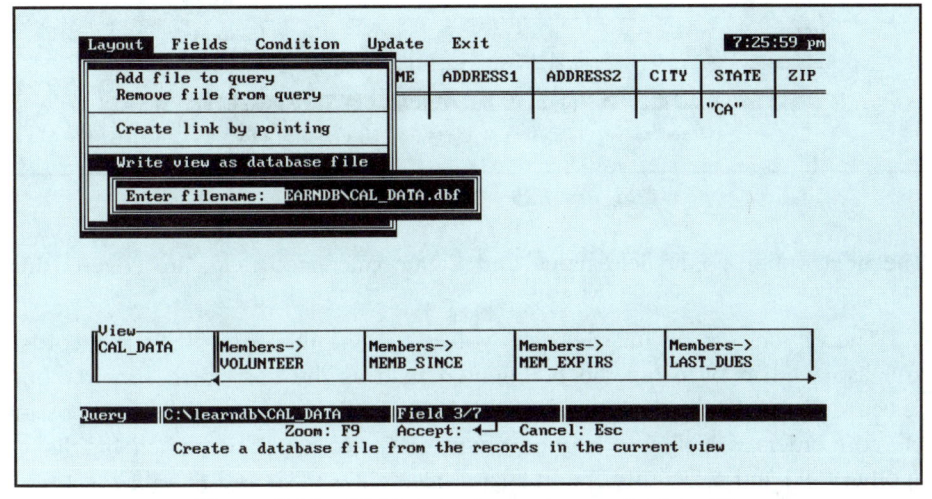

Figure 5.24 Writing the view as a new database file.

You have already seen how to use the next two options of this menu to add or edit the description of the query (which is displayed in the Control Center when the query is highlighted) and to save the query (without exiting from the Query screen).

The Fields Menu

The Fields menu is shown in Figure 5.25. The first two options on this menu duplicate the use of the **Field:F5** key. If the highlight is on a field of the file skeleton, use **Add field to view** to add the highlighted field to the view skeleton, just as you could by pressing **Data:F5**. If the highlight is on the view skeleton, use **Remove field from view** to remove the highlighted field from the view skeleton, just as you could by pressing **Data:F5**. Finally, if the highlight is under the file name of the file skeleton, both of these options are accessible, and you can use them to add or remove all of the fields in that file to the view skeleton, as you could by pressing **Data:F5** once or twice.

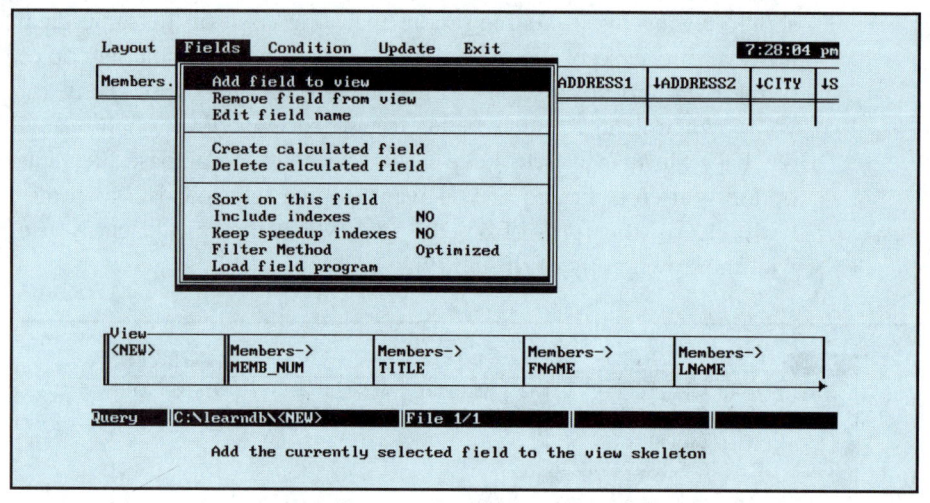

```
Layout   Fields   Condition   Update   Exit                    7:28:04 pm
Members. ┌─────────────────────────────┐ ADDRESS1  ↓ADDRESS2  ↓CITY  ↓S
         │ Add field to view           │
         │ Remove field from view      │
         │ Edit field name             │
         │                             │
         │ Create calculated field     │
         │ Delete calculated field     │
         │                             │
         │ Sort on this field          │
         │ Include indexes       NO    │
         │ Keep speedup indexes  NO    │
         │ Filter Method         Optimized │
         │ Load field program          │
         └─────────────────────────────┘

View
<NEW>        Members->      Members->      Members->      Members->
             MEMB_NUM       TITLE          FNAME          LNAME

Query   C:\learndb\<NEW>    File 1/1
             Add the currently selected field to the view skeleton
```

Figure 5.25   *The Fields menu.*

The next options, Edit field name and Create calculated field, are covered in Chapter 6.

The option Sort on this field lets you determine the order that the records are displayed in by using the highlighted field as the basis of a sort. If you select it, dBASE IV displays a picklist that lets you choose among the four possible sort orders, which you learned about in Chapter 4. If you then highlight another field and select this option again, this field is used as a tie-breaker if the values in the first field are the same in two records. When you select this option, dBASE displays the sort order that you chose in the field of the file skeleton. For example, in Figure 5.26, the query results would be sorted alphabetically by state; within each state, they would be sorted alphabetically by city; and within each city, they would be sorted in zip code order. Note that, in the fields, AscDict stands for ascending dictionary, DscDict stands for descending dictionary, Asc stands for ascending ASCII and Dsc stands for descending ASCII order. The number at the end of each indicates which fields are most important in determining sort order.

These abbreviations are just text that dBASE IV puts in the field. You could type these abbreviations in yourself rather than use the menu. You can also edit or delete them to change the sort order. If you delete one sort order and then use the menu to add another, dBASE IV keeps increasing the number, so that numbers may be skipped. Do not let this worry you, as the sort works properly even if numbers are skipped.

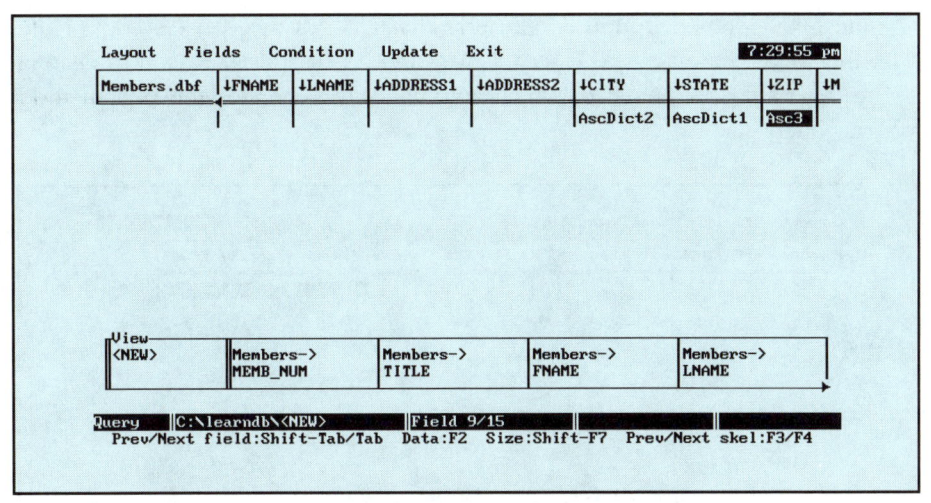

```
    Layout   Fields   Condition   Update   Exit                    7:29:55 pm
   ┌─────────┬──────┬──────┬─────────┬─────────┬──────┬──────┬─────┬──┐
   │Members.dbf│↓FNAME│↓LNAME│↓ADDRESS1│↓ADDRESS2│↓CITY │↓STATE│↓ZIP │↓M│
   ├─────────┼──────┼──────┼─────────┼─────────┼──────┼──────┼─────┤
   │         │      │      │         │         │AscDict2│AscDict1│Asc3│
   │         │      │      │         │         │      │      │     │



   ┌View─────────────────────────────────────────────────────────────
   │<NEW>    │Members->│Members->│Members->│Members->
   │         │MEMB_NUM │TITLE    │FNAME    │LNAME
   ├─────────┴─────────┴─────────┴─────────┴─────────
   │Query  │C:\learndb\<NEW>   │Field 9/15
    Prev/Next field:Shift-Tab/Tab  Data:F2  Size:Shift-F7  Prev/Next skel:F3/F4
```

Figure 5.26   *dBASE indicates which fields are the basis of a sort.*

Like the method of sorting that you learned about in Chapter 4, this method of sorting a query is slow if your file is large. If you have to use the query in sorted order more than once or twice, it is best to use indexes to determine the order, for the sake of better performance. You do this by using the final option on this menu.

If you select **Include indexes** from the Fields menu, dBASE displays either a **#** sign or an arrowhead next to each field that is the basis of an index. It also adds an extra field at the right of the fields menu for each index that is based on an expression rather than on a single field.

After you have included indexes in this way, you can choose a sort order based on one of these fields, just as you do on any field. You must select the order that is the same as the index order, and dBASE uses the index to order the records quickly when you execute the query.

An example of this is included in the next chapter, where you create a Quick Report based on an indexed query: see the section of Chapter 6 titled *A Sample Quick Report*. Figure 5.27 shows the query form from this exercise, so you can see how queries look when indexes are included and used as the basis of a sort.

The Keep speedup indexes option, which was covered above, lets dBASE save the indexes it creates to execute the query and update them rather than taking the extra time to rebuild them from scratch whenever you execute the query.

The Filter Method option is a feature that lets advanced users control the code that is generated by the query. Unless there is a special reason to change it, it can be left as Optimized, which automatically generates the best method for your query.

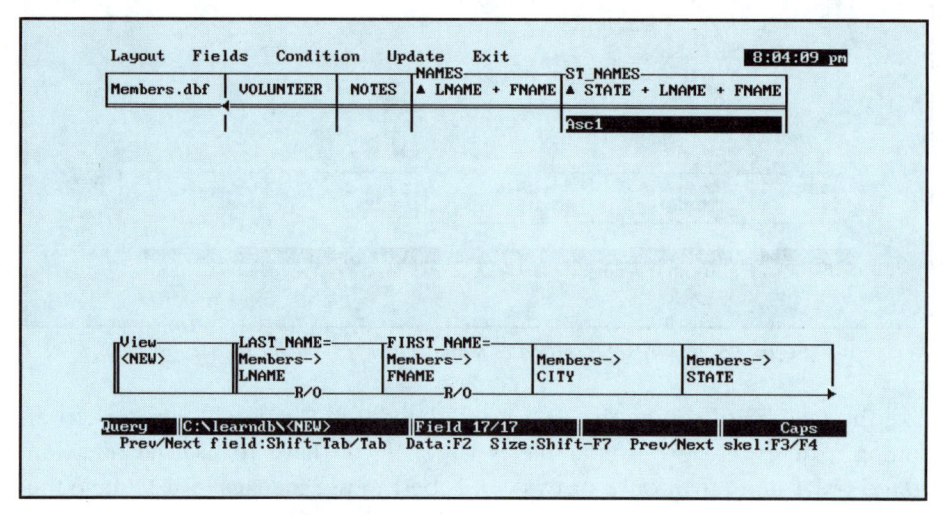

Figure 5.27 *An index used as the basis of a sort.*

The Condition Menu

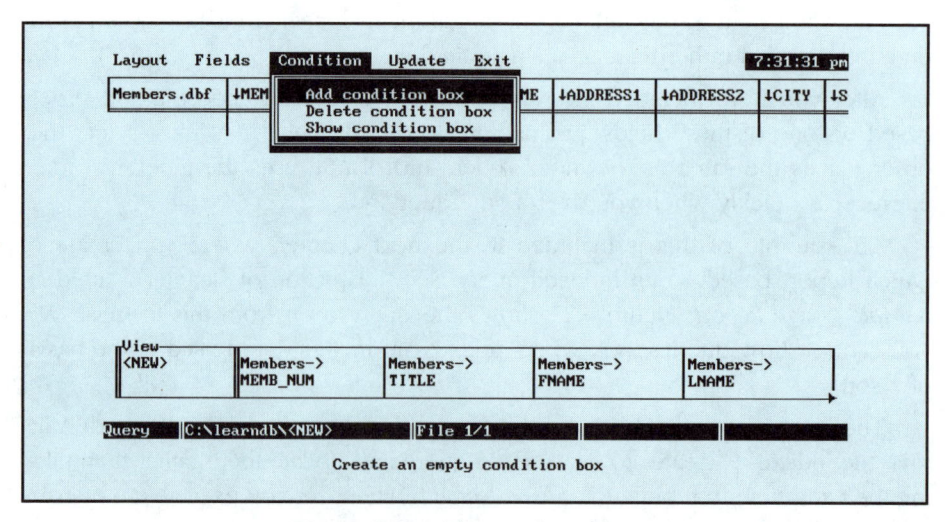

Figure 5.28 *The Condition menu.*

The Condition menu, shown in Figure 5.28, lets you add or delete a condition box, and to decide whether the condition box is shown or not. A condition box, as you can see in Figure 5.29, lets you type in any dBASE expression of a query as a condition, and the query filters out records that do not meet this condition, as well as those that do not meet the criteria entered under fields. Though this feature adds more power to the query screen, it reduces the ease of use that is its main advantage. A condition box is the only way to query memo fields, however, and there might be other cases where you would want to add an expression to the criteria entered in the query form. The condition box is covered in Chapter 11, which discusses dBASE expressions in detail.

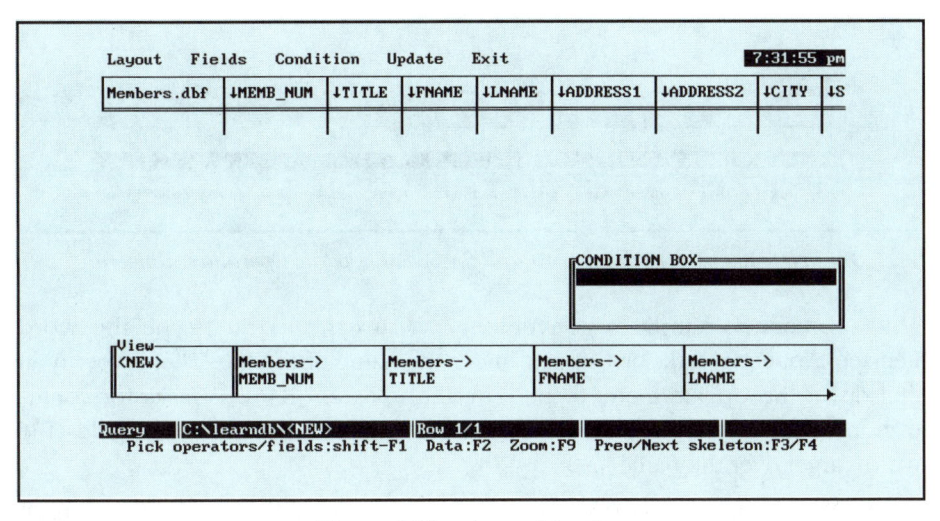

Figure 5.29 *A condition box.*

The Update Menu

The **Update** menu lets you perform operations on entire groups of records. The operations that can be performed are listed in the **Specify update operation** submenu, shown in Figure 5.30.

If you select one of the options from this submenu, dBASE IV first asks you to confirm that you want to remove the view skeleton, if there is one in the query screen. Because these operations update the database rather than displaying it, there is no need for the view skeleton, whose purpose is to determine which fields are displayed. If you confirm that you want to proceed with the update, dBASE IV adds the word Replace, Append, Mark, or Unmark under the name of the file in the file skeleton. It also adds the word Target over the name, to indicate that this is the file where the update will occur.

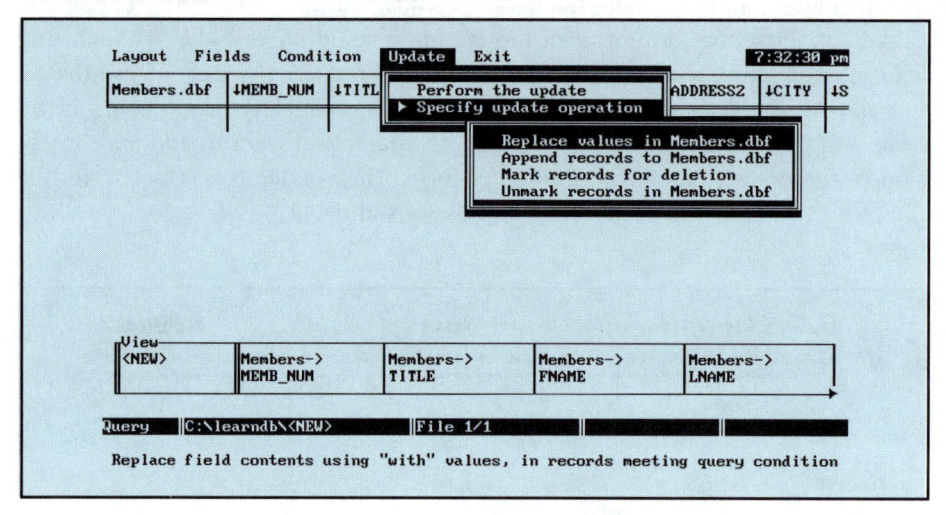

Figure 5.30 *The Update menu and the Specify Update Operation submenu.*

This submenu is simply a convenience. You can also just type the word Replace, Append, Mark, or Unmark under the name of the file. Then, when you pull down the Update menu to perform the update, dBASE IV asks for confirmation and, if you select **Proceed**, removes the view skeleton and adds the word Target over the name.

As you can see, it is best to create a new query to perform this sort of update, and not to use a query that you also use to display a view. First, add the criteria to limit the records on which the operation is performed. Then specify the update operation. Then select **Perform the update** from the Update menu.

If you are performing the Replace operation, you must also add a WITH operator under one of the field names. In its simplest form, the WITH operator is followed by a literal value. For example, if you wanted to start your volunteer program again from scratch, you could perform a Replace operation and type *with .f.* under the VOLUNTEER field. Likewise, you can fill in a date, character, or numeric field with a literal value, using the proper delimiters for the field type.

The Replace operation is even more powerful if you use the WITH operator followed by an expression. (dBASE expressions are covered in detail in Chapter 11.) For now, you can look at an example of a Replace operation using date arithmetic. You can use the operators + or - followed by a number to add or subtract that number of days from any date.

Imagine that you have decided to give all of your members from California an extra 30 days of membership for free. Try doing a Replace operation to change all their expiration dates:

1. Beginning from the Control Center with the MEMBERS file in use, select **<create>** from the Queries panel.

2. When the Queries Design screen appears, select **Specify update operation** from the Update menu, and select **Replace values in Members.dbf** from the submenu. Select **Proceed** from the prompt box to remove the view skeleton.

3. Move the cursor to the STATE field and type *"CA"*. Then move the cursor to the MEM_EXPIRS field and type *with mem_expirs + 30*. This query is shown in Figure 5.31.

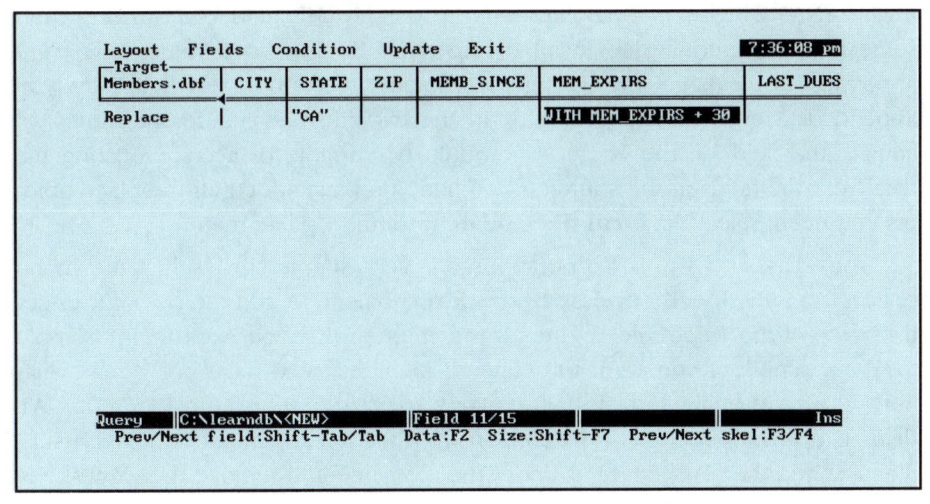

Figure 5.31 *The query for a replace operation.*

4. Select **Perform the update** from the Update menu to proceed. dBASE IV tells you that three records were replaced and that you should press **F2** to see the changes.

That is all there is to performing a Replace operation. Note that this example assumed that there was a database in use when you began. You can also use the query screen when there is no database in use, and select **Add file to query** from the Layout menu to add the file skeleton you need. Then dBASE IV does not have to remove the view skeleton.

To perform an Append operation, to add records from another database to the database you are using if the structures of the two are not the same, select **Specify update operation** from the Update menu and select **Append records to <*file name*>** from the submenu. (If the structures are the same, use the Append menu of the database design screen, covered at the end of Chapter 3.)

This is a complex operation that is just described briefly here. First, use the query screen and select **Specify update operation** and Append records to MEMBERS.dbf (for example) to add the Append operator under the name of the Target file that you want to add the records to. Then, select **Add file to query** from the Layout menu and add the name of the file that the records come from to the query screen. Then, add place holders to connect the fields of the two files. You can use any word as a place holder: for example, you might type *xyz* in the FNAME fields of both files, *abc* in the LNAME field of both files, and some other common value in all of the other fields whose values you want appended in the target file. Using placeholders to connect the fields lets you append data even though the fields in the two files have different names: of course, the fields in the Target file should be capable of accommodating the data from the fields in the source file. When you have added all the place holders you need, select **Perform the Update** from the Update menu.

The Mark and Unmark operations are very simple. Just select the menu option from the **Specify update operation** submenu to add the operator under the name of the Target file, and enter the criterion that you want them to apply to. For example, if you want to delete all members who have not given donations since the beginning of 1990, enter < {01/01/90} under the LAST_DONAT field, select **Mark records for deletion** from the Specify update operation submenu to add the Mark operator under the file name and remove the view skeleton, and select **Perform the update** from the Update menu.

Remember that this operation just marks the records and does not delete them. You can always unmark all or some of these records. For example, if you do not want to delete people who have not given donations as long as they are volunteers, then follow the previous update operation with another one where you enter the criterion .T. in the VOLUNTEER field and performing the Unmark operation.

The Exit Menu

The Exit menu, with which you are familiar, lets you either save or discard the changes you made in the query screen and return to the Control Center. You could do the same thing by pressing **Ctrl-End** or **Esc**.

Summary

In this chapter, you learned how to use the options of the **Go To** menu to search for single records in a database. You also learned how to use queries to filter data, search for records, and update the records in a database file. In the following chapter, you will learn even more about the power of queries, and also how to create quick reports and mailing labels.

Chapter 6

Quick Reports, Advanced Queries, and Mailing Labels

You have already learned most of what you need to know to do basic work with dBASE IV—creating a file, adding, editing, and deleting data, using sorts and indexes to determine the order of the data, and using queries to search for the data that you want.

The only basic feature of dBASE IV that you have not learned about yet is its ability to easily produce reports and other printed output.

This chapter covers two simple forms of printed output, which are all that you need for many common applications: quick reports, and mailing labels. You also learn some advanced features of the query screen, which you can use to get information such as group subtotals. In this chapter, you learn how to:

- Print quick reports and labels using options from the **Print** menu
- Generate quick reports based on database files or queries using the **Quick Report:F9** key
- Edit quick reports
- Create calculated fields to increase the power of your queries using field names, numbers, and arithmetic operators
- Design and create mailing labels
- Modify existing mailing labels
- Print mailing labels in any order your choose

If you are using Part 1 to get up and running with dBASE as quickly as possible, it is up to you to decide how to use this chapter and the next one. You only need to learn the parts that you feel are necessary for your own work. For example, if you think that quick reports are enough for your needs and that you do not need formatted reports, you could skip Chapter 7. Glance through these two chapters and decide which parts you need.

If you are going on to read the rest of this book, you should read both chapters thoroughly.

One thing that you will notice when you do the exercises in these two chapters is that dBASE IV generates code before printing reports or labels (or data entry forms, which are covered in Chapter 8). dBASE IV actually generates a program written in the dBASE language, which produces the report, labels, or data entry form that you laid out.

You do not need to know anything about programming to use these features, as the programs are generated and used automatically. If you are an experienced programmer, you can modify the programs that are generated and add new features. If you are a user, you should simply be aware that the extra time dBASE IV takes and the messages it displays on the status line describing its progress in generating the program are normal parts of using reports, labels, and forms.

The Print Menu

When you print reports or labels, you use the Print menu, shown in Figure 6.1.

In most cases, you can use the default settings on this menu. As a general practice, you should display your quick report, labels, or formatted report on the screen before printing, to make sure the print job is set up the way you want, for example, that the data fits on a single line. To preview your print job, select **View report on screen** from the Print menu. To print, simply select **Begin printing** from the Print menu.

The Print menu is also included as part of the dBASE IV word processor, and it is discussed at length Chapter 9. It does have some features that you should learn about now, although you may not need all of the Print menu options in everyday use.

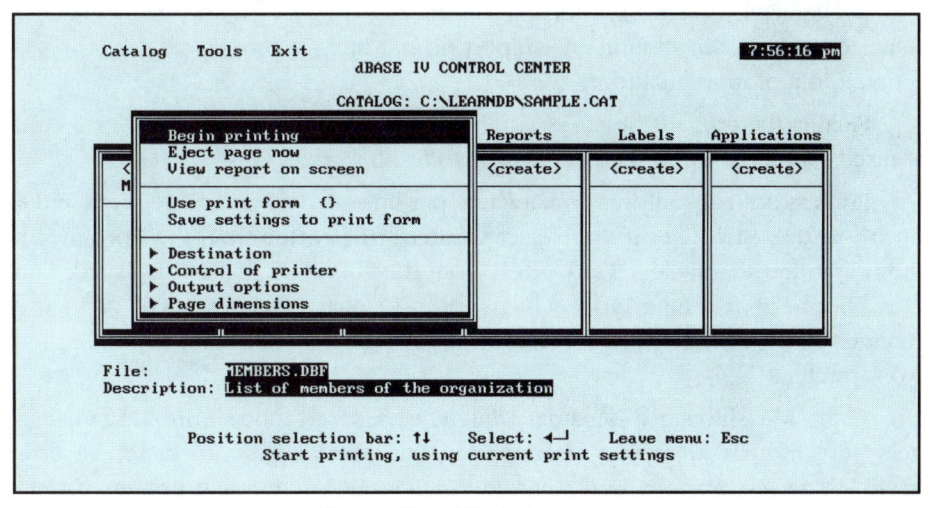

Figure 6.1   *The Print menu.*

In some cases, particularly with formatted reports, you will want to create a left margin. In most cases, though, you do not have to set margins; you can simply offset your printing from the left edge of the paper when you print. To do this, select **Print dimensions** from the Print menu and select **Offset from left** from the submenu. dBASE IV prompts you to enter an integer—you can edit the default of *0* to create the left margin you want. Ten spaces is a commonly used margin, as it is one-inch wide with most fonts. Of course, when you are designing the report, you must take into account the fact that you are planning to add a left margin, and make sure that the report fits on the page. Chapter 9 explains how to set margins within the word processor.

If you have an Apple LaserWriter or other PostScript printer, you must select **Control of printer** from the Print menu, and select **New page** from the submenu that appears until it cycles to AFTER. This makes the printer eject a new page only after it prints a report.

Some laser printers print 60 or 65 lines to the page, instead of the more common 66 lines per page, the dBASE IV default. To change the default to conform to your printer, select **Print dimensions** from the Print menu, and select **Length of page** from the submenu. dBASE IV prompts you to enter an integer; you can edit the default 66 to the number of lines you need.

If you have a printer that supports multiple fonts, you should not use a proportional font for dBASE IV reports. dBASE IV pads out empty spaces with the blank character, and proportional fonts give less space to the blank than to other characters, so columns in a report do not line up properly if the report is printed in a proportional font.

Finally, there might be cases when you want to use smaller type or a condensed font for a report that is too wide to fit on a page.

Printers normally allow 80 characters per line—10 characters per inch and 8 inches across each line. If you select **Control of printer** from the Print menu, however, and then select **Text pitch** from the submenu that is displayed, you can choose to use Elite type, which prints 12 characters per inch, or to use Condensed type, which prints from 16 to 20 characters per inch, depending on your printer.

With old-fashioned dot-matrix printers, condensed mode prints 132 characters per line. If you have a laser printer, you should experiment to see how many characters fit on a single line in condensed mode. Some printers do not support any condensed type, however, so you should experiment and see if dBASE IV prints in condensed mode on your printer before trying to create quick reports, reports, or labels that require condensed type.

Quick Reports

If you select **<create>** from the Reports panel of the Control Center, you can use the reports design screen (covered in Chapter 7) to create formal, presentation-quality reports. Yet many dBASE users never need reports that are this sophisticated. Some users spend all too much time learning about the Report Designs screen, and then never use most of its features.

dBASE IV does offer a simpler alternative. You can easily produce quick reports based on either queries or database files. In this section, you do a simple quick report based on a query, and in the next section, you move on to more advanced query features, which you can use for other purposes, such as finding group totals.

Printing a Quick Report

The mechanics of printing a quick report are extremely simple. The navigation line of the Control Center (and your function key template) indicate that **Shift-F9** is the Quick Report key.

You can print out all of the data in a database file or in a view simply by highlighting the appropriate name in the Data or Queries panel and pressing **Quick Report:Shift-F9**. dBASE IV displays the Print menu, described above, which you can use to print the quick report.

The data is listed in the same order that it appears in the file or view—and, as you will see, you can use indexed or sorted order. In addition to the data in the file or view, dBASE IV automatically includes a page number and the date at the top of each page of the quick report.

Of course, if you base a quick report on a database file, the data probably spreads across several pages and includes many fields that you do not need. The quick report feature is most effective when you use it to print a query that you have designed to use as the basis of the report.

Editing Column Headings

To make quick reports more readable you can edit column headings. To do this, simply select **Edit field name** from the Fields menu of the query screen. dBASE IV displays a prompt box where you can enter the new name of the field. As always, you can press **Esc** to cancel.

The new name you enter must be a valid dBASE field name, so it cannot be longer than ten characters and cannot include blank spaces. There is an advantage to producing quick reports with columns headed FIRST_NAME and LAST_NAME rather than FNAME and LNAME—if the names of the columns are easy to understand, those who read the printed report will find it easier to understand the data it contains.

Once you rename a field, you can edit its new name instantly any time you move to that field in the view skeleton, as you will see in the exercise below.

Changing names of fields in the view skeleton is useful not only for changing the headings of reports but also for changing column headings in the browse screen, if you want to make them easier for users to understand.

Remember that you can rename fields in the database file itself only by using the Database Design screen that you learned about in Chapter 2 of this book. For this reason, the **Edit field name** option of the Fields menu of the query screen is dimmed when the highlight is on a field of the file skeleton. You can only use this option to edit names of fields in the view skeleton, which determines how field names are displayed when you use this view but does not change the field names in the database file itself. (You can also use this option to change names of calculated fields in queries, which you learn about later in this chapter.)

A Sample Quick Report

You should have no trouble creating a simple quick report.

First, you must design a view with the fields you want in the report, making sure they fit on a printed page. If you want the fields in the report to appear in a specific order, you can first select **Sort on this field** from the **Fields** menu of the Queries Design screen. For greater speed, you can select **Include indexes**. You might have to create an index for the quick report or you might be able to use an existing index. Once the view that you want is saved, you can highlight its name in the Control Center and press **Quick Report:Shift-F9** to print it out at any time.

Since this is a feature of dBASE IV that you might want to use frequently in your own work, you should create a basic quick report as an exercise. This exercise also gives you experience in including indexes in a query, a feature that you learned about in Chapter 5 but did not try.

Create a quick report to list member's names, cities, and states, with the states listed alphabetically and, within each state, the members listed alphabetically by name. Before producing this report, you must create an index to order the results of the query.

If you look at the structure of your database file, you will see that the total width of the FNAME, LNAME, CITY, STATE, and ZIP fields adds up to 52 characters, so you will have no trouble fitting them in the width of a single sheet of paper.

1. Begin from the Control Center. To create the index you need, select **MEMBERS** from the Data panel, and select **Modify structure/order** from the prompt box.

2. Select **Create new index** from the Organize menu of the database design screen to call up the index definition submenu.

3. Select **Name of index** from this menu, and enter *ST_NAMES* as the name of the index.

4. Select **Index expression** and enter *STATE + LNAME + FNAME* as the index expression, as shown in Figure 6.2. Press **Ctrl-End** to create this index. Then press **Ctrl-End** again to return to the Control Center.

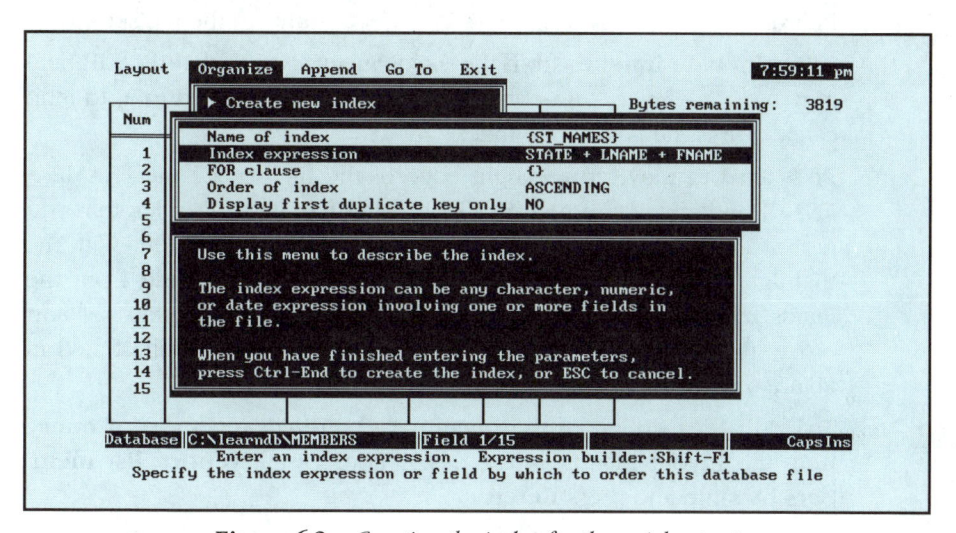

Figure 6.2 *Creating the index for the quick report.*

5. To create the new query, select **<create>** from the Queries panel. dBASE IV displays the queries design screen, with the highlight under Members.dbf.

6. Press **Field:F5** to remove all of the fields from the view skeleton.

7. Move the highlight to the LNAME field of the file skeleton, and press **Field:F5** to move it to the view skeleton.

8. Move to the FNAME field, and press **Field:F5** to move it to the view skeleton.
9. Move the highlight to the CITY, STATE, and ZIP fields of the file skeleton and press **Field:F5** to move each in turn to the view skeleton (or, if you find it easier, select them and move them as a group).
10. Now, rename some of the fields in the view skeleton, to give your report better column headings. Press **Next:F4** to move to the view skeleton and press **Home** to move to the LNAME field.
11. Select **Edit field name** from the Fields menu. dBASE IV prompts you to enter the field name. Type *last_name* and press **Enter**.
12. Then, press **Tab** to move to the FNAME field, select **Edit field name** from the Fields menu, and enter *first_name* as the new field name.
13. To have the report printed in proper order, first you must include the indexes in the file skeleton. Press **Prev:F3** to move to the file skeleton.
14. Select **Include indexes** from the Fields menu. Notice that the ZIP field now has a # sign (or an upward pointing arrowhead) next to it, to indicate that it is the basis of an index.
15. Press **End** to move to the right edge of the file, to see the LNAME + FNAME index and the new STATE + LNAME + FNAME index that you just created, both with the # sign (or arrowhead) to their left. With the highlight under this new index, select **Sort on this field** from the Fields menu, and select **Ascending ASCII** from the picklist of sort orders that dBASE IV displays. The final Query screen is illustrated in Figure 6.3.
16. To add a description of the query, select **Edit description of query** from the Layout menu. As the description, **Quick report: list members by state** and press **Enter**.
17. Press **Ctrl-End** or select **Save changes and exit** from the Exit menu. dBASE IV prompts you to enter a name for the query. Type *st_names* and press **Enter**.
18. You have returned to the Control Center with the name of this query highlighted. To test the quick report, press **Quick report:Shift-F9**.
19. In general, you should display the report on the screen before printing it, to make sure it is correct. Select **View report on screen** from the **Print** menu to preview the report, shown in Figure 6.4. Press **spacebar** until you return to the control center.

Chapter 6: Quick Reports, Advanced Queries, and Mailing Labels ◆ **143**

20. Since this is just an exercise, you probably do not want to actually print the report. If you do, make sure your printer is on, and then select **Begin printing** from the Print menu.

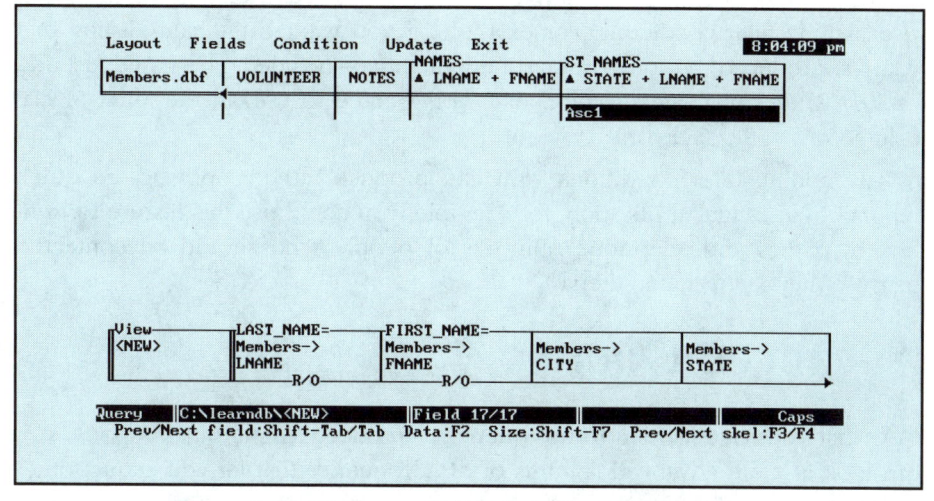

Figure 6.3   *The query used as the basis of the quick report.*

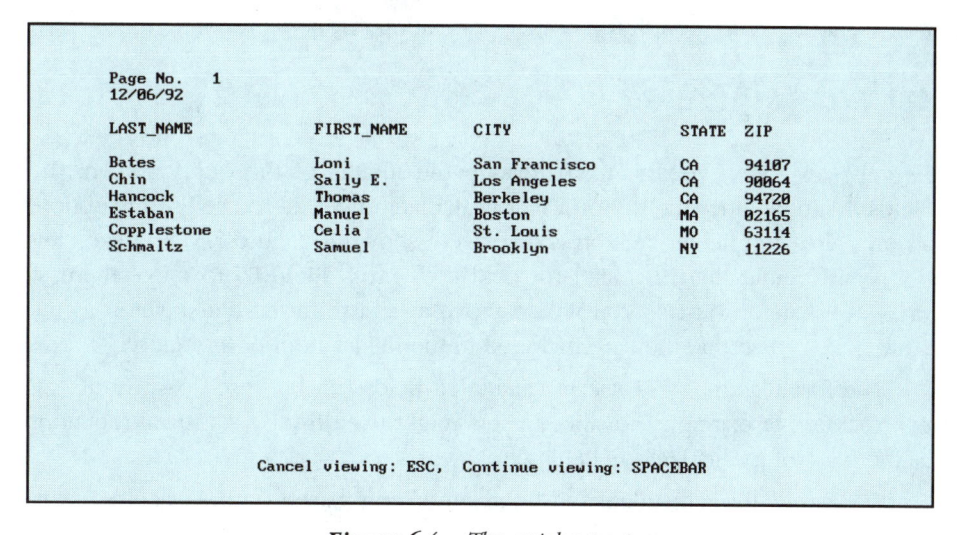

Figure 6.4   *The quick report.*

As you can see, the State names are arranged alphabetically. Within California (the only state with multiple members in your small sample database) the members are listed alphabetically by name.

Remember that the Queries that you use as the basis of quick reports can also include filter conditions. For example, if you wanted the same listing that you just produced, but only wanted new members included, you could just add >= {01/01/90} (or whatever cutoff date you wanted to use) in the MEM_SINCE column of the file skeleton.

By adding filter conditions, you can produce rather sophisticated quick reports. In an actual application, for example, you could use this feature to print lists of names and telephone numbers of people who should be contacted because they met certain criteria.

Advanced Queries

Now that you have learned to use queries to produce simple quick reports, you can look at more advanced features of dBASE queries that let you extract other kinds of information that are often included in formatted reports. Though you cannot format the data as elaborately as you can with the report generator, you can use these advanced query features to extract data that you need for internal use, without going through the bother of creating formatted reports.

Calculated Fields

As you saw when you glanced through the menus of the query screen, the Fields menu includes the option Create calculated field. If you select this option, a new calculated fields skeleton is displayed, shown in Figure 6.5. You can simply type formulas into this skeleton and then press **Field:F5** to move them to the view skeleton (just as you would move a field from the file skeleton to the view skeleton) so that they are included in the final output of the query.

The formulas that you use in calculated fields can be based on any dBASE expression. For example, advanced users might use dBASE's statistical functions as the basis of a calculated field.

Ordinarily, though, calculated fields are simply based on field names, numbers, and the arithmetic operators.

If you are basing the formula on fields that are the numeric or float data type, you can use the arithmetic operators listed in Table 6.1.

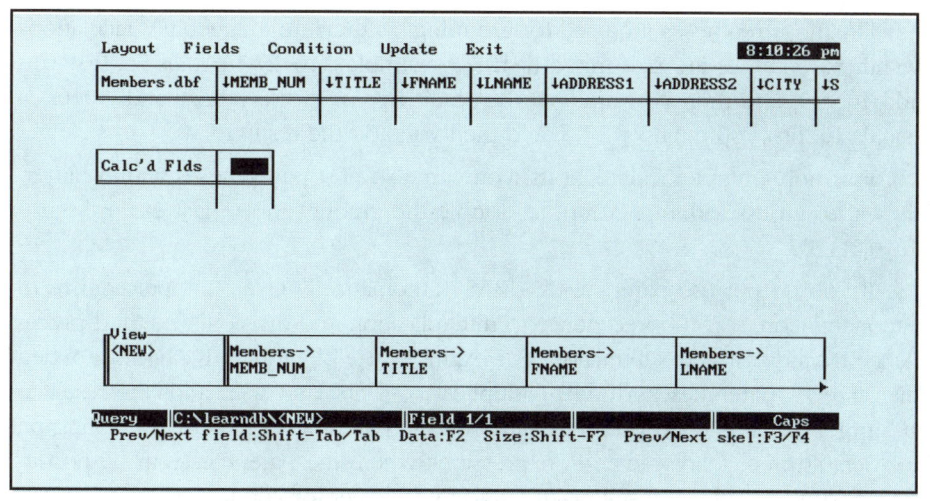

Chapter 6: Quick Reports, Advanced Queries, and Mailing Labels ◆ **145**

Figure 6.5   The calculated fields skeleton.

Table 6.1   The Arithmetic Operators.

+	addition
−	subtraction
*	multiplication
/	division
^ or **	exponentiation
( )	grouping

You probably recognize most of these operators. +, -, and / are used in ordinary arithmetic.

* is used to represent multiplication in many computer programs (instead of x, which is used in arithmetic). Note that you must include the * in dBASE—you cannot omit the multiplication sign as you do in algebra; for example, in algebra, you use 6a to mean six times the quantity represented by a, but in dBASE, you cannot use 6LAST_DUES instead of 6*LAST_DUES. You must include the *.

In algebra, *exponentiation*—that is, raising a number to a power—is represented by a superscript. Since many computer screens cannot display superscripts, dBASE uses ^ before the power to show that it should be above the line. It also uses **, since exponentiation is a step beyond multiplication. For example, nine cubed (nine to the third power) can be written as 9^3 or as 9**3.

Finally, parentheses are used for grouping, as they are in algebra. Calculations within parentheses are performed first. For example, (10+2)*3 equals 36: first you add 10 + 2, and then you multiply the result by 3. On the other hand, 10+(2*3) equals 16: first you multiply 2 * 3, and then you add the result to 10.

For more complex calculations, you can also nest parentheses within parentheses, to group within a group: to double the amount in the last example, use (10+(2*3))*2.

If you do not use parentheses, dBASE automatically gives first precedence to exponentiation, second precedence to multiplication and division, and third precedence to addition and subtraction. For example, 10+2*3 equals 16, because when there are no parentheses, dBASE multiplies 2 * 3 first and then adds the result to 10. In general, it is good practice to include the parentheses rather than relying on the default precedence—even in expressions where the parentheses make no difference to the result, they still make the formula easier for you to read.

Though we immediately think of numeric (or float) fields when calculations are mentioned, you can also use the + and - operators followed by a number (or numeric expression) to perform calculations with date fields. For example, MEM_EXPIRS - 30 gives you a date 30 days before the date in the MEM_EXPIRS field. In calculations involving dates, numbers represent number of days.

As an exercise, you can assume that you mail renewal notices to members thirty days before membership expires and add a calculated field to the CAL_NAMES query to indicate this date, so that, when you use this view, you see the date when the renewal notices must be mailed, rather than the actual expiration date.

1. Begin the exercise from the Control Center. Highlight **CAL_DATA** in the Queries panel. Press **Design:Shift-F2** to use the queries design screen

2. Select Create calculated field from the Fields menu. dBASE adds the calculated fields skeleton, and places your cursor where it can enter a formula.

3. Type *mem_expirs - 30* as the formula.

4. Press **Field:F5** to move the new field to the view skeleton. dBASE prompts you to enter a field name. Type *renewal* and press **Enter**. dBASE IV enters this name above the formula and includes the field at the end of the view skeleton.

5. Since you do not need both the expiration date and the renewal date, move to the MEM_EXPIRS field of the view skeleton, and press **Field:F5** to delete it.

Chapter 6: Quick Reports, Advanced Queries, and Mailing Labels ♦ 147

6. Press **End** to move to the far right of the view skeleton, so you can see the field you added, shown in Figure 6.6. Then press **Ctrl-End** or select **Save changes and exit** from the Exit menu to save the new query and return to the Control Center.

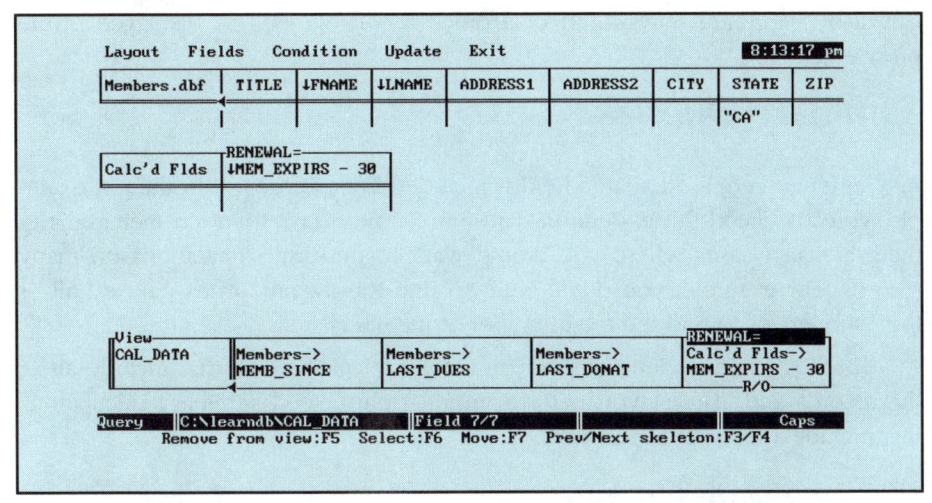

Figure 6.6 *A query including a calculated field.*

Figure 6.7 *The result of this query.*

7. Press **Data:F2** to see the result of the query in the Browse screen, and press **End** to see the calculated field you added, as shown in Figure 6.7. Then, press **Esc** to return to the Control Center.

Note that, because calculated fields can be included in the view skeleton, they can also be printed out as part of a quick report, as well as displayed in the browse screen.

Summary Queries

As you have seen, a calculated field is included in each record. In the last example, you calculated the expiration date minus thirty days for each member. But there are also cases where you would want to perform calculations on many records. For example, you might want to find the average dues paid by all of the members or to find the total number of members.

dBASE IV queries let you perform summary calculations that include all of the records and also let you perform more sophisticated summary calculations that include a number of records.

The Aggregate Operators

To perform a calculation that includes all of the records, you simply have to type one of the aggregate operators listed in Table 6.2 in the file skeleton, under the name of the field that you want summarized.

Table 6.2 *The aggregate (summary) operators.*

SUM	totals all of the values in the field
AVG or AVERAGE	averages all of the values in the field
MAX	finds the greatest value in the field
MIN	finds the smallest value in the field
CNT or COUNT	counts the total number or records

In early versions of dBASE IV, these aggregate operators may be used only in fields in the file skeleton, not in calculated fields. In versions 1.5 and later, they may also be used in calculated fields.

Obviously, you can find the sum or average only for numeric or float fields. You can find the maximum or minimum value for numeric, float, alphabetic, or date fields. You can use COUNT in any of these fields or in a logical field.

Chapter 6: Quick Reports, Advanced Queries, and Mailing Labels ◆ 149

For example, if you want to find the average dues paid by all of the members, use the query shown in Figure 6.8. The result of this query is shown in Figure 6.9. Notice that the result has data only in the LAST_DUES field. There is no way include a name, address, or data in any other field that applies to all of the records, unless you put a aggregate operator in that field in the query.

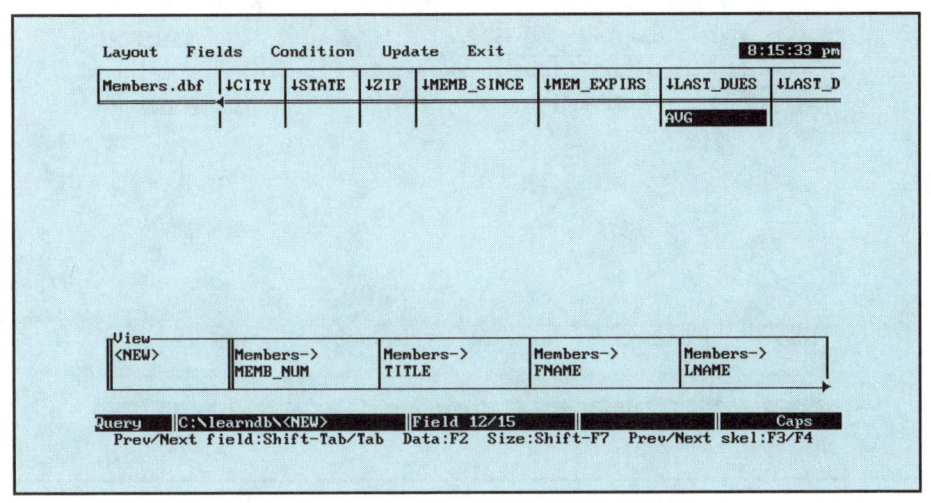

Figure 6.8 *A query to find the average dues.*

Figure 6.9 *The result of this query.*

Group Summaries

Often, you want summary data to apply to groups of records rather than to the entire database. For example, you might want to find the average dues paid by members in each state.

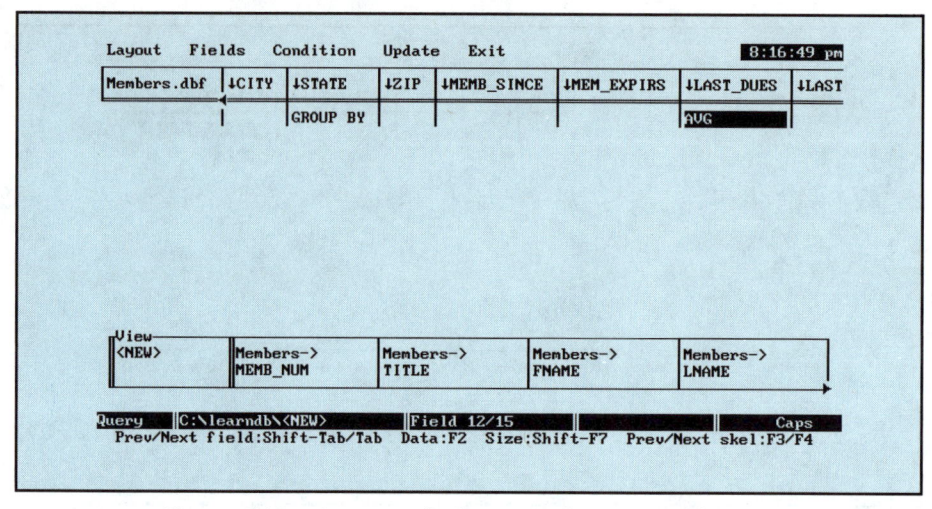

Figure 6.10   *A query to find average dues grouped by state.*

Figure 6.11   *The result of this query.*

To do this, you just have to include the GROUP BY operator in the field on which you want the grouping to be based, and include the appropriate aggregate operator in the field that you want summarized. Figure 6.10 shows a query to find average dues for each state, and Figure 6.11 shows the result of this query. Note that the result includes data only in the STATE and the LAST_DUES fields.

In early versions of dBASE IV, the GROUP BY operator may only be used only in fields that are in the file skeleton. In version 1.5 and later, it may also be used in the calculated field skeleton.

Filtered Summaries

You can also combine aggregate operators with filter conditions simply by placing the two values on the same line.

For example, Figure 6.12 shows a query for the average dues paid by members from California, and Figure 6.13 shows the result of this query.

These advanced queries can be used to extract the sort of information that you often find in reports. As you will see in Chapter 7, formatted reports can list individual records and also group them, give subtotals for groups, and give a grand total. This looks very impressive in a formal report, but if your reports are only meant for internal use, it can be easier to extract the same data using queries.

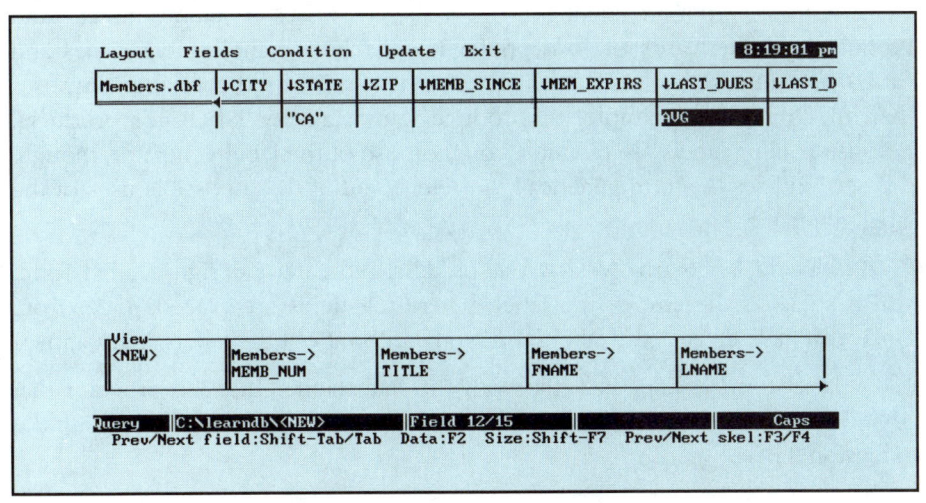

Figure 6.12 *A query combined with a filter condition.*

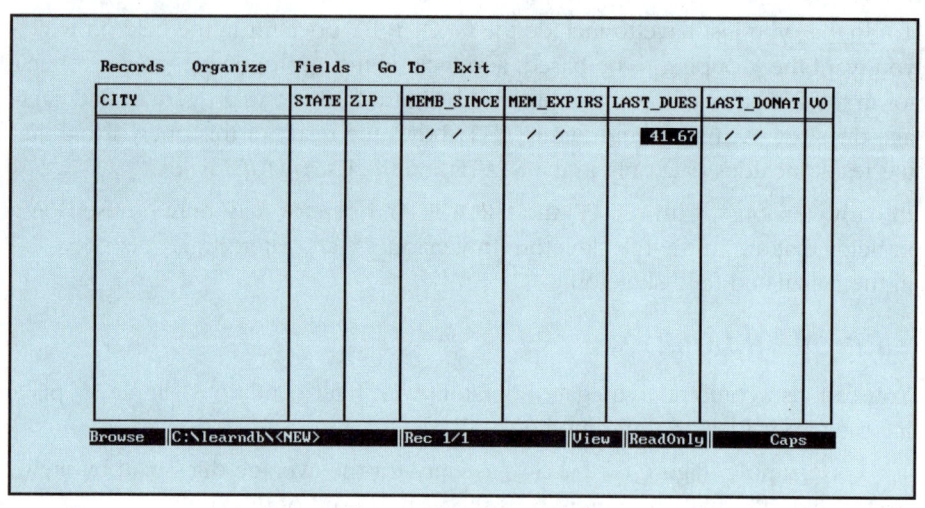

Figure 6.13 The result of this query.

Mailing Labels

As you will see, dBASE IV uses the word *labels* in a broad sense. The label generator not only produces mailing labels, it also addresses envelopes directly and produces Rolodex cards (if your printer is capable of handling envelopes and cards). Of course, the labels themselves can also be used for other purposes than mailings—for example, to produce name tags or labels for products. Because mailing labels are the most common use of the label generator, though, this section uses the term generically to refer to all of these possible uses of the label generator.

Producing labels involves two steps. First, you must design a label form, which specifies the size of the label, where the fields are placed, and so on. Once you have created the label form, you can print out the labels at any time.

A label form is kept in a file with the extension .LBL. The program that dBASE IV generates to produce the labels, the program is kept in a file with the extension .LBG.

Designing a Label Form

Before you define a label form, the database or view on which it is based must be in use. dBASE IV must know to which database the labels apply, so that it knows which fields may be placed on the label form when you are designing it.

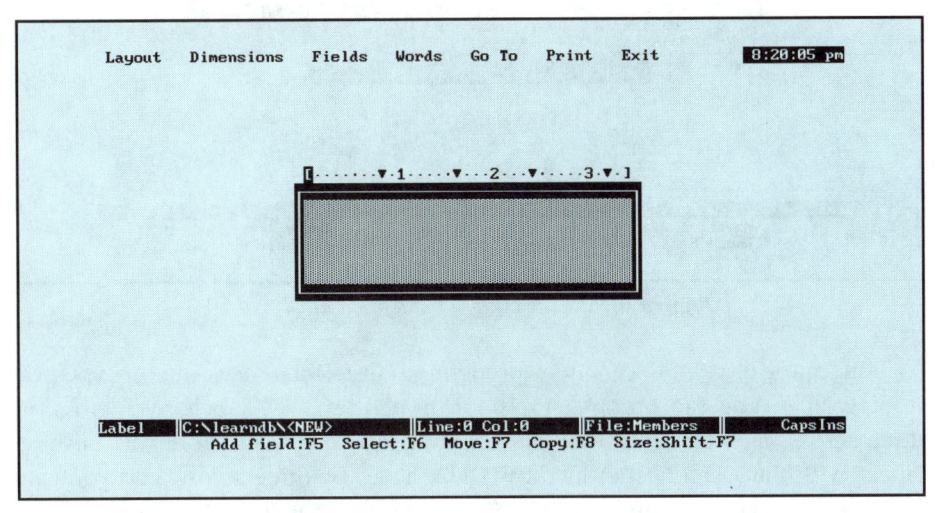

Figure 6.14   The Label Design screen.

Once the database is in use, you create the label form in the usual way: Select **<create>** from the Labels panel to use the labels design screen, shown in Figure 6.14. As you can see from the illustration, this screen actually displays a sample label, where you place fields and text. This screen includes the features of the dBASE IV word processor. Unlike other places where the word processor is used, however, the ruler here is displayed immediately above the label form (rather than at the top of the screen). In this case, it shows that the label is 3.5 inches wide.

Selecting a Label Size

This screen in the illustration represents just one of the standard predefined label sizes that you can use: it is 15/16 of an inch high by 3/12 inches wide, one label across the page, with one line skipped between labels the most common size of single-column labels used in tractor-feed printers.

dBASE IV also offers other standard predefined label sizes, which you can use by selecting **Predefined Size** from the Dimensions menu to use the submenu shown in Figure 6.15.

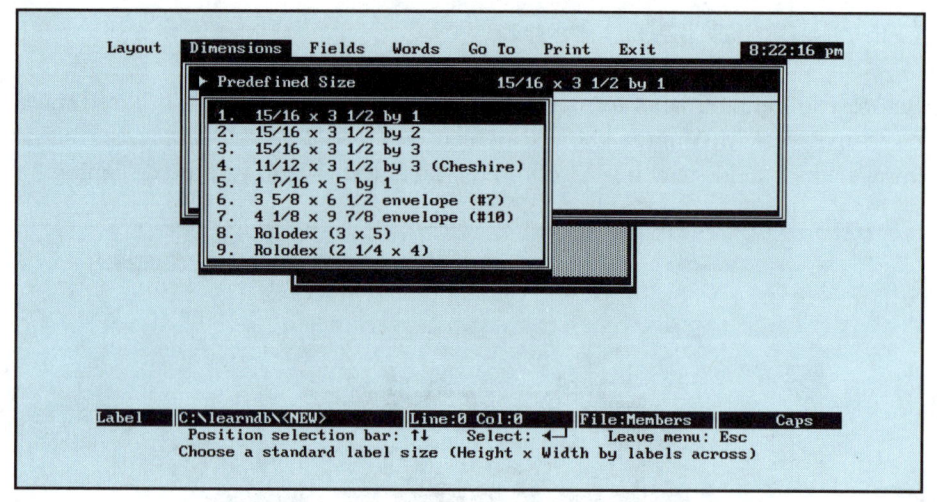

```
Layout   Dimensions   Fields   Words   Go To   Print   Exit           8:22:16 pm
         ▶ Predefined Size                  15/16 x 3 1/2 by 1
           1.  15/16 x 3 1/2 by 1
           2.  15/16 x 3 1/2 by 2
           3.  15/16 x 3 1/2 by 3
           4.  11/12 x 3 1/2 by 3 (Cheshire)
           5.  1 7/16 x 5 by 1
           6.  3 5/8 x 6 1/2 envelope (#7)
           7.  4 1/8 x 9 7/8 envelope (#10)
           8.  Rolodex (3 x 5)
           9.  Rolodex (2 1/4 x 4)



Label    C:\learndb\<NEW>         Line:0 Col:0      File:Members           Caps
            Position selection bar: ↑↓   Select: ↵     Leave menu: Esc
            Choose a standard label size (Height x Width by labels across)
```

Figure 6.15 *Selecting a predefined label size.*

As you can see, dBASE IV offers predefined sizes for five common types of mailing label. You can produce 15/16 of an inch by 3 1/2 labels two-across or three-across, as well as in a single-column. You can also produce Cheshire labels, which are 11/12 of an inch by 3 1/2 inches by three-across, and you can produce large single column labels, 1 7/16 inches by 5 inches.

In addition, if your printer handles them, you can address the two most common forms of envelopes, ordinary #7 envelopes and wide #10 envelopes, and you can produce the two common sizes of Rolodex card, 3-by-5 inches and 2-1/4-by-4 inches. The 3 by 5 setting can also be used to print index cards. If you select one of these predefined sizes, the Label definition screen changes accordingly—you can type on an area as large as the label, envelope, or card that you have selected.

If none of the predefined sizes is what you need, you can use the **Dimensions** menu to define your own label size. As you can see in Figure 6.16, when you select a predefined label size, this menu displays all of the specifications of that label size. The meaning of these menu choices, such as height of label and width of label is obvious, and the message line that is displayed when you move the highlight to one of these options gives you all of the explanation that you need to use them; for example, it tells you that the height of the label is measured in lines and may be any number from 1 to 255 and that the width of the label is measured in characters and may also be any number from 1 to 255.

To define a custom label size, simply select the predefined size that is closest to what you need, and make the changes that you need. For example, if you have single-column labels that are only 15/16 inches high but only 3 inches wide, select 15/16 x 3.5 by 1 as the predefined size. Then select **Width of label** from the Dimensions submenu and, when dBASE prompts you to enter an integer, enter *30*.

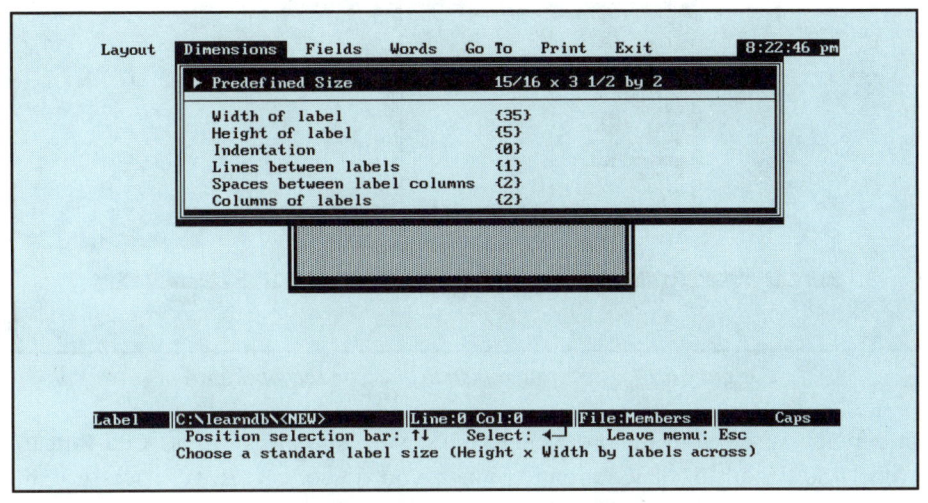

Figure 6.16 Defining a custom label size.

Laying Out the Label

Once you have the label size you need, add fields to the label much in the same way that you add fields to queries or reports—with the cursor where you want the field to begin, press **Field:F5**, or select **Add field** from the Fields menu. Using the mouse, you can simply double-click the location where you want to place the field. When you do any of these, the picklist shown in Figure 6.17, is displayed. Note that the database fields are displayed in alphabetical order. As you can see in Figure 6.17, you could also add calculated fields and predefined fields representing the current date, time, record number, and page number, however, these options are more useful in reports than in labels.

Once you have selected a field from this picklist, dBASE IV displays the menu shown in Figure 6.18, which lets you specify the display attributes for the selected field. This Display attributes menu is an advanced feature of the labels, reports, and form generator. It is generally not needed to produce labels, and it is covered in Chapter 7, because it is very useful in producing reports. It works exactly the same way in the label and report generators.

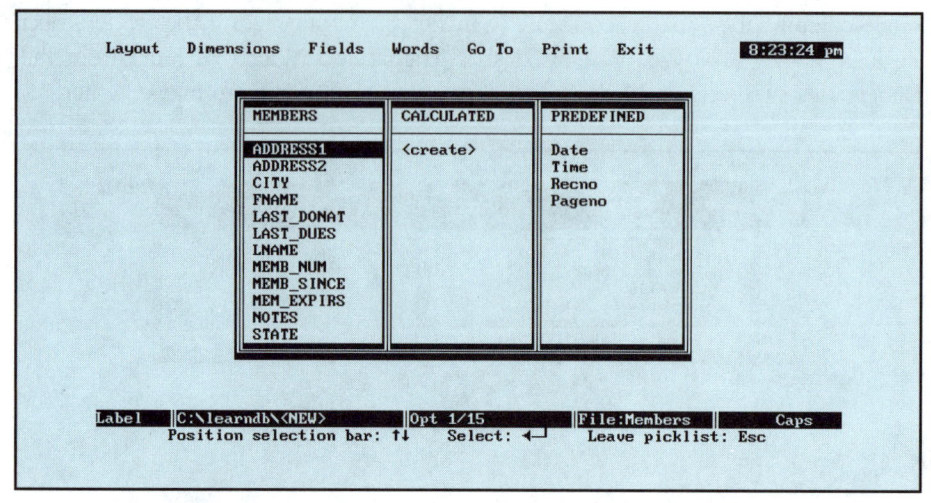

Figure 6.17   Selecting a field to place on the label form.

In general, when you are producing labels, you can simply press **Ctrl-End** to accept the default display attributes. When you do so, dBASE IV places a template representing this field on the work surface, as shown in Figure 6.19. This template contains enough Xs (or other characters) to represent the maximum number of characters in the field. When the label is printed, though, dBASE IV trims trailing blanks from the field, so that (for example) you have just John as the first name, rather than John followed by eleven blanks. If the field is to long to fit in the label, dBASE IV displays a message saying that it does not fit and will be truncated. That is, any characters that extend beyond the edge of the label are not printed.

In addition to placing fields, you can simply type text on the label. For example, type a blank space between the first name and the last name. Remember that blanks are trimmed from the field itself, and you do not want the label to read JohnSmith. Also to include a comma followed by a blank space after the city, and you may want to type some message on the label also. (If you are doing a mailing to people whose memberships have expired, for example, you could type the text *Please renew now!* directly on the label form.)

You can move around the work area using the mouse or the usual editing keys: the Arrow keys to move left, right, up or down, Home and End to move to the beginning or end of the current line, PgUp and PgDn to move to the top or bottom of the work surface or simply click any location with the mouse to move the cursor there. You will notice, though, that a field template is treated as a single character. You cannot move the cursor among the X's of the template; the entire template is highlighted when you move to it. As you move to a field template, the name of the field that it represents is displayed at the bottom of the screen.

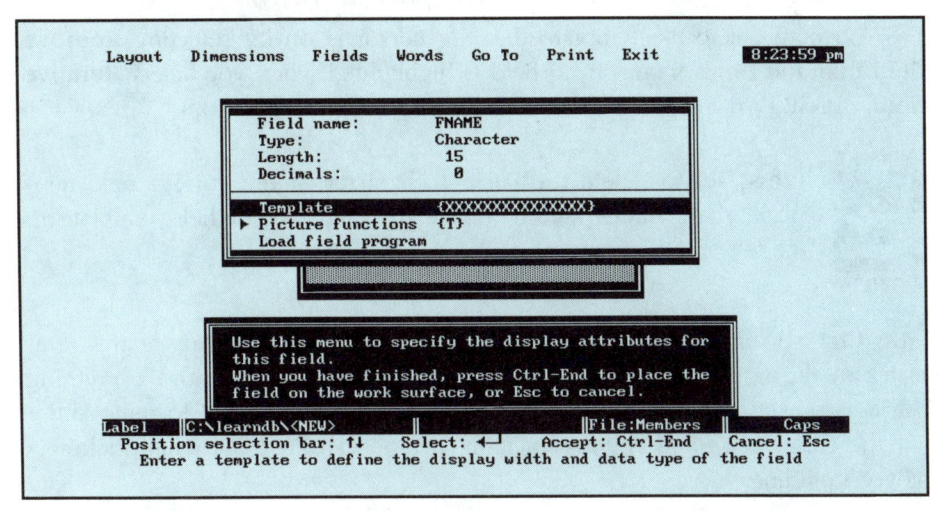

Figure 6.18 Press **Ctrl-End** to accept the default display attributes.

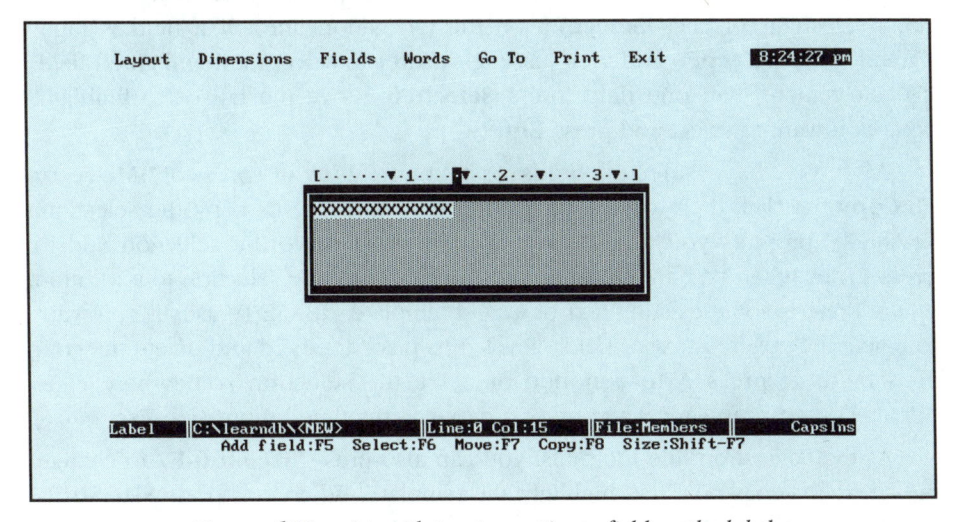

Figure 6.19 A template representing a field on the label.

Press the **Ins** key to toggle between insert mode and type-over mode. When you are in insert mode, the word Ins appears at the right edge of the status bar, and the cursor becomes larger. Type-over mode lets you type over existing text, but not over field templates. If you try to type over a template, text is inserted and the template is pushed right whether you are in insert or typeover mode.

You may delete the template that the cursor is on by selecting **Remove field** from the Fields menu. If no field is highlighted when you select **Remove field**, dBASE IV displays a picklist of fields for you to choose from.

SHORTCUT

Press **Del** to delete the current character or the current field template; press **Backspace** to delete the character or field template to the left of the cursor.

Press **Ctrl-N** to insert a new line at the location of the cursor. Any text or templates to the right of the cursor are moved to the new line, and everything below is moved down a line to make room for it. Press **Ctrl-Y** to remove the line the cursor is on and any text or templates on that line. Everything below is moved up a line.

After you have placed a field or typed in text, you can move it anywhere on the label. As the navigation line indicates, you press **Select:F6** to select fields and text on the label. dBASE IV prompts you to press **Enter** when you are done selecting (or click **Select:F6** on the navigation line). If a field is highlighted, press **Select:F6** and then just press **Enter** to select the highlighted field. To select more than one field, press **Select:F6**, move the cursor to highlight what you want to select and press **Enter**.

After you have selected fields or text in this way, press **F7:Move** or **F8:Copy** (or click them on the navigation line) to move or copy the selection. dBASE IV prompts you to use the cursor keys to move the selection and to press **Enter** when you are done. If you move or copy the selection to a location where there is some existing text or a field template, dBASE IV asks if you want to delete the covered text or fields. Press *Y* to place the field and delete the covered field, or press *N* to continue or place the selection somewhere else. Remember, you can cancel a copy or a move at any time by pressing **Esc**.

As the navigation line indicates, you can also press **Size:Shift-F7** to change the size of a template. First, highlight the template. When you press **Size:Shift-F7**, use the **Right Arrow** key to shorten and the **Left Arrow** key to lengthen the template, as indicated in the navigation line. Press **Enter** when you are finished. Or, if you are using the mouse, simply click the location where you want the template to end, instead of using the Arrow keys and pressing Enter. Again, you can press **Esc** to cancel the resizing. This feature is needed in reports more often than in labels, but you could use it with a mailing label to print just the first initial, rather than the entire first name. Shorten the template to one character, and type a period to its right.

As you will see in the next couple of chapters, the Reports Design screen and the Forms Design screen are very similar to the Labels Design screen. Fields are placed in the same way, the editing keys are used in the same way, and moving, copying, and resizing are done in the same way.

There is one other feature of the labels design screen, however, which only works for labels. If a line of the label is blank, dBASE automatically ignores that line and adds an extra blank line at the bottom of the label instead. In your sample database, many people have just one-line addresses, but dBASE IV does not print a blank line in the middle of the label at the location of the ADDRESS2 field. This feature gives you more attractive mailing labels.

Other Features of the Menu System

Once you have designed the label that you want, you can enter a description of it in the familiar way, by selecting **Edit description of label design** from the Layout menu. The Layout menu also contains an option to **Use different database file or view**. If you made a mistake and opened the wrong file or view before creating the labels, use this option to change the file or view the labels are based on.

Finally, the Layout menu contains an option to **Save this label design**. If you select this option, dBASE prompts to you edit the name of the file. You can press **Enter** to save the design under its current name and then return to the labels design screen. This is useful so that the design is not lost in case of power failure. You should save your work periodically if you are working on a label form that takes a long time to design. You can also edit the file name and then press **Enter** in order to change the name of the file. This is useful, for example, to modify an old label form in order to create a new one with another name (without destroying the original when you save the modified version). A similar option appears on the Layout menu of many dBASE IV screens.

You can save and name the file in the familiar way, by pressing **Ctrl-End** or by selecting **Save changes and exit** from the Exit menu. You can also cancel the design at any time by pressing **Esc** or selecting **Abandon changes and exit** from the Exit menu.

Rather than saving the labels and printing them from the Control Center, you also can print the labels directly from the labels design screen, as it includes the Print menu. This menu is particularly useful for previewing the labels as you are designing them. To preview the labels select **View labels on screen** from the Print menu

This version of the Print menu has one extra option: Generate sample labels. This helps you check the alignment of the labels in your printer by printing a sample label (or a row of sample labels, if your labels are more than one-across) consisting of rows of Xs. If they are not lined up correctly on your label form, realign the forms in your printer and try again. Once the label forms are lined up properly, you can actually print the labels. This feature is useful if you are using a tractor-feed printer.

The Print menu, Words menu, and Go To menu are parts of the dBASE IV word processor. The word processor is covered in detail in Chapter 9, but you do not need all of dBASE's word processing power to type a label that is only a few lines long.

Modifying the Label Form

Once the label form has been designed and saved, its name is displayed in the Labels panel of the Control Center.

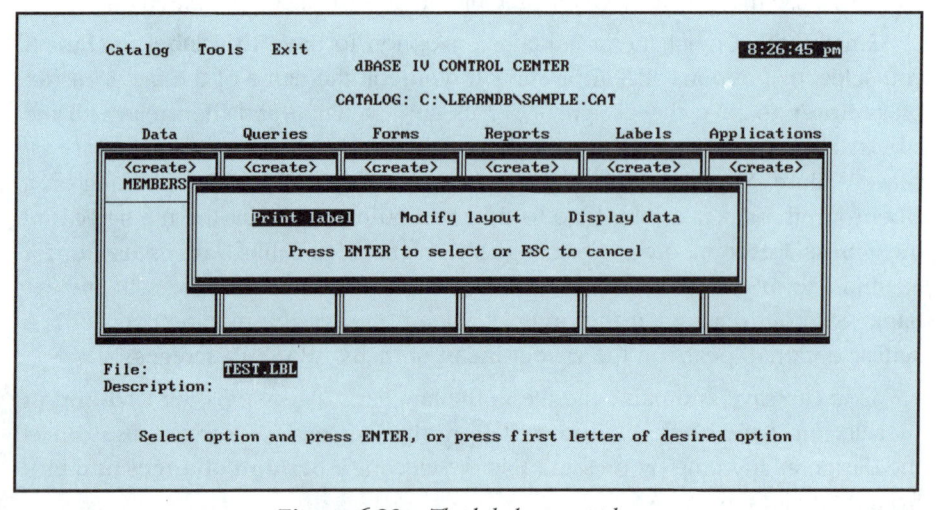

Figure 6.20 *The labels prompt box.*

Select the name of the label form from the Labels panel to display the prompt box shown in Figure 6.20. As you can see, one option is Modify layout. Select this to return to the Label definition screen, with the layout that you specified earlier. Then modify this layout in any way you want and save it. Selecting **Display data** from this prompt box simply displays a Browse screen with all of the data from the database file or the view on which the label form is based.

Rather than using the prompt box, you can simply highlight the name of the label you want to modify and press **Design:Shift-F2** to return to the labels design screen to modify the layout. You can display a Browse screen of the database file or the view on which the label form is based by highlighting the name of the label form and pressing **Data:F2**.

Printing Labels

As you have seen, this prompt box also contains the option **Print label**, and if you select this option, dBASE IV displays the Print menu. Finally, as you know, the Print menu is included in the labels design screen itself.

You can also call up the Print menu by highlighting the name of the label form and pressing **QuickReport:Shift-F9**.

As with quick reports, you generally should select **View labels on screen** from this menu to preview the labels before actually printing them. Then, after aligning the forms in the printer (as described above) select **Begin printing**.

Printing Filtered Labels

You can print labels for selected records by using a query before printing the labels. You can use any query to print mailing labels, as long as it includes all of the fields that are used on the label.

For example, imagine that you do regular mailing to the volunteers in your sample database. You could create a query that includes all the fields in the view skeleton and has .T. in the VOLUNTEER field of the file skeleton. When you want to print the labels, first select the query's name in the Queries panel of the Control Center in order to use it; then, select the name of the label form in the Labels panel and print the labels for all the Volunteers.

Printing Mailing Labels in Order

It is common to print mailing labels in zip code order, for bulk mailing. If you are producing Rolodex cards, you might want them in alphabetical order.

To print labels in order, simply use the appropriate index to order the records of the file. To do this you select the file from the Data panel, select **Modify structure/order** from the prompt box, and select **Order records by index** from the Organize menu. Labels are printed out in index order.

If you are printing from a query, include indexes in the Query Design screen and use the appropriate index to determine the order of the records, as you learned to do in Chapter 5.

In either case, labels are printed out in the same order that records would be displayed in the Browse screen. Just use an index or design a view to display the records in the proper order, and the labels are printed out in that order.

Sample Labels

You may never need the advanced features of the Display attributes menu (covered in detail in Chapter 7) or of the word processor (covered in Chapter 9) to produce labels. You have learned all you need to know to produce labels for most real applications, and you should solidify what you have learned in this chapter by producing labels for the sample membership application.

In the exercise, imagine that you want to print standard-sized two-column labels. When you are done, you can test the result by viewing the labels on the screen or by printing them on ordinary printer paper. If you would like, you may alter the instructions and design the labels to fit on your own label paper instead.

Note that, when it is needed to make the locations on the label form clear, these instructions tell you to use the cursor movement keys to move the cursor and then to place the field, but you can also simply double click that location.

1. First, use the database by selecting **MEMBERS** from the Data panel of the Control Center and selecting **Use file** from the prompt box. Then select **<create>** from the Labels panel to use the labels design screen.

2. To use the desired size, select **Predefined Size** from the Dimensions menu. Then select **15/16 x 3 1/2 by 2** from the submenu.

3. The cursor is in the first column of the first row of the label. To place the name there, Press **Field:F5**, select **FNAME** from the picklist, and press **Ctrl-End** to accept the default display attributes and place the field.

4. Then, press the **Spacebar** to leave a space between the first and last name. Press **Field:F5**, select **LNAME** from the picklist, and press **Ctrl-End** to accept the default display attributes. dBASE displays a warning at the bottom of the screen that says: *Insufficient space on row, field truncated*. Remember that this label is thirty-five spaces across, and the FNAME field (with fifteen characters), the LNAME field (with twenty characters) plus the blank space between them take up a maximum of thirty-six characters. You will probably never have a name that fills the entire width of both the FNAME and the LNAME field, so truncated data will not be a problem.

5. Now, try making an instructive error. You should move the cursor to the left edge of the second line. Instead, press **Enter**. Because there is no space to its right, the cursor is still on the LNAME field, and, if you are in insert mode, that field is moved to the second line. If you pressed **Enter** and moved the field to the second line, press **Select:F6** and **Enter** to select the field. Then press **Move:F7**, use the Arrow keys to move it back to its proper position, and press **Enter** again.

6. Add the rest of the address. Move the cursor to the left edge of the second line. Press **Field:F5**, select ADDRESS1 from the picklist, and press **Ctrl-End** to place this field on the second line.

7. Move to the left edge of the third line. Then press **Field:F5**, select ADDRESS2 from the picklist, and press **Ctrl-End** to place the field.

8. Move to the left edge of the fourth line, press **Field:F5**, select CITY from the picklist and press **Ctrl-End** to place it. Type , (a comma followed by a space), to separate the city and state names.

9. Then press **Field:F5**, select STATE from the picklist, and press **Ctrl-End** to place it.

10. Press the **Spacebar** once. Then press **Field:F5**, select **ZIP** from the picklist, and press **Ctrl-End** to place it. The label form should look like Figure 6.21.

11. Select **Edit description of label design** from the Layout menu. When dBASE IV prompts you to Edit the description of this .lbl file, type *General purpose two-column mailing labels*, and press **Enter** to return to the work space.

164 ♦ teach yourself...dBASE IV

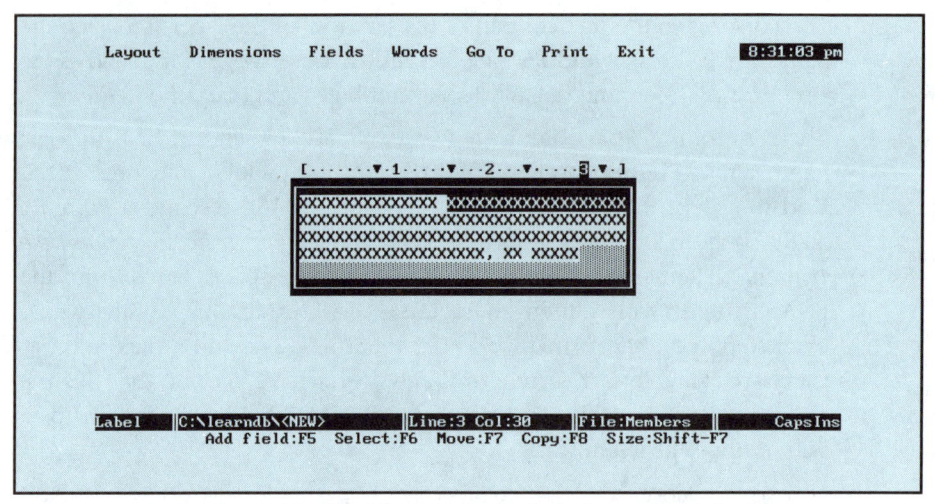

Figure 6.21   *The label form with templates for name and address.*

12. To save the label form, press **Ctrl-End**. dBASE IV prompts you for the name to save it as Type *two_col* and press **Enter**. dBASE takes a moment to generate the label program and returns to the Control Center.

13. Now, imagine that you decide to modify your standard labels so that they include the membership expiration date on the first line. The highlight should be on TWO_COL in the Labels panel of the Control Center. Press **Design:Shift-F2** to return to the label design screen.

14. The cursor is in the first column of the first row of the work surface. Press **Ctrl-N** to insert a new row, moving everything down a row. The cursor should still be in the first row.

15. Press **Tab** twice. Type *expires* followed by a blank space. Press **Field:F5**, select MEM_EXPIRS from the picklist, and press **Ctrl-End** to accept the display attributes and place the field. Note that the template for a date field is MM/DD/YY, rather than the X's that are used for character fields. The label form now looks like Figure 6.22.

16. To save the changes, press **Ctrl-End**. dBASE IV takes a moment to generate the program and then returns you to Control Center.

17. To produce the labels in zip code order, select **MEMBERS** from the Data panel, and select **Modify structure/order** from the prompt box. Then select **Order records by index** from the Organize menu, and select **ZIPS** from the picklist. Press **Esc** and press *Y* to confirm in order

to return to the Control Center. (It is best to press **Esc** to return in case you inadvertently made changes to the database structure, the index is opened, but changes are not saved.)

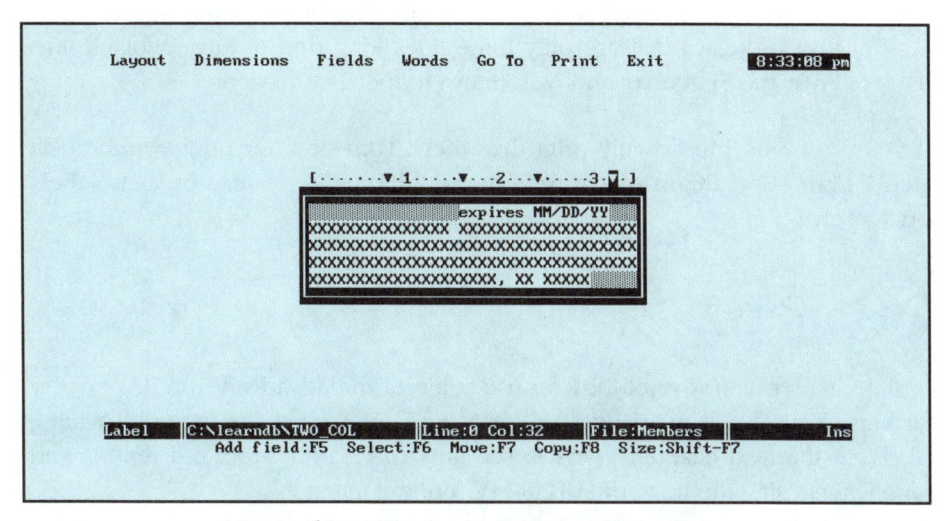

Figure 6.22   *The final label form with templates.*

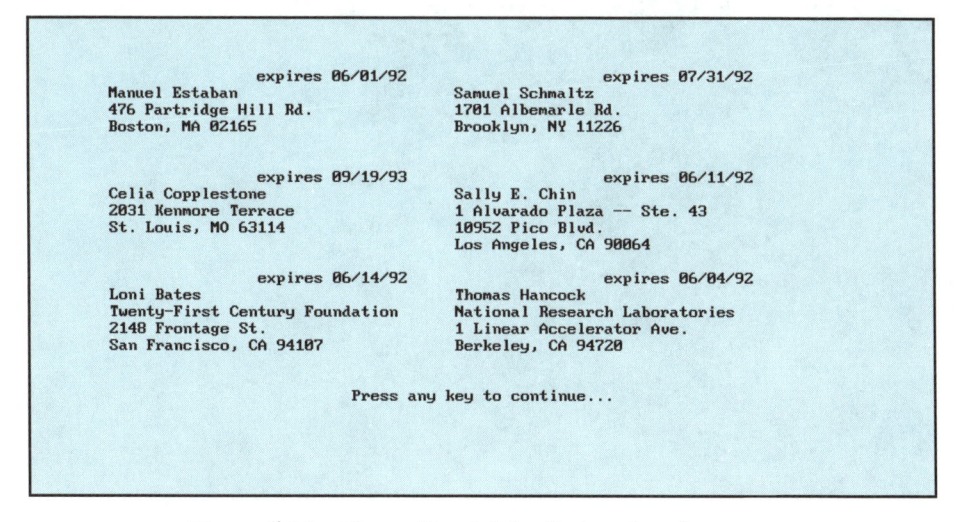

Figure 6.23   *The mailing labels, displayed on the screen.*

18. Select **TWO_COL** from the Labels panel, and select **Print label** from the prompt box. When the Print menu appears, select **View labels on screen** to preview the labels. The labels are shown in Figure 6.23. Note that they are in zip code order, that the expiration date is indented enough that it does not interfere with your reading the address, and that addresses that are only three lines long do not have a blank line. Press the **Spacebar** until you return to the Control Center.

If you want, you can actually print the labels. Turn on your printer and repeat Step 17, but select **Begin printing** from the Print menu (instead of **View labels on screen**).

Summary

In this chapter, you learned how to use some of the advanced dBASE IV query features. You also learned how to create and print quick reports and mailing labels. In the next chapter, you will see how to create customized reports and form letters using the powerful dBASE IV report generator.

Chapter 7

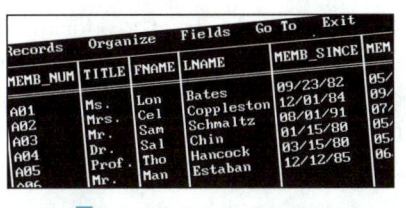

Formatted Reports

You have already learned to produce quick reports and generate mailing labels based on data contained in dBASE databases or views. In this chapter, you are be introduced to additional power and functionality when you learn how to create formatted reports.

In this chapter, you learn how to:

- ◆ Design a basic formatted report
- ◆ Identify the various types of report bands
- ◆ Create an instant report with the quick layout feature
- ◆ Identify the three different types of formatted report layouts: Column layout, Form layout, and Mailmerge layout
- ◆ Edit the generated report to obtain exactly the results you want
- ◆ Use the Display attributes menu to add templates and picture functions
- ◆ Add graphics, such as boxes or lines, to make a report easier to understand
- ◆ Group records in a report by adding Group Bands
- ◆ Further organize a report by nesting groups
- ◆ Save, preview, and print a formatted report

The overall process of producing reports is similar to the process of producing labels. First, you must use the database or view that the report is based on, so dBASE IV knows which fields can be included in the report. Then, select **<create>** from the Reports panel to use the reports design screen, which is described in detail throughout this chapter.

When you have finished designing the report and have named and saved it, you can produce it any time, just as you produce labels.

As with labels, you can modify a report that has already been created by highlighting its name and pressing **Design:Shift-F2,** or by selecting it and then selecting **Modify layout** from the prompt box. (If you highlight the report and press **Data:F2** or if you select **Display data** from the prompt box, dBASE IV displays a browse screen with all of the data in the current database or view.)

You can also produce filtered reports by creating a query that includes only the records you want, and then using this query (rather than the database file) before creating the report. (As with labels, the view must include all the fields that are used in the report.)

Likewise, you can produce reports with records in a specified order just as you do labels. Before producing the report, select the database file from the Data panel, select **Modify structure/order** from the prompt box, and use the picklist to select the index that you want. If the report is based on a view, include the indexes in the Query Design screen and select the one you want to use to order the records as the sort order of the query. In either case, the records in the report are printed in the same order as the records in the database or view.

Printing records in order is more important for reports than for mailing labels. You do not always need labels in zip code order, but you will often want your reports in a specific order. Often, you will have to create specific indexes just for reports.

Report forms are kept in files with the extension .FRM. When dBASE IV generates a program to produce the report, it keeps the program in a file with the extension .FRG.

The Basics of Report Design

Designing a report form is also very much like designing a label form. You add and remove fields, type text, use the editing keys, resize templates, and select, move, and copy fields and text in exactly the same ways.

Report Bands

The feature of the reports design screen that makes it unique is that it is organized in horizontal areas called *bands*. The band in which you type text or add a field determines how the final report uses that text or field.

When you select **<create>** from the Reports panel, the reports design screen appears with empty bands and with the Layout menu displayed. First look at the initial screen without the Layout menu in the way, shown in Figure 7.1, to get the basic idea of how report bands work.

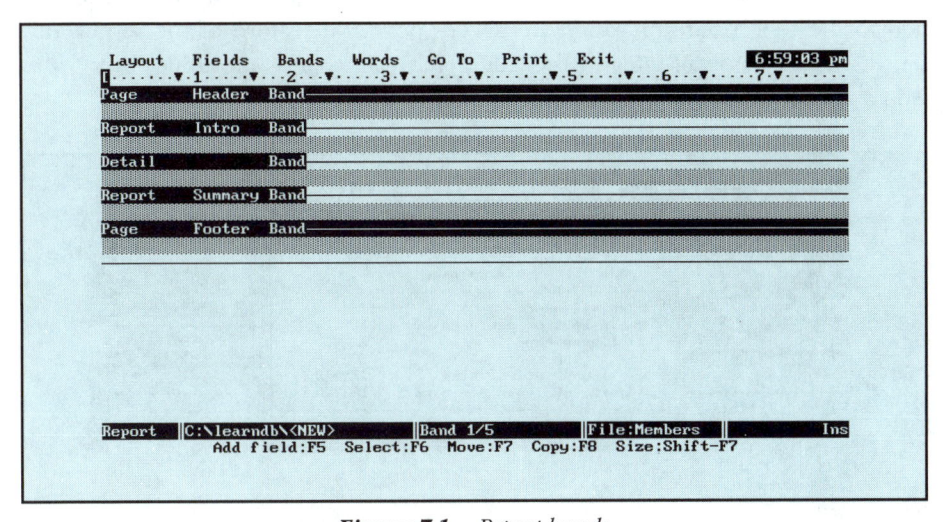

Figure 7.1   Report bands.

As you can see in Figure 7.1, the Reports Design screen contains the following types of bands:

- **Page Header Band**: Any text you type or fields you place here is displayed at the top of each page of the report as a header.
- **Report Intro Band**: Any text or fields you place in the Report Intro Band is displayed only once in your report, at the beginning. It is useful to add an introduction to the data contained in the report or to add a title page.
- **Detail Band**: The heart of the report. Fields that you place and any text that you type here are repeated for each record in the report. For exam-

ple, if you place the name and address field templates in this band, the report includes all of the names and addresses of all the records in the database or view on which the report is based.

- **Report Summary Band**: Anything in the Report Summary Band is displayed only once in your report, at the end. It can be used for totals, averages, or to summarize the information contained in the report.
- **Page Footer Band**: Like the Page Header Band, any text or fields placed here are displayed at the bottom of each page of the report as a footer.

In addition, there is one more type of band called a *Group Band* that you can add to the report. Group bands are a very powerful feature of the report and are discussed in detail later in this chapter. Group bands are added using the Add a group band option of the Bands menu, shown in Figure 7.2.

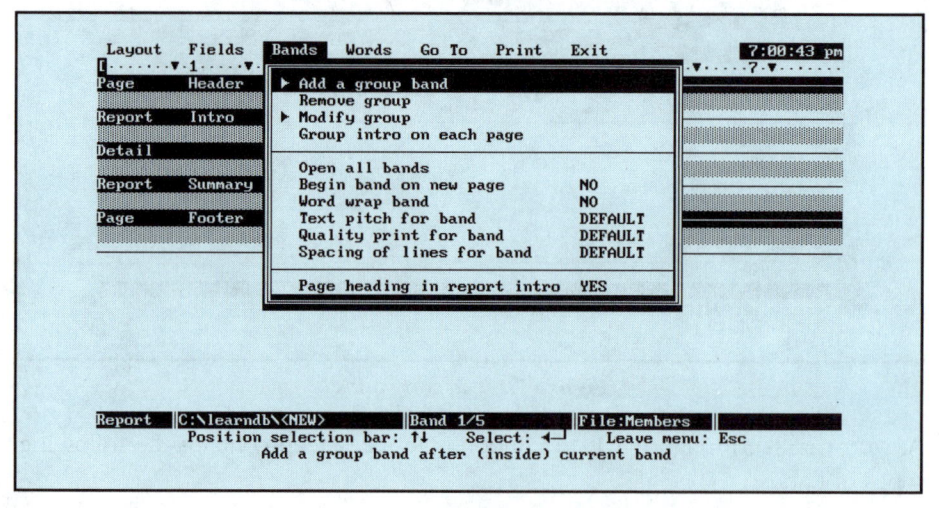

Figure 7.2 *The Bands menu.*

You can move among the bands by using the usual cursor movement keys or the mouse. When you move the cursor to a band, the line containing the name of that band is highlighted.

Though each band is displayed having only one line, you can expand a band to whatever size you need:

- To add a line, press **Ctrl-N** or select **Add line** from the Words menu. You can also add a line by just pressing **Enter** if you are in insert mode.

- To remove a line, press **Ctrl-Y** or select **Remove line** from the Words menu. Doing this deletes any text or fields on the line.

Closing and Opening Bands

When you add extra bands, the reports design screen can sometimes become cluttered making it difficult to work. To remedy this situation, you can *close a band* (that is, hide it temporarily) by moving the cursor to the line with that band's name and pressing **Enter**. Closing a band leaves the band border (the line with its name) on the screen but makes the contents of the band disappear.

To make the band's content reappear, move the cursor to its border and press **Enter** again.

You can also select **Open all bands** from the Bands menu to open all bands in the report that are temporarily closed.

Bands that are closed are not printed when you print the report. If you have closed bands while working on the report, it is a good idea to select **Open all bands** before printing or saving the report, to make sure that all bands are included when you print the report.

Word Wrap

Selecting **Word wrap band** from the Bands menu toggles word wrap from the default NO to YES. You do not want word wrap in most bands, since data is arranged in columns or in some other fixed form. If you want to type a report introduction that is a few paragraphs of background information, you should use the word wrap feature in that band. As you will see, word wrap is ON by default in form letters, to let you type text.

Space in the bands where nothing has been typed is ordinarily shaded to indicate that the word wrap is off. If you turn word wrap on, the shading disappears.

To use word wrap to type text, you must add a right margin, as described in Chapter 9.

Apart from wrapping at the right margin, though, there are other differences in the way the word processor works when word wrap is ON and when it is OFF. The most important differences are:

- When word wrap is off, dBASE IV usually keeps fields in their original positions, so they remain aligned. If you add text to the left of a field template, for example, even if you are in insert mode, the field template is not pushed to the right unless there is text in all of the spaces to its left. If there are any blank spaces, text that comes before the field template is pushed right into those spaces, but the template itself does not move until all blank spaces to its left are filled. If you are in word wrap mode, on the other hand, templates are pushed right or pulled left whenever you insert or delete text to their left. They are simply treated as part of the text you are typing.

- When word wrap is off, each line is treated as a separate unit. If you move to the left edge of the screen and press **Backspace** or **Left Arrow**, for example, dBASE IV displays an error message saying you cannot move beyond the edge of the screen. When word wrap is on, all of the lines in the band are treated as a single unit. If you move to the left edge of the screen and press **Backspace**, for example, you delete the separation between the two lines, so text and templates on the second line are moved to the end of the first line. You can do the same thing by moving to the end of a line and pressing **Del**, just as you can with most word processing programs.
- When word wrap is off, pressing **Tab** moves the cursor around the screen without affecting text or field templates. When word wrap is on, pressing **Tab** pushes text and field templates to the right.

As you will see in the exercise, you can take advantage of some of these features of word wrap to make it easier to lay out a report, even if you are not actually using the word wrap feature to type lengthy text.

Other Features of the Bands Menu

Selecting **Begin band on new page** toggles the setting from the default no to yes. You might want to begin a band on a new page, for example, if you want the report introduction on a separate page, just make the band following the Report Intro Band begin on a new page. In some reports, you may want each group to begin on a new page—select the **Begin band on new page** option in the Group Intro band.

The dBASE's IV Print menu, covered in detail in Chapter 9, lets you select text pitch, quality of print, and spacing of lines for the report as a whole. The next three options on the Bands menu let you select these for an individual band, if you want a particular band to have a different look from the rest of the report. For example, you might want most of the report to be in condensed type, so all of the data fits across the page, but want the introduction to be in standard type, so it is more readable. Leaving these options on DEFAULT leaves the current band with the same print settings as the entire report.

Selecting **Page heading in report intro** lets you determine whether the heading is included on the first page of the report, above the report introduction.

Quick Layouts

When you first select **<create>** in the Reports panel of the Control Center, the reports design screen is displayed with the **Layout** menu pulled down. This menu gives you the option of selecting **Quick layouts.** There are some reports that include only a few fields, and you would produce them by placing each field individually on the Reports Design screen. For many reports, though, it is easier to begin with a quick layout and then simply remove the fields you do not want.

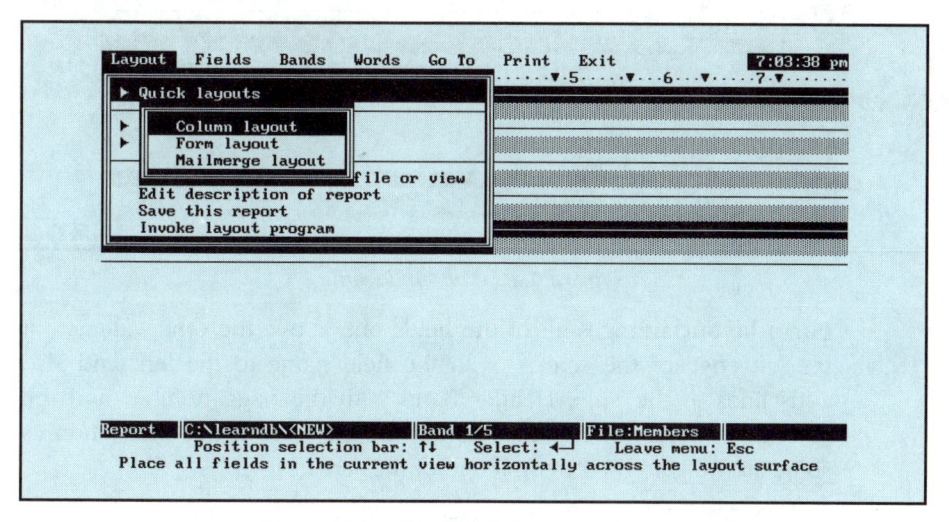

Figure 7.3   The Quick Layouts submenu.

To use a quick layout, when the Layout menu appears, you can press **Enter** to select Quick layout, the first option on this menu, and use the submenu shown in Figure 7.3 to select a Quick layout. If you want to place fields one by one, you can press **Esc.**

As you can see in Figure 7.3 three Quick layouts are available:

- **Column layout** arranges all of the fields in columns across the screen with the field name in the Page Header Band above each column, as shown in Figure 7.4. As you can see, it also adds lines in the Page header band with the page number and the date. (Not all fields can be seen in this illustration, as some are beyond the right edge of the screen.) The maximum width of the report is 255 spaces, and if your fields take up more space than this, dBASE IV displays a message saying that it has truncated the data that did not fit.

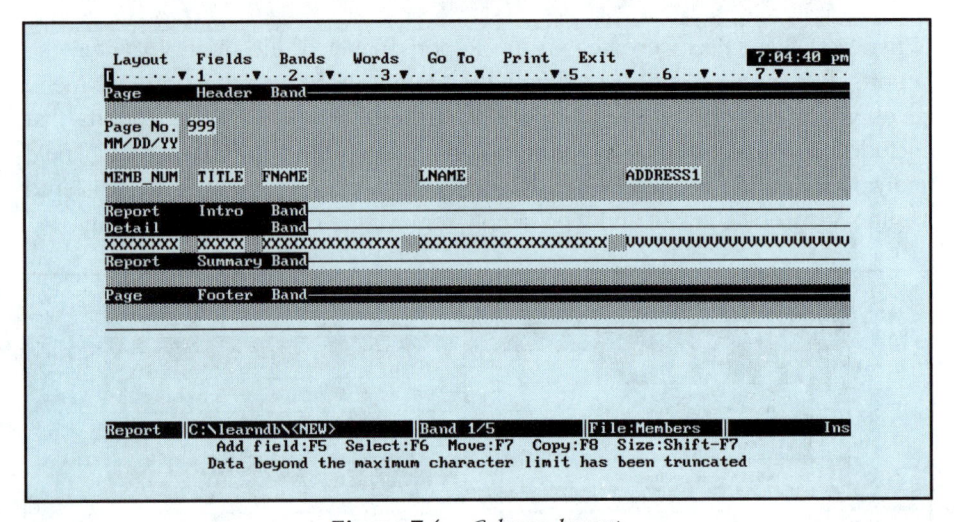

Figure 7.4   *Column layout.*

- **Form layout** arranges all of the fields one above the other, aligned at the left edge of the screen, with the field name to the left, and also adds lines in the Page Header Band with the page number and the date, as in Figure 7.5. (Not all fields can be seen in this illustration as some are beyond the bottom edge of the screen.)
- **Mailmerge layout**, which is used to write form letters, is shown in Figure 7.6. This layout does not place fields on the form. Instead, it includes no lines in the header, footer, intro, and summary bands, it gives you extra lines in the Detail Band, and it turns word wrap on in this band (indicated by the fact that the band is not shaded). After adding margins, you simply type a letter in the Detail Band, and place fields (such as name and address) wherever you want them in the letter. The letter is repeated for each record in the report, using the name and address (and other fields, if you include them) from that record. In

this layout, the Begin band on new page feature also is on for the detail band, so each letter automatically begins on a new page.

Figure 7.5 *Form layout.*

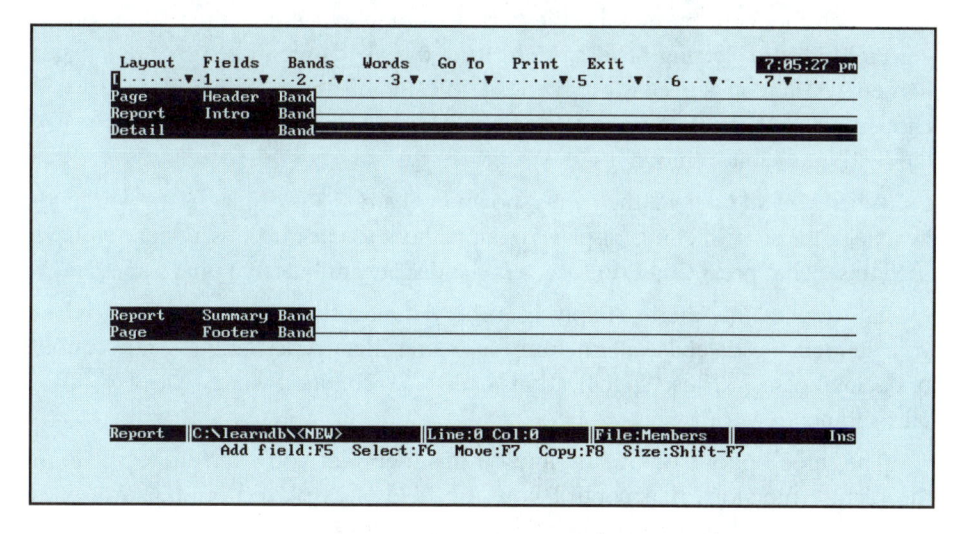

Figure 7.6 *Mailmerge layout.*

Notice, in all of these layouts, that only data contained in the Detail Band is repeated. In Column layout, the field names display in the Page Header Band, so they are displayed only once at the top of the page. In Form layout, the field names are displayed in the Detail Band, so they are repeated for each field. In the Mailmerge layout, the field names are placed in the Detail Band when the letter is typed, so they are repeated for each record: that is, a letter are printed for each person in the database file or view.

These quick layouts do not change the capabilities of the report generator. They just set it up so you can get started with less work. The Column and Form layouts just place all of the fields and field names for you. And the Mailmerge layout just changes the width of the bands and changes the default setting of the Detail Band for Word wrap band and for Begin band on new page. You could do the same things by manually, using only the features of the report generator that you learned in the previous section, though it would take a bit more time. These three quick layouts are an excellent example of the versatility that the banded reports design screen gives you.

Field Display Attributes

You can control a field's display attributes when you first add the field to the reports work surface. You can also change the display attributes of a field already on the form by moving the cursor to highlight it and then either pressing **Field:F5** or selecting **Modify field** from the Fields menu. If no field is highlighted when you select **Modify field**, dBASE displays a picklist to let you choose which field to modify. Using the mouse, you can simply double-click the field you want to modify.

When you add a field, the menu shown in Figure 7.7 is displayed. (If you modify a field, the same menu is displayed, but without the instructions.) After you have used this menu, press **Ctrl-End** to accept the display attributes you have specified.

The top of this menu simply lists the definition you gave this field when you defined the database's structure—its name, data type, length, and number of decimal places. These specifications cannot be changed via the Display attributes submenu.

The three options below the line on this menu let you alter the template or the picture functions that control how the field is displayed, and also let you suppress the display and printing of repeated values.

The difference between templates and picture functions is very simple. Templates include one character for each character in the field—they let you control the display on a character-by-character basis. A picture function, on the other hand, consists of a single character that controls how the entire field is displayed.

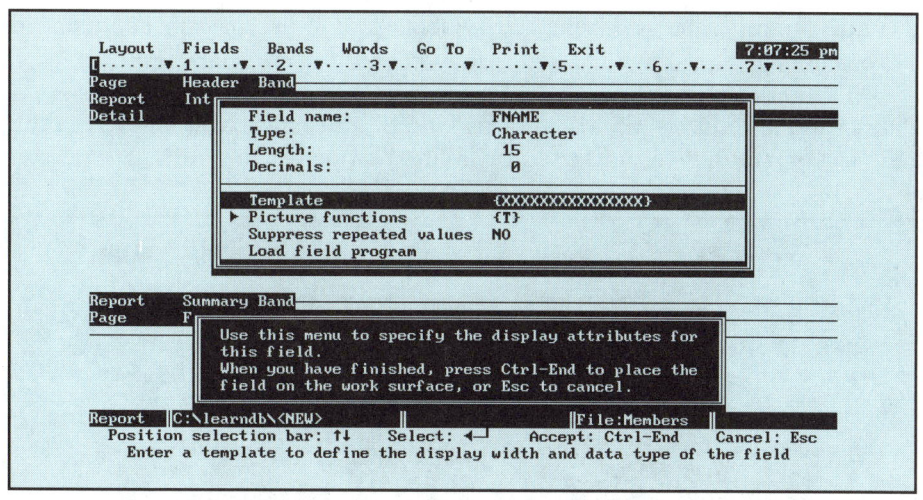

```
           Layout    Fields    Bands    Words    Go To    Print    Exit            7:07:25 pm
           [......▼..1......▼...2...▼....3.▼......▼......▼.5....▼...6...▼....7.▼.....
           Page          Header    Band
           Report        Int┌──────────────────────────────────────────────┐
           Detail           │  Field name:            FNAME                │
                            │  Type:                  Character            │
                            │  Length:                15                   │
                            │  Decimals:              0                    │
                            │ ┌──────────────────────────────────────────┐ │
                            │ │ Template                 {XXXXXXXXXXXXXXX}│ │
                            │ │▶ Picture functions       {T}              │ │
                            │ │ Suppress repeated values NO               │ │
                            │ │ Load field program                        │ │
                            └─┴──────────────────────────────────────────┴─┘

           Report       Summary Band
           Page         F ┌──────────────────────────────────────────────┐
                          │ Use this menu to specify the display attributes for │
                          │ this field.                                  │
                          │ When you have finished, press Ctrl-End to place the │
                          │ field on the work surface, or Esc to cancel. │
                          └──────────────────────────────────────────────┘
           Report    ║C:\learndb\<NEW>          ║            ║File:Members
              Position selection bar: ↑↓   Select: ◄┘    Accept: Ctrl-End    Cancel: Esc
                 Enter a template to define the display width and data type of the field
```

Figure 7.7 *Specifying a field's display attributes.*

Templates

As you know, the default template for a character field is a series of Xs, one for each character in the field. Select **Template** from the Display attributes submenu to edit the template.

One use of the template is to control the number of characters that is displayed. If you edit the template by deleting Xs, no more characters are displayed than the number of Xs remaining in the template. (When you were creating labels, you learned that you can also resize the template right on the screen by highlighting it, pressing **Size:Shift-F7**, pressing the **Right Arrow** to make the template shorter or the **Left Arrow** to make the template longer, and pressing **Enter** when you are done. If you resize the template in this way, the template on the **Display attributes** menu changes accordingly.) If the template is not large enough to hold the contents of the field, its final letters are truncated. For example, if you use one **X** as the template for the FNAME field, the report displays only the first initial (that is, the first letter of the first name).

You can use other symbols in the template besides X. When you edit a template, dBASE IV displays a list of template symbols.

Figure 7.8 shows the list of template symbols that dBASE IV displays for a character field. Notice that the description of most of these begins with the word "Accept." That is because these symbols are meant to be used in data entry forms (which are discussed in Chapter 8 of this book) to validate the data that is entered.

178 ◆ *teach yourself...dBASE IV*

Apart from X, the only template symbols on the list that are important in Reports are ! to capitalize a character, and Other to insert a character.

Any other character you use besides the template symbols is inserted directly in the display, but you must use the picture function R, covered in the next section, for these characters to be inserted properly.

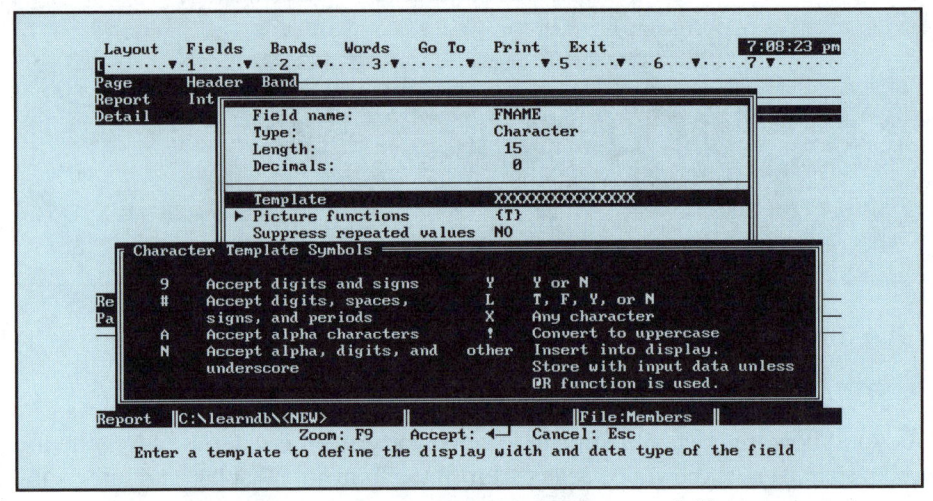

Figure 7.8 Template symbols for character fields.

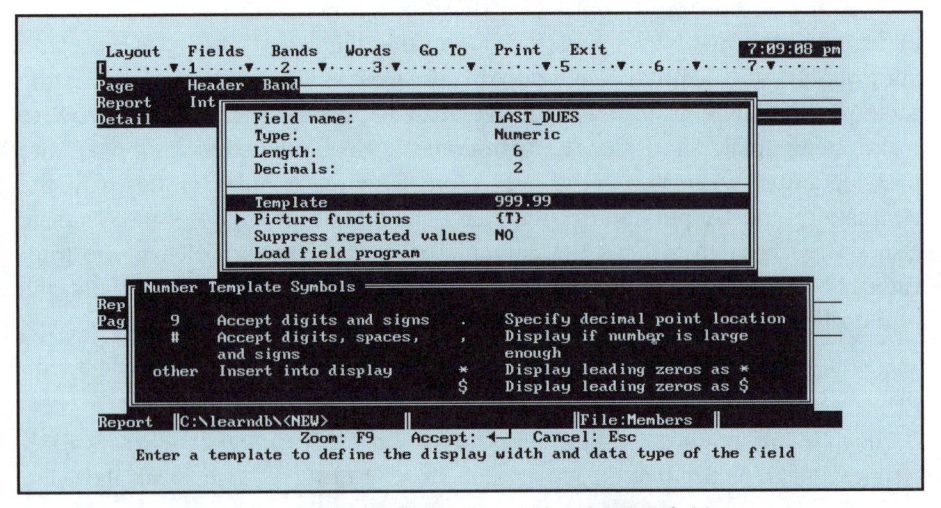

Figure 7.9 Template symbols for numeric fields.

The template symbols for numeric fields are shown in Figure 7.9 and Table 7.1. As you can see, the default template uses 9s to represent the digits and, if the number has decimal places, includes the decimal point. Note that, unlike character fields, numeric fields can be misleading if the template is not long enough to display the entire integer. For example, if you had one 9 as the template and the value were 100, then it would be very misleading just to display 1. With numeric fields, dBASE IV displays an asterisk in the number field in a case like this, to show that the actual number does not fit (rather than truncating the entry, as it does with character fields).

On the other hand, if the template can display the entire integer but not all of the decimal places, the number is rounded off to the closest value that fits in the template, since this can be done without a very misleading distortion of the value. It is sometimes handy to edit the template to suppress the display of the decimals and decimal point, so the number is rounded off to the nearest integer.

Apart from 9s, most of the symbols here are also meant for data entry forms. The ones relevant to reports are shown and described in Table 7.1.

Table 7.1 *Number template symbols.*

9	Use 9s to represent digits and signs, including the decimal point.
#	Use #s to represent digits, spaces, and signs. Use # instead of 9 if your numeric data includes some blank spaces.
,	Add commas to insert them in the numbers if they are large enough. For example, 999,999.99 includes the comma between the hundreds and thousands column if the number is greater that 1,000 but omits it if the number is less.
*	Use asterisks instead of 9s to display leading 0's as *'s.
$	Use dollar signs instead of 9s to display leading 0s as $s.
Other	Any other character is inserted in the display, as in character fields.

The * and $ are sometimes used for security. The usual 9 template simply omits leading zeros and leaves blank spaces in their place, but in some cases (for example, if you are printing checks) this can allow fraud: someone can type numbers in those blank spaces to make the amounts look larger. For this reason, some financial applications replace the leading zeroes with asterisks or repeated dollar signs instead of blank spaces.

NOTE: Do not use the $ template to add a single dollar sign before a number: as you will see, there is a picture function that does that.

By default, date fields are displayed using the template MM/DD/YY, to show that the month, then the day, then the year is displayed. This template is dimmed on the Display attributes menu, and it cannot be selected and changed. (You can change the date display by selecting **Settings** from the Tools menu of the Control Center, which is discussed in more detail in Chapter 9.)

Logical fields have the default template of Y. The other Template options for logical fields are not relevant to reports. Templates for memo fields are made up of Vs or Hs, for reasons discussed in the section on picture functions, below.

Picture Functions

When you select **Picture functions** from the Display attributes submenu for a field, dBASE IV displays a menu of possible picture functions, and you can select any one to toggle it on or off. The menu includes a brief description of the picture function followed by the character that represents that picture function. This book, however, refers to these options with the character first and then the description, because it's good to get into the habit of referring to these functions by character.

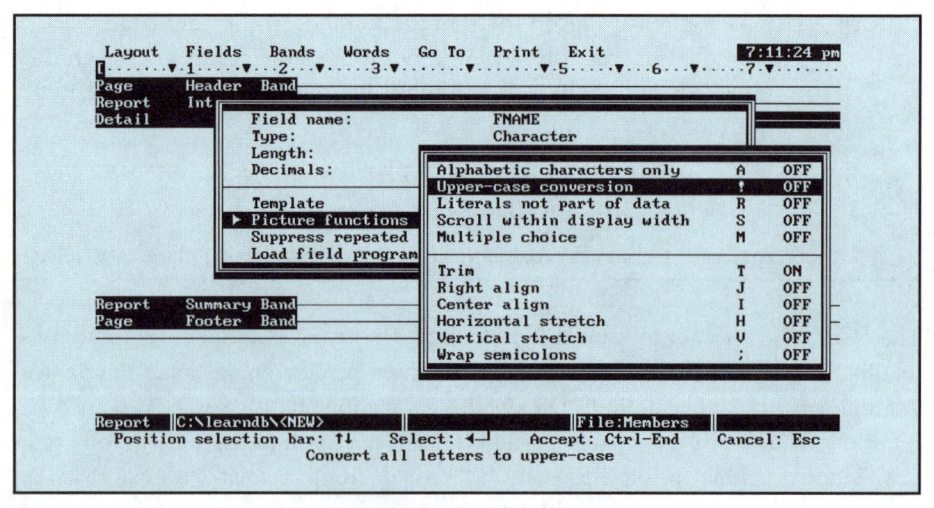

Figure 7.10 *The picture functions submenu for character fields.*

All of the characters representing the functions that are on are listed to the right of the Picture functions options on the Display attributes menu. You may have notice that, by default, the letter T appears on the Display attributes menu for character fields. This is the TRIM function, which removes leading and trailing blank spaces from the field. Trailing blanks are automatically trimmed, as you saw when you created labels, because this function is on. You can turn it off if you want to keep the blanks.

Select **Picture functions** from the Display attributes menu of a character field to display the Picture functions submenu shown in Figure 7.10. The message line at the bottom of the screen describes the function of the template that is highlighted. Again, most functions are meant for data entry screens, but the ones relevant to reports are summarized in Table 7.2.

Table 7.2 *Picture functions*

!	Upper-case conversion	Capitalizes all of the characters in the field. Using this function is like using a template with ! for each character. In either case, non-alphabetic characters are not affected.
R	Literals not part of data	Inserts characters used literally in the template, rather than overwriting data.
T	Trim	Removes leading and trailing blanks.
J	Right align	Places data at the right edge of the template's width.
I	Center align	Centers data within the template's width.
H	Horizontal stretch	If the template has been shortened this displays all of the data in the field, even if it requires going beyond the edge of the template on the same line.
V	Vertical stretch	If the template has been shortened, this displays all of the data in the field within the defined width of the template, even if it means printing on additional lines.
;	Wrap semicolons	Wraps data at semicolons.

> **NOTE** R Literals not part of data, needs more explanation. The description of it is misleading, because it refers to its use in forms; in reports, this option would be better described as "Insert literals in data." Remember that you learned in the last section that other characters you use in templates are inserted directly in the display. If this picture function is not used, these literal characters overwrite the data rather than being inserted in it. For example, a Social Security number could be stored as 051387189, and when the report is produced you could use the template XXX-XX-XXXX, so the Social Security number is displayed as 051-38-7189. You must turn R ON, however, for the hyphens to be inserted in this way. If you do not, the hyphens overwrite characters in the field rather than being inserted. Now that disk space is cheap and abundant, people rarely bother to save storage space in this way, and this picture function is not used as often as it was when disk space was at a premium.

Note that picture functions are needed only for Right align or Center align, since character data is normally aligned at the left edge of the field template.

Since memo fields are variable-length character fields, the picture functions available for them are the same as for character fields, but there are different default settings. As you can see in Figure 7.11, the Horizontal stretch or Vertical stretch functions are automatically on for memo fields, so the variable content of a memo field are printed out in the report in its entirety.

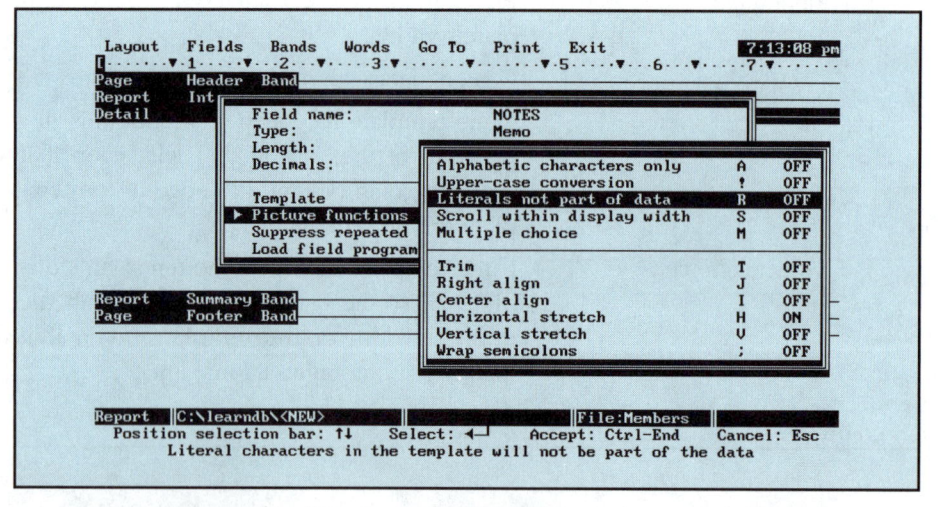

Figure 7.11 *The picture function submenu for memo fields.*

Horizontal stretch is needed only in word wrap mode, to stretch the template so all of the memo's contents fit right in the text; like everything else, it is wrapped when you reach the end right margin. Vertical stretch is needed only when you are not in word wrap mode. If the memo's contents are too long, it wraps onto the next line in a column that is the width of the template you created, rather than extending beyond the edge of that column.

For this reason, the picture function automatically toggles to **Vertical stretch** when you switch out of word wrap mode and then toggles back to **Horizontal stretch** when you switch back to word wrap mode.

When one of these picture functions is used, the Xs in the field template representing the function in the report automatically change to Vs or Hs, for Vertical or Horizontal stretch. In addition, the template becomes inaccessible on the Display attributes menu. Thus, the template is inaccessible by default on the Display attributes menu for Memo fields.

When Horizontal stretch is on, there is no need to change the template's width, since the width expands to fit the amount of text in the field. When Vertical stretch is on, though, you will probably want to change the template to determine the width of the column. Even though the template is inaccessible on the Display attributes menu, remember that there is another way of resizing templates—move the cursor to highlight the template on the report screen and press **Size:Shift- F7**, then use the Left Arrow key to make the template shorter or the Right Arrow key to make it longer or move the mouse pointer to desired location and click.

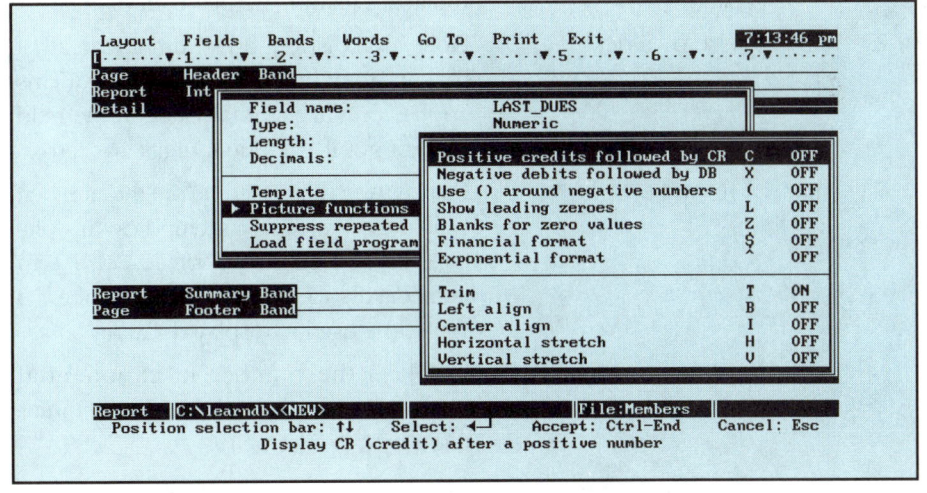

Figure 7.12   *The Pictures Functions submenu for numeric fields.*

If you select **Picture functions** from the Display attributes menu of a numeric field, dBASE IV displays the Picture functions submenu shown in Figure 7.12.

Notice that the options below the line are the same for numeric fields as the functions for character fields, described above, with a couple of minor differences: TRIM is not on by default, and Left align (rather than Right align) is now available as an option, as numeric fields are generally right-aligned by default.

The options above the line are specific to numeric fields, and all of them are relevant to reports, though most are not used frequently. The options as described in Table 7.3.

Table 7.3 *Numeric picture function options.*

C	Positive credits followed by CR	Prints the letters CR (for credit) to the right of any positive number.
X	Negative debits followed by DB	Prints the letters DB (for debit) to the right of any negative number.
(	Use () around negative numbers	Puts negative numbers in parentheses rather than using the minus sign, as is commonly done in accounting.
L	Show leading zeroes	Includes leading zeroes to fill up the entire width of the field, rather than replacing leading zeroes with blanks.
Z	Blanks for zero values	Does not display any number at all if the number in the field is zero. (This applies only if the total value in the field is zero, not if individual digits are zero.)
$	Financial format	Displays the dollar sign before the number. Unlike the $ symbol in templates, this picture function displays a single dollar sign immediately to the left of the number. It should be used to display dollar amounts.
^	Exponential format	Displays the number in exponential (scientific) notation, as a number multiplied by a power of 10.

T	Trim	OFF by default for numeric fields, as you do not generally want to remove the leading blanks from numeric fields and run them together, as you often do with character fields.
B	Left align	Available for numeric fields, taking the place of J Right align on the menu for character fields, because numeric fields are normally aligned to the right if no alignment is specified.

Some of these, such as $, are indispensable. Others are also sometimes useful.

You should be careful with C and X, which display the abbreviations CR and DB to the right of positive and negative numbers. Not all credits are positive and not all debits are negative in double-entry accounting. The menu descriptions of these functions are a bit misleading, as they imply that the abbreviations are only used with "positive credits" and "negative debits." Actually, they are used with all positive and negative numbers. Use these Picture functions only if you know enough about accounting to understand when CR and DB should be used.

Picture functions are not available for date or logical fields.

Suppressing Repeated Values

The Suppress repeated values option of the Display attributes menu is very easy to understand. If you select this option to toggle the setting to YES, the contents of a field are not displayed if they are the same as the contents of the previous record.

An example should make this clear. Remember that you created an index earlier to list records by state with the names of the members listed alphabetically within each state. Imagine that you are producing a report that uses this index and has the state's names in the left column. It would be easier to read this report if a state's name were listed only in the first record for that state, rather than being repeated in every record. Selecting Suppress repeated values as a display attribute of the state field produces this effect.

This feature is often used for reports on relational databases, which usually include repetitive data in many fields. It is rarely needed for reports on simple databases.

Other Features of the Report Generator

Other Types of Fields

When you add a field to a report, dBASE IV displays the picklists shown in Figure 7.13. In addition to the fields from the database file, you can also add predefined fields, calculated fields, and summary fields. Predefined and calculated fields are also available in the labels design screen, but they are covered here because it is more common to use them in reports. Summary fields are used in the Report Summary Band and in Group Summary Bands of reports.

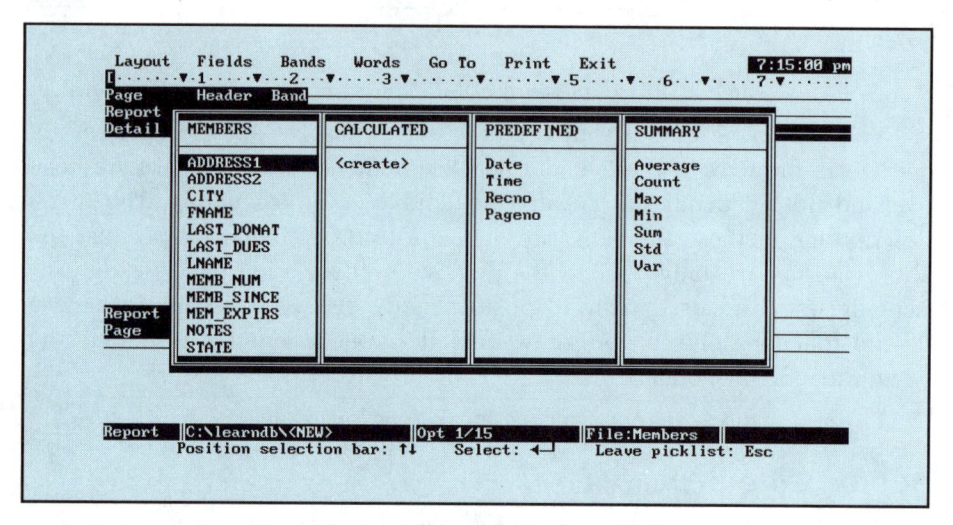

Figure 7.13   *Types of fields used in reports.*

The use of the predefined fields is self-evident. Add them to include the current date, the current time, record numbers, or page numbers in the report.

Both summary fields and calculated fields are similar to features you have already learned working with advanced queries.

The options in the Summary panel include operators like the aggregate operators that you used in queries to calculate the average value, count the number of records, find the maximum or minimum value, or find the sum of the values in a field for the entire database file or for a group of records. In addition, Std and Var calculate the standard deviation and variance of the values in a field. These are primarily useful for statistical applications.

Calculated fields are based on expressions that determine their value. Most calculated fields just need to use field names and the arithmetic operators, which you learned when you added calculated fields to queries in Chapter 6.

If you need to review this material, see the sections in Chapter 6 entitled *Calculated Fields* and *Aggregate Operators*.

When you place a summary field or a calculated field, you use the Display attributes menus shown in Figure 7.14 and Figure 7.15. Both let you enter a name and a description for the field.

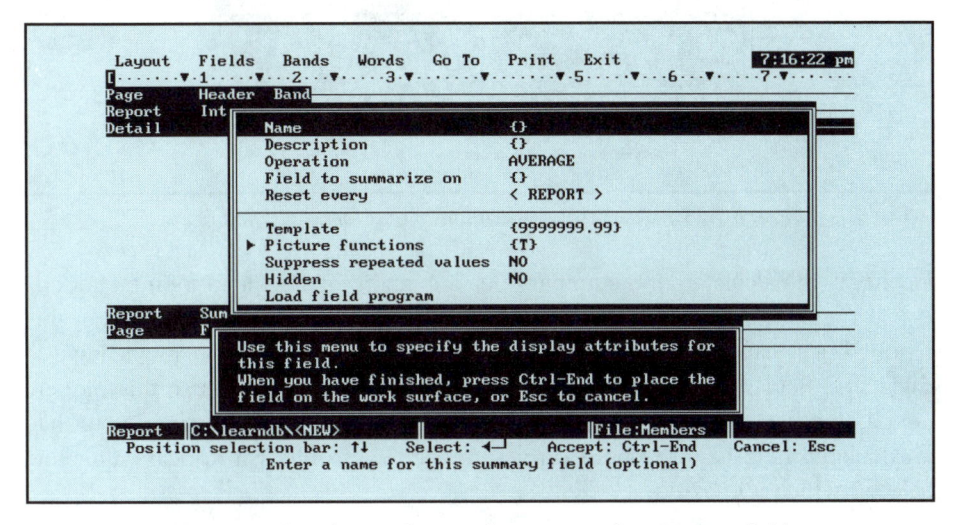

Figure 7.14   *The Display Attributes menu for summary fields.*

The menu for a calculated field lets you enter an expression that determines its value. Expressions are covered in detail in Chapter 11, but for most calculated fields, you can simply use expressions made up of field names and the arithmetic operators, as you learned to do in Chapter 6.

The menu for a summary field lets you select **Operation** to choose from a picklist of the different summary operators (with the one you chose when you created the field as the default operation). Select **Field** to choose from a picklist of fields in the database, to determine which one should be summed, averaged, counted, or whatever. Select **Reset every** to choose from a picklist that lets you determine to which records the summary applies. It includes REPORT (to be used if the field summarizes the entire report up to that point), PAGE (to be used if the field summarizes only the records since the beginning of the page), and, if you have created groups, it also includes the names of the fields on which the groups are based, so you can create summary fields for them.

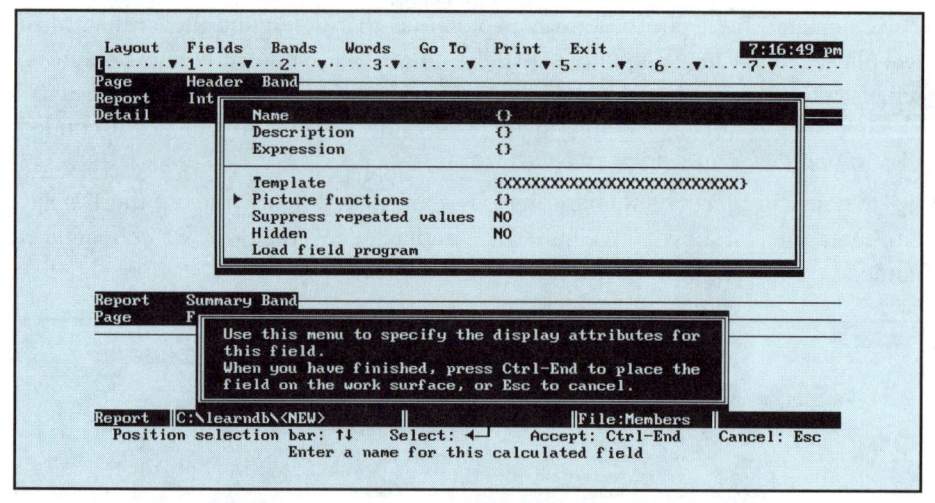

Figure 7.15 *The Display Attributes menu for calculated fields.*

Finally, both calculated and summary fields contain the display attribute Hidden. If you toggle this from the default NO to YES, the field is not displayed on the report, but it can still be used in calculations. For example, you might have a calculated field in each record that is hidden. Then you could use this hidden field as the basis of a summary field in the report or group summary. Note that a calculated field can be based on a summary field only if it appears after the field on which it is based.

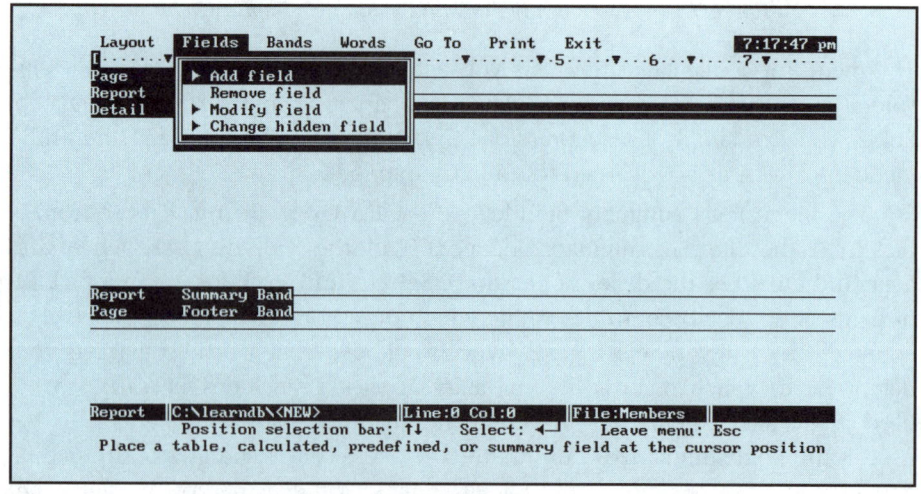

Figure 7.16 *The Fields menu.*

The Fields menu, shown in Figure 7.16, includes an option to Change hidden field. If you select this option, it displays a picklist of all hidden fields in the report. Select one to use its display attributes menu again. You can modify its display attributes just as you do the display attributes of any field—the only difference is that you must use this picklist to select it, as you cannot highlight it on the screen because it is hidden.

The other features of the Display attributes menus for calculated and summary fields are the same as those for ordinary database fields, covered above.

Adding Graphics

The Layout menu has options that let you add simple graphics, such as boxes and lines, to the report.

To use these features, simply select **Box** or **Line** from the Layout menu. In either case, dBASE IV displays the submenu that lets you draw the box or line using a single line, a double line or any other character. If you select **Using specified character**, DOS displays a picklist of all of the ASCII characters, and you can select any one. Both the submenu and picklist are shown in Figure 7.17.

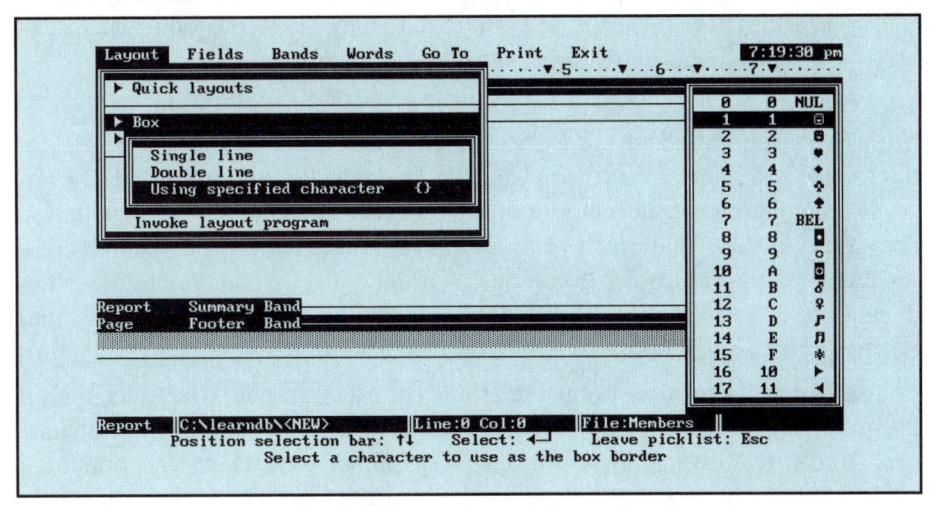

Figure 7.17   *Defining a box or line.*

After you have selected Single line, Double line, or Using specified character, dBASE IV prompts you to move the cursor to the upper-left corner of the location where you want the box to appear or where you want the line to begin and press **Enter**. After you have pressed **Enter**, use the Arrow keys to move the cursor and draw the line or box. If you are drawing a line, you can move the cursor at random, left, right, up, or down, and the line is drawn wherever you move it. You can draw irregular lines as well as straight ones. If you are drawing a box, you must begin at one corner and move the cursor to the diagonally opposite corner. A box is filled in between the two corners, and the entire box expands or contracts as you move the cursor. Press **Enter** to stop drawing when the box or line is complete. Using the mouse, you can simply make the menu selection and then click and drag from one corner to the other.

After it is drawn, a box is treated as a single object, like a field. When you move the cursor to it, the entire box is highlighted. If you press **Del** while the box is highlighted, the box is deleted.

A line, on the other hand, is treated as separate characters. If you move the cursor on it, only the width of one character is highlighted. If you press **Del**, only that one character-width is deleted.

> **NOTE** Which graphics characters you can use depends on your printer. Some common printers, including Epson-compatible dot-matrix printers, do not support DOS line drawing characters. If you include single or double lines in your report, they substitute other characters instead and ruin your report.

No printers support all of the DOS characters that are available in the picklist that you use to select a specified character. In particular, the first 26 ASCII characters are control characters, and they may make your printer do strange things. For example, ASCII character 13 is the carriage-return character, though it is represented by a musical note. If you use it to draw a box, your printer does not draw a pretty box made of musical notes. Instead, it sends carriage returns and starts printing at the left margin whenever character 13 is sent.

If you have seen your printer print lines or other graphic characters, then it is safe to use the single- or double-line feature or those specific graphic characters. Otherwise, you might want to test your printer by creating and printing a sample report with just a graphic feature, to see if it works, before causing yourself trouble by using that graphic character in a full-fledged report.

Margins

You probably have noticed that the menu system of the reports design screen includes the Words, Go To, and Print menus that are also included in the Labels

Design screen, the memo editor, and other screens that let you use the dBASE IV word processor. These advanced word processing features are covered in detail in Chapter 9.

Before you produce form letters, you should learn some of these advanced word processing features. In particular, you must set margins before you print a form letter. Word wrap does not work unless you add a right margin.

You can produce most reports, apart from form letters, without setting the margins. As you learned in Chapter 6, you can offset the report from the left edge of the page when you print it, rather than set formal margins. Just design the report so it begins in the first column, at the left edge of the screen. Then, before you print the report, select **Page dimensions** from the Print menu and **Offset from left** from the submenu to enter an offset that dBASE IV uses as the left margin when it prints the report: 10 is a common margin. Since a standard page is eighty characters wide, you can make the report extend from column 0 to about column 63, in order to leave space for the offset of 10 to the left and a margin of 7 to the right.

To become more accomplished at creating reports and to create form letters, read the section on the word processor in Chapter 9, including the section on setting margins. While you are learning, however, the simple method you have already learned is adequate.

Saving Your Work

The Layout and Exit menus, with which you are already familiar from other screens, have options that let you save your work.

The Layout menu includes an option to Edit description of report, which (as you know) lets you create the description that is displayed when the report name is highlighted. It also includes the option, Save the report, which lets you save your work without leaving the Reports Design screen. Since reports often take a long time to design, it is a good idea to save them periodically, so that you do not lose all of your work in case of a power failure or other computer failure. Since dBASE IV prompts you for the name to save as, you can also use this option to rename the report. If you are creating a new report by modifying an old one and you want to keep the old one under its original name, just save the new one under a different name.

The **Layout** menu also includes the option **Use different database file or view.** If you select this, dBASE IV displays a picklist of all the available files and views in the current catalog, and you can choose the one you want to use as the basis of the report.

Finally, the Exit menu includes the familiar options Save changes and exit and Abandon changes and exit. As always, you can just press **Ctrl-End** or **Esc** rather than selecting these options.

A Sample Report

As you can see, the report generator is very powerful, and you should create a sample report to solidify your understanding of what you have learned so far before going on to learn about groupings in the next section.

The exercise begins by using the Form layout from the Quick layouts submenu. After you are done with it, you might want to experiment on your own with the column reports and form letters. As you know, the way you place fields and type text is the same with all of the quick layouts, but they do have different feels—particularly the mailmerge layout, where word wrap is turned on and you type a long body of text.

When it is needed to make locations clear, these instructions tell you to use the keyboard to move the cursor to the location and then place the field. You can also simply double-click these locations.

1. Begin from the Control Center. If it is not already in use, select **MEMBERS** from the Data panel and select **Use file** from the prompt box. Then select **<create>** from the Reports panel.

2. The reports design screen should appear, with the Layout menu already pulled down. Press **Enter** to select **Quick layouts** from the **Layout** menu. Then select **Form layout** from the **Quick layouts** submenu. This initial layout is shown in Figure 7.18.

3. Begin by getting rid of some fields and text that you do not need. Move the cursor down to the line with the MEMB_NUM field and press **Ctrl-Y** to delete the entire line. Note that everything below moves up a line.

4. Press **Ctrl-Y** again to delete the entire line with the TITLE field.

5. Then press **Ctrl-Y** again to delete the entire line with the FNAME field, since you want the name on a single line with the last name first.

6. If necessary, move to the far left of the line with the LNAME field and press **Del** to delete the L, leaving NAME as the field title.

7. Then move to the right of the text on the line, and type a comma followed by a blank space to separate the last from first name. To add the

first name on this line, press **Field:F5**, select **FNAME** from the MEMBERS field list, and press **Ctrl-End** to accept the default field attributes. (Of course, you could have moved the FNAME field rather than deleting and placing it.)

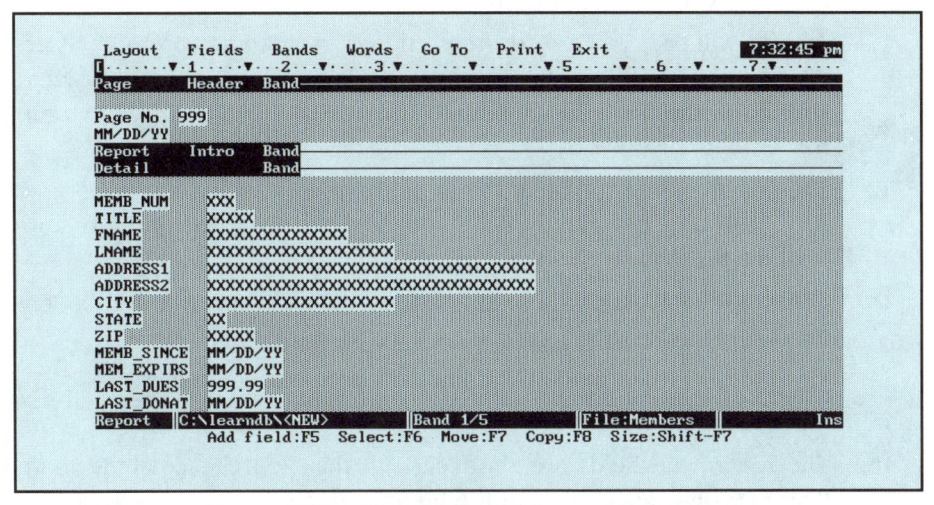

Figure 7.18 *The initial quick layout for the report.*

8. Move the cursor to the 1 at the end of the name of the ADDRESS1 field and press **Del** to delete that character, leaving ADDRESS as the name of the field. Then, move to the left edge of the second address line, the line with the ADDRESS2 field, and press **Del** until you delete the entire name of that field.

9. Up to now, you wanted to delete or change field names without the field templates moving, to keep the fields lined up. Now, though, you must do some things that require you to move the field templates. You want to indent all of the lines below the name to make each new record stand out. You also want to combine data that is now on two lines. You cannot do these things easily unless you are in word wrap mode. Try it to see. Move the cursor to the left edge of the line with the ADDRESS1 field. Look at the status bar to make sure you are in insert mode: it should say Ins at its far right; if it does not, press **Ins**. Then press **Tab** to try to indent everything on the line: nothing moves except the cursor. Press **Home** to move back to the left edge of the line and press **Spacebar.** The text moves a space, but the field tem-

plate does not. Press **Backspace** to delete the blank space you just added.

10. Try to combine the data on two lines. Press **Backspace** again, and dBASE IV just beeps and displays a message saying you cannot move beyond the left edge of the layout.

11. As you will see, you can do these things in word wrap mode. Select **Word wrap band** from the Bands menu. Wait a moment until the band shading in the band disappears, to indicate that is now in word wrap mode.

12. The cursor should still be at the far left edge of the first ADDRESS line. Press **Tab** and the entire line is indented the width of one tab stop, both the text and the field template.

13. Move to the far left of the second address line, and press **Tab** to indent the field template.

14. Move to the far left of the CITY line, and press **Tab** to indent it.

15. Move to the far left of the STATE line, and press **Tab** to indent it.

16. The rest of the fields are short enough that you can combine more than one on a line. Move to the far left edge of the line with the ZIP field, and then press **Backspace.** This deletes the break between lines, so that ZIP is now right after the state field template on the previous line, with the cursor still on the Z of the word ZIP, where it was before.

17. Press **Tab** twice to move the word ZIP and the field template to the right.

18. Move to the left edge of the next line and then press **Tab** to indent the MEMB_SINCE field. Then edit the field name so it reads MEMBER SINCE instead of MEMB_SINCE—just move the cursor to the underscore, press **Del** to delete it, and type *ER* followed by a blank space.

19. Move to the right edge of this line, and then press **Del** to delete the line break and move the MEM_EXPIRS up to this line, to the right of the MEMB_SINCE field template. Press **Tab** to line it up the field name under the name ZIP on the previous line. Then edit the field name so it reads MEMBERSHIP EXPIRES instead of MEM_EXPIRS.

20. Move to the left edge of the next line, and then press **Tab** to indent the LAST_DUES field name and template.

21. Edit the name so it reads LAST DUES without the underscore.

Chapter 7: Formatted Reports ♦ **195**

22. Move to the right of this line. Then press **Del** to move the LAST_DONAT field up to the same line. Press **Tab** to line up the field name, and then edit the field name so it reads LAST DONATION.

23. Move to the left edge of the next line, and then press **Tab** to indent the line.

24. Move to the left edge of the next line, and then press **Tab** to indent this line. Note that the Notes field template changed from Vs to Hs when you shifted to word wrap mode; that is, it changed from vertical to horizontal stretch (which is what you want when you are including a memo within word-wrapped text).

25. In this case, though, you do not want the memos to continue indefinitely to the right. You want any extra text from the memo to be lined up immediately below the text on the first line of NOTES. Thus, you should switch out of word wrap mode again to change the field back to Vertical stretch. To do this, select **Word wrap band** from the Bands menu again to toggle the setting back to NO. dBASE takes a moment before the shading appears. Note that the NOTES field mask has turned to Vs again.

26. Alter the NOTES field template to print more of the memo on each line. Move the cursor to this field template. All of the Vs should be highlighted. Then press **Size:Shift-F7**, press the **Right Arrow** key until the template is 40 characters long, so its right edge is lined up under the right edge of the MEMBERSHIP EXPIRES field template, and then press **Enter** (or, using the mouse, just click at that location).

27. To make the screen more readable, skip a line between the address and the other data. Move the cursor up so it is to the right of the ZIP field template, and press **Ctrl-N** to push everything below down one line. You have now finished laying out the detail band, and the reports design screen should look like Figure 7.19.

28. You should get into the habit of saving your work periodically when you do a procedure as long as this one, especially at natural breaks in your work. Select **Save this report** from the Layout menu, and when dBASE prompts you for the name, enter *standard* (since this is your standard, general-purpose report). dBASE IV takes a moment to generate the report before returning you to the reports design screen.

29. You can also enter a description of the report: select **Edit description of report** from the Layout menu, and when dBASE IV prompts you to

Edit the description of this .frm file, type *General purpose report listing membership data* and press **Enter** to return to the reports design screen.

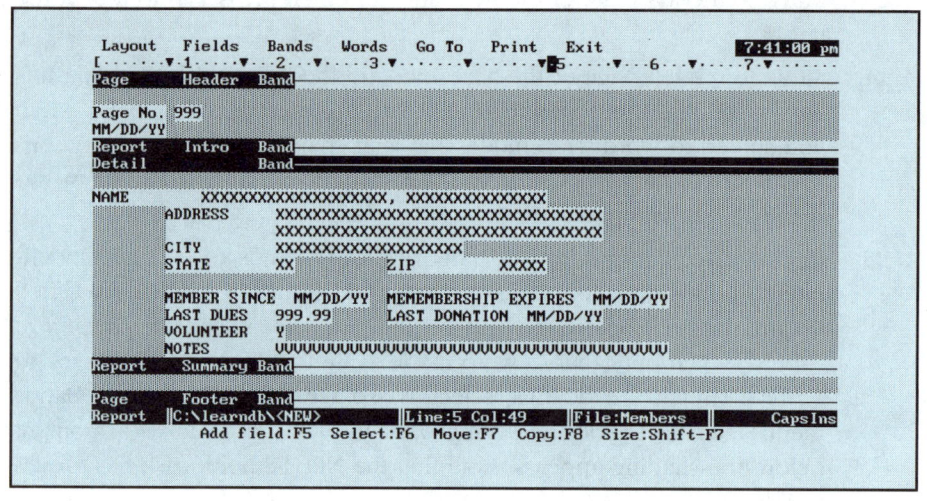

Figure 7.19 *The layout of the detail band.*

30. To add a footer, move to the cursor to the Page Footer band, make sure you are in Insert mode, and press **Enter** to add a second line to the footer band; then type *General membership report*. If you were designing an actual report, you would probably want to redesign the header and perhaps design a more elaborate footer, but since this is an exercise, you can use this simple footer and leave the header as it is.

31. To add a report summary that lists the number of members and the average dues, first move the cursor to the Report Summary Band and press **Enter** four times to make the band five lines wide.

32. Move the cursor to the next to the last line of the band, indented two spaces from the left.

33. Press **Field:F5**. Select **Count** from the SUMMARY field list. When the Display attributes menu appears, select **Template**, and edit the template so it consists of only six 9s (assuming that the organization will always have less than a million members), press **Enter** to accept the new template value, and press **Ctrl-End** to place the field.

34. Now press **Spacebar**, type *members total, paying average dues of*, and press **Spacebar** again.
35. Now press **Field:F5**. Select **Average** from the SUMMARY field list.
36. Select **Field to summarize on** from the Display Attributes menu, and select **LAST_DUES** from the picklist of fields.
37. Select **Picture functions** from the Display attributes menu. Select both **Financial format** and **Trim** from the Picture functions submenu, to add a dollar sign and trim zeroes, so there is no extra space separating this field from the rest of the sentence. Then press **Ctrl-End** to accept these picture functions
38. Press **Ctrl-End** again to place the template.
39. To highlight the summary, you can draw a box around it. Select **Box** from the Layout menu, and select **Double line** from the submenu. Press **Up Arrow** and **Home** to move the cursor to the left edge of the first line of the summary band, and then press **Enter** to begin drawing the box.

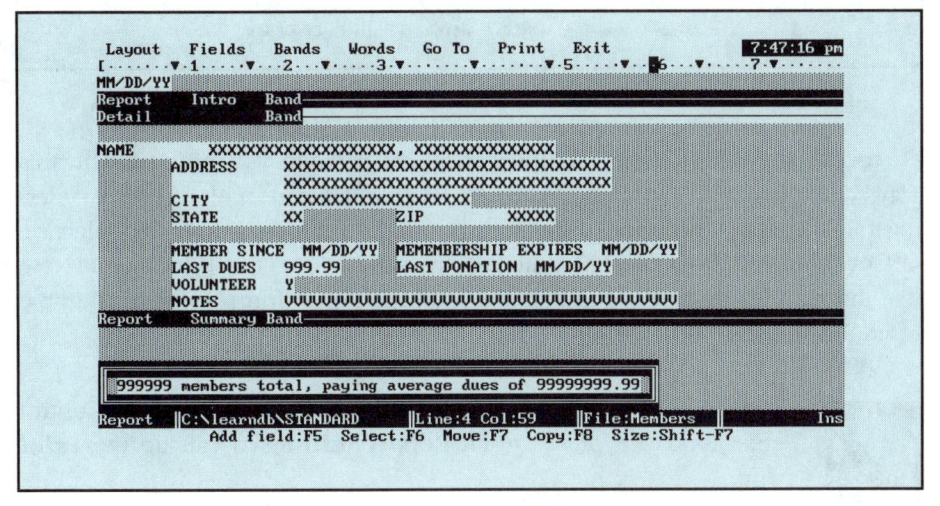

Figure 7.20   *The final layout of the report.*

40. Press the **Down Arrow** key once and press **End** to stretch the box to the end of the text on that line. Then press the **Down Arrow** once and **Right Arrow** once to extend the box around the text, and press **Enter** to stop drawing. (Alternatively, just click and drag with the mouse to place the box.) The final report is shown in Figure 7.20.

41. To test the report, select **View report on screen** from the Print menu. Press **Spacebar** to see the entire report and return to the report form screen. The final screen of the preview, with the report summary is shown in Figure 7.21.

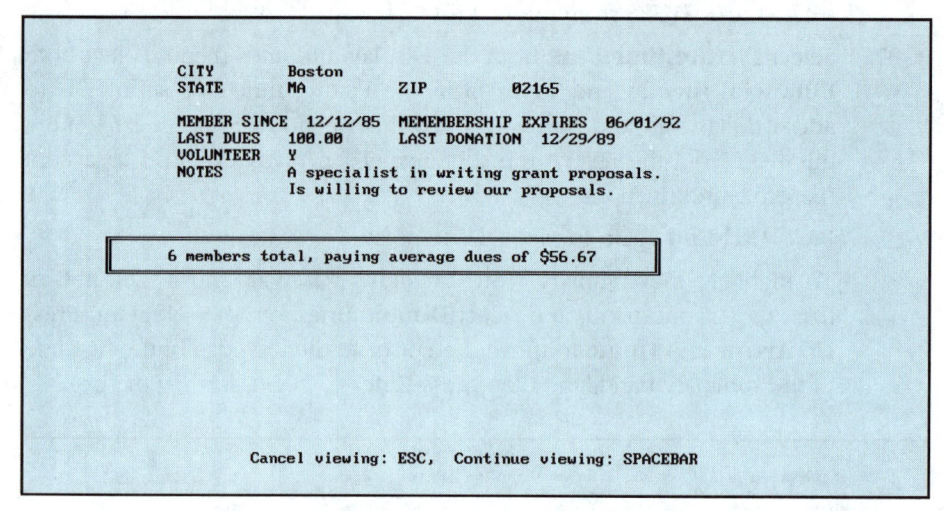

```
CITY        Boston
STATE       MA          ZIP         02165

MEMBER SINCE 12/12/85  MEMEMBERSHIP EXPIRES  06/01/92
LAST DUES    100.00    LAST DONATION  12/29/89
VOLUNTEER    Y
NOTES        A specialist in writing grant proposals.
             Is willing to review our proposals.

6 members total, paying average dues of $56.67



                Cancel viewing: ESC,  Continue viewing: SPACEBAR
```

Figure 7.21 *Previewing the report.*

Of course, the report is not in alphabetical order when you preview it in this way. When you actually print it, you will use the database with an index ordering the records. When you print it, you will also add a margin by selecting **Offset from left** from the Page dimensions submenu of the Print menu. Note that the report only extends to column 59 of the report form, so there is ample room for margins.

NOTE If you highlight the report name in the Reports panel of the Control Center, you can press **Quick Report:Shift-F9** to call up the **Print** menu.

Grouping the Records in Reports

Now you want a report with members from each state listed separately, with a summary that tells you the number of members from each state. dBASE IV makes it easy for you to organize your report in groups and to add separate introductions and summaries for each group.

To add this sort of grouping to your report, select **Add a group band** from the Bands menu to display the submenu shown in Figure 7.22. (If the cursor is in the Detail Band, this option is dimmed. You may be in any other band when you add a group.)

As you can see from the illustration, a group can be based on:

- **Field value**: If you select this option, dBASE displays a picklist of fields and you choose which field the group is based on. If you choose **STATE**, for example, there is a separate group for each state.

- **Expression value**: If you select this option, dBASE IV lets you enter an expression to use as the basis of the group. For example, if you want a new group whenever the first letter of the member's name changes, enter an expression that evaluates to the first letter of the LNAME field. (Expressions are covered in Chapter 11.)

- **Record count:** If you select this option, dBASE IV lets you enter an integer, and this number of records is made into a separate group. For example, to make a long report more readable, you might want to group every five records.

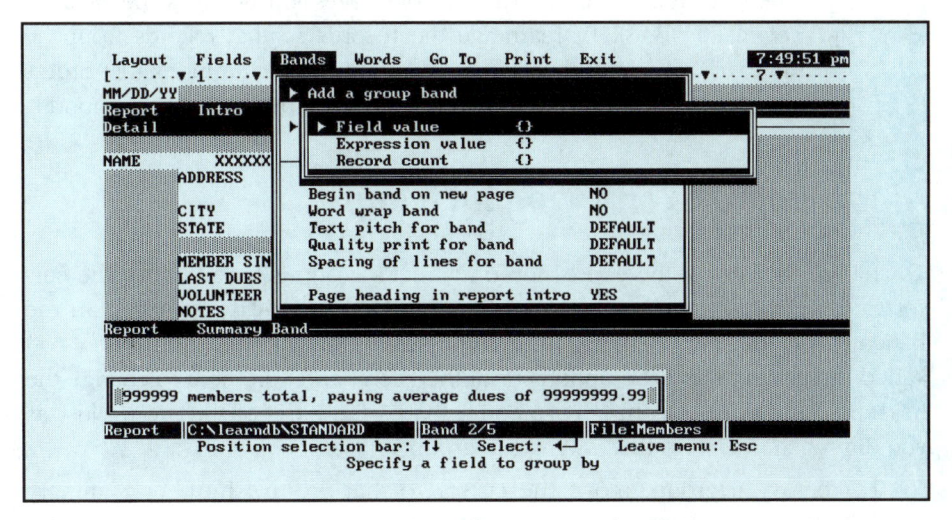

Figure 7.22 Adding a group band.

You can use only one of these as the basis of each group. If you make an entry for one, any entry that you might have in another is automatically removed. (However, as you will see soon, you can add more than one group, which could be based on different options.)

When you add a group band in one of these ways, bands for Group Intro and Group Summary are added to the Reports Design screen. These bands can be treated just like the Report Intro and Report Summary Bands. For example, you can add summary fields in the group summary band. They could also be left as blank lines, so the report skips lines between groups; for example, if you were grouping every five records to make the report readable, you would probably want to leave a blank line in the Group Summary band and leave nothing in the Group Intro band, so that the report skips a single line after each group of five records.

Ordinarily, the group introduction is printed only once at the beginning of each group. If groups are several pages long, though, there are some cases when you might want the group introduction repeated at the top of each page. To add this feature, move the cursor to the Group Intro band and select **Group intro on each page** from the Bands menu.

> **NOTE** If you are basing a group on a field or expression, you must remember that adding a group band makes dBASE IV begin a new group whenever the value of that field or expression changes, but it does not make dBASE IV rearrange the records so that records from the same group are together. It is up to you to create an index that orders the records properly and to use this index before printing the report.

Modifying or Removing a Group

To change the field or the expression on which a group is based, move the cursor to that group's Intro or Summary Band and select **Modify group** from the Bands menu. dBASE IV displays the same submenu that was used when you added the group. Select the options from this menu and edit them to change the field, the expression, or the record count that is the basis of the group, just as you did when you were first adding the group

To remove a group, move the cursor to that group's Intro or Summary Band. Then select **Remove group** from the Bands menu, and press Y to confirm that you want to delete the group's bands.

A Sample Report with Groups

Try grouping your membership report by state. You should still have the layout for this report displayed on the reports design screen, where you left it at the end of the last exercise. If you do not, highlight STANDARD in the Reports panel and press **Design:Shift-F2**.

1. Make sure the cursor is not in the Detail Band, and select **Add a group band** from the Bands menu.
2. Select **Field value** from the submenu, and select **STATE** from the pick-list of field names. dBASE IV adds band names Group 1 Intro Band and Group 1 Summary Band, as shown in Figure 7.23.

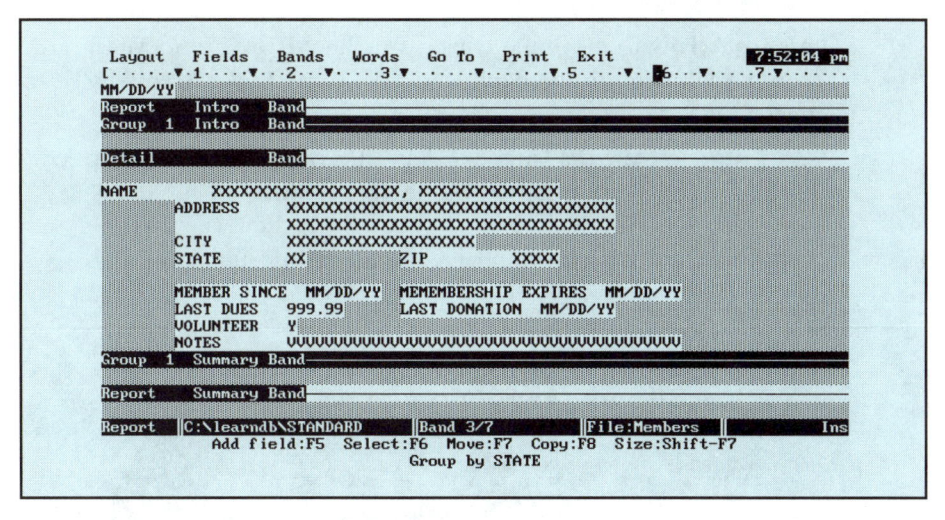

Figure 7.23   Group Intro and Summary bands added to the report.

3. Leave the Group Intro Band blank, but add a Group Summary that is similar to the Report Summary Band. Move the cursor to the Group 1 Summary Band. Press **Enter** four times, so it has five lines in all. Press **Up Arrow** to move the cursor to the third line of the band and, if necessary, **Home** to move to the left edge. Press **Right Arrow** four times to indent a bit.
4. Now, add a summary similar to the report summary you added earlier. Press **Field:F5**, select **Count** from the SUMMARY field list, shorten the template to 999999. and press **Ctrl-End** to place the field.

5. Then press **Spacebar**, type *members from* and press **Spacebar** again.
6. Then press **Field:F5**, select **STATE** from the MEMBERS field list, and press **Ctrl-End** to place the field.
7. Then type *, paying average dues of* and press the **Spacebar**.
8. Then press **Field:F5**, select **Average** from the SUMMARY panel.
9. Select **Field to summarize on** and select **LAST_DUES** from the picklist.
10. Select **Picture functions**, select **$ Financial Format** and **T Trim** from the Picture functions submenu and press **Ctrl-End.**
11. Press **Ctrl-End** to place the field.
12. To add a box, select **Box** from the Layout menu and select **Single line** from the submenu.
13. Press **Up Arrow** to move the cursor up a line, **Home** to move the cursor to the left edge of the band, and then press **Right Arrow** twice to indent a bit.
14. Press **Enter** to start drawing. To draw the box, press **Down Arrow**, End, **Right Arrow**, **Down Arrow**, then press **Enter** to stop drawing.

Figure 7.24 shows both this group summary and the report summary band.

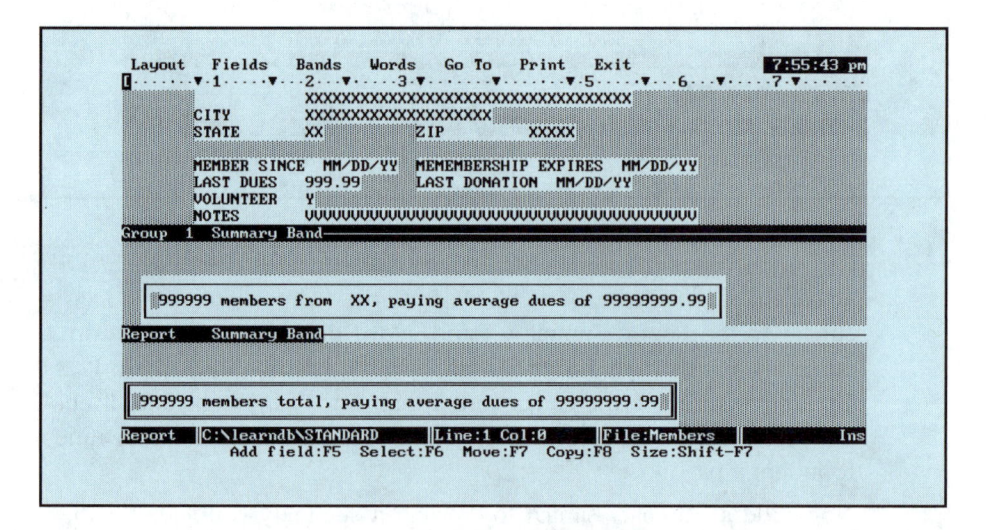

Figure 7.24 *The Group and Report Summary bands.*

15. Now that the report is designed, save it under a new name: call it BY_STATE. Select **Save this report** from the Layout menu. Edit the report name so it reads C:\LEARNDB\BY_STATE (dBASE IV automatically adds the .FRM extension) and press **Enter**.

16. Select **Edit description of report** from the Layout menu, and enter *Membership report grouped by state* as the description.

17. Press **Ctrl-End** to save changes and return to the Control Center.

18. As it happens, you already have the index you need to put the records in the proper order to produce this report. Select **MEMBERS** from the Data panel of the Control Center, and select **Modify structure/order** from the prompt box.

19. Select **Order records by index** from the Organize menu, and select **ST_NAMES** from the picklist of indexes.

20. Then press **Esc** and *Y* to return to the Control Center.

21. Now that the records are ordered by state (and ordered alphabetically by name within each state), you can test the report. Select **BY_STATE** from the Reports panel and select **Print report** from the prompt box. Then select **View report on screen** from the Print menu. One screen of the report preview is shown in Figure 7.25.

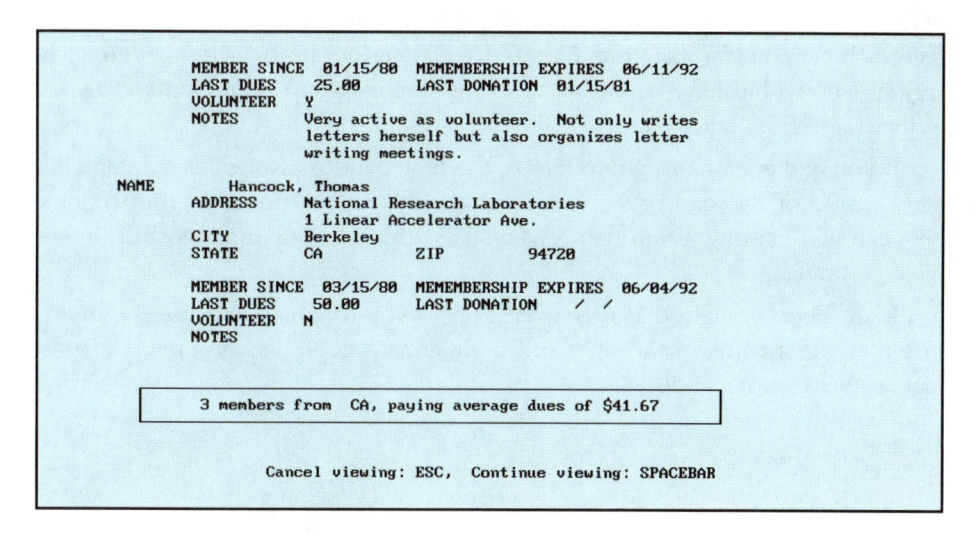

Figure 7.25 *Previewing the grouped report.*

22. If you want, you can actually print the report rather than just previewing it. First, select **Offset from left** from the Page dimensions submenu of the Print menu and enter *10* as the left margin. Then select **Begin printing** from the Print menu.

Nested Groups

It is also easy to add subgroups within groups. For example, if you had a large database file, you might want records grouped by state and, within each state, grouped by zip code. And, within each zip code, you might want every five records grouped. This is called *nesting* groups.

When you select **Add a group band** from the Bands menu, a new group is added *inside* of the band where the cursor is. (Remember that you cannot add a group band when the cursor is in the Detail Band.)

Thus, if you want the records to be grouped by zip code within each state, put the cursor in the Group Intro Band based on the STATE field, and then add a new group band based on ZIP field. The band is added inside of the band based on STATE, indicating that the records are grouped by STATE and, within each state, are grouped by ZIP code.

On the other hand, if you had put the cursor in the Page Header Band or Report Intro Band when you added the new group band, the new group band would be outside the state band. You might do this if you wanted to group records by region (for example, East and West) and group by states within each region. You would have to create an expression to group by region and use it as the basis of the outer band.

If you add even more group bands, the new band is always placed immediately inside of the band where the cursor is, so you can add group bands between two existing group bands as well as adding a new innermost or outermost grouping.

Remember, though, that it is always up to you to create and use the index that puts the records in the right order for grouping. Nested groupings of this sort require complex indexes.

Summary

In this chapter, you learned how to create and work with custom formatted reports using the dBASE IV report generator. This concludes Part 1 of this book. You should now be up and running and able to use all the basic features of dBASE IV from the Control Center.

If you continue to Part 2, you will learn how to create custom data entry forms with the forms generator and generate quick applications of your own using the dBASE IV Applications Generator. You will also learn more about some of the advanced features of dBASE IV, such as the word processor and more options of the Print menu and the Tools menu, covered in Chapter 9, and the ability to work with relational databases, discussed in Chapter 10.

Part 3 of this book introduces you to dBASE language the and the fundamentals of dBASE programming.

Part 2

ADDING POWER

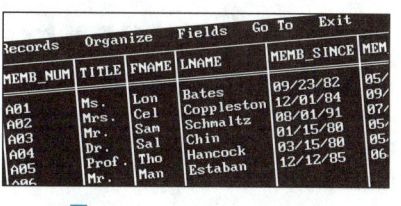

Chapter 8

Forms and Quick Applications

This chapter begins Part 2 of this book. Now that you know the basic features necessary to be up and running with dBASE IV, you will be introduced to some of the program's more advanced features. In this chapter, you design a custom form to accept data entry for the MEMBERS database and create a menu-driven application to accompany it.

In this chapter, you learn:

- How to create and modify a custom data entry form from the Control Center

- How to create and run a quick application using the dBASE IV applications generator

About Custom Forms and Applications

This chapter covers two features of dBASE IV: custom forms and quick applications, which are often used to set up the program so that users who are not familiar with dBASE IV can work with it easily.

First, you create a custom data entry form using dBASE's forms layout screen. A data entry form makes it easier for the user to add or edit data. You can rearrange the fields to resemble existing paper forms and add any help text that you want, so the screen is easier for an inexperienced user to understand than the usual dBASE IV Browse or Edit screen. It also lets you control the display of data and validate data that is entered by using field templates, like the templates used in reports. This feature makes forms useful for experienced users as well.

Second, you generate a quick application. Once you have created a form, it is very easy to create a quick application that uses that form as part of a menu-driven system, so that an inexperienced user can perform all of the usual tasks of file maintenance simply by choosing options from the menu without knowing anything about dBASE IV.

Forms

The Forms Design screen is almost identical to the Reports Design screen you worked with in the previous chapter. However, it is much simpler and should be easy for you to learn. You can use only one quick layout, the forms layout.

As in the Reports Design screen, you can add, delete, move, and resize field templates.

You also enter and edit text as you did in the Reports Design screen, but in non-wordwrap mode. The Forms Design screen does not have a word wrap mode, as it is used only for creating screen-oriented data-entry forms and not for typing a body of text.

To validate data—that is, to control what data may be entered—you use a popup menu to edit templates and add picture functions that is similar to the Display attributes menu that you already used to control the display of data in the reports design screen.

After you have created and saved the custom data-entry form, you can use it in the usual ways. You can highlight its name in the Control Center and press

Data:F2, or select it and then select **Display data** from the prompt box. The dBASE IV edit screen is displayed using the form *you* designed, rather than the default dBASE IV edit screen. The usual edit menus are included, and so you should allow a line for them at the top of the screen when you design the form.

You can also modify a data-entry form in the same way that you have modified other dBASE IV forms. Highlight its name in the Control Center and press **Design:Shift-F2**, or select it and select **Modify layout** from the prompt box.

The screen that you use to design the form is saved in a file with the extension .SCR (short for screen form). The program that dBASE IV generates from the forms, which is actually used for data entry, is saved in a file with the extension .FMT (short for format).

The Menu System of the Forms Design Screen

The Forms Design screen is so similar to the Reports Design screen that you should be able to understand it just by glancing at its menu system.

If you begin from the Control Center by using a database file or a view and then selecting **<create>** from the Forms panel, dBASE IV displays the forms design screen with the Layout menu pulled down, as in Figure 8.1. (If you do not use a database file or view first, dBASE IV highlights Use different database file or view on the Layout menu instead, so you can choose the file on which you want the report to be based.)

Notice that the menu system is the same as the reports design screen's, except that there is no Bands menu. Bands are not needed to layout a screen form.

The Layout Menu

Note that in the illustration the message line for the Quick layout option says *arrange all fields in the current view vertically on the layout*, indicating that there is only one quick layout available, which is the same as the forms layout of the reports design screen.

The next two options, Box and Line, work just as they do in the reports design screen. If you select one of these, dBASE IV displays the same submenu, letting you select single-line, double-line, or a specified character, and then lets you draw a box or line by using the cursor keys, just as when you create reports.

The next three options also work in familiar ways. If you select **Use a different database file or view**, dBASE IV displays a picklist of available databases and views for you to choose from. If you select **Edit description of**

form, dBASE IV lets you enter a new description or edit the current description of the form. If you select **Save this form**, dBASE IV prompts you to enter the name that the form should be saved as.

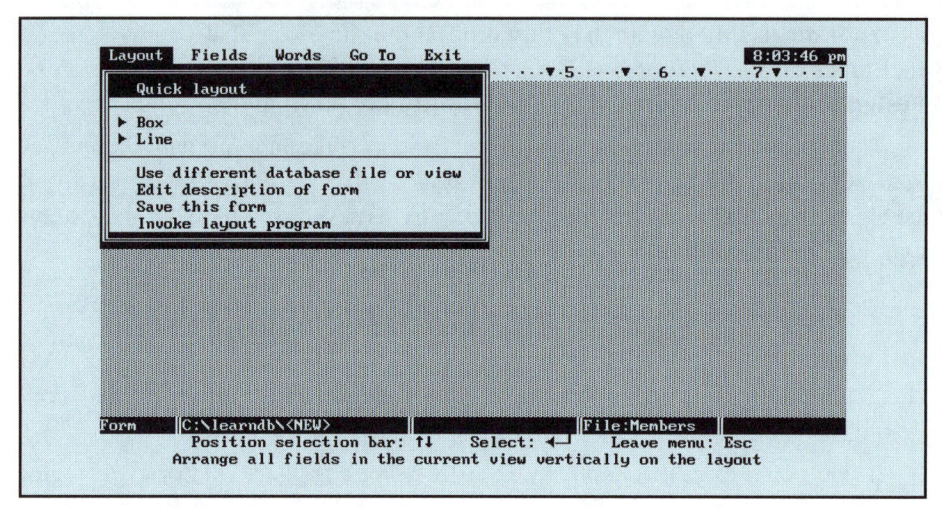

Figure 8.1   The initial Forms Design screen and Layout menu.

The Fields Menu

The Fields menu, shown in Figure 8.2, lets you add, remove, or modify a field, like the Fields menu of the Reports Design screen. If you select **Add field**, dBASE IV displays a field list, as shown in Figure 8.3, which lets you add a field from the database file (or view) on which the report is based or lets you add a calculated field. If you select **Modify field** or **Remove field**, dBASE IV lets you modify or remove the field that is currently highlighted. If no field is highlighted, it displays a list of fields for you to choose from.

As with the reports design screen, you can also add a field by moving the cursor to where you want the field to be placed and pressing **Field:F5**, remove a field by highlighting it and pressing **Del**, and modify a field by highlighting it pressing **Field:F5**.

The Fields menu also has an Insert memory variable option. Memory variables are discussed in Part 3 of this book.

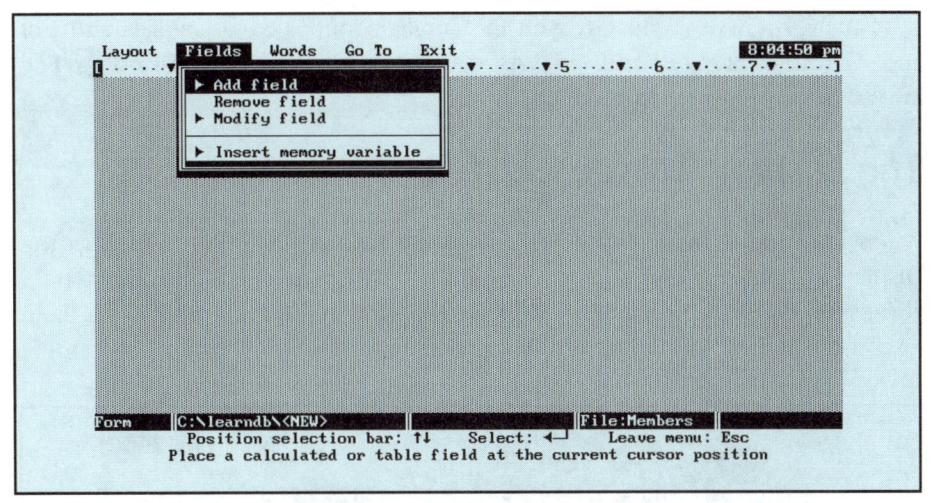

Figure 8.2   The Fields menu.

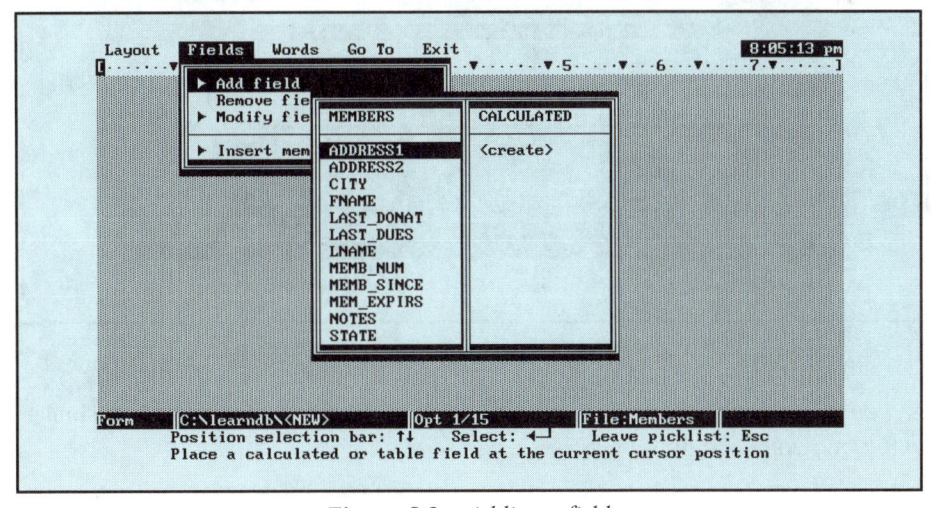

Figure 8.3   Adding a field.

Other Features of the Menu System

The next two menus are the Words and Go To menus, the menus for the word processor, which are included in many other screens. These menus are covered in Chapter 9, and they are not really needed for the small amount of text that you type on a data entry form.

Finally, the Exit menu give you the familiar options Save changes and exit and Abandon changes and exit. As usual, you can press **Ctrl-End** or **Esc** instead of using these menu options.

The Display Attributes Menu

When you add a field to the Forms Design screen, dBASE IV displays the Display attributes menu, shown in figure 8.4. If you are modifying a field already on the screen, dBASE IV displays the same menu, but without the help text, just as it does in the Reports Design screen.

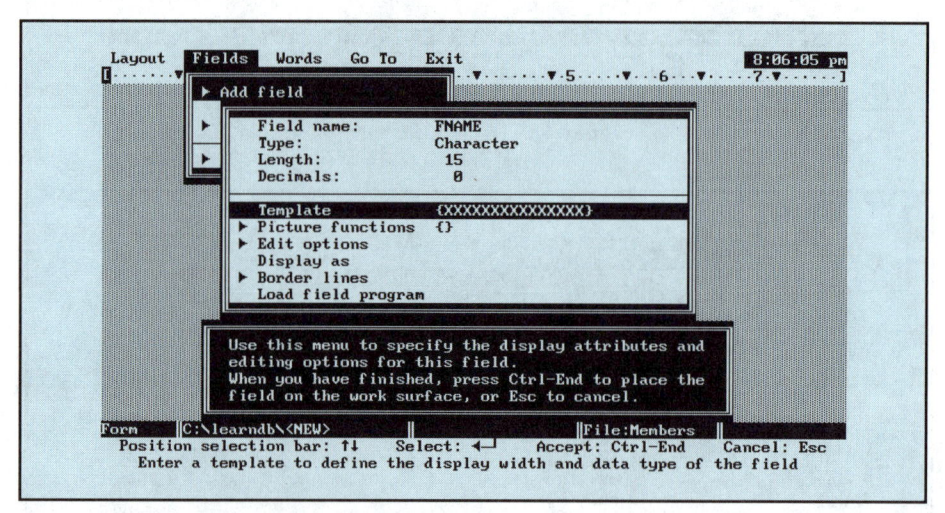

Figure 8.4   *The Display Attributes menu.*

As you can see, this menu lets you use templates and picture functions, similar to the one you used in the reports design screen.

It also has choices for Edit options, a very powerful feature that gives you added control over the data that is entered. The options Display as and Border lines are used only for memo fields and are dimmed on the menu for other fields.

Templates are used to control the data on a character-by-character basis, and picture functions are used to control the entire field, just as they are used in reports.

Custom data entry forms are used both for adding new data to the database and for viewing and editing data that is already in the database, so templates and picture functions can be used to control the way that existing data is displayed as well as to control what new data may be entered.

Templates

If you select **Template** from the Display attributes menu for characters fields, you can use templates with the symbols shown in Figure 8.5.

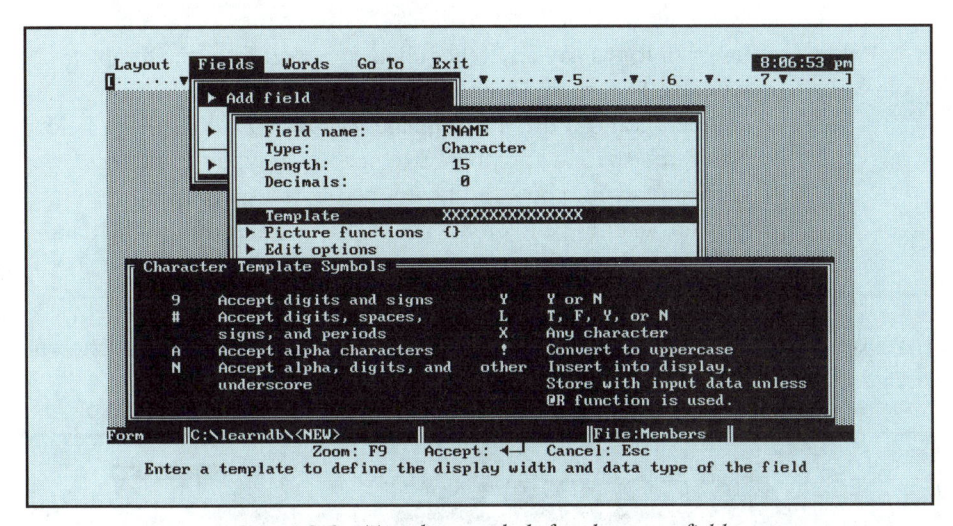

Figure 8.5 Template symbols for character fields.

Notice that all of the symbols except the last two determine what sorts of characters dBASE accept. For example, if you use the template symbol 9, dBASE only accepts numbers—more precisely, digits or the plus or minus sign—for that character. If you try to enter anything else, it beeps and refuses to move the cursor to the next field. Thus, you can use the template 99999 for the ZIP field, since it is a character field that must be made up of five digits.

The uses of the character template symbols to restrict data entry is fairly clear.

Table 8.1 Character template symbols for character data.

9 or #	Allows numbers to be entered. Nine accepts only digits and the plus or minus sign. # also accepts spaces and periods.
A	Allows only letters to be entered.
N	Allows letters, numbers, and the underscore to be entered, but does not allow special characters such as & or @.

Y or L   Allows logical values to be entered. Y lets the user enter only Y or N. L lets the user enter T, F, Y, or N. In either case, the letters entered may be small or capital.

X   Allows any character to be entered.

!   Converts letters to upper case. This symbol lets you enter any character, and if the character is alphabetic, it capitalizes it (if it is not already capitalized).

Other   Inserts into display any other character apart from the template symbols. For example, if you have a field for Social Security number, you can use the template 999-99-9999 to display a field with three spaces, a hyphen, two spaces, a hyphen, and four spaces. Only numbers can be entered in the spaces, and the hyphens cannot be altered. (The hyphens are stored in the database file unless you use the picture function R, described below.)

The Display attributes menu for numeric fields lets you use the templates shown in Figure 8.6

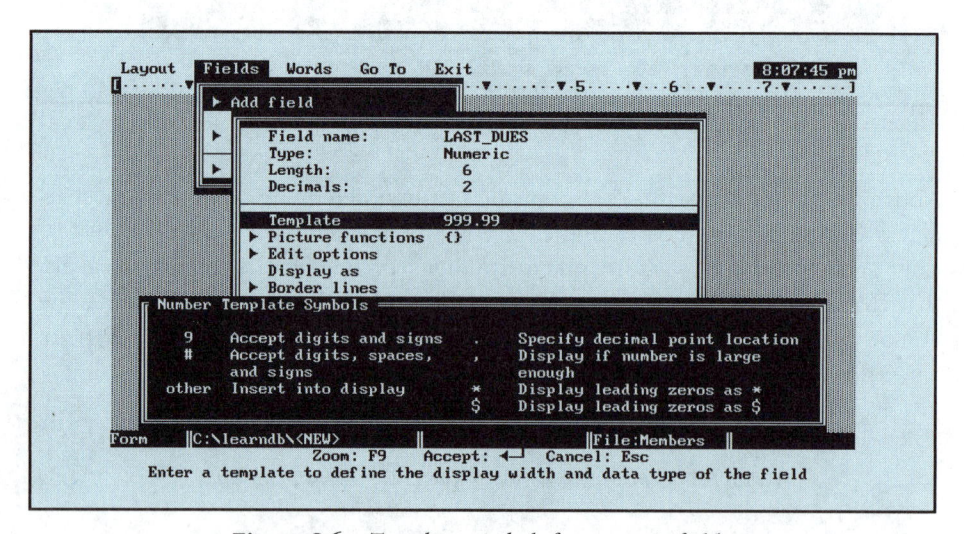

Figure 8.6   *Template symbols for numeric fields.*

Notice that the symbols * and $ control the way that numbers are displayed. They pad out the display with the symbol * and $ instead of leading blanks, just as they do in reports.

The symbols used to control the data entered in numeric fields are the same as some of those used for character fields. Nine lets the user enter only digits or signs, # lets the user enter digits, signs, spaces, and periods, and other characters are inserted in the display.

In addition, you can use the template to indicate the position of the decimal point.

Note that apart from the decimal point, other characters inserted in the display are not stored in the database file, as they are with character fields. Numeric fields cannot store characters.

NOTE

The Display attributes menu for logical fields lets you use the template symbols shown in Figure 8.7. These are the same as some of the symbols used in the character fields. L lets the user enter T, F, Y, or N and is the default for logical fields. Y lets the user enter only Y or N. Other characters are inserted literally in the display.

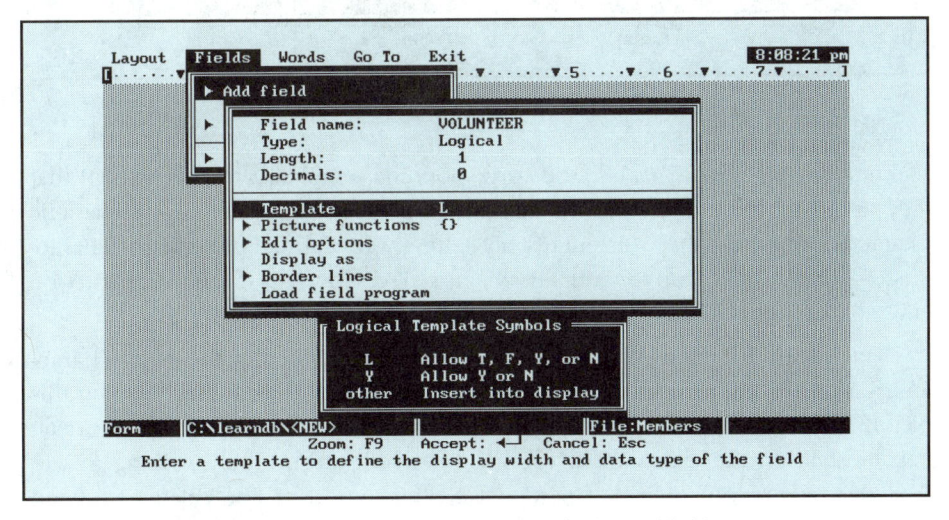

Figure 8.7 Template symbols for logical fields.

Date fields use the Template MM/DD/YY and memo fields use the template MEMO. Neither of these can be altered by using the Display attributes menu.

Picture Functions

Picture functions are used in forms, as they are in reports, to control the entire field, unlike templates, which control only one character at a time.

The Picture functions menu for character fields is shown in Figure 8.8. Only the functions that are relevant to designing forms are described here.

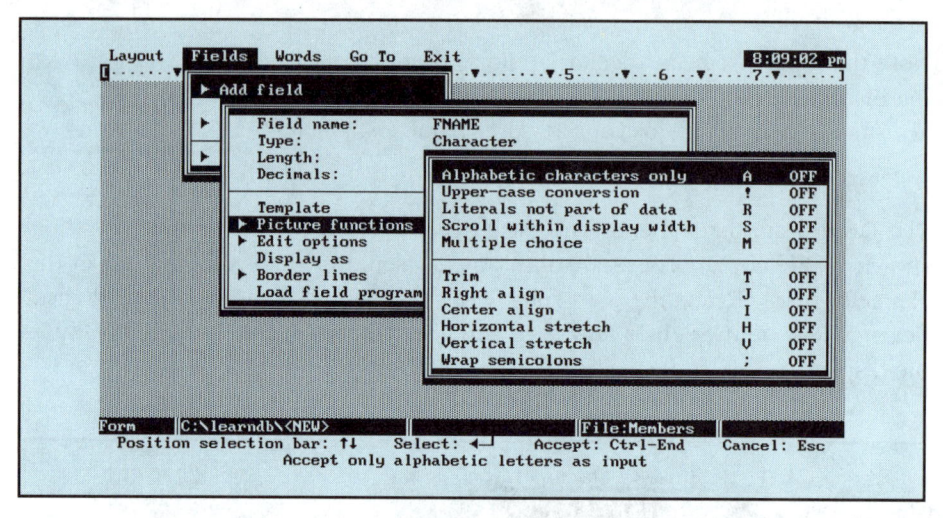

Figure 8.8 *Picture functions for character fields.*

The first two options work like the corresponding template symbols, except that they apply to the entire field rather than to a single character. A—Alphabetic Characters only lets the user enter only letters, not numbers or special characters. !—Upper-case conversion allows upper or lowercase characters to be entered but automatically capitalizes all letters.

The option R Literals not part of data determines whether the other characters, such as hyphens, used in templates are saved in the database. Turning this picture function ON makes you do extra work. Later, when you use the data, you must insert the character. It used to be worth the trouble of doing this to save disk space, but now that hard disks offer abundant and relatively cheap storage, this option is rarely used.

The picture function S—Scroll within display width is useful if you do not have enough room on the screen to hold certain fields but you still want the user to be able to enter data that is the full width of the field. When you select this function to toggle it on, dBASE IV prompts you to enter a scroll width. As long as the function is on, it displays the field with just the width you entered, but the user can still enter data that is the full width of the template. The data scrolls within the width you entered as you move the cursor, so it can all be edited or seen. Thus, you can leave the template its full width and select this option to crowd fields onto the screen without limiting the amount of data that can be entered or edited.

The picture function M—Multiple Choice offers one of the best ways of ensuring that only valid data is entered—you can restrict the user to a list of predefined multiple choice entries. If you select this option, dBASE IV prompts you to enter a string containing the choices. Enter the list of choices separated by commas. When choices are entered, the option automatically toggles on. If the multiple choices are deleted, it toggles off. Then, the user can press the **Spacebar** to cycle among the choices that you allowed. You will use this feature when you create your own custom form later in this chapter.

Figure 8.9 shows the picture functions available for numeric fields.

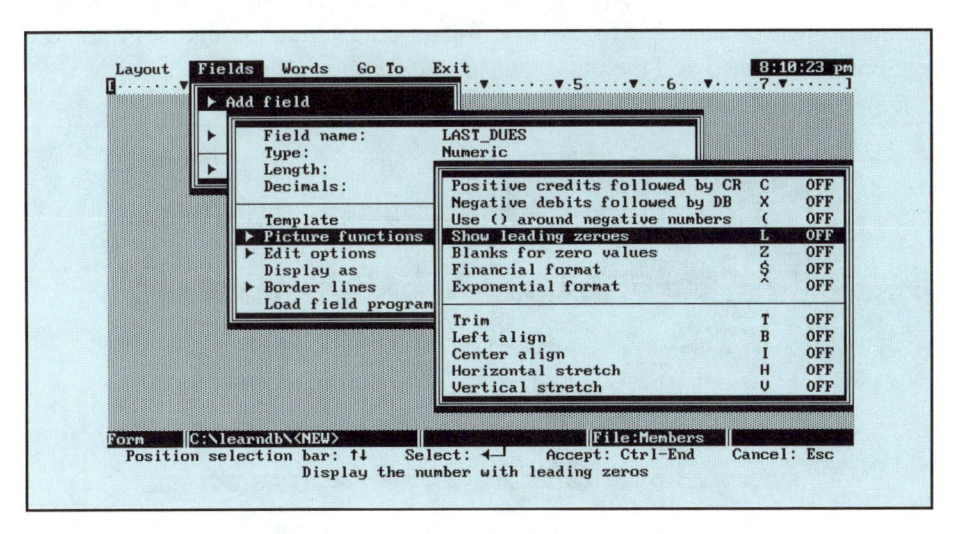

Figure 8.9   *Picture functions for numeric fields.*

Those that are used with forms control the way that existing data is displayed rather than validating data as it is entered, and they work in forms as they do in reports. Only the functions relevant to data entry forms are discussed here.

Table 8.2   *Picture functions for numeric data.*

L	Show leading zeroes	Displays leading zeroes instead of leading blanks, if the number does not fill the entire width of the field.
Z	Blanks for zero values	Displays a blank field instead of displaying a zero in the field if the value is zero.
F	Financial format	Displays a dollar sign (or other currency sign) before the value.
^	Exponential format	Displays the value in exponential (or scientific) notation, as a number times a power of 10.

Picture functions are not available for date, logical, or memo fields.

Edit Options

Edit options are a very powerful feature of dBASE IV. The same Edit options menu, shown in Figure 8.10, is used for all data types, though some of the options are dimmed and therefore unavailable for memo fields.

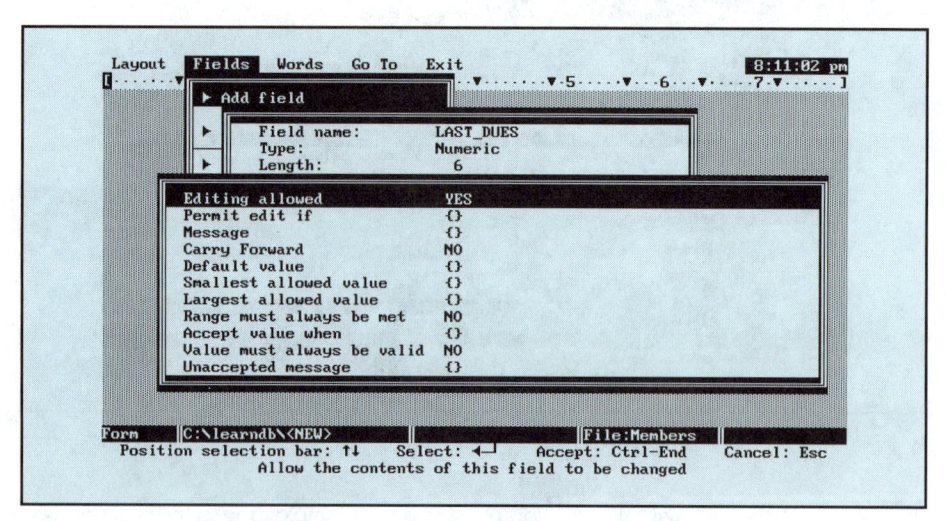

Figure 8.10   *The Edit Options menu.*

Select **Editing allowed** to toggle to NO to make it impossible for the user to change the data currently in the field or to enter data in this in appended records. The data in the field is dimmed when you use the form, to show that it is inaccessible.

Select **Permit edit** if to enter an expression to determine whether editing the field is allowed. You must enter a logical expression when you use this option: (expressions are discussed thoroughly in Chapter 11). For example, if you select **Permit edit if** for the City field and enter the expression STATE="CA", the user will be able to edit city names only if the state is California. If the member is from another state, the cursor skips the CITY field. If you are appending records, you will not be able to type in the CITY until after you have typed CA into the STATE field, and so in this example the records should be arranged on the form with STATE before CITY.

Select **Message** to enter a help message line that is displayed at the bottom of the screen when the user moves the cursor to the specified field.

Select **Carry forward** to make the data entered in this field in one record (when you are adding new records) appears as its default value in the following record. This default value can be edited or can be accepted by pressing **Enter**. For example, if new memberships come in by state—a list from California, a list from New York, and so on—you can toggle Carry forward to YES for the STATE field. Then you only need to type in the state name for the first entry from each state and you can press **Enter** to confirm that state name for the rest of the members from the state.

Select **Default value** to enter a value that always appears in the field initially when you are adding new records. For example, if most of the new members of your organization are from California, you can enter CA as the default value for the STATE field. Then, when you enter new records, you can just press **Enter** to confirm this value for most members. When you want to enter a member from another state, you can type over the default CA in the STATE field.

Select **Smallest allowed value** or **Largest allowed value** to do the obvious—specify the maximum or minimum value that may be entered in the field. These options can be used with Character and Date fields as well as with Numeric fields. Select both of them to specify a range of values.

Two options that follow can be used in conjunction with each other. Select **Accept value when** to enter a logical expression that must be True for dBASE to permit you to enter a value. Select **Unaccepted message** to enter the error message that dBASE IV displays on the bottom line of the screen if you try to violate the specified condition.

Using Memo Fields in Forms

In addition to templates, picture functions, and edit options, the Display attributes menu has two options that are available only for Memo fields.

Select **Display as** to toggle between MARKER and WINDOW. By default, a memo field is displayed as a marker—the user sees only a small field with the work MEMO in it, as you do in the ordinary Browse or Edit screen. Instead, you can choose to use a window, which lets the user see some of the text that is in the memo field.

After you toggle this selection to WINDOW, dBASE IV places a large memo window in the center of the screen. To fit this window into the data entry form, you must do the following:

- **Resize the window.** Move the cursor to it if necessary. The entire window is highlighted when the cursor is on it. Then press **Size:Shift-F7**. The cursor moves to the lower-right corner of the window. Using the keyboard, you can make the window smaller by pressing the **Up Arrow** or **Left Arrow** (or other cursor movement keys), or make the window larger by pressing the **Down Arrow** or **Right Arrow** (or other cursor movement keys). Press **Enter** to stop resizing the window when you are done. Using the mouse, simply click at the location indicting the size.

- **Move the window to the proper location on the form.** Make sure the cursor is still on the window, and the window is still highlighted. Move the window by pressing **Move:F7**. The cursor moves to the upper-left corner of the window and you can now move the window simply by pressing the arrow keys or other cursor keys. When the window is positioned where you want, press **Enter** to stop the process.

If you are using a window for the memo field, you might also want to select **Border lines** from the field's Display attributes menu to select the type of line that is used as the window's border. dBASE IV displays the familiar submenu that you use when you draw boxes or lines, so you can choose to use a single line, a double line, or a specific character as the window's border.

The window displays whatever portion of the actual memo field happens to fit inside it: only this position of the memo can be viewed from the data entry form. To edit the memo field, you must use it in much the same way that you use any memo field. After you have moved the cursor to the window, press

Ctrl-Home to scroll within the window and edit the text in the memo field. As you do this, the rest of the record is still visible while you edit the memo. Alternately, you can press **Zoom:F9** to use the full-screen memo editor to view and edit the memo field. Using the mouse, simply double-click the window. In any case, press **Ctrl-End** when you are done editing the memo.

A Sample Form

Now, you can create a sample data entry form to make it easier for someone who knows nothing about dBASE IV to maintain the MEMBERS file. In the last section of this chapter, you use this form as the basis of a Quick Application, and in Chapter 14, you use the same form as part of a dBASE program.

Before creating the form, you must think about the intended user. The design may differ depending on whether the form is meant for an advanced dBASE user or a beginner. In particular, you should think about whether the form will include the status bar and the menu. The dBASE IV system menu might be extremely confusing to a beginner, for example.

If you are planning to use the form in a program, as you will see in Chapter 14, you can use the dBASE command SET STATUS OFF to get rid of the status bar. Unfortunately, there is no command to let the user add new records without having access to the menu.

Nevertheless, you can conceal the menu simply by creating some feature of the data entry form that is displayed over it, for example, a box that takes up the top line of the screen. The user can still access the menu in the usual way—for example, pressing **Alt-E** still pulls down the Exit menu—but the menu bar is not visible at the top of the screen to confuse the user.

When you design the sample form, assume that the user is a beginner, so that the menu should be covered up in this way. You must also add messages telling the user to press Ctrl-U to save changes and exit, and to press PgUp and PgDn to move through the file. Assuming that the user already knows the use of the Arrow keys and the basic editing keys such as Del and Ins, this help is enough to perform simple data entry.

If you let the user delete and undelete records by pressing Ctrl-U, you may want to leave the status bar ON so that the user knows whether the record is already marked for deletion.

When you design the form, then, you do not leave the top line blank for the menu, but leave space to allow for the status bar.

1. Begin from the Control Center with the MEMBERS file in use. Then select **<create>** from the Forms panel to use the forms design screen.

2. The Layout menu should already be pulled down. Select **Quick layout**. dBASE IV displays the initial layout, shown in Figure 8.11, with all of the fields of the database and their names one above the other on the screen.

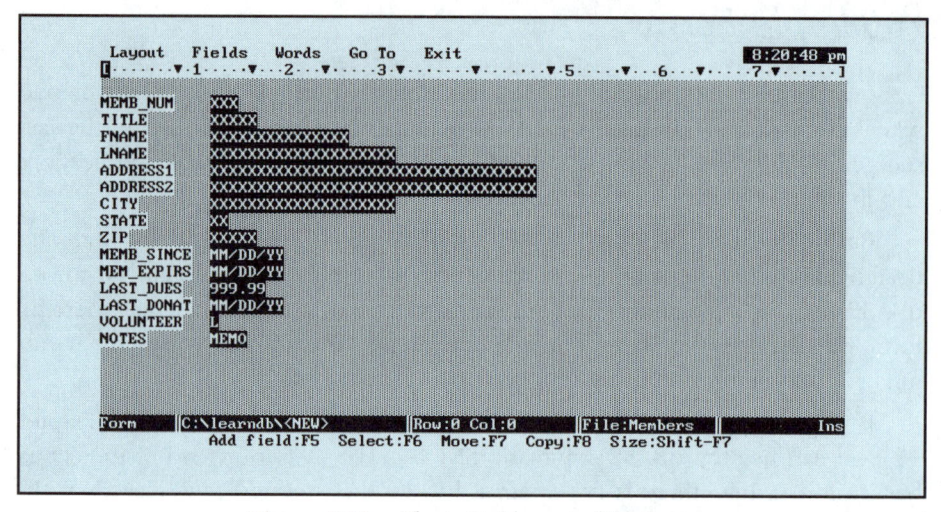

Figure 8.11   *The initial layout of the form.*

3. Begin by changing the names of fields, where necessary. Edit the field name MEMB_NUM so it reads MEMBER NUMBER, and press the **Spacebar** three times to add three spaces between it and the field space.

4. Edit FNAME so that it reads FIRST NAME. Leave the template in place, lined up with the other field templates, rather than adding spaces.

5. Edit LNAME so that it reads LAST NAME.

6. Edit ADDRESS1 so it reads ADDRESS. Delete the name ADDRESS2 (but not the template for this field).

7. The field templates following the address remain lined up in the final form, so you must add extra spaces before some of their names. First go down and edit MEM_EXPIRS so it reads MEMBERSHIP EXPIRES and add three spaces between it and the template.

8. Now, move the cursor back up to the line with MEMB_SINCE, edit it so that it reads MEMBER SINCE, and add nine spaces before the template that it is lined up above the template for MEMBERSHIP EXPIRES.

9. Then edit LAST_DUES so it reads LAST DUES and add twelve spaces to line its template up.
10. Edit LAST_DONAT so it LAST DONATION and add eight spaces to line up its template.
11. Finally, edit VOLUNTEER so it reads VOLUNTEER (Y/N) and add six spaces to line up its template.
12. Now you can move the field names and templates to the position where you want them on the screen. First press **PgUp** to move to the first line and press **Ctrl-N** twice to move all of the field names and templates down two lines.
13. Then move the cursor to the first letter of TITLE. Press **Select:F6**. Press **End** to select the entire line, and press **Enter** to complete the selection.
14. Then press **Move:F7**. Use the Arrow keys (or the mouse) to move the selected text and field up a row and to move it to the right until there are only three spaces between the right edge of the template and the right edge of the screen. The status line should say the cursor is a Row:3, Col: 60. Press **Enter**. Note that, when you select it in this way, dBASE IV includes a blank space to the right of the template. If this space makes you line it up improperly, press **Move:F7** again and line it up with three spaces between the right edge of the screen and the final X of the template.
15. Finally, select just the word **TITLE** and move it right so there are only three spaces between it and the template. Since it covers part of its previous location, dBASE asks you to confirm that you want to delete covered text and fields. Press *Y.*
16. Select and move the LAST NAME field name and template in the same way, so they are to the right of the FIRST NAME field. Move it far enough right so that the final X of the template is also three spaces away from the right edge of the screen. The cursor should be at Row:5, Col:45.
17. To fit both address fields on one line, you must alter their display width. Do this using the picture function S Scroll within display width, so the user can still enter, edit, or view data that is the full width of the field. Put the cursor on the first address field template and press **Field:F5**.
18. Select **Picture functions** from the Display attributes menu and select **S Scroll within display width** from the submenu. When dBASE IV

prompts you to enter the scroll width, enter *30*. Then press **Ctrl-End** twice to return to the Forms Design screen, and note the template for the first address field is now displayed as only thirty Xs.

19. Now, do exactly the same to the second address field template to make it five characters shorter also. Select the template of the second ADDRESS field, move it up one line, and line it up also so there are three spaces between it and the right edge of the screen. The cursor should be at Row:7, Col:47.

20. Now, move the STATE and ZIP fields so they are on the same line as the CITY field. First, select the STATE field name and template and move them to the right of the CITY field, so the S of STATE is lined up under the L of LAST NAME. Then select just the template of this field and move it so there are only three spaces between it and the field name.

21. Now, select the ZIP field name and template. Move them up two lines and far enough right that the right edge of the template is line up under the right edge of the name and address templates; the cursor should be at Row:9, Col:60. Then select just the field name ZIP and move it right until only three spaces are left between it and the template.

22. Finally, you can delete one of the two lines you just left blank. Press the **Down Arrow** to move the cursor down a row, and then press **Ctrl-Y** to delete the blank line. The locations of the fields at this point is shown if Figure 8.12.

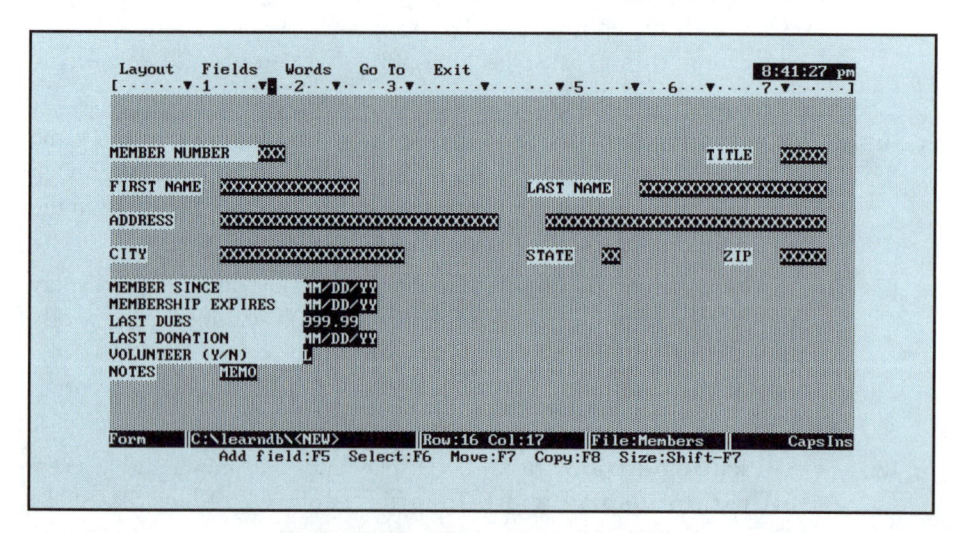

Figure 8.12   *The location of the fields.*

Chapter 8: Forms and Quick Applications ◆ **227**

23. Now you can create a window for the NOTES field. Move the cursor to the MEMO template, then press **Field:F5**.

24. Select **Display as** from the Display attributes menu to toggle to WINDOW, and press **Ctrl-End**. dBASE IV places a large window in the center of the screen. Move the cursor to highlight this window. Then press **Size:Shift-F7** to resize the window. Press the **Up Arrow** until the window has only two rows of Xs in it, and press the **Left Arrow** to move the cursor until it is only twenty Xs across, the cursor should be at Row:4, Col:35. Press **Enter** to accept that size.

25. Press **Move:F7**, and use the Arrow keys to move the window until its upper edge is on the same line as the NOTES field name and its right edge is lined up under the right edge of the field template above it. Then press **Enter**.

26. Now, select the field name NOTES and move it down one line. The final location of the field name and memo window is shown in Figure 8.13.

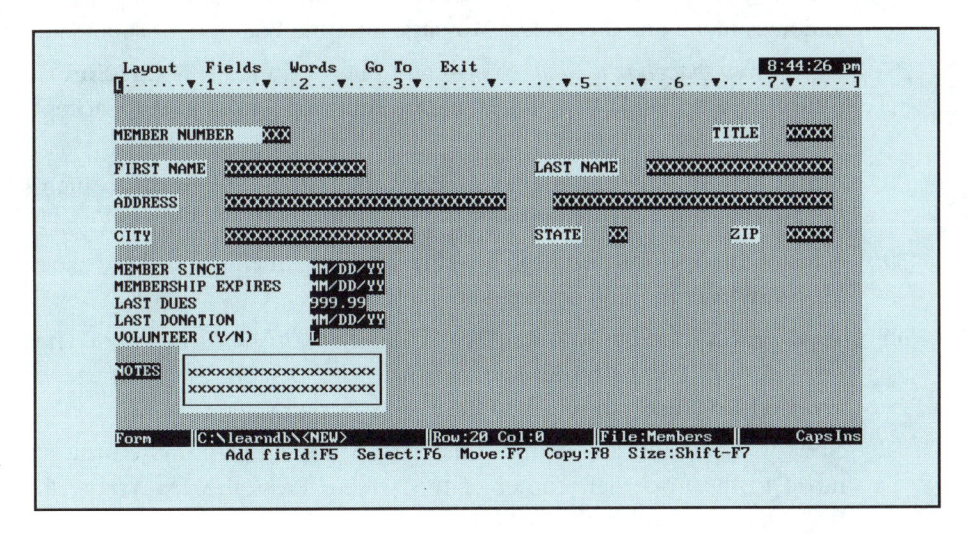

Figure 8.13 *The Memo window placed on the form.*

27. Now, you can alter the display attributes of fields where it is necessary. First, change the template of the MEMBER NUMBER field in order to validate the data. Move the cursor to that field template. Press **Field:F5**.

28. Select **Template** from the Display attributes menu. Edit the template so it reads !99, and press **Enter**. Then press **Ctrl-End**.

29. Add a picture function to the State field, to make sure it is properly capitalized. Move the cursor to that field template. Press **Field:F5**.
30. Select **Picture functions** from the Display attributes menu.
31. Select **! Upper-case conversion** from the Picture functions submenu, and press **Ctrl-End** to accept it. Press **Ctrl-End** again to accept the Display attributes menu. (Of course, you could have used the template !! instead to do the same thing as this Picture function.)
32. Make the TITLE field multiple choice, since the word TITLE by itself might confuse users. Move the cursor to this field. Press **Field:F5**.
33. Select **Picture functions** from the Display attributes menu.
34. Select **Multiple choice** from the submenu. When dBASE prompts you to enter the choices, type *Mr., Ms., Mrs., Miss, Dr., Prof.* and press **Enter**.
35. Press **Ctrl-End** to return to the **Display attributes** menu.
36. You should also add a help line for this field, so the user knows how to use the multiple choice feature. Select **Edit options** from the Display attributes menu and then select **Message** from the Edit options submenu.
37. Type *Press spacebar to view choices* and press **Enter**. Press **Ctrl-End** to return to the Display attributes menu and **Ctrl-End** again to accept these attributes.
38. Add a help line for the memo window also. Move the cursor to highlight that window. Press **Field:F5**.
39. Select **Edit options** from the Display attributes menu and then select **Message** from the Edit options submenu.
40. Type *Press Ctrl-Home to edit, F9 to Zoom, and Ctrl-End when done* and press **Enter**. Press **Ctrl-End** to return to the Display attributes menu and **Ctrl-End** again to return to the Forms Design screen.
41. Now, you can add a heading to the screen. Press **PgUp** and **Home** to move to the upper-left corner of the screen. Press the **Up Arrow** to make sure you are on the first line.
42. Select **Box** from the Layout menu, and select **Double line** from the submenu. Press **Enter** to position the upper-left corner of the box.
43. Press the **Down Arrow** twice and press right arrow until the right edge of the box is lined up above the right edge of the field templates; the cursor should be at Row:2, Col:76; press **Enter** to complete the box. (With a mouse, you could also click and drag to create this box.)

44. Now, move the cursor to Row 1, Col 24 and type *Edit the MEMBERS database file*.

45. Finally, you can add help text, with the basics of how to use this screen. Move the cursor to Row 11, Col 38. Select **Box** from the Layout menu and select **Double line** from the submenu. Press **Enter** to start drawing. Move the cursor to Row 19, Col 76 and press **Enter** to complete the box.

46. Now, move the cursor to Row 13, Col 42 and type *PgUp/PgDn: Previous/Next Record*.

47. Move the cursor to Row 15, Col 46 and type *Ctrl-U: Delete/Undelete*.

48. Move the cursor to Row 17, Col 42 and type *Ctrl-End: Save Changes and Exit*. The final layout of the data entry form is shown is Figure 8.14.

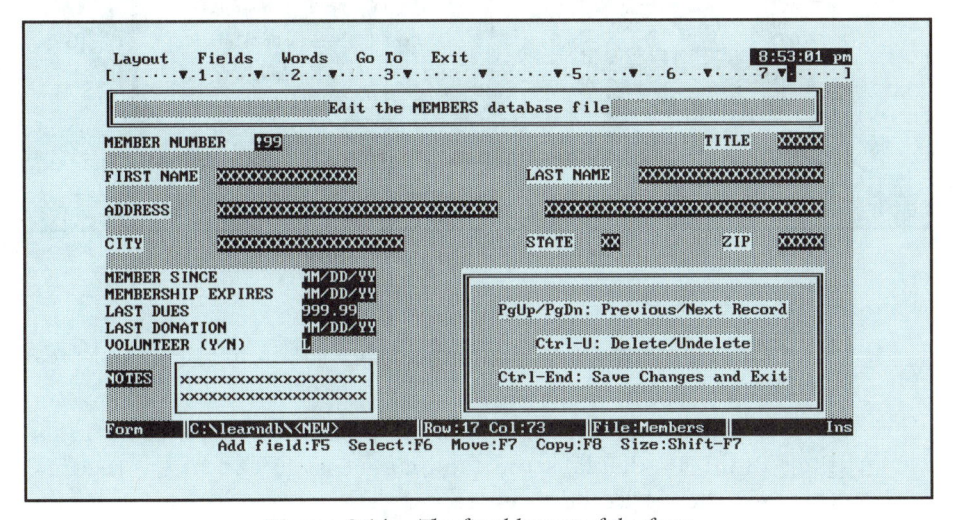

Figure 8.14 *The final layout of the form.*

49. Select **Edit description of form** from the Layout menu.

50. Type *Enter or edit data for all fields of the MEMBERS file* and press **Enter**. Then press **Ctrl-End** to save the form. When dBASE IV prompts you to enter its name, type *membform* and press **Enter**. After taking a moment to generate and compile the program for this form, dBASE returns you to the Control Center.

51. The new form is already highlighted. To test it, press **Data:F2**. The current record in the file is displayed. If necessary, press **PgUp** until Member A01 is displayed.

52. Move the cursor to the first address field. Note that the entire address is too wide to be displayed in the field, but that you can scroll to view it all.

53. Move the cursor to the memo window, and notice that the help line that you entered is displayed at the bottom of the screen, as in Figure 8.15.

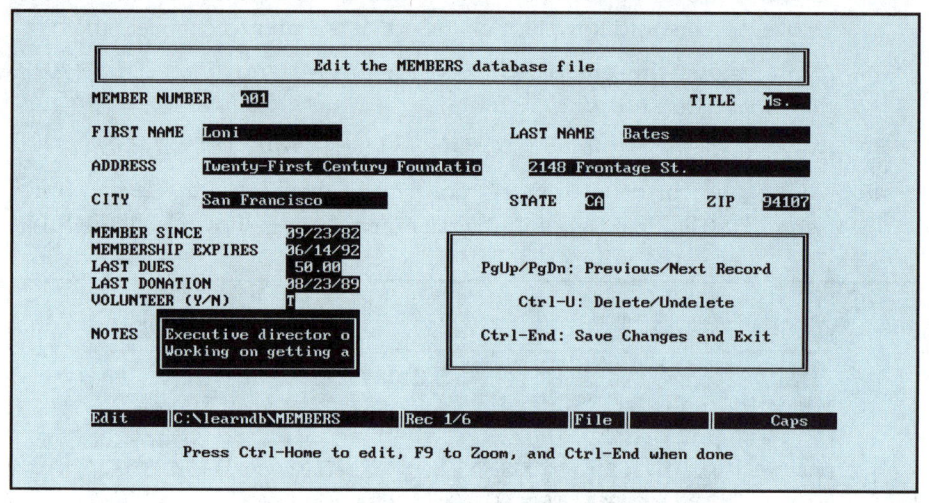

Figure 8.15 *Using the new data entry form.*

54. Press **Ctrl-Home**, try scrolling through the data in the field, and press **Ctrl-End** when you are done.

55. Press **PgDn** repeatedly. When you get beyond the final record in the file, dBASE IV displays the familiar message. Add new records? (Yes/No). Press *Y* to add a new record.

56. Try adding data to test the features of the various fields: for example, try entering all letters in the MEMBER NUMBER field—dBASE IV just beeps.

57. Enter a valid member number and move to the TITLE field—note the help line and press **Spacebar** to cycle through the choices you entered.

58. Then move the cursor to the STATE field and try entering small letters. Note that they are automatically capitalized.

59. When you are done testing the features of this form, press **Esc** to return to the Control Center without saving this new record.

Quick Applications

Now that you have created a data entry form to make it easier for an inexperienced data entry person to work with the database, it's not difficult to use the applications generator to create an entire menu-driven application. Generating a quick application is simple, but the applications generator has some advanced features that can be complex. In some cases, it would be harder to generate an application than to write a program. Advanced features of the applications generator are not covered in this book.

To generate a quick application, you first select **<create>** from the Applications panel of the Control Center. A prompt box gives you the option of writing a program or generating an application.

After you select **Applications generator** from the prompt box, dBASE IV displays the Application definition form shown in Figure 8.16.

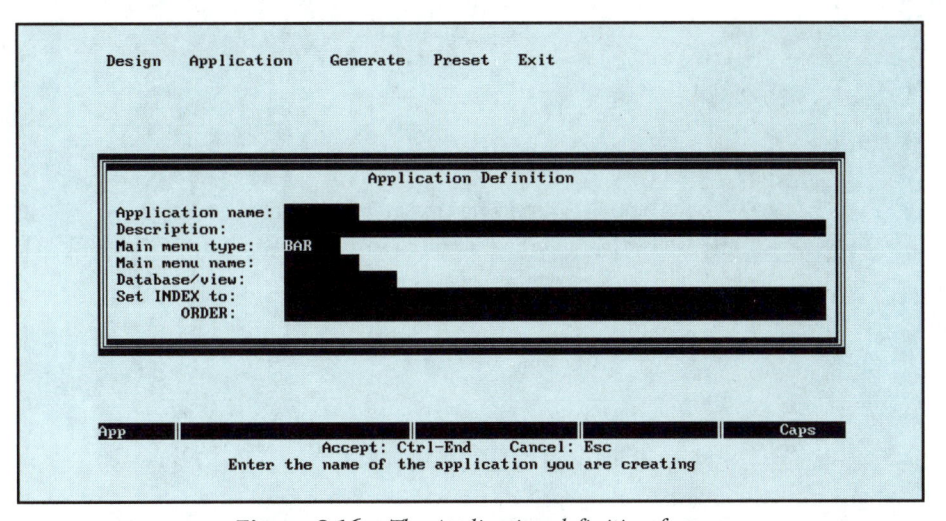

Figure 8.16 *The Application definition form.*

Before going on to use the menu system, fill out the form with the following data:

- **Application name:** The name of the application, which is displayed in the Applications panel of the Control Center.
- **Description:** A description that is displayed when the file name is highlighted (also included as a note in the generated code).

- **Main menu type:** The type of menu for the application. Press the **Spacebar** to cycle among BAR (a light-bar menu), POP-UP (pop-up menus like those used in dBASE IV itself), and BATCH (an advanced option that lets you create a batch process for the menu).
- **Main menu name:** A name for the main menu.
- **Database/view:** The database file or view that will be used in the application.
- **Set INDEX to:** The index file that will be used in the application.
- **ORDER:** The controlling index that determines the order of the records.

After you have filled out this form, press **Ctrl-End**. dBASE IV displays an application object that you may use as a sign-on banner (to display the program name and perhaps your name and copyright before the program begins) shown in Figure 8.17.

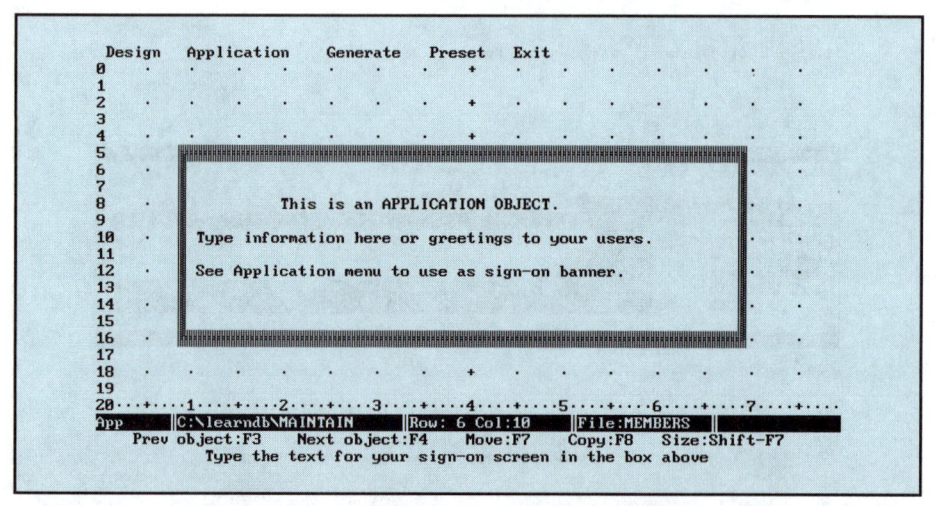

Figure 8.17 The initial Applications design screen.

You may simply ignore the applications design screen, though, and select **Generate quick application** from the **Applications** menu to display the form shown in Figure 8.18.

This form has already been filled out with the application, database file, and index names that you entered when you began. You can also fill in the names of all of the forms you might use: a screen format, report format, and label format files (or press **Pick:Shift-F1** to select from a pick list of available objects). When you press **Ctrl-End** to indicate that you have finished filling out the form, dBASE IV generates the program code necessary for the application. That's all you need to do to create a quick application.

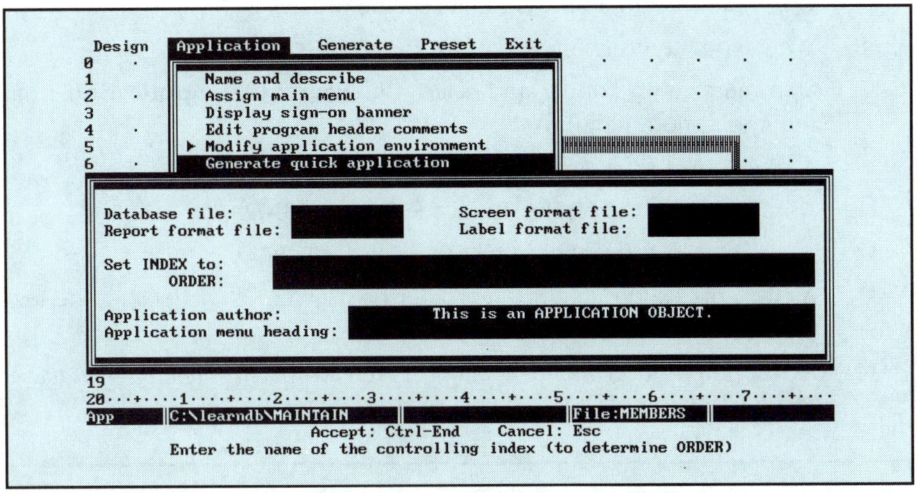

Figure 8.18   *Generating a quick application.*

Once you have created the quick application, you an use it or modify it by selecting its name from Applications panel of the Control Center. When you select the application's name, dBASE IV displays a prompt box with the options Run application and Modify application. You may also modify the application's design by highlighting its name and pressing **Design Shift-F2**.

Try creating a quick application that uses the data entry form you have already designed.

1. Beginning from the Control Center, select **<create>** from the Applications panel. Then select **Applications generator** from the prompt box.
2. The Application definition form is displayed. As the application name, enter *MAINTAIN*.
3. As the description, enter *General purpose quick application to maintain MEMBERS file*.
4. Leave the Main menu type as BAR.

5. At the Database/view, enter MEMBERS.
6. At Set INDEX to, enter MEMBERS.
7. At ORDER, enter NAMES. (Remember that the actual name of the production .MDX file is the same as the name of the database file—NAMES is the name of the index tag that sets the order.)
8. When you are done filling out this form, press **Ctrl-End**.
9. Skip the sign-on banner and select **Generate quick application** from the Application menu.
10. As the name of the screen format file, enter *MEMBFORM*.
11. As the name of the report format file, enter *STANDARD*.
12. As the name of the label format file, enter *TWO-COL*.
13. As the application author, enter your own name (after deleting the text already on that line, if necessary).
14. As the application menu heading, enter *Maintain Members Database*. The final form is shown in Figure 8.19.

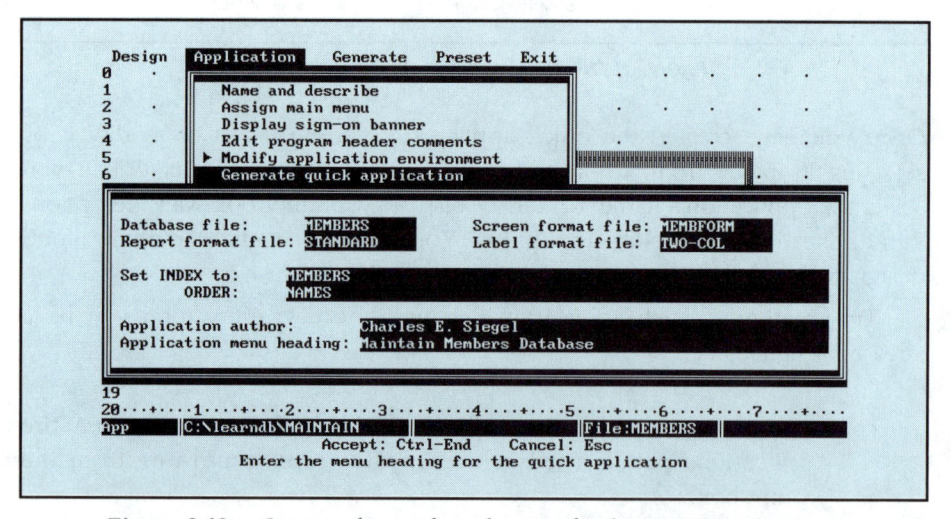

Figure 8.19 *Creating the quick application for the MEMBERS database.*

15. Press **Ctrl-End**, and then press *Y* to confirm. Wait while the program is being generated. When you are prompted, press any key to return to the applications generator menu system. Press **Esc** to remove the menu, and then press **Ctrl-End** to return to the Control Center.

16. To test the new application, select **MAINTAIN** from the Applications panel. Then select **Run application** from the prompt box and press Y to confirm that you want to run the application. dBASE IV displays the menu shown in Figure 8.20.

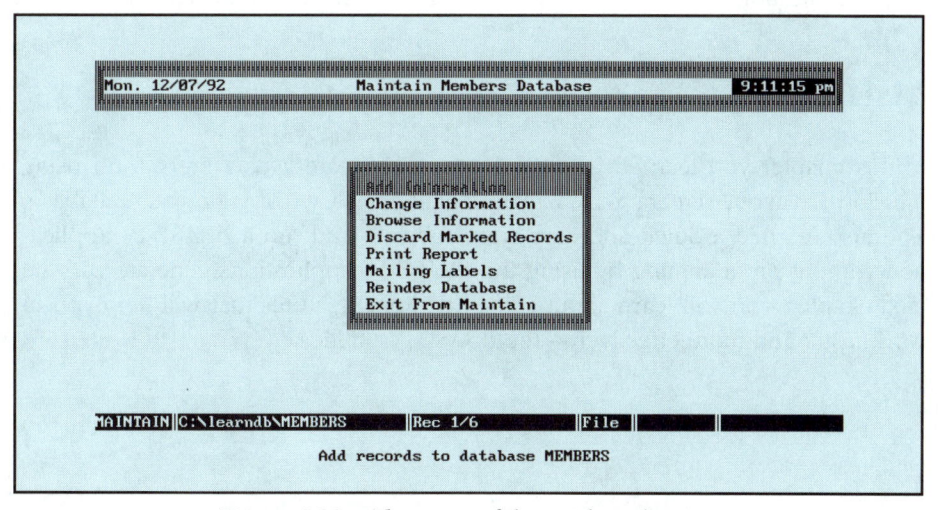

Figure 8.20 The menu of the quick application.

17. Move the light bar through the menu choices and notice the help line at the bottom of the screen. The menu options are self-explanatory. Select **Change Information** from this light bar menu to edit the database file using the MEMBFORM data entry form. Try paging through the records and tabbing through the fields of the data entry form, and test it in any you want. Press **Esc** to return to the light bar menu when you are done.

18. Select any other options from this menu to test any feature of the quick application that interest you. When you are done, select **Exit from Maintain** from the light bar menu to return to the Control Center.

You probably have noticed that quick applications have their limitations. You can use only one report form and one label form, for example. Because you can use only a single index to order the records, you can use the records in alphabetical order but cannot print labels in zip code order or print your grouped report, which requires indexing in order of state and name.

When you learn programming, you might want to try modifying the programs created by the applications generator to get around some of these limitations. It is very easy, for example, to change index order before printing reports or labels and to change it back afterwards. And even without programming, quick applications are adequate for many simple tasks of file maintenance.

Summary

In this chapter you learned how to design and create a data entry form using the Forms Layout screen, which makes it easier to work with your database. You also learned a quick and easy way to create and run a dBASE IV application without programming by using the dBASE IV applications generator. In the next chapter, you will learn about some additional features that will help you to work faster and more effectively—the dBASE IV utilities.

Chapter 9

Utilities

This chapter covers the dBASE IV utilities—features of the program that are not essential to its main function of managing data, but that give you extra power and ease of use.

In this chapter, you learn about the following dBASE IV utilities:

◆ The word processor, which has been mentioned frequently throughout this book

◆ The Print menu and its many options for printing quick reports, previewing reports on screen, and controlling the printed appearance of a document

◆ The various options of the Tools menu including options for macro creation, import and export of data, dBASE IV environment settings, and a menu-driven DOS shell that you can use to perform many DOS commands

The Word Processor

You already worked with the dBASE IV word processor when you edited memo fields and when you used the Labels Design screen, the Reports Design screen, and the Forms Design screen. It is also used in the Macro Editor and the Text file editor, which you will look at later in this chapter, and in the program editor, which you will use beginning in Chapter 13. There are minor differences among these implementations of the word processor. The version of the word processor used for labels, nonword wrap bands of reports, and forms is sometimes called the *layout editor* because it is used to layout the design of a screen as well as to edit text. The version of the word processor used for editing programs, memo fields, word-wrap bands of reports, and macros is sometimes called the *program editor*. It is exclusively a text editor. This chapter, however, covers the word processor in a way that lets you use all of its implementations.

Note also that when you edit memo fields, word-wrap bands of reports, or macros, the word processor is in word wrap mode; when it reaches the right margin, the text automatically continues on the next line, like an ordinary word processor. Other versions of the word processor do not need word wrap. You obviously do not want word wrap on data entry forms or mailing labels, for example, and you will see in Chapter 13 that word wrap would interfere with editing programs.

In the past, you used just the most basic features of the word processor: the basic cursor movement keys and the essential features of the Print menu.

The word processor also lets you use other editing keys for more power and includes the Go To menu, which lets you move the cursor to a specific word or phrase, and the Words menu, which lets you format the text and make other adjustments to the text.

For most uses—for example, for mailing labels and most memos and reports—you do not need all of the power of the word processor. Though you might find one of its features handy on occasion, you can get by with the basics that you learned in earlier chapters.

The features of the word processor covered in this chapter, however, are indispensable for editing form letters and are very useful for editing programs and for editing memo fields in applications that use them to store long documents.

You can skim through the descriptions of its features in this chapter and just learn only those features that you think you will need. Come back to this chapter later if you find that you have a practical use for other features of the word processor.

Editing Keys

In earlier chapters, you used some standard keys for editing, such as **Del** to delete a character. The editor includes a few extra editing keys: for example, **Ctrl-T** to delete from the position of the cursor to the end of the word.

It also lets you use alternative keys instead of the standard editing keys. For example, **Ctrl-G** instead of **Del** to delete the character the cursor is on. These alternative keys are based on the WordStar word processing program, and if you are familiar with WordStar, you will find them natural to use. Some people prefer them to the conventional editing keys, because you can use them without removing your hands from the main section of the keyboard.

All of the editing keys, including these alternatives, are listed in Table 9.1.

Table 9.1   *The editing keys.*

Home or **Ctrl-Z**	Moves the cursor to beginning of the current line
End or **Ctrl-B**	Moves the cursor to end of the current line
PgUp or **Ctrl-R**	Moves the cursor to top of the current screen or scrolls up a screen
PgDn or **Ctrl-C**	Moves the cursor to bottom of text on the current screen or scrolls down a screen
Ctrl-PgUp	Moves the cursor to the beginning of document
Ctrl-PgDn	Moves the cursor to the end of document
Right Arrow or **Ctrl-D**	Moves the cursor one character right
Left Arrow or **Ctrl-S**	Moves the cursor one character left
Up Arrow or **Ctrl-E**	Moves the cursor one line up
Down Arrow or **Ctrl-X**	Moves the cursor one line down
Ctrl-Right Arrow or **Ctrl-F**	Moves the cursor to the beginning of the next word
Ctrl-Left Arrow or **Ctrl-A**	Moves the cursor to the beginning of the last word
Insert or **Ctrl-V**	Toggles between insert and overwrite modes

Del or **Ctrl-G**	Deletes the character the cursor is on
Backspace or **Ctrl-H**	Deletes the character to the left of the cursor
Ctrl-Backspace	Deletes the word to the left of cursor—the whole word if cursor is to the right of the word, part of the word if the cursor is on the word
Ctrl-T	Deletes the from cursor position to the end of the word
Ctrl-Y	Deletes the current line
Ctrl-N	Inserts a new line
Tab or **Ctrl-I**	Moves the cursor to thenext tab stop
Enter	Ends the paragraph and moves the cursor to the next line (inserts a new line if in insert mode)
Ctrl-End or **Ctrl-W**	Saves changes and exits
Esc or **Ctrl-Q**	Abandons changes and exits

In addition to these editing keys, you can use the function keys to move and copy text. You have already learned about these keys when you were working with the labels, reports, and forms editor. They are summarized in Table 9.2.

Table 9.2 Use of the function keys for moving and copying text.

Select:F6	Select text
Move:F7	Move selected text
Copy:F8	Copy selected text

When you press **Select:F6**, dBASE IV prompts you to Complete selection with ENTER. Move the cursor until all of the text you want to select is highlighted and then press **Enter**. You can also select larger blocks of text by pressing **Select:F6** repeatedly. How much text is selected depends on which screen you are using.

As you know, you can also use the mouse to move the cursor or to select text. Simply click a location in the text to move the cursor there. Click and drag to select text. Pull the pointer beyond the bottom or the top of the screen to scroll.

To move or copy selected text, just move the cursor to where you want it to go and press **Move:F7** or **Copy:F8**.

You can also delete an entire block of text by selecting it, and then pressing **Del** (or **Ctrl-G**). dBASE IV asks for confirmation before deleting the block of text.

Finally, the dBASE IV word processor lets you use the function keys to search for text, as summarized in Table 9.3.

Table 9.3 Use of the function keys to search for text.

Find:Shift-F5	Searches for text—dBASE IV prompts you to enter the string to search for
Find Next:Shift-F4	Searches for the next occurrence of the text
Find Prev:Shift-F3	Searches for the previous occurrence of the text
Replace:Shift-F6	Replaces text—dBASE prompts you to enter the text to search for and the replacement text and, each time it finds the text, asks for confirmation before replacing

These function keys are similar to the Forward search, Backward search, and Replace options of the Go To menu, covered later in this chapter.

The Words Menu

The Words menu contains one of the main differences among the various implementations of the word processor. The Words menu for labels, reports, and data entry forms (that is, for the layout editor), shown in Figure 9.1, contains far more options than the Words menu used for other screens (for the program editor), shown in Figure 9.2. Not all of the options of the Words menu of the Layout editor are activated on all of the screens where they are displayed, however. Only the options that are relevant to that particular screen are activated.

The extra features let you format labels, reports, and forms to determine how they are printed or how they are displayed on the screen. In other screens, the Words menu is simply used for editing plain text files (such as memo fields and programs), and so it does not need the options for formatting.

242 ♦ *teach yourself...dBASE IV*

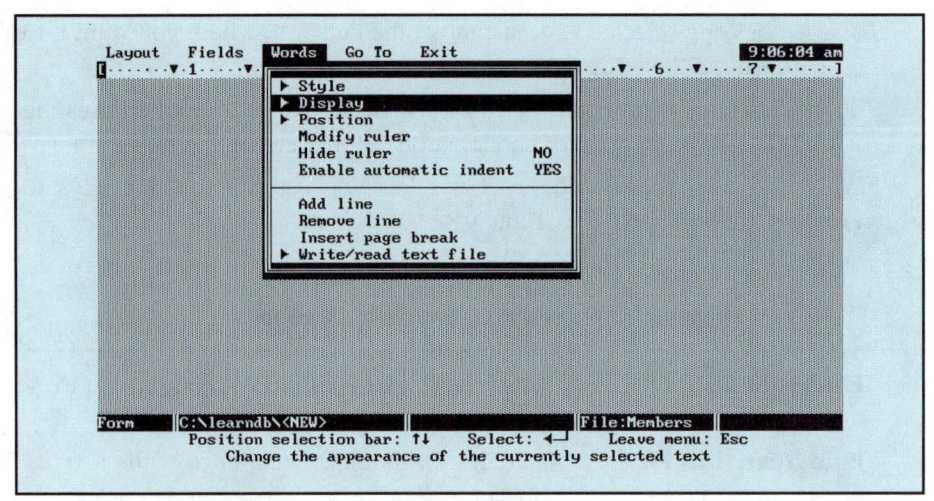

```
Layout   Fields   Words   Go To   Exit                          9:06:04 am
[.......▼.1.....▼.▶ Style          .........▼...6...▼...7.▼.....]
                   ▶ Display
                   ▶ Position
                     Modify ruler
                     Hide ruler                  NO
                     Enable automatic indent     YES

                     Add line
                     Remove line
                     Insert page break
                   ▶ Write/read text file




Form   C:\learndb\<NEW>                        File:Members
       Position selection bar: ↑↓    Select: ←   Leave menu: Esc
          Change the appearance of the currently selected text
```

Figure 9.1   *The Words menu for labels, reports, and forms.*

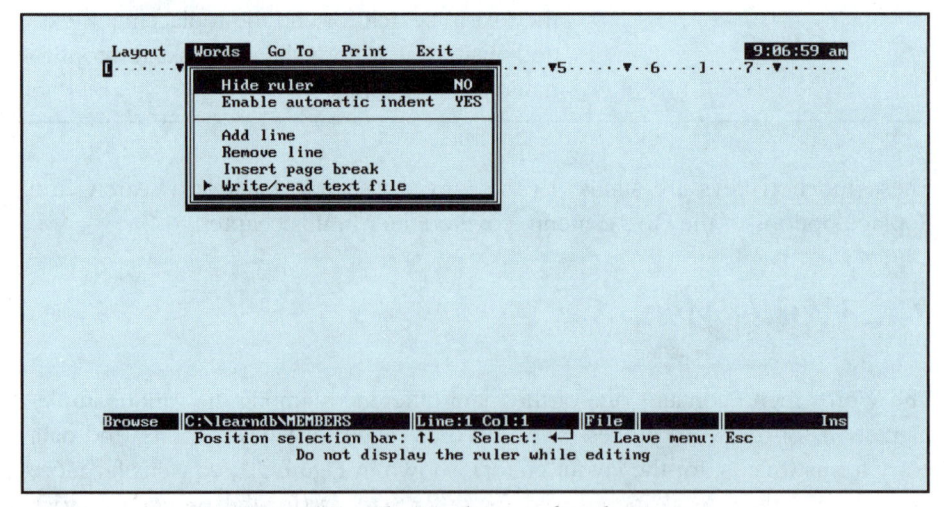

```
Layout   Words   Go To   Print   Exit                           9:06:59 am
[.......▼  Hide ruler                  NO       .▼5.....▼..6...]....7.▼.....
           Enable automatic indent     YES

           Add line
           Remove line
           Insert page break
         ▶ Write/read text file




Browse  C:\learndb\MEMBERS    Line:1 Col:1    File                      Ins
       Position selection bar: ↑↓    Select: ←   Leave menu: Esc
              Do not display the ruler while editing
```

Figure 9.2   *The Words menu for other screens.*

The Style and Display Submenus

If you select **Style** from the Words menu it lets you use the Style submenu, shown in Figure 9.3, to select a print style. As you can see in the illustration, Normal is ON by default. You can toggle on the other options to print in boldface, underlined, italics, superscript, or subscript. There are also spaces for five other options, which you can use if you have a laser printer that supports more fonts. Their settings can be assigned in the CONFIG.DB file, covered in the Appendix. Styles can also be combined, for example, to produce boldface that is also underlined.

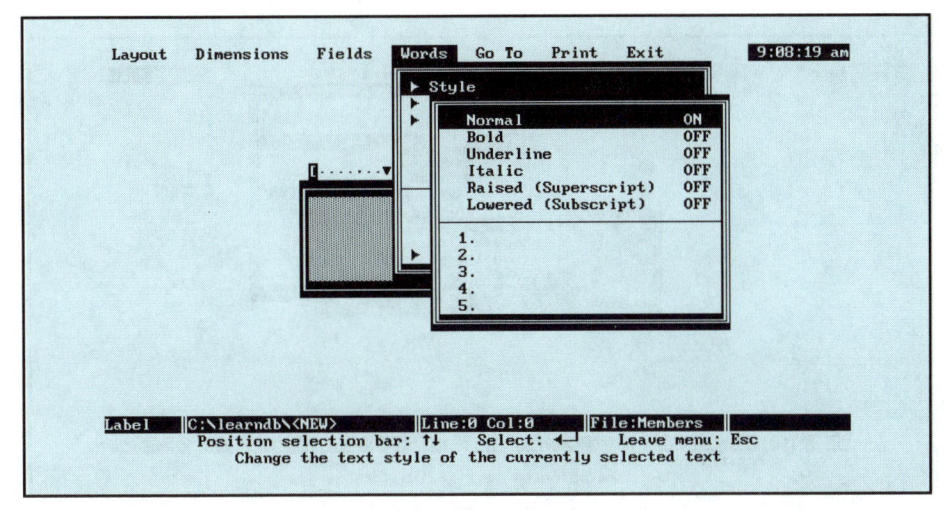

Figure 9.3 *The Style submenu.*

First select the text and fields whose style you want to change. Press **Select:F6** and highlight the text and fields you want using the cursor keys: dBASE IV prompts you to press **Enter** to complete the selection or select the text by clicking and dragging with the mouse. Once the text is selected, select **Style** from the Words menu and select the style you want from the Style submenu.

Style is dimmed on the Words menu of the forms design screen, as it applies to printing and not to screen display. Instead, the forms screen activates the Display option, which lets you control screen display.

If you are using a monochrome monitor, selecting Display lets you select display attributes such as intensity, reverse video, underline, and blink. If you are using a color monitor, it lets you select colors. These submenus are like ones used by the Display option of the Tools menu, discussed later in this chapter. First, select the text and fields whose display you want to change, then select **Display** from the Words menu, and then select the attribute or color that you want to use.

The Position Submenu

Select **Position** from the Words menu to display the submenu shown in Figure 9.4, which lets you center the selected text or align it at the left or right margin. As usual, you must select the text before making this menu selection.

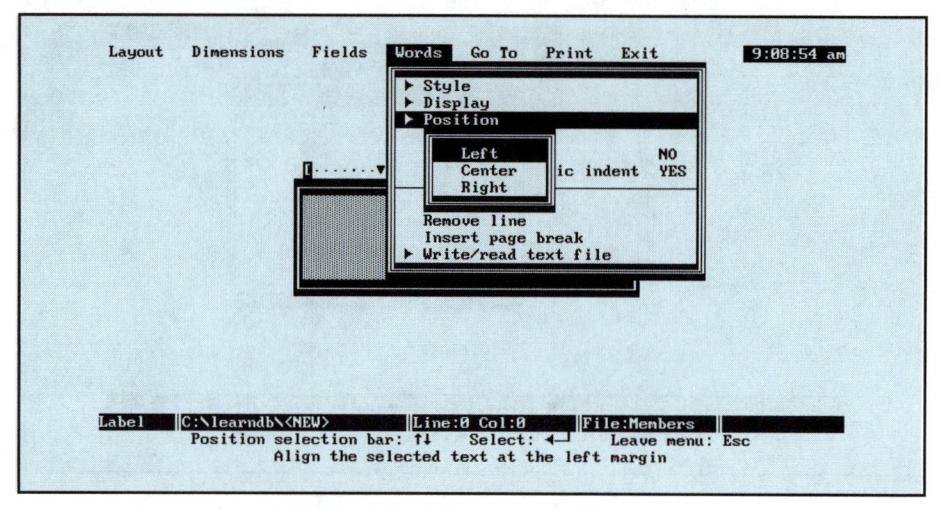

Figure 9.4 *The Position submenu.*

Modify Ruler: Setting Margins and Tabs

If you select Modify ruler from the Words menu, the cursor moves from the screen to the ruler.

You can move the cursor to different positions on the ruler by using the Arrow keys or Spacebar. Press **Ctrl-Right Arrow** or **Ctrl-Left Arrow** to move it eight spaces right or left.

Once the cursor is where you want it, you can add a left or right margin by pressing [(left square bracket) or] (right square bracket).

You can also create an indent (where the text is to the left of the initial margin) or an outdent (where the text is to the right of the initial margin) by typing [where you want the margin and typing # where you want the indent or outdent.

Tab stops are displayed as triangles on the ruler. You can set tab stops by typing ! where you want a new tab stop to be; to remove a tab stop, use **Del** or **Backspace** to delete the triangle. To set tabs at a regular interval, type =, and dBASE IV prompts you to enter the number of spaces you want between tabs. If you enter **0**, there will be no tabs.

When you have added the settings you want, press **Enter** or **Ctrl-End** to leave the ruler and return to the screen—or press **Esc** to abandon the changes and return to the screen.

Other Features of the Words Menu

You have looked at all of the options that are displayed on only the labels, reports, and forms screens. The other features of the Words menu are fairly simple.

Select **Hide ruler** to toggle the setting to YES, which makes the ruler disappear from the top of the screen, and back to NO, which makes it reappear.

Select **Enable automatic indent** to toggle automatic indent on and off, also indicated by the word YES or NO to the right of the menu option. If automatic indent is on and you are at the beginning of a paragraph, pressing **Tab** resets the margin to that tab stop. You can unindent—that is, move the margin left—by pressing **Shift-Tab**. Automatic indent works only when you are in insert mode. It is particularly useful in programming.

You are already familiar with the next two options, Add line and Remove line. As you know, you can also add or remove a line by pressing **Ctrl-N** or **Ctrl-Y**.

Selecting Insert page break makes the printer start a new page at the point where the page break is inserted. The page break is inserted above the line where the cursor is currently located, and is indicated by a heavy, dashed line. It can be removed simply by moving the cursor to the page break indicator and pressing **Del**.

Selecting Write/read text file displays a submenu with the option Write selection to file, which lets you save the current document as a plain ASCII text file, and the option Read text from file, which lets you import plain ASCII text files. In either case, dBASE IV prompts you to enter the name of the file you want to write to or read from, as you can see in Figure 9.5. If you are reading from a file, the navigation line tells you that you can press **Shift-F1** to select the file name from a picklist of available text files rather than typing its name. The picklist lists files with the extension .TXT, but you can read or write plain text files with any extension.

If you read a text file, dBASE IV inserts it into the current document, at the location of the cursor. It does not overwrite what is already in the document.

ASCII text files can be created or used by many programs, and so this option is very useful to let you interchange data with other programs. For example, if you have used your regular word processing program to take notes, you can use them in dBASE IV memo fields without retyping them. First, use your word processing program to save them as ASCII text files. Then use this feature of the dBASE IV word processor to read the appropriate text file into the memo field of each record.

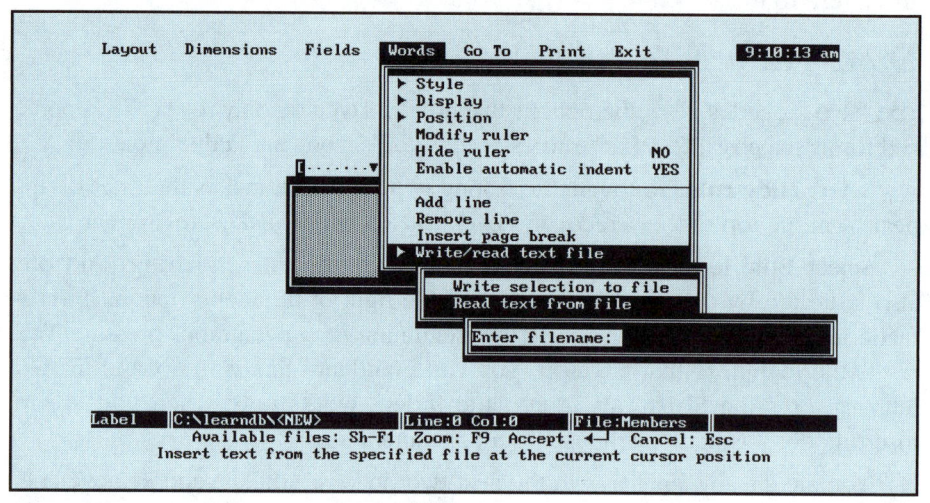

Figure 9.5 *Reading a text file.*

The Go To Menu

The Go To menu, shown in Figure 9.6, lets you move the cursor through the text and to search for and replace text.

If you select **Go to line number**, dBASE IV prompts you to enter a line number, and it moves the cursor to the line in the document that you entered.

If you select **Forward search**, dBASE IV prompts you to enter the text string that you want to search for, as in Figure 9.7. It moves the cursor to the next occurrence of that text, following the current location of the cursor.

If you select **Backward search**, dBASE IV prompts you to enter the text string in the same way, but it moves the cursor to the previous occurrence of that text, before the current location of the cursor.

You can continue to select forward or backward search over and over again until you have gone through all of the occurrences of the text in the document. dBASE IV keeps the text that you entered as the default search string, so you just have to press **Enter** after making the menu selection to search for it again.

Chapter 9: Utilities ◆ **247**

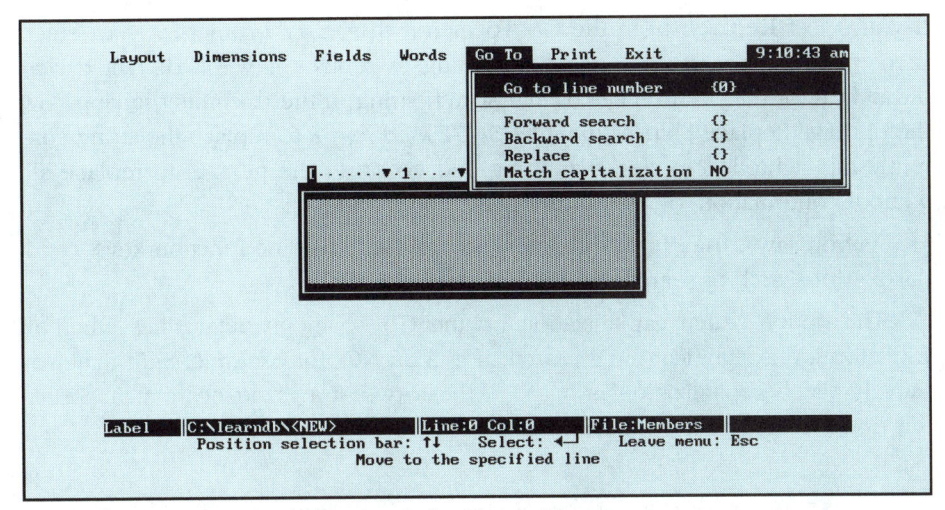

Figure 9.6 The Go To menu.

With either a forward or a backward search, dBASE IV wraps from the end to the beginning of the document. It acts as if the first occurrence of the search string in the document followed its last occurrence, so you can cycle through the document and find all occurrences of a string, no matter where the cursor is located when you begin.

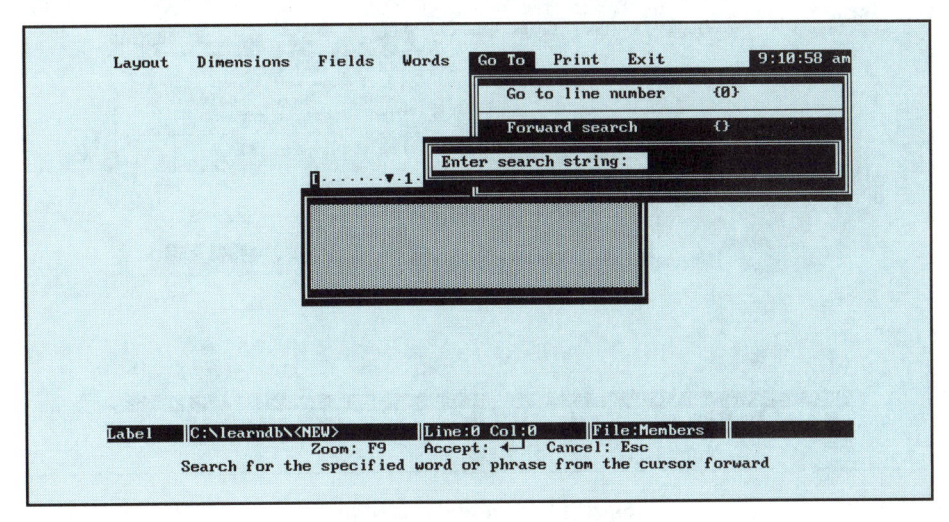

Figure 9.7 Searching for text.

If you select **Replace** from the Go To menu, dBASE IV prompts you to enter both the string to search for and the string to replace it with. Then it cycles through all of the occurrences of that search string in the document, giving you the options: Replace/Skip/All/Quit (R/S/A/Esc). Press R to replace the string currently highlighted, S to skip that string and go on to the next, A to replace all without confirmation, or **Esc** to cancel the command.

As you saw earlier in this chapter, you can also use the function keys to do this sort of search or search and replace operation.

The option Match capitalization on the Go To menu determines whether capitalization is significant in a search. If it is on NO, for example, SAM matches sam. If Match capitalization is on YES, these two strings do not match. Select this option to toggle it from YES to NO.

The Print Menu

When you print most anything—for example, quick reports, mailing labels, formatted reports, or program files—dBASE IV displays the Print menu, shown in Figure 9.8. By changing settings on this menu, you can control how the document is printed.

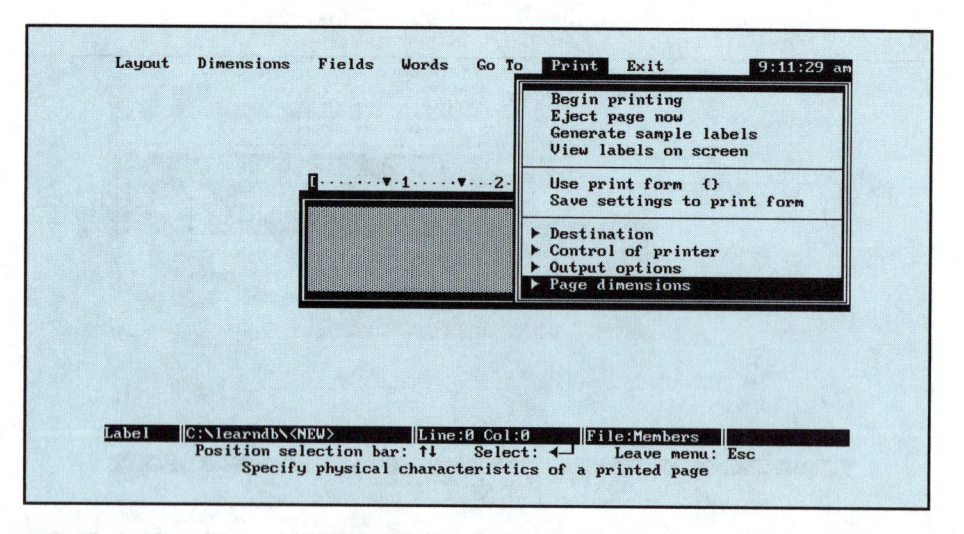

Figure 9.8 *The Print menu.*

The Basics

The first three options on this menu let you control the basic, physical features of printing.

If you select **Begin printing**, the document is printed, using all of the current settings of this menu and its submenus.

If you select **Eject page now**, the printer ejects the current page, so that it is ready to begin printing at the top of a new page. As you will see in the section *Controlling the Printer*, by default, dBASE IV automatically ejects a page before printing but not afterwards. If you use the dBASE IV default settings, then after a report is finished printing, you may want to select **Eject page now** to eject the final page, which may have printing only on part of it. If you change the dBASE IV default settings, then you can select this option to eject a page whenever necessary.

You can also eject a page by pressing the *Form Feed* button on your printer. The Eject page now menu option is just a convenience.

As you know, if you are using the Print menu with quick reports, labels, or formatted reports, you can select **View report on screen**, and dBASE IV displays a preview of the printed report on the screen, one screen at a time, so you can make sure the appearance of the report is what you want. One limitation of this preview feature is that the screen can only display eighty characters across, so anything beyond that is wrapped to the next line. The standard printer also displays eighty characters, but if you are using a wide carriage printer or using Elite or Condensed print, then you cannot display a *what-you-see-is-what-you-get* (WYSIWYG) preview on the screen.

In other screens within the dBASE IV Print menu, the option **Line numbers** is included instead of **View report on screen**. Select this option to toggle it from NO to YES. If this option is turned on, each line of the printout will be numbered. If you are printing a program listing, for example, line numbers can be a help in debugging.

Print Forms

The next two options on the Print menu let you save all of the print settings that you have chosen in a print form or to use other settings that you have saved in an earlier print form. These options are useful if you print different documents with complex sets of options. They save you the trouble of doing all of these settings by hand each time you print.

Once you have selected all of the options that you want, select **Save settings to print** form to save all of the current settings. dBASE IV prompts you to enter the name of the print form you want them saved in, as you can see in Figure 9.9. A print form is kept in a separate DOS file, with the extension .PRF.

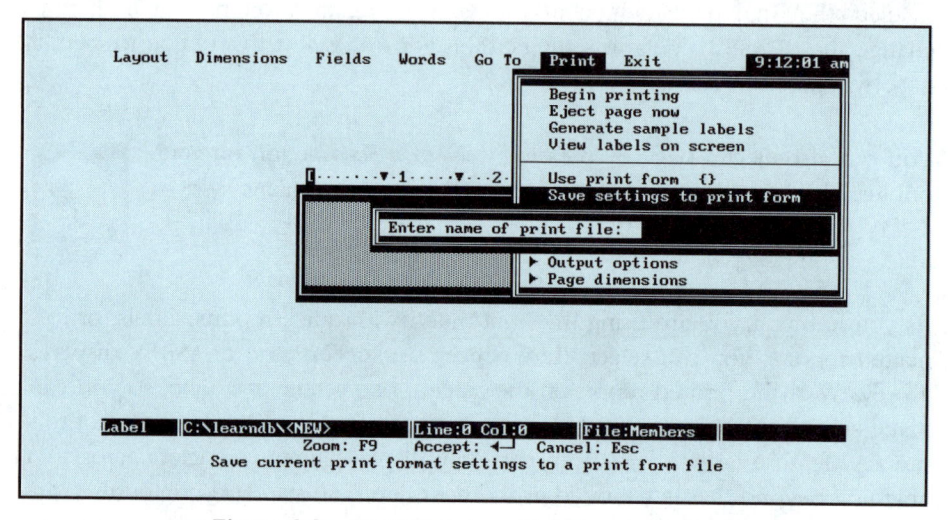

Figure 9.9 Saving printer settings in a print form.

When you save a formatted report or mailing labels for the first time, if you altered the printer settings while designing the report, dBASE IV automatically asks you if you want to save the settings to a print form.

By default, when you are creating a formatted report or mailing labels, dBASE IV gives a print form the same name as the report or label with the extension .PRF added. You can press **Enter** to use the suggested name, or you can edit the name and then press **Enter**. If you use this menu option to save the print settings for a quick report, you will find it easiest to follow the same convention and use the query name followed by the extension .PRF.

To use an existing print form, select **Use print form** from the Print menu. dBASE IV displays a picklist of print forms, and you simply select one.

To change the settings of a print form you created earlier, first select **Use print form** from the menu and select the print form you want from the picklist. Then make the needed changes in the settings, save the print form under its existing name, and select **Overwrite** from the prompt box to replace the old form with its altered version.

Controlling Printing

The final four options on the Print menu let you control the printed output in a variety of ways.

Specifying the Destination

If you select **Destination** from the **Print** menu, dBASE IV displays the submenu shown in Figure 9.10. As you can see from the illustration, the default settings of this menu send output to a generic printer without echoing the output to the screen.

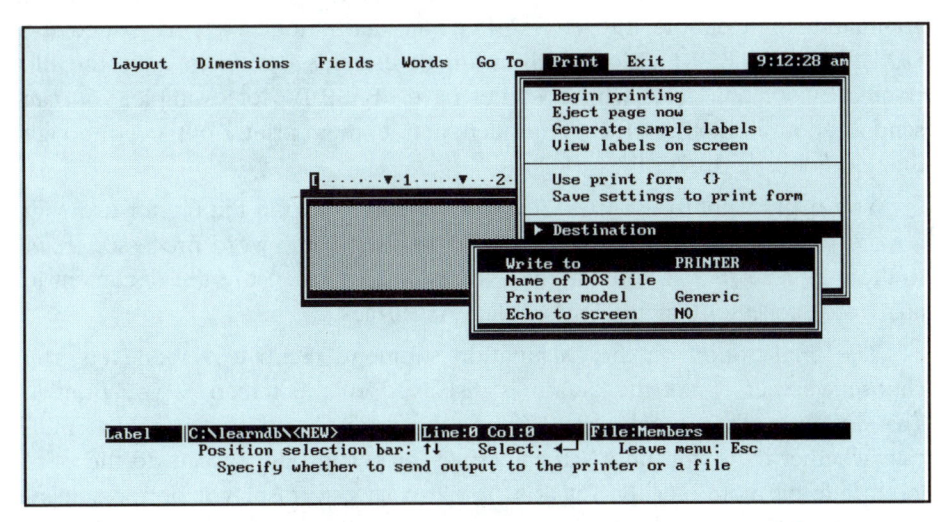

Figure 9.10   The Destination submenu.

By selecting **Write to** from the Destination submenu, you can toggle from PRINTER to DOS FILE as the destination of the output. The reasons that you might want to send the output to a DOS file rather than directly to the printer are discussed in a moment.

When you toggle **Write to** to the DOS FILE setting, the option Name of DOS file becomes accessible, and dBASE IV suggests a name based on the name of the database file, label, or report that you are printing. If Generic is selected as the printer model, the DOS file has the default extension .PRT. If ASCII text is selected as the printer model, the DOS file has the default extension .TXT. Select **Name of DOS file** from the Destination submenu to change the suggested name of the DOS file.

By selecting **Printer model** from the Destination submenu, you can toggle between Generic and ASCII Text. (There will be additional choices of printers if you installed other printer drivers using DBSETUP. For more information, see Appendix A.)

If you select Generic, the output includes any printer codes you inserted by using the Control of Printer submenu, which will be discussed in a moment. If you select ASCII Text, printer codes are stripped away, so that only ASCII characters remain.

If you print the document to a file in Generic form, with printer codes included, this file can be printed from the DOS prompt by using the PRINT command: for example, PRINT SAMPLE.PRT (assuming that you named the DOS file SAMPLE.PRT). You might want to use this option to have the file printed by someone else who does not have dBASE IV; for example, you can send a report to another office by modem and let them print it out, even though they do not have dBASE IV.

You might want to use the ASCII Text option to export the file for use with a word processor that can import plain ASCII files. Some word processors refer to these as *DOS files*. If you use this option, you can then use the document in any word processor that can import plain ASCII files.

The final option on the Destination submenu, Echo to screen, lets you choose whether or not the output is displayed on the screen as you print it. This option is also a toggle, and NO or YES are displayed on the right to indicate whether there will be a screen display or not. dBASE IV can do the print job a little bit more quickly if it does not also have to display it on the screen, but many people prefer having the screen display so that they can keep track of the print job's progress.

Controlling the Printer

Selecting **Control of Printer** from the Print menu lets you use the Control of Printer submenu, shown in Figure 9.11.

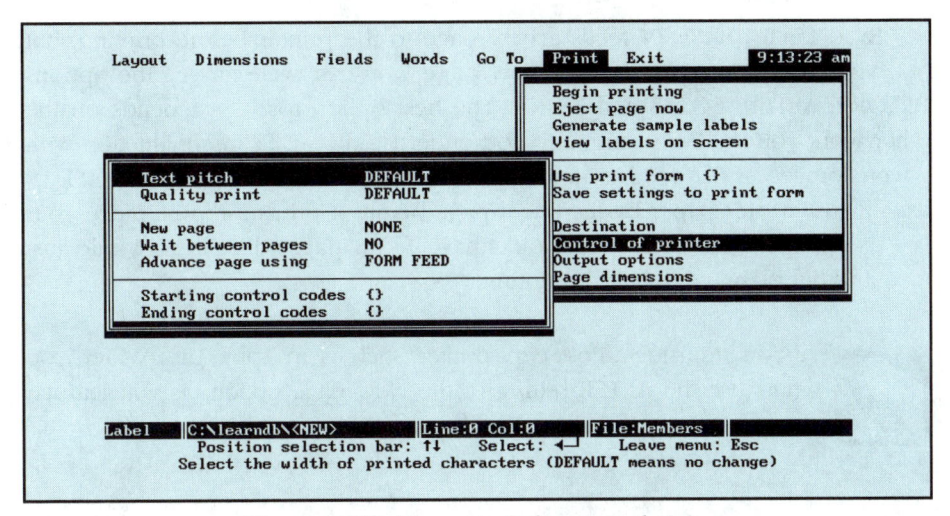

Figure 9.11   *The control of printer submenu.*

Initially, the selection for Text pitch is DEFAULT, which means that the pitch (the size) of the text is whatever you have selected using the switches of your printer. By selecting Text Pitch, you can toggle to

- **PICA**: prints ten characters to the inch, the standard type on most ordinary printers.
- **ELITE**: prints twelve characters to the inch.
- **CONDENSED**: prints from sixteen to twenty characters per inch, depending on your printer.

Elite and condensed type are very useful for fitting wide reports on a single page width. Of course, they work only if your printer includes these fonts.

The Quality print option is useful if you have a dot matrix printer that has both a draft mode that prints quickly and a letter-quality or near-letter quality mode that prints more slowly but produces a better result. The initial DEFAULT selection prints in whatever mode is set by the switches of your printer. By selecting **Quality print** from the Control of printer menu, you can also set Quality print as YES or NO, to make the printer use near-letter quality or draft quality print, regardless of the setting of its switches.

The next three selections on the Control of printer menu control the way the pages are fed to the printer.

By default, dBASE IV feeds a new page to the printer before printing, but not when it is done. By selecting **New page**, you can cycle among the options BEFORE, AFTER, BOTH, and NONE. The best option for you depends on the other work you do. For example, if you often use dBASE IV in conjunction with a word processor that feeds a new page after it finishes printing, then dBASE IV usually just wastes paper by feeding a page before it prints a report. Since your last use of the word processor would have fed a page, dBASE IV would just feed another blank page before printing.

NOTE If you are using a PostScript printer, such as an Apple LaserWriter, you must use the AFTER setting of the New page option, as you learned when you were first introduced to the Print menu in Chapter 6.

NOTE Use the New page setting that is most convenient for you. Remember, though, that by default, dBASE IV does not feed a page when it finishes the report. If you are not printing another dBASE IV report immediately afterwards, you may have to select **Eject** from the Print menu or press your printer's **Form Feed** button to get the final page of the report. If you do not eject the final page of the report, and you later use some other program to print, it might begin printing on the bottom of the last page of the dBASE IV report.

By selecting **Wait between pages** from the Control of printer submenu, you toggle this feature between YES and NO. If you have a printer which you must hand-feed a new sheet of paper to print each new page, then set this option to YES. It can also be useful if you are hand-feeding envelopes or other special forms to the printer. Except in these special cases, though, leave it at the default setting of NO.

By selecting **Advance page using**, you can determine whether dBASE IV begins a new page by sending a Form Feed to your printer or by sending a number of Line Feeds to your printer and advancing it to the top of the next page line by line. Leave this option on the default FORM FEED unless you have some special reason to toggle to LINE FEEDS.

The final two options of the Control of printer submenu, Starting control codes and Ending control codes, let you use other special features of your printer by sending it control codes before or after printing. Select either one and dBASE IV prompts you to enter a string. The control code that you enter appears between the curly brackets, and you can edit it by selecting the option again. Printer control codes are a difficult technical subject. You must enter them just as they are indicated in your printer's manual, with special non-printing characters, such as {ESC} enclosed in curly brackets. In general, you should avoid using printer codes unless you are knowledgeable about the subject.

Output Options

Selecting **Output options** from the Print menu lets you use the Output options submenu, shown in Figure 9.12.

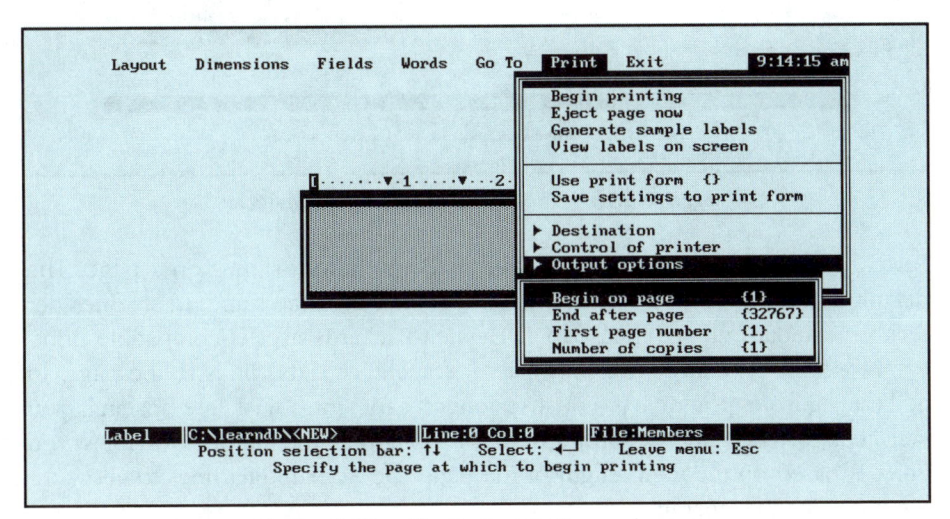

Figure 9.12 *The Output Options submenu.*

As you can see from the illustration, this submenu is fairly simple. If you select any of its options, dBASE IV prompts you to enter an integer.

Select **Begin on page** to specify which page dBASE IV begins printing with, select **End after page** to specify which is the final page that dBASE IV prints, select **First page number** to specify what number dBASE IV gives to the first page, and select **Number of copies** to determine how many copies of the report dBASE IV prints.

Page Dimensions

Select **Page dimensions** from the **Print** menu to use the **Page dimensions** submenu, shown in Figure 9.13.

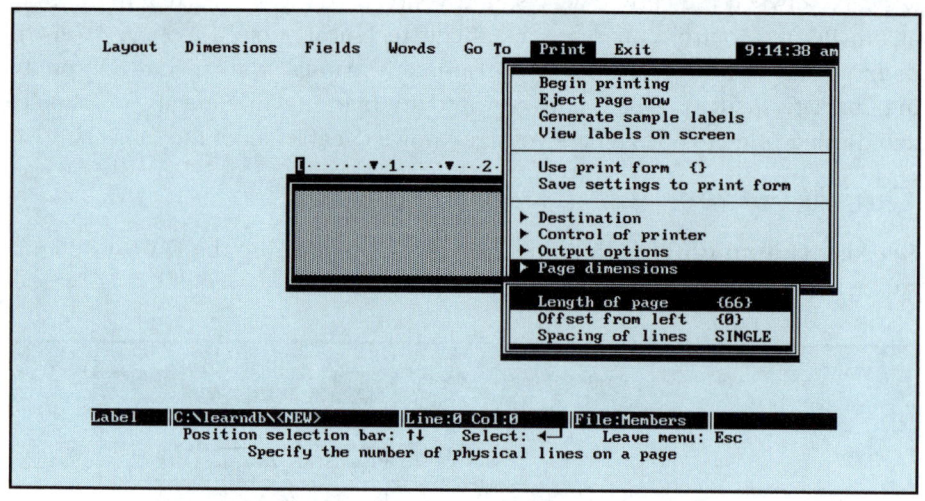

```
Layout    Dimensions    Fields    Words    Go To    Print    Exit        9:14:38 am
                                                    Begin printing
                                                    Eject page now
                                                    Generate sample labels
                                                    View labels on screen
                   ▼···1···▼···2·                   Use print form       {}
                                                    Save settings to print form
                                                  ► Destination
                                                  ► Control of printer
                                                  ► Output options
                                                  ► Page dimensions
                                                    Length of page      {66}
                                                    Offset from left    {0}
                                                    Spacing of lines    SINGLE

Label   C:\learndb\<NEW>         Line:0 Col:0      File:Members
             Position selection bar: ↑↓   Select: ↵   Leave menu: Esc
                    Specify the number of physical lines on a page
```

Figure 9.13 *The Page Dimensions submenu.*

Selecting **Length of page** lets you specify the number of lines on a page. The default of sixty-six lines assumes that your printer uses the standard six lines per inch on standard eleven inch paper. Hewlett-Packard LaserJet-compatible printers, however, generally print sixty-six (or sometimes sixty) lines to the page. In addition, if your printer lets you use longer paper or adjust line spacing, you can change this value accordingly. Remember that the number of lines you enter is based on the total length of the page. Do not subtract lines to allow for the top or bottom margin.

N O T E As you know, selecting **Offset from left** lets you enter an integer to determine whether what you are printing should be indented from the left edge of the page; the default is 0 for no offset. This offset is different from the left margin that the dBASE IV word processor lets you set by using the ruler. If you print a document with a margin and also use Offset from left, dBASE IV adds the width of the margin to the width you specified for the offset to determine how much total white space to leave on the left of the page.

The Tools Menu

Working from the Control Center, you can press **Alt-T** or use the mouse to access the Tools menu, shown in Figure 9.14. As you can see, this menu lets you create macros, import or export data, use DOS utilities, protect your data, and change some of the settings that control your working environment.

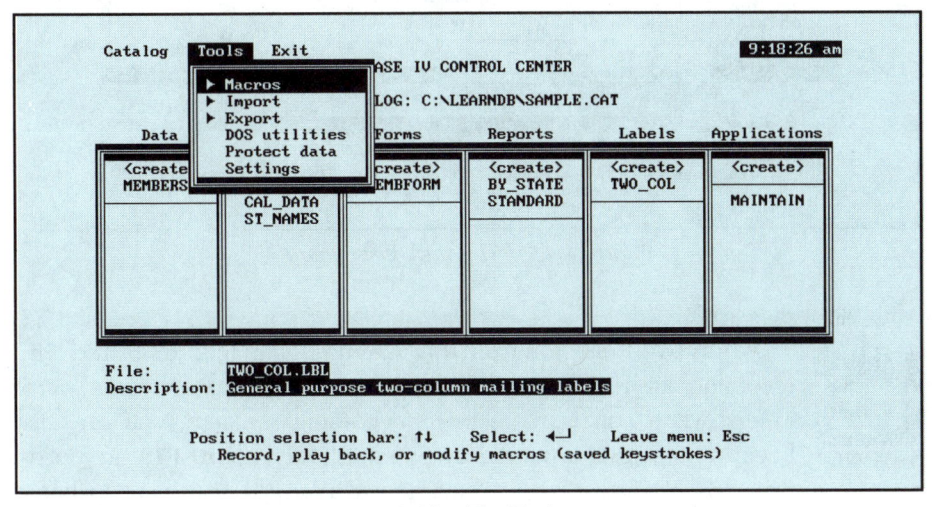

Figure 9.14 The Tools menu.

Macros

A macro records a series of keystrokes. By executing the macro, you can run those keystrokes automatically, without entering each one by hand. Needless to say, this can save you a great deal of time and of repetitive work if you must use the same series of keystrokes repeatedly.

The keystrokes that you record can include menu choices (such as Alt-C to use the Catalog menu from the Control Center) or text (such as your return address, so that you can begin form letters by using this macro, rather than typing the address in by hand), or a combination of both menu choices and text entry. Because a macro can only record keystrokes, the mouse is turned off while you are recording.

When you select **Macros** from the Tools menu, you use the Macros submenu, shown in Figure 9.15.

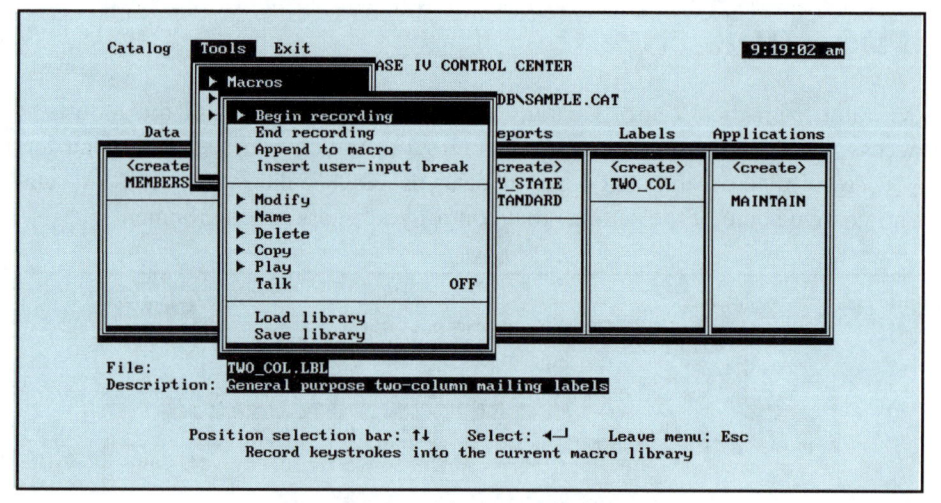

Figure 9.15 *The Macros submenu.*

SHORTCUT

The first two selections on this menu, Begin recording and End recording, are fundamental. Since you are not always at the Control Center when you want to begin recording a macro, you can also begin recording at any time by pressing **Macro:Shift-F10**. If you do this, dBASE IV displays a prompt box asking if you want to begin recording or to cancel.

NOTE

When you begin recording, dBASE IV displays a list of all of the keys that you can assign macros to, with the names of those macros that are already assigned to letters. You can assign a macro to any of the letter keys, from a to z, or to any of the function keys, from F1 to F9. As you will see, you can play macros more quickly if they are assigned to function keys than if they are assigned to letters so you should reserve the function keys for the most frequently used macros.

After you assign a key to the macro, a message is displayed at the bottom of the screen indicating that it is recording a macro and that you should press **Shift-F10 E** to end recording. Perform whatever operation that you want the Macro to record, and when you are done, press **Macro:Shift-F10**. dBASE IV displays a prompt box, and you may press *E* or **Enter** to end recording.

After you are done recording, you can play the macro at any time. If you assigned it to a function key from F1 to F9, press **Alt** plus that function key to play it instantly. If you assigned it to a letter, press **Alt-F10**: dBASE IV prompts you to enter the letter of the macro you want to play and plays it after you enter the letter.

You must remember that when you use the macro, dBASE IV simply executes the keystrokes that you recorded. You must be using the right screen and have the cursor in the right place for the macro to do what you want it to do. If you are at the Control Center and play the macro that contains text that you often type in memo fields, for example, dBASE IV just beeps once for each keystroke in that text, just as it would if you typed those keys by hand while you were at the Control Center.

The other essential features of the Macros submenu are the options Load library and Save library. You must use these options to reuse macros in later dBASE IV sessions.

Select **Save library**, and dBASE IV prompts you to enter a file name for the macro library. All of the macros that you have created so far in the current session with dBASE IV are saved in this library. If you do not use Save library, the macros you create are lost when you quit the current dBASE session.

Select **Load library** to reuse macros that you saved previously. dBASE IV displays a picklist that lets you select macro libraries in the current directory or move to other directories to select macro libraries there.

You can have many macro libraries with different names. You might have one that you use for form letters, another for reports, another for programming, and so on.

The other options on the Macros submenu are essentially utilities that make macros more powerful or easier to manage:

- **Append to macro**: lets you add more keystrokes to the end of an existing macro.
- **Insert user-input break**: lets the user input keystrokes in the middle of the macro. When the user presses **Macros:Shift-F10**, the macro continues to execute where it left off.
- **Modify**: lets you use the word processor to edit the contents of a macro.
- **Name**: change the name of a macro. By default, the macro is named after the letter key or function key that activates it. You can give it a more descriptive name to make it easier for you to remember what it does.

- **Delete**: delete an existing macro.
- **Copy**: create a new macro that is a copy of an existing one. If you want a new macro similar to an existing one, for example, you can copy it and then edit the copy to incorporate the changes.
- **Play**: plays a macro. As you know, you can also use Alt-function key or Alt-F10 followed by a letter key to play back a macro.
- **Talk**: displays each keystroke as the macro executes it.

Appending to a macro is difficult because you make this selection from the Control Center, but you must move to the location where the macro ended before you continue to add more keystrokes at the end. This leaves the keystrokes that you used to move to that location in the middle of the macro, where they do not belong. You must edit the macro to remove them.

If a macro is virtually all text—for example, if it is a stock paragraph that you use in many form letters—you can use the word processor to edit it and change the text without much trouble. Macros that involve menu choices, though, are difficult to edit. The macro editor records the keystrokes that you made, but it is up to you to remember what they mean. For example, if you record a macro to exit from the Control Center to the dot prompt, it appears in the editor as {Alt-e}e. This macro records the Alt-E that you used to pull down the Exit menu, followed by the E that you pressed to select Exit to dot prompt from that menu. If you want to change this macro so it quits to DOS instead, you can edit it so it reads {Alt-e}q.

SHORTCUT

With complex macros, it is obviously difficult to remember what keystrokes are needed to make changes. If you want to change most macros, it is usually easiest to start again from scratch and rerecord them from beginning to end.

NOTE

The options for appending to a macro or editing a macro are tricky and are best to avoid in most cases.

Import/Export

dBASE IV has tools to import data from a number of other programs and to export data both to other programs and to three different types of text files.

Chapter 9: Utilities ◆ **261**

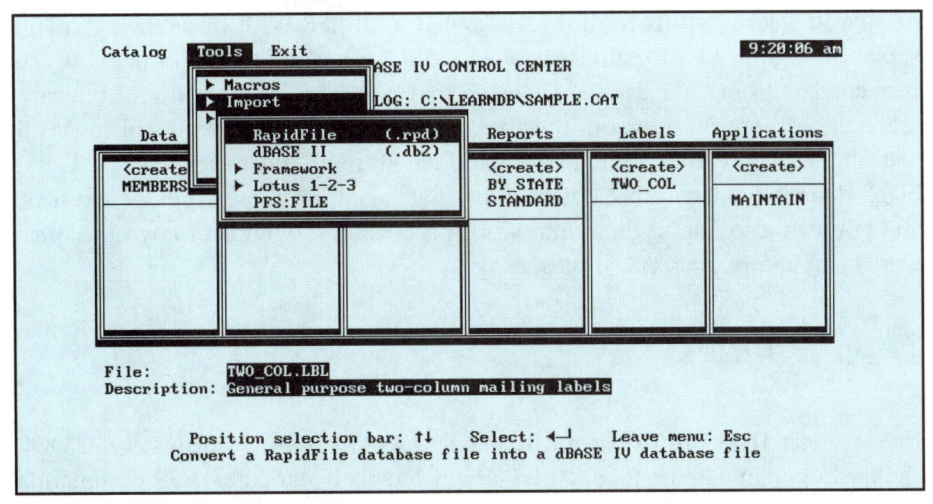

Figure 9.16 *Importing data.*

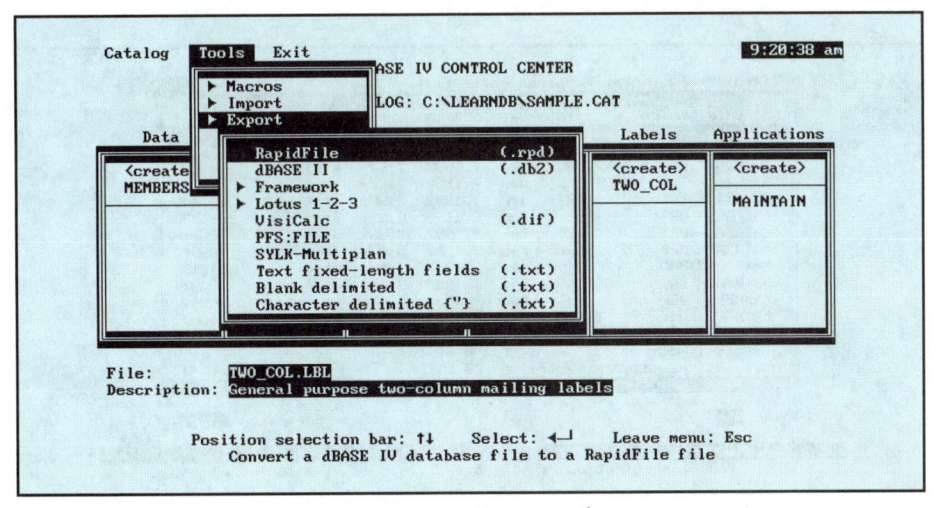

Figure 9.17 *Exporting data.*

If you select **Import** from the Tools menu, dBASE IV displays the menu shown in Figure 9.16. (Versions of dBASE IV earlier than 1.5 include fewer formats.) It can convert the data from any of the programs listed so that it can be used by dBASE IV. Just select the program where the data originates, and dBASE IV displays a picklist to let you select the name of the file that you want to import.

If you select **Export** from the Tools menu, dBASE IV displays the submenu shown in Figure 9.17. (Again, versions before 1.5 include fewer formats.) It can convert data from your database files so that it can be used by any of the programs listed here. In addition, the Export menu lists three types of plain ASCII text file that you can export data to: fixed-length fields, character delimited, and blank delimited. Many other database programs can use these types of text files, and you can also import them into word processing programs or any other programs that accept plain ASCII files.

DOS Utilities

If you select **DOS utilities** from the Tools menu, dBASE IV displays the DOS shell, shown in Figure 9.18. This screen lets you execute DOS commands directly, and it also gives you a menu-driven method of executing the most important DOS commands.

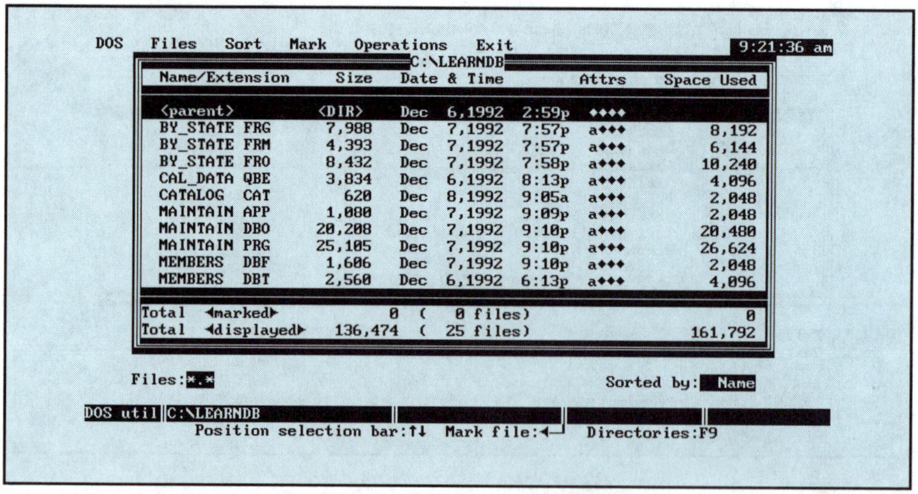

Figure 9.18 *The DOS shell.*

This screen lists all of the files and subdirectories of the current directory. Each file includes the file name and extension, the size of the file in bytes, the date and time that the file was last changed, the attributes of the file and the disk space that the file uses. (The disk space is larger than the actual size of the file because disk space is allocated by sectors, rather than by individual bytes.)

You can move among subdirectories by selecting the parent directory or a subdirectory of the current directory to move to it. In this way, you can eventually move to any subdirectory of the disk. To move more among directories more quickly, press **F9** (as the navigation line says). dBASE IV displays a diagram of the entire directory tree of the current disk and you can select any directory to move to it.

A powerful feature of this screen is that it lets you execute commands on groups of files. You can mark a file simply by selecting it—move the highlight to it and press **Enter** or simply click it with the mouse. When you mark a file, a small triangle is displayed to its left. If a file is already marked, you can unmark it by selecting it. As you will see, you can also use the menu system to mark and unmark groups of files.

Once the files you want are marked, you can use the menu system to perform certain operations on all of them.

The DOS Menu

The DOS menu, shown in Figure 9.19, lets you enter commands in text form, rather than using the shell's menu system to select them.

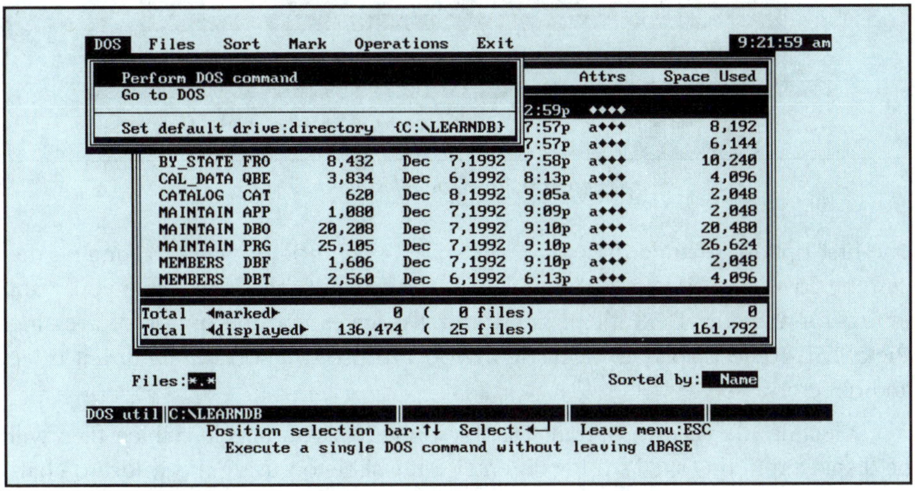

Figure 9.19 *The DOS menu.*

If you select **Perform DOS command**, dBASE IV prompts you to enter a single DOS command.

If you select **Go to DOS**, dBASE IV lets you use what it calls a DOS window—a full screen with a DOS prompt, like the one DOS itself lets you use. Enter as many commands as you want. When you are done, type *exit* to return to dBASE IV.

If you select **Set default drive:directory**, dBASE IV lets you enter the full path name of the directory that you want to use as the current directory.

The Files Menu

The Files menu, shown in Figure 9.20, lets you choose which files are displayed.

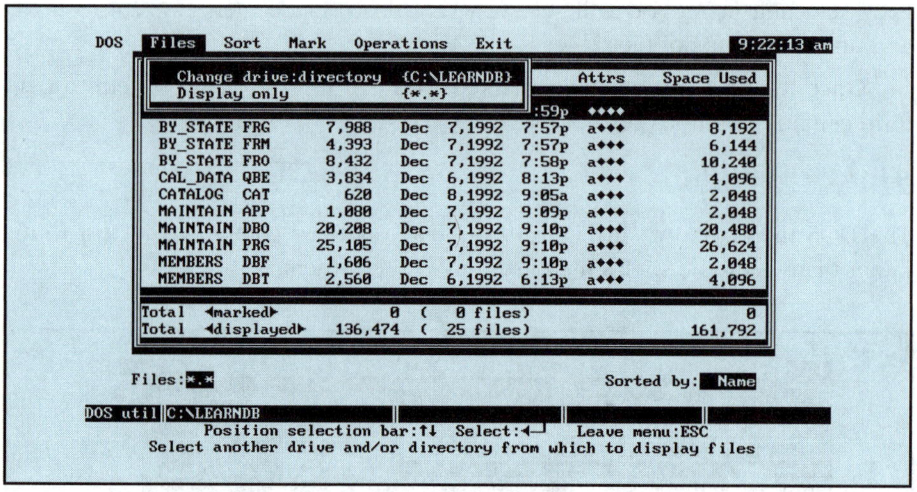

```
DOS  Files  Sort    Mark    Operations   Exit                    9:22:13 am
            Change drive:directory   {C:\LEARNDB}    Attrs      Space Used
            Display only             {*.*}
                                              :59p   a***
            BY_STATE  FRG     7,988   Dec   7,1992   7:57p  a***      8,192
            BY_STATE  FRM     4,393   Dec   7,1992   7:57p  a***      6,144
            BY_STATE  FRO     8,432   Dec   7,1992   7:58p  a***     10,240
            CAL_DATA  QBE     3,834   Dec   6,1992   8:13p  a***      4,096
            CATALOG   CAT       620   Dec   8,1992   9:05a  a***      2,048
            MAINTAIN  APP     1,080   Dec   7,1992   9:09p  a***      2,048
            MAINTAIN  DBO    20,208   Dec   7,1992   9:10p  a***     20,480
            MAINTAIN  PRG    25,105   Dec   7,1992   9:10p  a***     26,624
            MEMBERS   DBF     1,606   Dec   7,1992   9:10p  a***      2,048
            MEMBERS   DBT     2,560   Dec   6,1992   6:13p  a***      4,096
      Total  <marked>             0  (   0 files)                        0
      Total  <displayed>    136,474  (  25 files)                  161,792

      Files:*.*                                      Sorted by: Name
DOS util C:\LEARNDB
              Position selection bar:↑↓  Select:↵   Leave menu:ESC
         Select another drive and/or directory from which to display files
```

Figure 9.20 *The Files menu.*

The first option, Change drive:directory, gives you another way of changing the current drive and directory. If you select it, it lets you enter the drive you want in text form, as the DOS menu does, and also gives you the option of pressing **Pick:Shift-F1** to display a picklist that you can use to choose the current drive and directory.

Selecting the second option, Display only, lets you specify which files will be displayed in this shell's list. You enter a file skeleton using the wildcard characters * to represent any file name or extension and ? to represent any single character. Thus, the default *.* displays files with any name and any extension—that is, all files. If you want to display only backup files with the extension .BAK, you can select this option and enter the file skeleton *.BAK.

The Sort Menu

The Sort menu, shown in Figure 9.21, determines the order in which files are displayed.

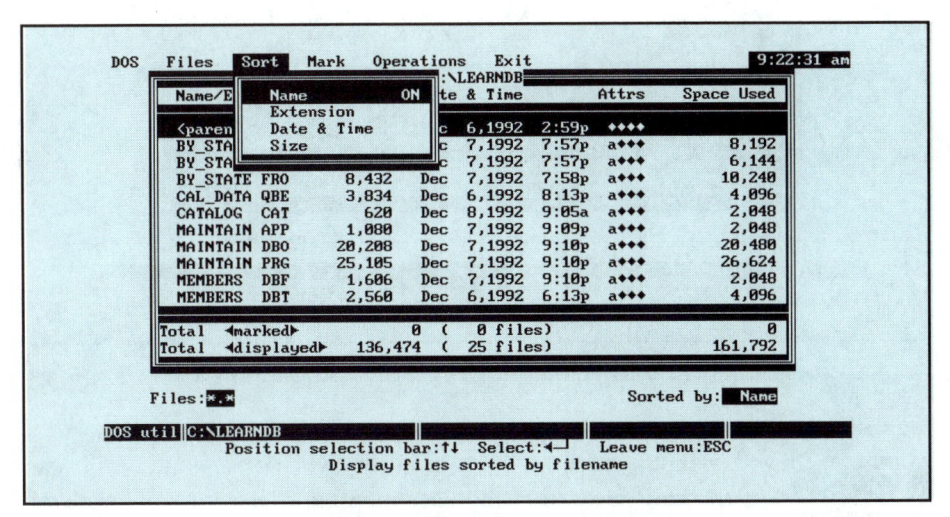

```
DOS    Files   Sort    Mark    Operations   Exit              9:22:31 am
                                :\LEARNDB
        Name/E  Name          ON  te & Time        Attrs    Space Used
                Extension
        <paren  Date & Time      c  6,1992  2:59p  ••••
        BY_STA  Size             c  7,1992  7:57p  a•••        8,192
        BY_STA                   c  7,1992  7:57p  a•••        6,144
        BY_STATE FRO     8,432  Dec  7,1992  7:58p  a•••       10,240
        CAL_DATA QBE    3,834   Dec  6,1992  8:13p  a•••        4,096
        CATALOG  CAT      620   Dec  8,1992  9:05a  a•••        2,048
        MAINTAIN APP    1,080   Dec  7,1992  9:09p  a•••        2,048
        MAINTAIN DBO   20,208   Dec  7,1992  9:10p  a•••       20,480
        MAINTAIN PRG   25,105   Dec  7,1992  9:10p  a•••       26,624
        MEMBERS  DBF    1,606   Dec  7,1992  9:10p  a•••        2,048
        MEMBERS  DBT    2,560   Dec  6,1992  6:13p  a•••        4,096

        Total  <marked>        0  (    0 files)                     0
        Total  <displayed>  136,474  (  25 files)                161,792

        Files: *.*                                 Sorted by: Name
DOS util C:\LEARNDB
         Position selection bar:↑↓   Select:↵   Leave menu:ESC
                    Display files sorted by filename
```

Figure 9.21 *The Sort menu.*

By default, the files are listed alphabetically by name. You can see that ON is to the right of the Name option in the menu.

Select **Extension** to list files alphabetically by extension, so that (for example) all the .DBF files, all the .DBT files, all the .QBE files and so on will be listed next to each other.

Select **Date & Time** to list files in the order that they were last changed, with the oldest at the top of the list.

Select **Size** to list files in the order of their size, with the smallest first.

The Mark Menu

The Mark Menu, shown in Figure 9.22, lets you mark groups of records. The options Mark all and Unmark all let you mark or unmark all of the files that are currently displayed. Selecting **Reverse marks** unmarks all of those that are currently marked and marks all those that are currently unmarked.

266 ♦ teach yourself...dBASE IV

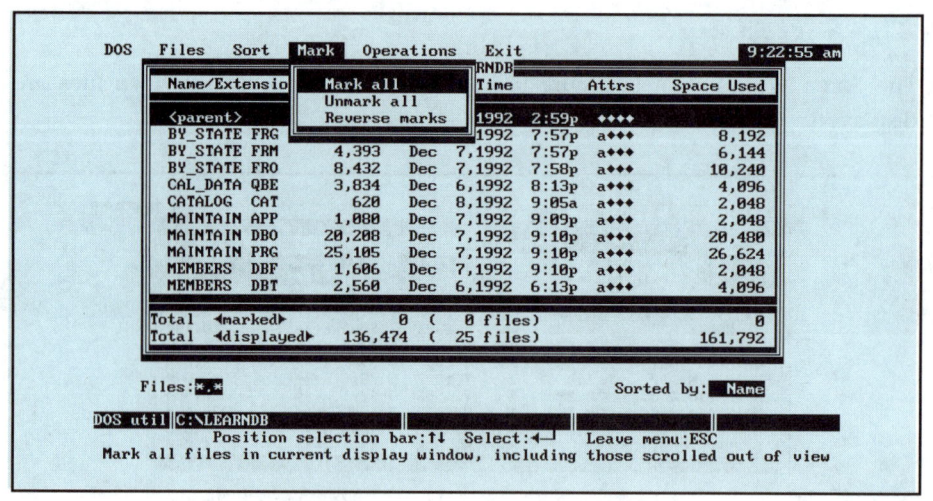

```
   DOS    Files    Sort    Mark    Operations    Exit              9:22:55 am
                          ┌─────────────┐ RNDB
        Name/Extensio     │ Mark all    │ Time         Attrs     Space Used
                          │ Unmark all  │
           <parent>       │ Reverse marks│ 1992   2:59p  ♦♦♦♦
           BY_STATE FRG   └─────────────┘ 1992   7:57p  a♦♦♦        8,192
           BY_STATE FRM        4,393    Dec  7,1992   7:57p  a♦♦♦        6,144
           BY_STATE FRO        8,432    Dec  7,1992   7:58p  a♦♦♦       10,240
           CAL_DATA QBE        3,834    Dec  6,1992   8:13p  a♦♦♦        4,096
           CATALOG  CAT          620    Dec  8,1992   9:05a  a♦♦♦        2,048
           MAINTAIN APP        1,080    Dec  7,1992   9:09p  a♦♦♦        2,048
           MAINTAIN DBO       20,208    Dec  7,1992   9:10p  a♦♦♦       20,480
           MAINTAIN PRG       25,105    Dec  7,1992   9:10p  a♦♦♦       26,624
           MEMBERS  DBF        1,606    Dec  7,1992   9:10p  a♦♦♦        2,048
           MEMBERS  DBT        2,560    Dec  6,1992   6:13p  a♦♦♦        4,096

          Total  ◄marked►           0   (    0 files)                      0
          Total  ◄displayed►  136,474   (   25 files)                161,792

          Files: *.*                                 Sorted by: Name
  ┌─────────┬─────────────┬────────────┬─────────────┬───────────┐
  │DOS util │C:\LEARNDB   │            │             │           │
  └─────────┴─────────────┴────────────┴─────────────┴───────────┘
                  Position selection bar:↑↓  Select:◄┘   Leave menu:ESC
          Mark all files in current display window, including those scrolled out of view
```

Figure 9.22   The Mark menu.

SHORTCUT If you want to mark all of your .BAK files, for example, you can select **Display only** from the Files menu and enter the file skeleton *.BAK to display only the .BAK files. Then select **Mark all** from the Mark menu to mark them all. Then select **Display only** from the Files menu and enter *.* to display all the files again, with the .BAK files marked.

SHORTCUT If you want to mark all of your files except for the files with the extension .BAK, do the steps listed in the last paragraph to mark all of the files with that extension. Then select **Reverse marks** from the Mark menu to unmark the .BAK files and to mark all of the other files. (This assumes that no files were marked to begin with. To make sure that none were marked before you started, you could first have used *.* and selected **Unmark all** from the Mark menu.)

Marks made using the DOS shell are kept only as long as you continue to use the DOS shell. When you return to the Control Center, all files are unmarked.

The Operations Menu

The Operations menu, shown in Figure 9.23, lets you perform the basic operations Delete, Copy, Move, and Rename. If you select any of these options, dBASE IV displays the submenu shown in Figure 9.24, so you can choose to perform the operation on the single file that is currently highlighted, on all files that are marked, or on all files that are displayed.

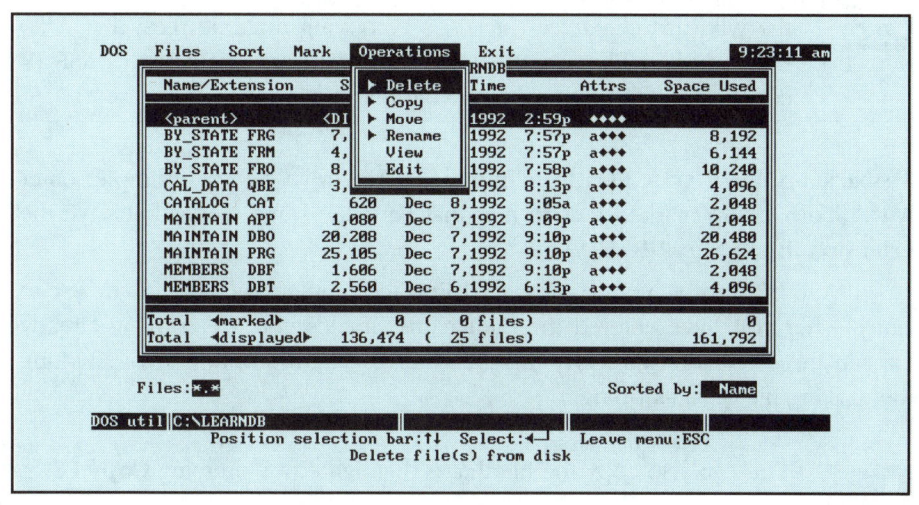

Figure 9.23 *The Operations menu.*

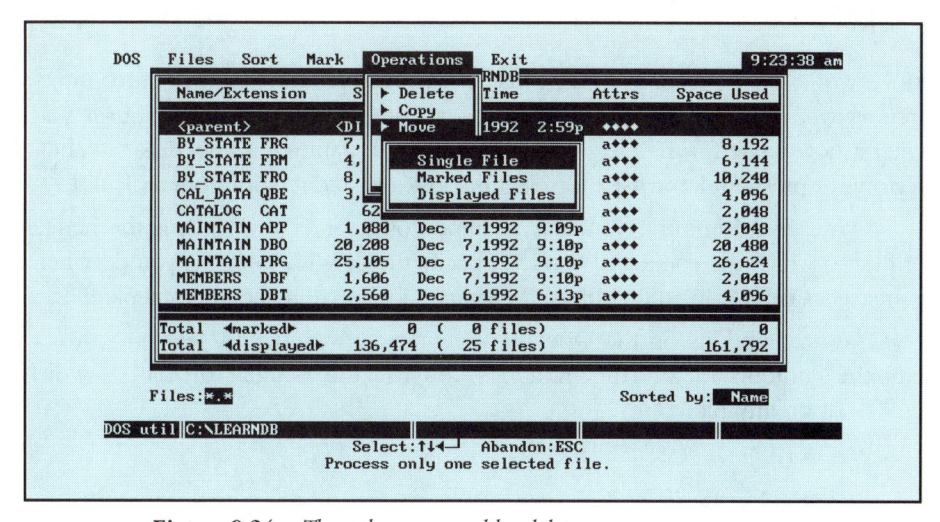

Figure 9.24 *The submenu used by delete, copy, move, rename.*

Selecting **Delete** deletes files permanently from the disk. Selecting **Copy** copies files to another disk or directory. When you select it, dBASE IV prompts you to enter the directory to copy the files to. You may type in the path name of the directory or press **Pick:Shift-F1** to select the directory from a picklist.

> **NOTE** Enter the path name of the directory followed by a file name if you are copying a single file or followed by a file skeleton that contains the wildcard character * if you are copying multiple files. If you do not include a file name that uses this wildcard character, dBASE IV copies all of the files to the one file that is named.

To back up all of your files to a floppy disk in drive A:, for example, enter A:*.*. To back up marked files to files that have the same names but have the extension .BAK, enter *.BAK.

dBASE IV prompts you to press **Ctrl-End** to complete the copying or **Esc** to cancel after you have entered the path name. If files you are copying already exist in the destination directory, dBASE IV gives you the option of overwriting the existing file or of skipping it.

> **SHORTCUT** You can also copy the file that is highlighted by pressing **Copy:F8**.

Move works a bit like Copy except that it removes the file from the source directory as well as copying it to the destination directory. It also does not let you enter a new name for the file. Simply type the path name of a new disk or subdirectory, or press **Pick:Shift-F1** to select the disk or subdirectory from a picklist.

If you select **Rename**, dBASE IV prompts you to enter a new name for the file or files to which the command applies. Specify the new file name as you do when you select **Copy**, using the * wildcard character if you are renaming multiple files.

The final options on the Operations menu, View and Edit, let you view or edit the contents of any file. Edit lets you use the familiar dBASE IV word processor on any file.

You will have trouble understanding the contents of many files, though, and you should be very cautious about editing any files except DOS text files. Most files have codes in them that are used by the programs that created them, and if you inadvertently change one of these, the file will probably not work properly.

The Exit Menu

The Exit menu of the DOS shell has only one option, Exit to Control Center. There is no choice of saving or abandoning changes, as changes are made permanently while you are working with the DOS shell. You can also return to the Control Center by pressing **Esc** (but not by pressing **Ctrl-End**).

Protect Data

Select **Protect data** from the Tools menu to add security measures that control access to your data. You can add log-in security, which prevents unauthorized users from using dBASE IV, file and field access security, which determines which users can access which files and fields, and data ecryptions, which codes dBASE IV files so unauthorized users cannot read them.

These options are used primarily on networks. See your network administrator for more information on when you should use them.

Settings

The Settings option lets you control the dBASE IV environment. The default settings are generally best for working from the Control Center, but changing settings becomes very important in programming.

After you select **Settings** from the Tools menu, you can use the Options menu to change miscellaneous environment settings or the Display menu to change settings that are related to screen display.

The Options Menu

The Options menu is shown in Figure 9.25, with the default settings that dBASE IV uses if you make no changes to the environment. As you can see, most of its options toggle ON and OFF. Just move the highlight to the option you want to change, and press **Enter** or **Spacebar** to toggle from the current setting. Other options of this menu prompt you to enter an integer or let you cycle among options.

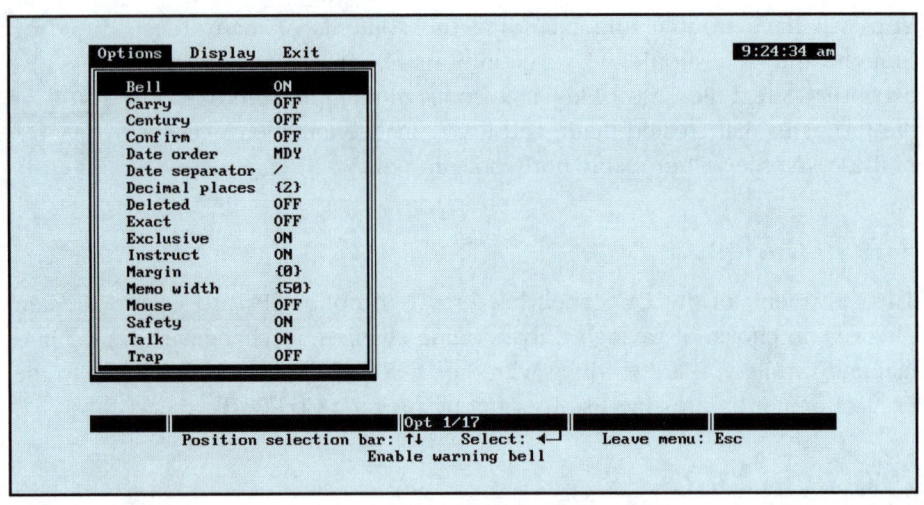

```
Options  Display  Exit                              9:24:34 am
         Bell            ON
         Carry           OFF
         Century         OFF
         Confirm         OFF
         Date order      MDY
         Date separator  /
         Decimal places  {2}
         Deleted         OFF
         Exact           OFF
         Exclusive       ON
         Instruct        ON
         Margin          {0}
         Memo width      {50}
         Mouse           OFF
         Safety          ON
         Talk            ON
         Trap            OFF

                         Opt 1/17
         Position selection bar: ↑↓   Select: ↵    Leave menu: Esc
                         Enable warning bell
```

Figure 9.25 *The Options menu.*

The effects of these settings are listed below. In most cases, the non-default settings are described, as you are already familiar with the effect of many of the default settings from the work you have done with dBASE IV. Compare these descriptions with the settings that you are accustomed to using.

- **Bell**: sounds a warning beep. If it is OFF, dBASE IV does not sound a beep when you press an invalid key or come to the end of a data entry field.

- **Carry**: copies data from a preceding record to a new record. The data that you enter in one record is carried to the next record if it is ON when you are appending new records to a database file. This is similar to the Carry forward menu option discussed earlier.

- **Century**: determines whether the century is included in the years of date fields. If it is ON, years are displayed with four digits (1991).

- **Confirm**: determines whether you must press **Enter** before data is accepted in a data entry field. If it is ON, dBASE IV beeps but does not move automatically to the next field when an entry fills a field. You must press **Enter** to confirm the entry and go to the next field.

- **Date order**: lets you change the date display from the default MDY, which displays date fields month first, then day, then year, to DMY or YMD.

- **Date separator**: lets you cycle from the default / to - or . to separate the month, day, and year in date fields.

- **Decimal places**: lets you enter an integer from 0 to 18 to determine how many decimal places are displayed by default in numbers.
- **Deleted**: ignores records marked for deletion. If it is ON, records that are marked for deletion are ignored.
- **Exact**: determines if strings must be identical for there to be a match. If it is ON, strings must be identical in length as well as content for there to be a match.
- **Exclusive**: determines file access rights. If it is ON, other users in a network may not access an open file.
- **Instruct**: determines whether prompt boxes are displayed. If it is OFF, dBASE IV does not display prompt boxes when you select objects in the Control Center. For example, selecting a database file immediately uses the file. To see the data or modify the structure, you must press **Data:F2** or **Design:Shift-F2**.
- **Margin**: determines the left margin for printed output by allowing you to enter an integer.
- **Memo width**: determines the width of the column used by default to display memo fields by allowing you to enter an integer.
- **Safety**: determines the display of a confirming message before overwriting files. If it is OFF, dBASE IV overwrites existing files without a warning.
- **Talk**: determines the display of results of operations. If it is OFF, dBASE IV does not display added information on commands that it executes when you are working from the dot prompt.
- **Trap**: if it is ON, dBASE IV activates the debugger when it finds an error in a program.

Some of these options, such as setting Safety OFF, are dangerous and should be avoided, unless you have a special reason to use them.

The options to determine the display of dates may be used in combination to display dates fields in any order, with any separator, with or without the century.

The Display Menu

The Display menu, shown in Figure 9.26, lets you control the way dBASE IV displays elements of its screens, such as normal text, messages, highlights, boxes, information, and fields.

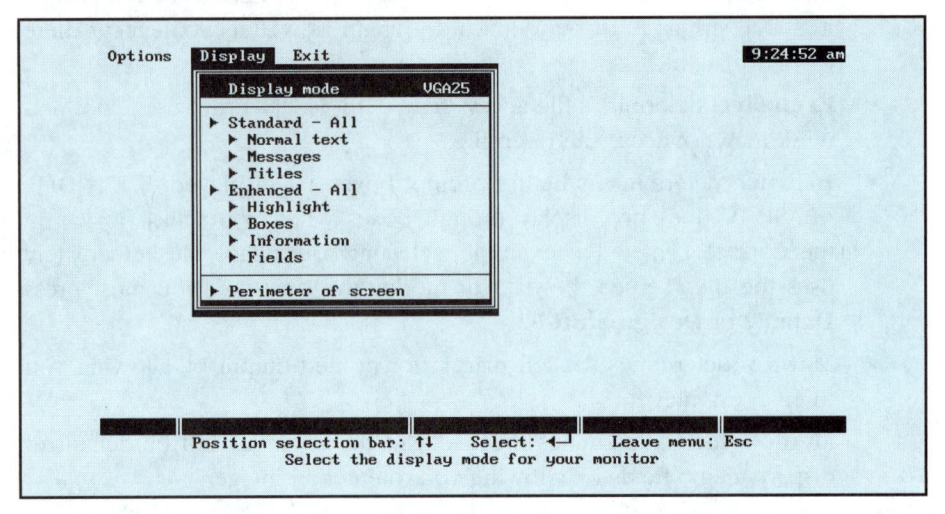

Figure 9.26 *The Display menu.*

The submenu that dBASE IV displays depends on whether you have a monochrome or color monitor. If you have a monochrome monitor, it lets you select Intensity, Underline, Reverse video, and Blink. If you have a color monitor, it lets you select among sixteen foreground and eight background colors.

For example, imagine that you have a monochrome monitor and you want the highlights to be in intense display instead of in reverse video. Select **Highlight**. Reverse video is on by default. Turn it off. Turn Intensity ON, and press **Ctrl-End** to accept the setting. Then, when you move the highlight among menu choices, dBASE IV displays them in intense (enhanced) display instead of in reverse video.

You can select **Display mode**, to use the Display submenu for either monochrome or color only if your system supports more than one type of monitor. This option is inactive on most systems.

The Exit Menu

The Exit menu has only one option, Exit to Control Center. You can also press either **Esc** or **Ctrl-End** to exit to the Control Center. Both have the same effect, as changes are always saved.

Summary

In this chapter you learned how to use additional features of the dBASE IV word processor and options on the Print menu and the Tools menu that can increase your ability to use dBASE IV effectively. In the next chapter you are introduced to the real power of a database management system—relational databases.

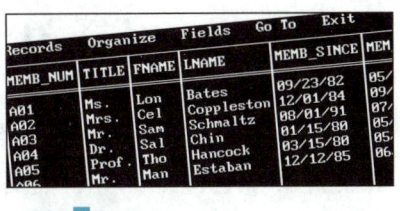

Chapter 10

Relational Databases

In the first part of this book, you learned the fundamentals of how to construct a simple database to handle data that has a one-to-one relationship among fields. In Chapter 2 you were introduced to the basics of analyzing your data and you learned about the three different types of relationships among fields: one-to-one, one-to-many, and many-to-many. Now you will see how to work with relational databases to manage more complex data.

In this chapter you learn how to:

- Reduce duplication of data through data normalization
- Identify data having one-to-many and many-to-many relationships
- Create a sample relational database
- Use key fields to link data contained in different files
- Create a query to join related files
- Use a query to create filters, sort, or index in relational databases
- Create formatted reports on relational databases

About Relational Databases

Before computers became widely used in business, a personnel department might have kept records with the name, address, Social Security number, and date hired for each employee. A payroll department might have kept records with the name, address, Social Security number, hourly wages, and hours worked for each employee. A training department might have kept files recording the name, address, Social Security number, and training courses taken by each employee. The same basic information—name, address, and Social Security number—may have been kept in a dozen different files by a dozen different departments. If a record changed—for example, if an employee moved—it would have been necessary to change the employee's address in all of the places files were kept. As you can see, this resulted in a great deal of extra work.

When large business first began the process of computerizing their records, an unexpected benefit was discovered.

At first, many businesses tended to create computer records containing the same information in the same form they had been accustomed to using. They soon discovered, however, that because of the ability of a computer to quickly process large amounts of data, it was no longer necessary for duplicate data to be maintained in several departments. Computer scientists found that it was necessary to keep only one central copy of the duplicated information (in this example, name, address, and Social Security number), and a computer could quickly locate it and combine it with the other information that each department needed.

Relational databases emerged as the most powerful and easiest to use method of combining data in this way. The basic idea of the relational database is that the data is broken down into separate files that are related using a common *key field*. For example, one file could hold employees' names, addresses, Social Security number, and an employee number that is used as a key field. Another file could have just employee numbers and training courses. To produce a report for the training department, the computer reads the file that lists training courses and employee numbers, and looks in the other file to find the name, address, and Social Security number for each employee number. Because it can look up data effortlessly, the computer can produce the same report as the training department always used, without keeping a separate copy of the name, address, and Social Security number for that department.

Normalizing Data

The process of breaking down your data into multiple files in order to reduce duplication of data is called *data normalization*. There are elaborate rules for normalizing data based on set theory, which are covered in advanced books on database design. In most cases, though, you just need to use common sense and to remember the basic rule that the fields in any single file should be in a one-to-one relationship.

When you analyze the data you need to work with, you might find that fields are in two other possible relationships besides the one-to-one relation that you need: you might find one-to-many or many-to-many relationships.

The One-to-Many Relationship

You have already considered the one-to-many relationship when you first analyzed the MEMBERS database. Remember that this file only keeps track of the date of the last donation. In the simple database you created, you could not keep track of all donations because one member might give more than one donation. This is a typical one-to-many relationship.

You can handle it by breaking down the database into two files, like those shown in Table 10.1. As you can see from this example, "many" can mean any number from zero up. Some people give no donations, some give one, and some give more.

Table 10.1 *A One-to-many relationship.*

DONATIONS FILE:

MEMB_NUM	DATE	AMOUNT
A01	01/01/88	100.00
A01	05/15/89	50.00
A01	02/10/90	50.00
A02	08/16/91	100.00
A04	12/30/89	150.00
A04	12/28/91	150.00
A06	01/15/91	30.00

MEMBERS FILE:

MEMB_NUM	TITLE	FNAME	LNAME	ADDRESS1
A01	Ms.	Loni	Bates	Twenty-First Century Fund
A02	Mrs.	Celia	Copplestone	2031 Kenmore Terrace
A03	Mr.	Samuel	Schmaltz	1701 Albemarle Rd.
A04	Dr.	Sally E.	Chin	1 Alvarado Plaza—Ste. 43
A05	Prof.	Thomas	Hancock	National Research Laboratory
A06	Mr.	Manuel	Estaban	476 Partridge Hill Rd.

Look at this database, so that you can see clearly how dBASE relates the two files. For example, when it sees a record in the DONATIONS file with the member number A04, it looks up the record in the MEMBERS file with the same member number, so it can fill in the name, address, and other data on the member who gave that donation.

For this reason, the file that is on the "one" side of the one-to-many relation is sometimes called the *detail file* or the *look-up file*: it fills in the missing details for each record in the file on the "many" side of the relationship.

The file on the "many" side of the relationship is called the *controlling file*, because it controls how many records will be in the queries or reports that combine the two files. With the sample data listed above, for example, a report on donations would have three records for member A01, one for each record in the controlling file. Each record would have the data from the DONATIONS file with that member's name and other details from the MEMBERS file added to it.

NOTE The key field in the detail file must be unique for the database to work properly. You cannot have two different records in the MEMBERS file with the same MEMB_NUM, or dBASE would not know which to use for the name and address. On the other hand, records in the file on the "many" side of the relationship can and often does have more than one record with the same MEMB_NUM. This does not create any problem in looking up the data.

The Many-to-Many Relationship

A database meant to keep track of which students are enrolled in which classes at a college is a typical example of a many-to-many relationship: each student takes many classes, each class has many students in it.

The way to deal with this sort of database is by breaking it up into three files, one with data on students, one with data on classes, and one with data on enrollments that links the other two, as shown in Table 10.2:

Table 10.2 *A Many-to-many relationship.*

STUDENTS:

STU_NUM	FNAME	LNAME	ADDRESS
A001	James H.	Spero	101 First St.
A002	Cynthia	Bingham	456 Main St.
A003	Ann	Chandler	5690 Cedar St.

CLASSES:

CLAS_NUM	TITLE	ROOM	HOURS
X01	Intro. To Spanish	441 Boylan Hall	Tu-Th:11-12
X02	Advanced Spanish	823 Low Hall	M-W-F:9-10
X03	Biochemistry	451 Chemistry Hall	Tu-Th:3-5
X04	Computer Science	1243 Evans Hall	M-Tu-W-F:9-11

ENROLLMENTS:

STU_NUM	CLASS_NUM	GRADE
A001	X01	B+
A001	X03	A-
A001	X04	C
A002	X02	A+
A003	X02	B-
A003	X03	B+

Notice that the computer can combine these files to extract any data that you need. For example, if you want to see which classes Ann Chandler is taking, look in the STUDENTS file to find that her number is A003, then look in the ENROLLMENTS file to find that the student with that number is taking classes X02 and X03. Then look in the CLASSES file to find the names, rooms and hours of the classes with those numbers. On the other hand, to find who is taking Biochemistry, begin in the CLASSES file to find that it is class number X03, then go to the ENROLLMENTS file to find the student numbers of the students taking X03. Finally, go to the STUDENTS file to find the names and addresses of the students taking the course.

Note that both the STUDENTS and the CLASSES files are in a one-to-many relation with the linking ENROLLMENTS file. One student or one class may have many enrollments. One enrollment must consist of just one student and one class.

Both STUDENTS and CLASSES are used as detail files by the ENROLLMENTS file, to look up the names and addresses of students or the names, locations, and hours of classes, so both STUDENTS and CLASSES must have unique key fields. You cannot have two records in the STUDENTS file with the same STU_NUM, for example, because dBASE must be able to look up the students' name and address in the STUDENTS file and find only one name and address for each.

Of course, grades also go in the ENROLLMENTS file, because there is one grade for each enrollment of a student in a class.

More Complex Data

Many databases are even more complex, and you should look briefly at the complex data that you may run across in some actual applications, though you should not try to master this sort of application yet.

Imagine, for example, that the sales representatives at your business each deal with many customers, that each customer makes many purchases, and that each purchase includes many inventory items.

Table 10.3   *A complex database.*

SALESREPS:	EMPL_NUM, FNAME, LNAME, ADDRESS ...
CUSTOMERS:	CUST_NUM, EMPL_NUM, CONTACT, COMPANY_NAME, ADDRESS ...

SALES:	INVOICE_NUM, CUST_NUM, DATE, DISCOUNT
ITEMS_SOLD:	INVOICE_NUM, ITEM_NUM, QUANT_SOLD
INVENTORY:	ITEM_NUM, PRICE, DESCRIPTION ...
(WAGES:	EMPL_NUM, DATE, HOURS_WORKED, ...)

Table 10.3 outlines the structures of the files that you might use to hold this data. (To make it easier to read, some of the file and field names used are longer than you could actually use in dBASE.)

The SALESREPS file holds the basic data on your sales representatives: their employee numbers, names, addresses, and so on.

The CUSTOMERS file holds the basic data on your customers: their customer numbers, the company names, addresses, your contact person at each company, and also the employee number of the Customer Sales Representative you have assigned to deal with this customer.

We are assuming a one-to-many relation between Sales Representatives and Customers: each customer deals with just one sales representative, and each sales representative deals with many customers. Thus, EMPL_NUM must be unique in the CUSTREPS file but not in the CUSTOMERS file.

The SALES file includes an INVOICE_NUM as its key field, plus the CUST_NUM of the customer to whom the sale was made, the date of the sale, and the discount on the sale (assuming that the sales representative can negotiate a discount on each sale). Note that, since sales are in a one-to-many relationship with Customers, CUST_NUM must be unique to each record in the CUSTOMERS file but is repeated in several records in the SALES file. When you bill for the sale, for example, you use the CUSTOMERS file as the look-up file to find the name and address of the company you bill, and there had better be only one company to bill.

You do not include the individual items sold in the record of that sale in the SALES file, however, because there is a one-to-many relationship between sales and items sold. In fact, you do not know how many items will be sold in each sale, so you could not put items sold in the SALES file—you would not know how many fields to have for them.

Instead, you break down the data about each sale into the SALES file plus a separate file of ITEMS_SOLD, which has the INVOICE_NUM of the sale plus the ITEM_NUM of the item and the quantity of that item sold in that sale.

Other data about the item is kept in an INVENTORY file, with the ITEM_NUM, PRICE, DESCRIPTION, and presumably other data about each item (such as the number in inventory).

Notice that SALES and INVENTORY are actually in a many-to-many relationship. Each sale includes many inventory items, and each inventory item is sold in many sales. The ITEMS_SOLD file relates these two in the same way as the ENROLLMENTS file related students and classes in the previous example. ITEMS_SOLD is in a many-to-one relation with both SALES and INVENTORY: The INVOICE_NUM in the ITEMS_SOLD file is used to look up data about the sale in the SALES file, and the ITEM_NUM in the ITEMS_SOLD file is used to look up data about the item in the INVENTORY file.

Those five files are needed to hold data about your sales. Just in case the database still seems too simple, though, the WAGES file is included in parentheses to point out that, in a real-life application, you might also have to keep data about the hours that your sales representatives and other employees worked, their hourly wages, and so on.

Ignoring the WAGES file, though, you might want to trace the logic of how the other files are connected. For example, you can produce a report with the sales of each sales representative by finding all of the CUSTOMERS with the EMPL_NUM of that sales representative in their records, all of the SALES with the CUST_NUM of those customers in their records, all of the ITEMS_SOLD with the INVOICE_NUMS of those sales in their records, and finding the price and description of each of the ITEMS_SOLD by looking up the record with its ITEM_NUM in the INVENTORY file.

The Key Field

Notice that in all of the examples you have looked at, even this very complex one, you finally break down the data into several files with one-to-many relationships among one another. In the example in this chapter, you just work on a simple database with a one-to-many relationship, to keep track of members' donations, but even the most complex data is finally analyzed into multiple one-to-many relationships, all of which dBASE handles in the same way as the simple one you will look at.

Only one other point should be mentioned before you go on to create a sample relational database—what to use as the key field. Novices sometimes look for some unique key that already exists in their data to use as the key field.

For example, if no two people in the list have the same name, they may be tempted to use LNAME as the key.

Never use a meaningful key field of this sort. What if someone new joins with the same name as someone already in the file? And what if people change their names, for example because they get married? You not only have to change the name in the lookup file: you also have to change every key field in the controlling file, so it still relates to the right record in the lookup file. This could lead to errors and it could be a major task if you have a complex database with a large number of controlling files that use details from the same lookup file. It creates just the sort of duplication of data entry that a relational database is meant to avoid.

It is best to use an arbitrary value as the key field, such as an employee number. The only meaningful value that you might use as a key field is the Social Security number, since it is assigned arbitrarily, it is unique to each person, and it never changes. This could create problems, though, if the database contains records on people who do not have Social Security numbers: for example, people who are residents of other countries.

Creating the Database

As a sample relational database, add to your MEMBERS database a second file to hold donations. Records in the DONATNS file only need to have the member number, the date of the donation, and the amount of the donation. The MEMBERS file is the detail file, where dBASE IV looks up the name and address of the member who gave each donation.

Before creating a new file for donations, you should create a new Catalog to hold this relational database, and you should modify the structure of the MEMBERS file. The MEMBERS file no longer needs a field to hold the date of the last donation, since you will be keeping track of all the donations. It also needs to be indexed on MEMB_NUM.

NOTE: As you will see when you use a query to join the MEMBERS and DONATNS file, indexes of the MEMB_NUM fields of both are included. If you do not create or include indexes for the key fields that relate the two files, dBASE IV automatically creates temporary indexes each time that you execute the query. This indexing is transparent to the user, but it takes extra time whenever you execute the query. For better performance, you should create the indexes yourself and include them in the query, so they are updated during data entry and are ready for use when the query is executed.

1. First, modify the structure of MEMBERS and save it under a different name. It cannot have the same name, as it will be used again in its original form in a later chapter. Select **MEMBERS** from the Data panel and select **Modify structure/order** from the prompt box. Press **Esc** to get rid of the Organize menu.

2. Then select **Save this database file structure** from the Layout menu.

3. When dBASE IV prompts you with Save as:, change the file name to MEMBERS2. Leave the path name and extension as they are. Then press **Enter**.

4. To index on the MEMB_NUM field, move the highlight to the Index column and type *Y*.

5. Now, move the highlight down to the LAST_DONAT field, and press **Ctrl-U** to delete it.

6. Finally, press **Ctrl-End** to save the changes and *Y* to confirm and return to the Control Center.

7. Select the new MEMBERS2 file and select **Close file** from the prompt box.

8. Then move the highlight to MEMBERS2 again and select **Remove highlighted file from catalog** from the Catalog menu. Press *Y* to confirm that you want to remove it from the Catalog, and press *N* to indicate that you *do not* want to delete it from the disk. (You had to close the file first because dBASE IV does not remove an open file from the Catalog.)

9. Select **Use a different catalog** from the Catalog menu.

10. Then select **<create>** from the picklist of catalogs and, when dBASE IV prompts you to **Enter name for new catalog**, type *relatnl* and press **Enter**.

11. Select **Add file to catalog** from the Catalog menu, and select **MEMBERS2.DBF** from the picklist of files. As its description, enter *Detail file on members*.

Now that you have created a new catalog to hold the relational database and added the data in the members file to it, you can create the second file of this database and enter some sample records in it.

1. Select **<create>** from the Data panel.
2. For field 1, enter MEMB_NUM as the field name, keep Character as the type, enter *3* as the width, and type *Y* in the Index column.
3. For field 2, enter *date* as the field name, press *D* to enter Date as the type, 8 is automatically entered as the width, press **Enter** to keep N in the index column.
4. For field 3, enter *amount* as the field name, type *N* to enter Numeric as the type, enter *7* as the Width and *2* as the number of decimal places. Keep N in the Index column. The structure of this file is shown in Figure 10.1.

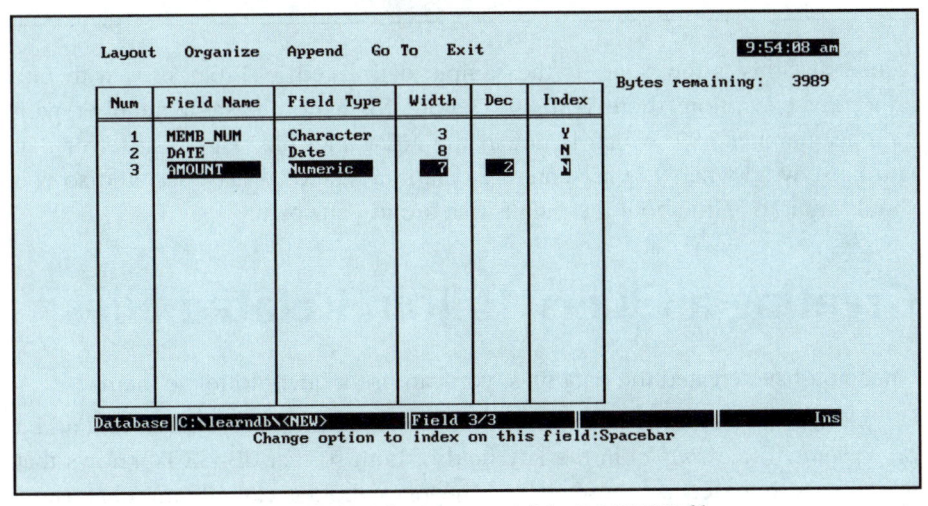

Figure 10.1   *The Structure of the DONATNS file.*

5. Now, select **Edit database description** from the Layout menu, and when dBASE IV prompts you to *Edit the description of this .dbf file*, type *List of donations by members* and press **Enter**.

6. Finally, press **Ctrl-End** to save your work. When dBASE IV prompts you for the name to Save as, type *donatns* and press **Enter**.
7. When dBASE IV asks you whether you want to add records now, press Y to go to the edit screen. As sample data, enter the records listed in Table 10.4. Press **Ctrl-End** to return to the Control Center when you are done.

Table 10.4 Sample data for the DONATNS file.

MEMB_NUM	DATE	AMOUNT
A01	01/01/88	100.00
A01	05/15/89	50.00
A01	02/10/90	50.00
A02	08/16/91	100.00
A04	12/30/89	150.00
A04	12/28/91	150.00
A06	01/15/91	30.00
A99	10/07/91	1000.00

Notice that this is the same as the sample data listed in Table 10.1, with one important exception: there is also a record for a non-existent member with member number A99, which is not in the MEMBERS file. This is an error that you must avoid when you are entering data in a relational database, and so you should try it to learn about the pitfalls that are in your path.

Creating a Query to Join Related Files

Once you have created the data files, you can use a query to relate them.

All you have to do is use both file skeletons on the query screen and add a *place holder* (or *example*) in the key field of both so that dBASE IV knows that the relation is based on these fields. The place holder can be any characters, such as abc or HELLO, as long as it is the same in the two key fields that are related and is not used in other fields.

You can easily add these place holders by selecting **Create link by pointing** from the Layout menu. When you make this selection, dBASE IV adds the word LINK1 to the current field and prompts you to move the cursor to a second field and press **Enter** in order to add the word LINK1 there also. If you are using a more complex database and need to create more than one relation, it uses the words LINK2 for the second, LINK3 for the third, and so on.

You can add any or all of the fields in both files to the view skeleton. If fields in the two files have the same name, dBASE IV prompts you to enter an alternate name for one of them: this new name is only used in the view skeleton, which cannot have two fields with the same name. The name of the field does not change in the actual file.

In dBASE IV version 1.0 and 1.1, the query that joins two files in this way is read-only. You can use it to extract data from the related files, but not to change these files. In later versions, you can edit the view.

1. At the Control Center, first make sure the DONATNS file is in use. It should be above the line in the Data panel. Then select **<create>** from the Queries panel.

2. The queries design screen for the DONATNS file appears. Select **Include indexes** from the Fields menu: a # or arrowhead appears before the MEMB_NUM field to indicate that it is indexed.

3. Select **Add file to query** from the Layout menu, and select **MEMBERS2.DBF** from the picklist that is displayed.

4. Press **Field:F5** to add all fields of MEMBERS2 to the view skeleton. dBASE IV prompts you to enter a new name for the MEMB_NUM field, since its name is the same as a field already in the view skeleton. Just type *B* to change its name to MEMB_NUMB and press **Enter**. All the fields are added to the view skeleton.

5. Select **Include indexes** from the Fields menu to include the indexes in this file also. Note the **#** or arrowhead before MEMB_NUM.

6. Now, relate the two files. Move the cursor to the MEMB_NUM field of the MEMBERS2 file skeleton. Then select **Create link by pointing** from the Layout menu. dBASE IV adds the word LINK1 to the current field, and the navigation line prompts you to press **Enter** to finish.

7. Move the cursor to the MEMB_NUM field of the DONATNS file, and press **Enter** to make dBASE IV add the word LINK1 there also. That is all you need to relate the two files and include all the fields of both in the resulting view, as shown in Figure 10.2.

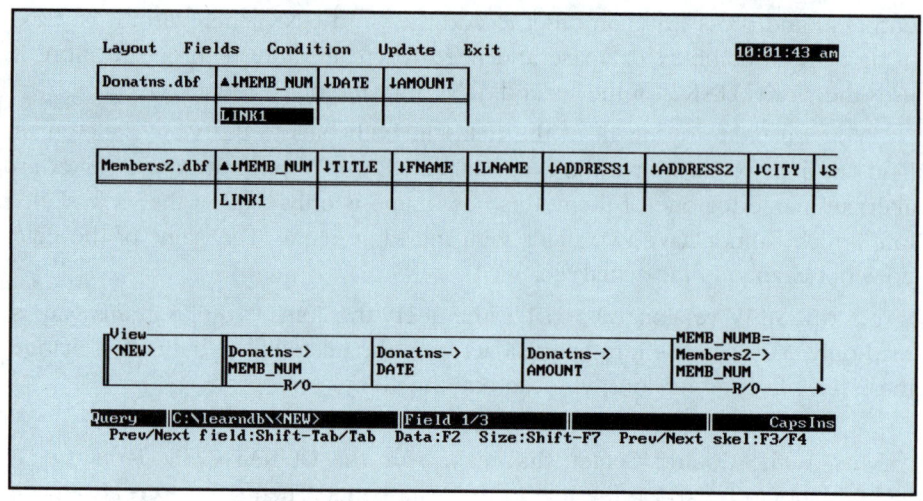

Figure 10.2 *A query relating the two files.*

8. Select **Edit description of query** from the Layout menu, and as the description of the file, type *Relates DONATNS and MEMBERS2 files and includes all fields in view* and press **Enter**.

9. Then press **Ctrl-End** to save your work, and when dBASE IV prompts you for the name to save as, type *dons_dtl* and press **Enter** to return to the Control Center.

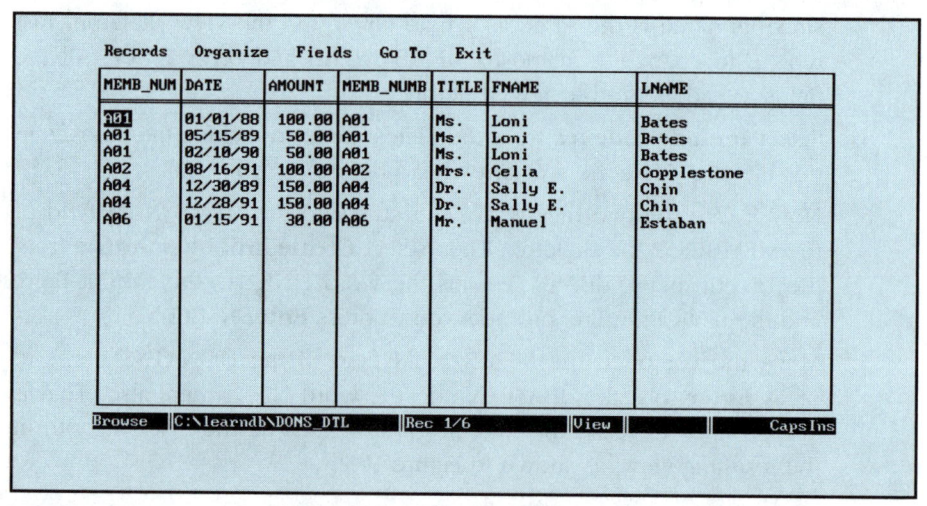

Figure 10.3 *The data from this view.*

10. Now, press **Data:F2** to see the result of this query. dBASE IV displays the Browse screen shown in Figure 10.3.

Note that the browse screen has a record for each record in the controlling5 DONATNS file; the same details from the MEMBERS2 file are repeated for records with the same MEMB_NUM. But it does not have a record for the donation with MEMB_NUM A99, the member number entered incorrectly.

By default, a view that relates two files has a record only when the common key field appears in both files. It leaves out the members who did not give donations, and it also leaves out the donations that do not have corresponding members.

Including All Records

There are times when you want a view that includes all of the records from the look-up file. You might want to produce a donations report that included all of your members, for example, so you could see who has given a donation and who has not.

As a general rule, you should *always* include all records from the controlling file in any view. There should not be any records from the controlling file that do not have a corresponding record in the detail file, so all of the records should appear in the view even if they are not included explicitly—but, as you know, things are not always what they should be. It is good to include all records from the controlling file explicitly, to make it easier to detect errors.

You can include all of the records from any file in a view simply by using the operator *Every* before the place holder in the key field of that record.

Try changing your query to make the lost donation reappear:

1. Press **Design:Shift-F2** to return from the Browse screen to the queries design screen. (Or, if you have already returned to the Control Center, highlight **DONS_DTL** in the Queries panel and press **Design:Shift-F2**.)

2. The cursor should already be on the place holder LINK1 in the DONATNS file skeleton. If it is not, move it there. Edit this place holder so it reads *Every LINK1*. If you are not in Ins mode and you inadver-

tently type over part of the word LINK1 when you try to add Every, do not worry; just retype any letters you typed over. LINK1 was added by pointing, but it can just as well be typed in.

3. The query now looks like Figure 10.4. Press **Data:F2** to see the Browse screen in Figure 10.5.

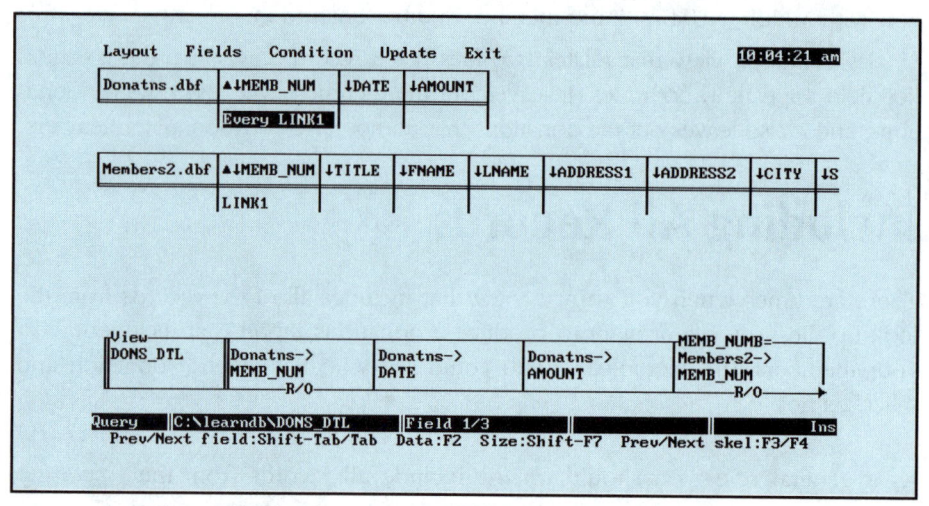

Figure 10.4   *The query with the every operator.*

Figure 10.5   *The result of this query.*

The mysterious donation with MEMB_NUM A99 has appeared, and you can see that an error was made in data entry, as there is not a corresponding record in the MEMBERS2 file.

If you wanted a query that included all members, you could use Every in just the same way with the MEMB_NUM of the MEMBERS2 file.

Working with a Relational Database

Once you have set up the view that joins the two files, you can work with it much as you work with other views. You can move the pointer through the browse window to view your data, create queries that filter out certain records, index or sort records, and produce reports as you have with single-file databases.

Viewing and Editing Data

You can move through the Browse window to view the data just as you do with any database file, using the cursor movement keys and the mouse.

In versions 1.0 and 1.1 of dBASE IV, this view is read only, and so you cannot add or edit the data using this view. You must use the individual database files.

In versions 1.5 and 2.0 of dBASE IV, however, you can add or edit data using this view as you do with any view.

You must be very careful not to edit the key field in the detail file when you edit a view of a relational database in this way, as changing this key field can cause very substantial loss of data. In fact, it is best not to include the key field of the detail file in the view, to make sure it is not altered by mistake. This field is not needed, because it merely duplicates the key field of the controlling file.

Finding Specific Records

You can use the query to create a filter in a relational database just as you do with any other database. Enter the criterion under any field of any file skeleton, and you will filter records out of the resulting view that do not match.

Figure 10.6 shows a query with a criterion in the controlling file, to list only donations given since the beginning of 1991, and Figure 10.7 shows the result of that query.

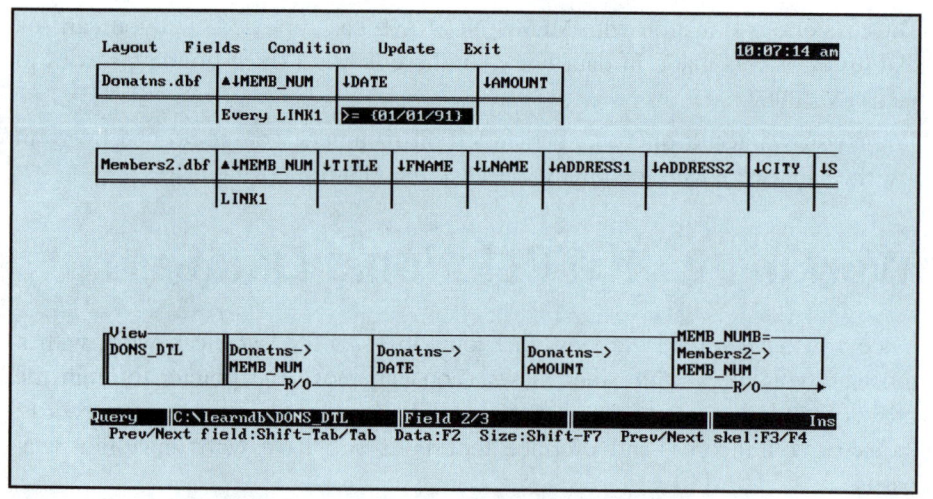

```
Layout    Fields    Condition    Update    Exit              10:07:14 am
┌──────────┬──────────┬──────────┬──────────┐
│Donatns.dbf│↕MEMB_NUM │↓DATE     │↓AMOUNT   │
│          │Every LINK1│>= {01/01/91}│       │
└──────────┴──────────┴──────────┴──────────┘

┌──────────┬──────────┬────────┬───────┬───────┬─────────┬─────────┬─────┬──┐
│Members2.dbf│↕MEMB_NUM│↓TITLE │↓FNAME │↓LNAME │↓ADDRESS1│↓ADDRESS2│↓CITY│↓S│
│          │LINK1     │        │       │       │         │         │     │  │
└──────────┴──────────┴────────┴───────┴───────┴─────────┴─────────┴─────┴──┘

┌View────────┬──────────┬──────────┬──────────┬MEMB_NUMB=──┐
│DONS_DTL    │Donatns-> │Donatns-> │Donatns-> │Members2->  │
│            │MEMB_NUM  │DATE      │AMOUNT    │MEMB_NUM    │
│            │───R/O──  │          │          │────R/O─────│
└────────────┴──────────┴──────────┴──────────┴────────────┘
Query    C:\learndb\DONS_DTL    Field 2/3                    Ins
  Prev/Next field:Shift-Tab/Tab  Data:F2  Size:Shift-F7  Prev/Next skel:F3/F4
```

Figure 10.6   *A query with criterion in the controlling file.*

```
Records    Organize    Fields    Go To    Exit
┌─────────┬────────┬────────┬─────────┬──────┬─────────┬──────────────┐
│MEMB_NUM │DATE    │AMOUNT  │MEMB_NUMB│TITLE │FNAME    │LNAME         │
├─────────┼────────┼────────┼─────────┼──────┼─────────┼──────────────┤
│A02      │08/16/91│ 100.00 │A02      │Mrs.  │Celia    │Copplestone   │
│A04      │12/28/91│ 150.00 │A04      │Dr.   │Sally E. │Chin          │
│A06      │01/15/91│  30.00 │A06      │Mr.   │Manuel   │Estaban       │
│A99      │10/07/91│1000.00 │         │      │         │              │
└─────────┴────────┴────────┴─────────┴──────┴─────────┴──────────────┘
Browse   C:\learndb\DONS_DTL   Rec 4/8           View              Ins
```

Figure 10.7   *The result of this query.*

Figure 10.8 shows a query with the criterion in the lookup file to find only donations from members from California, and Figure 10.9 shows the result of that query, though in Figure 10.9, you cannot see the state on the screen, if you try the query you will see that only California members are included.

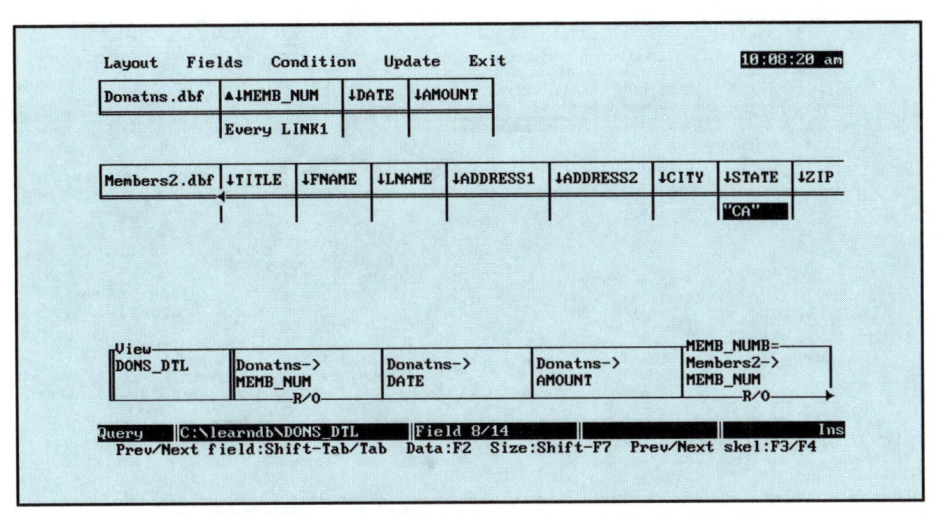

Figure 10.8 A query with the criterion in the lookup file.

Figure 10.9 The result of this query.

Finally, Figure 10.10 shows a query that has an AND relation between fields in the two files, to find donations from members from California that were given since the beginning of 1991, and Figure 10.11 shows the result of that query.

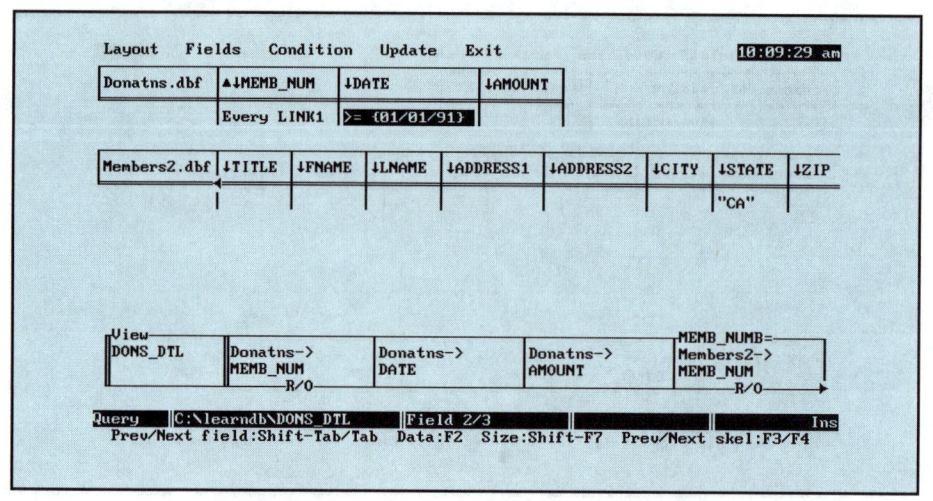

Figure 10.10   *A query with criteria in both files.*

Figure 10.11   *The result of this query.*

As you can see, you can enter criteria in the two file skeletons just as if they were a single file skeleton.

If you want to enter a criterion in the same field that has a place holder, just add a comma after the place holder to separate it from the criterion.

Chapter 10: Relational Databases ◆ **295**

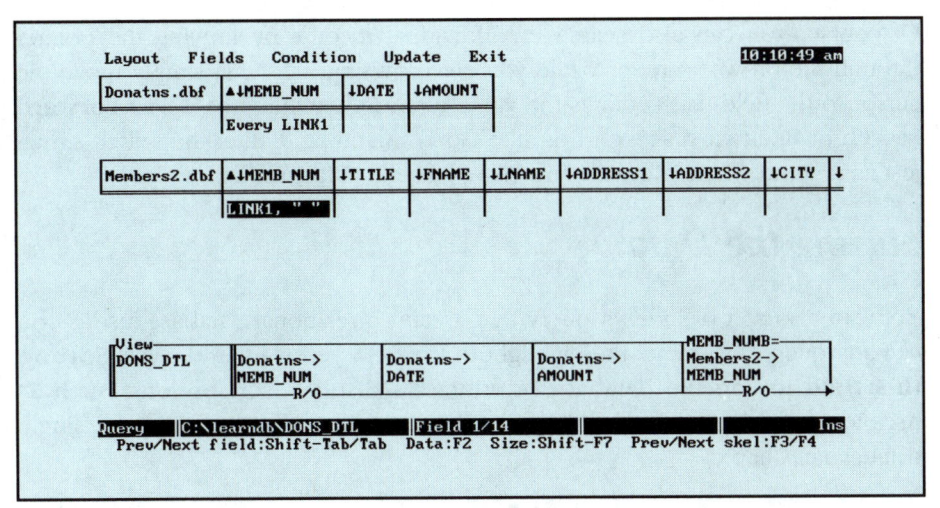

Figure 10.12 A query to find data entry errors.

Figure 10.13 The result of this query.

For example, Figure 10.12 shows a query that is useful to check for data entry errors, it finds records in the DONATNS file that do not have a corresponding record in the MEMBERS2 file. You can see in Figure 10.13 that this view isolates the record in the DONATNS file with detail fields that are blank. This record matches the criterion " " entered for the member number of the MEMBERS2 file.

NOTE

Of course, you can also search for individual records by moving the pointer through the browse screen. While you are browsing the view, simply move the cursor to the field that contains the value you are searching for, select **Forward search** or **Backward search** from the Go To menu, and enter the search string, just as you did when you were browsing a single database file.

Sorting the Data

You can also sort or index a query that creates a relational database just as you can any query. Just move the highlight to the field you want and select **Sort on this field** to sort the database. A submenu displays sort options (such as Ascending ASCII and Descending ASCII) as it did when you sorted a single database in Chapter 4.

> **NOTE** For better performance, use indexes rather than sorting. Create an index for the order that you want, include it in the field skeleton, and use it as the basis of the sort, as you did when you were working with a single file.

As an example, assume that you want donations listed by members' names in alphabetical order, with the donations of each member listed by date. In Chapter 11, you will learn to use expressions to create indexes based on mixed data types, like this one. For now, you can simply use a sort.

1. Beginning from the Control Center, highlight **DONS_DTL** and press **Design:Shift-F2** to use the queries design screen.
2. Move the cursor to the LNAME field of the MEMBERS2 file skeleton. Select **Sort on this field** from the Fields menu and **Ascending Dictionary** from the submenu.
3. Then move to the FNAME field, select **Sort on this field** from the Fields menu and **Ascending Dictionary** from the submenu.
4. Finally, move the cursor to the DATE field of the DONATNS file.
5. Then select **Sort on this field** from the Fields menu and select **Descending ASCII** from the submenu (to list the donations beginning with the most recent).
6. Select **Save this query** from the Layout menu and press **Enter** to keep the same name. The query is shown in Figure 10.14.

Chapter 10: Relational Databases ◆ **297**

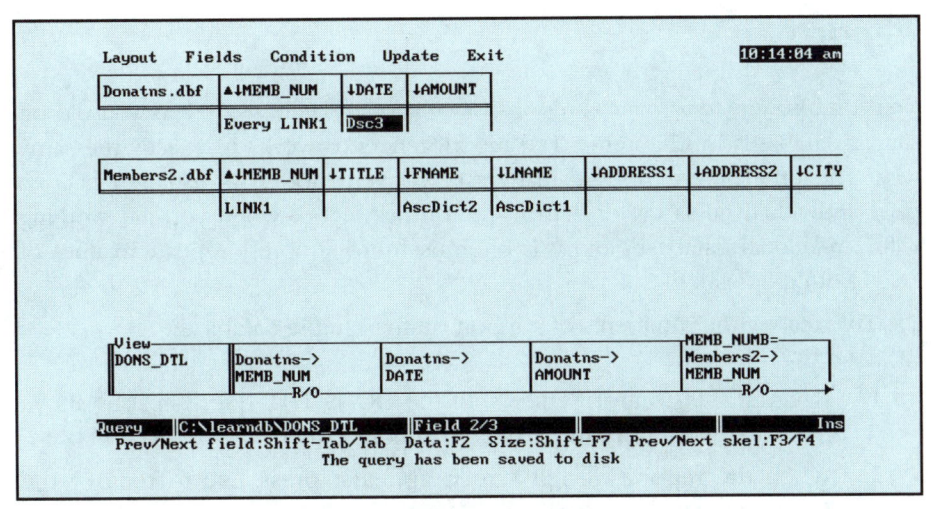

Figure 10.14 A sorted query.

7. To test the query, press **Data:F2**, to display the Browse screen shown in Figure 10.15. Then press **Esc** to return to the Control Center.

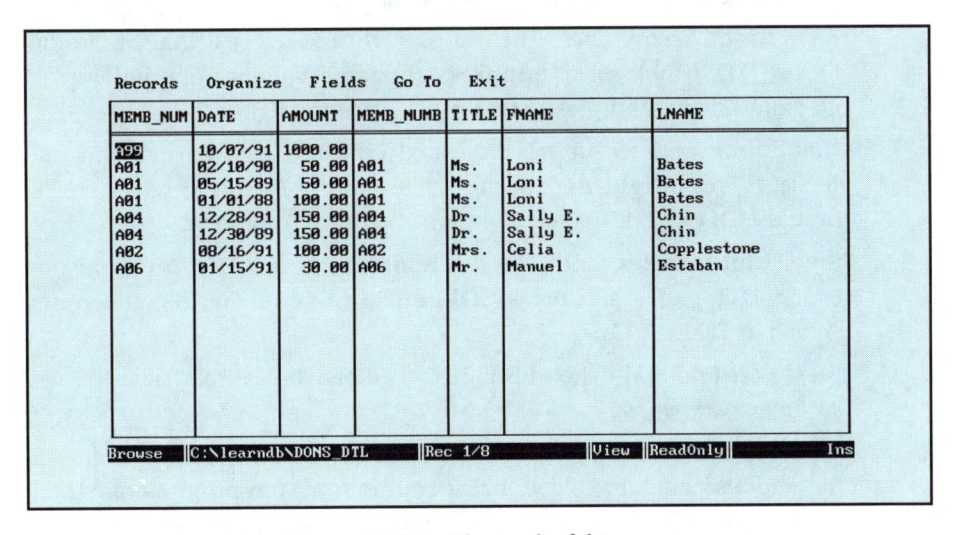

Figure 10.15 The result of this query.

Reports

You can also create formatted reports on relational databases just as you did on simple databases in Chapter 7. The report generator works in exactly the same way. The only differences are matters of convenience. It is usually easier to place individual fields rather than using a quick layout when you are working with a relational database, and it is often useful to suppress repeated values of fields from the detail file.

Try creating the rudiments of a report on the sample database:

1. Begin at the Control Center with the DONS_DTL query in use (above the line). Select **<create>** from the Reports panel.

2. When the reports design screen appears, press **Esc** to remove the **Layout** menu. Then press the **Down Arrow** five times to move the highlight into the Detail Band.

3. Press **Field:F5**, select **LNAME** from the DONS_DTL field list, select **Suppress repeated values** from the Display attributes menu to toggle it to YES, and then press **Ctrl-End** to place the field.

4. Press **Right Arrow** once. Then press **Field:F5**, select **FNAME** from the DONS_DTL panel, select **Suppress repeated values** from the Display attributes menu, and press **Ctrl-End** to place the field.

5. You do not want to suppress repeated values for the donation amount or date. Press **Right Arrow** once. Then press **Field:F5**, select **DATE** from the DONS_DTL panel, and press **Ctrl-End** to place it.

6. Press **Right Arrow** once, press **Field:F5**, select **AMOUNT** from the DONS_DTL panel, and press **Ctrl-End** to place it. The report form is shown in Figure 10.16.

7. Press **Ctrl-End** and, when dBASE IV prompts you for the name to save as, enter *donbymem*.

8. After you have returned to the Control Center, select **DONBYMEM** from the Reports panel and select **Print report** from the prompt box. Then select **View report on screen** from the Print menu. The preview of the report is shown in Figure 10.17. Notice that names are listed in alphabetical order, and that all of the donations for each member are listed on the lines next to and under each name. (The first line, with no name, is our mysterious entry for member number A99: since the name

is blank, it comes first in sort order.) Press the **Spacebar** until you return to the Control Center.

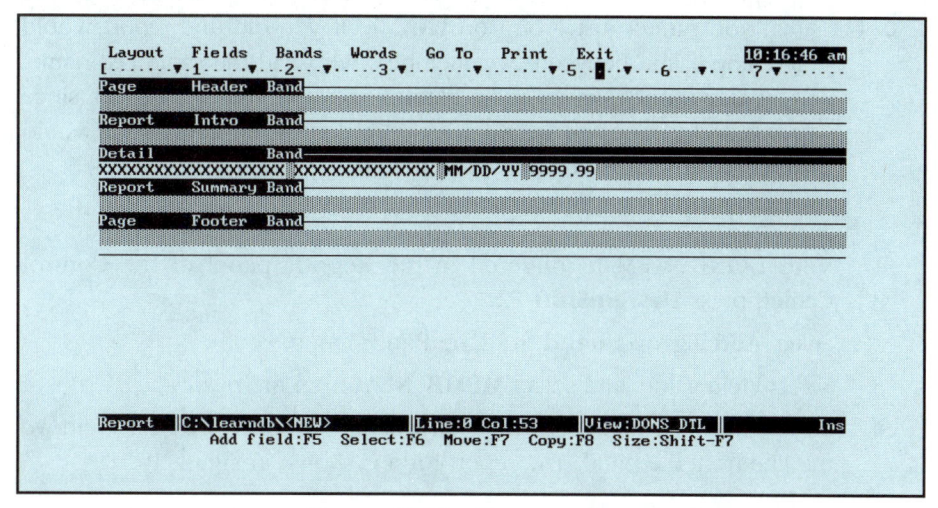

Figure 10.16   The report form.

Figure 10.17   The output of the report.

In an actual application, you would want to improve this report by adding a page header or footer, and a report introduction and perhaps a summary.

NOTE You might also want to skip lines between members. You can do this by grouping on member number and just putting a blank line in the group summary, so the report skips a line after each name. (Note that you cannot just group on LNAME. If you did, the report would not skip a line between two members who had the same last name. You also cannot simply add a blank line within the detail band, since it would be repeated between each record of the view, so it would separate donations made by the same member.)

1. With DONBYMEM highlighted in the Reports panel of the Control Center, press **Design:Shift-F2.**
2. Select **Add a group band** from the Bands menu.
3. Select Field value, and select **MEMB_NUM** from the picklist.
4. Move the cursor into the Group Intro Band, and press **Ctrl-Y** to remove the line from the band. The report form is shown in Figure 10.18.

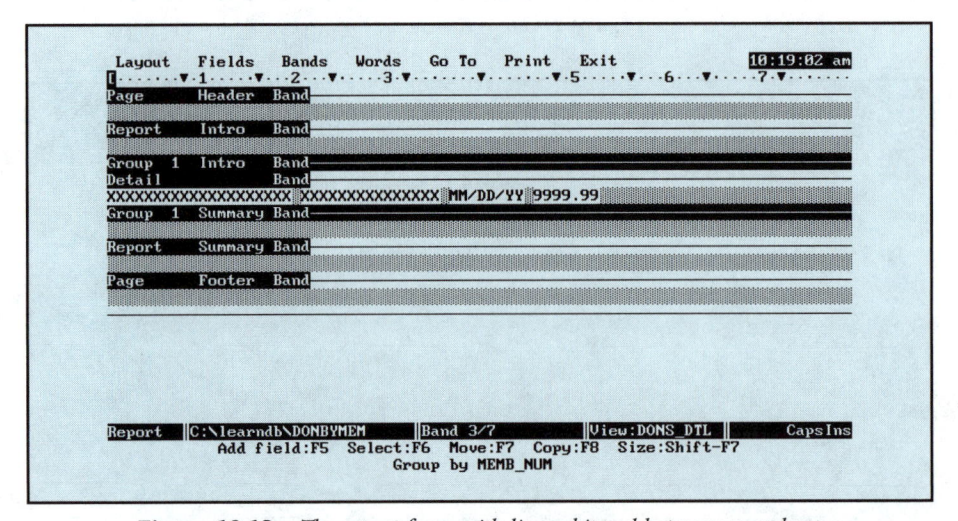

Figure 10.18 The report form with lines skipped between members.

5. Then press **Ctrl-End** to save the report and return to the Control Center.
6. Select **DONBYMEM** from the Reports panel, and select **Print report** from the prompt box. Then select **View report on screen** from the **Print** menu. The output is shown in Figure 10.19. Press the **spacebar** until you return to the Control Center.

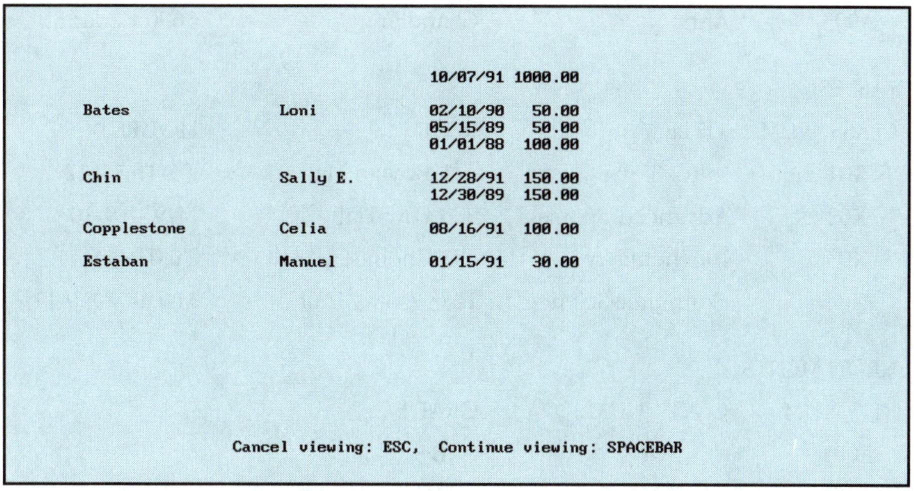

```
                              10/07/91 1000.00
         Bates        Loni    02/10/90   50.00
                              05/15/89   50.00
                              01/01/88  100.00
         Chin         Sally E. 12/28/91 150.00
                              12/30/89  150.00
         Copplestone  Celia   08/16/91  100.00
         Estaban      Manuel  01/15/91   30.00




         Cancel viewing: ESC,  Continue viewing: SPACEBAR
```

Figure 10.19   *The output of this report.*

Of course, you could also add a summary field in the Group Summary Band to calculate the total donations by each member, a summary field in the Report Summary Band to calculate total donations—and you could also add graphics, calculated fields, and any other feature that you may want to use in a formatted report.

More Complex Data

Now that you understand how to link database files, you should not have any problem working with more complex data. Since the techniques are the same, there is no need for you to go through another exercise. Instead, just think about setting up a database for enrollments, like the one described at the beginning of this chapter.

Look again at the sample data for this database, shown in Table 10.5.

Table 10.5   *A many-to-many relationship.*

STUDENTS:

STU_NUM	FNAME	LNAME	ADDRESS
A001	James H.	Spero	101 First St.
A002	Cynthia	Bingham	456 Main St.

| A003 | Ann | Chandler | 5690 Cedar St. |

CLASSES:

CLASS_NUM	TITLE	ROOM	HOURS
X01	Intro. To Spanish	441 Boylan Hall	Tu-Th:11-12
X02	Advanced Spanish	823 Low Hall	M-W-F:9-10
X03	Biochemistry	451 Chemistry Hall	Tu-Th:3-5
X04	Computer Science	1243 Evans Hall	M-Tu-W-F:9-11

ENROLLMENTS:

STU_NUM	CLASS_NUM	GRADE
A001	X01	B+
A001	X03	A-
A001	X04	C
A002	X02	A+
A003	X02	B-
A003	X03	B+

Now, imagine that you want to create a query that lists all of the students, the classes each took during the semester that is recorded in this database, and the grades each received in each class.

The query needed to link the files in this way is shown in Figure 10.20. Notice that there are two links, one from the ENROLMTS file to the STUDENTS file and one from the ENROLMTS file to the CLASSES file; the indexes for these key fields are included in all the files. The query is sorted by students' names, so the data is listed by student, as you can see in Figure 10.21.

The view skeleton in the example includes only the students' names, student numbers, the class numbers, class titles, and the grades, to make the browse screen easy for you to understand. In a real application, you might prefer to create a view that includes all of the fields from the STUDENTS and CLASSES files, and to design reports based on that view that include just the fields you need. As long as the query is sorted by students' names—or, perhaps for other purposes—by student number, all of the records for each student will come one after another, which is what you need for a report on students. (You might also want a view with the EVERY operator in the STU_NUM field of the

STUDENTS file, to get a listing of all students, even those who did not take classes during this semester.)

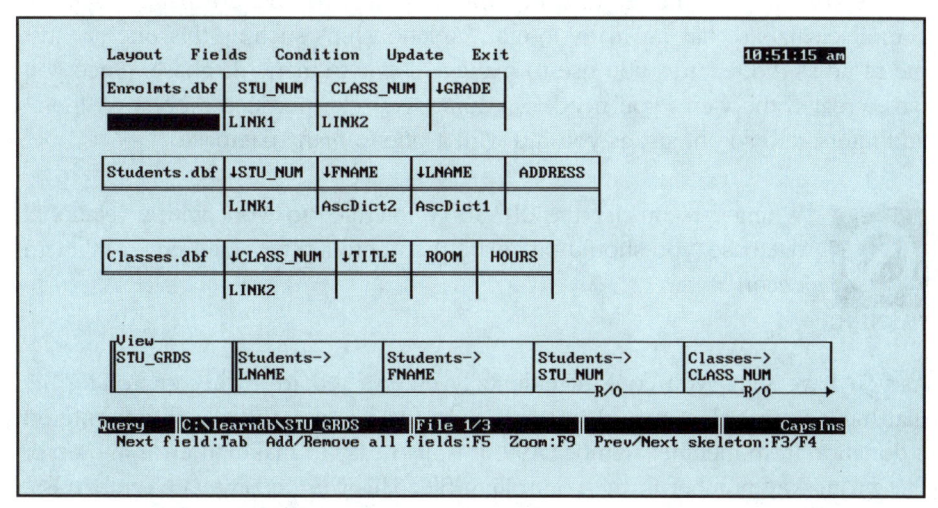

```
 Layout    Fields   Condition   Update   Exit              10:51:15 am
   Enrolmts.dbf  STU_NUM   CLASS_NUM   ↓GRADE
                 LINK1     LINK2

   Students.dbf  ↓STU_NUM  ↓FNAME     ↓LNAME     ADDRESS
                 LINK1     AscDict2   AscDict1

   Classes.dbf   ↓CLASS_NUM  ↓TITLE   ROOM   HOURS
                 LINK2

  ┌View─────────────────────────────────────────────────────────
  │STU_GRDS  Students->  Students->  Students->   Classes->
  │          LNAME       FNAME       STU_NUM      CLASS_NUM
  │                                         R/O              R/O

  Query   C:\learndb\STU_GRDS       File 1/3                CapsIns
   Next field:Tab   Add/Remove all fields:F5   Zoom:F9   Prev/Next skeleton:F3/F4
```

Figure 10.20   *A query to list students' classes and grades.*

```
 Records   Organize   Fields   Go To   Exit
 LNAME       FNAME        STU_NUM  CLASS_NUM  TITLE              GRADE
 BINGHAM     CYNTHIA      A002     X02        ADVANCED SPANISH   A+
 CHANDLER    ANN          A003     X02        ADVANCED SPANISH   B-
 CHANDLER    ANN          A003     X03        BIOCHEMISTRY       B+
 SPERO       JAMES H.     A001     X01        INTRO. TO SPANISH  B+
 SPERO       JAMES H.     A001     X03        BIOCHEMISTRY       A-
 SPERO       JAMES H.     A001     X04        COMPUTER SCIENCE   C




 Browse   C:\learndb\STU_GRDS       Rec 1/6        View  ReadOnly   CapsIns
```

Figure 10.21   *The result of this query.*

On the other hand, if you wanted to create a query to list classes and the students enrolled in them, you would link the databases in the same way but sort the view by CLASS_NUM, so that all of the records for each class come one after another. Then you can get a report on classes—for example, one listing the students enrolled in each and their grades.

As you can see, the features of dBASE IV that you use to manage a more complex database having many-to-many relationships such as this one are just the same as the features you use to manage a one-to-many database. Once you have created the views you need, of course, you can produce reports on them, add filters, and so on, just as you did with a one-to-many database.

WARNING
Whenever you use the dBASE IV interface to work with a relational database, you should be aware that there are two fatal errors that can occur.

As you have seen, you could accidentally enter a record in the controlling file that has no equivalent record in the lookup file—as you did when you entered a donation from member number A99. It is also easy to make an error and enter the wrong key number in the controlling file. This can become very embarrassing when you have to send out thank-you letters to members who gave donations, and you have no name or address for some and the wrong name and address for others. It is even worse if you are working with a database of clients, for example, and bill the wrong people for your services.

You should always double check the data you entered in the controlling file. Remember you can use a query like the one illustrated in Figure 10.12 to find records with no corresponding record in the lookup file.

WARNING
An even worse error can occur if you mistakenly change the key field in an existing record in the look-up file. Imagine if you change someone's member number in the MEMBERS2 file so that it is the same as the number of another member. Then you have no way of knowing which of those two members gave which donations: you have one group of donations with no corresponding member and another group of donations with two corresponding member records. You should always keep careful backups of your look-up file, in case this problem occurs.

Summary

In this chapter, you learned how relational databases help you manage your data more efficiently by eliminating duplication of data. You created a sample relational database and used it to learn how to link database files and create queries and formatted reports. This takes dBASE IV about as far as it can go using the Control Center. In Part 3 of this book you will learn how to use the dBASE programming language and to work at the dot prompt.

Part 3

THE dBASE LANGUAGE

Chapter 11

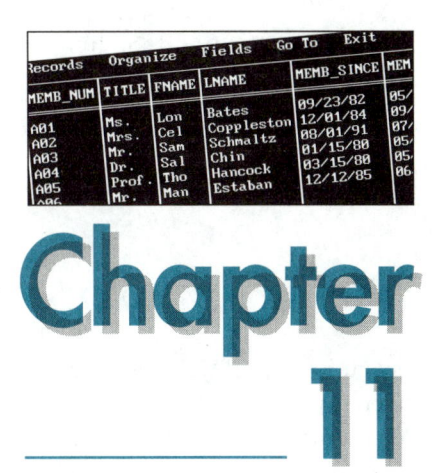

dBASE Expressions

Now you have taken dBASE IV about as far as it can go using only the menu-driven interface. In Part 3 of this book, you begin to add more power to your work by using the dBASE language's expressions and commands.

Chapters 11 and 12, the first half of Part 3 of this book, introduce expressions and commands for someone who might want to use them with the menu-driven interface or through the dot prompt. Chapters 13 and 14 add dBASE commands that are used exclusively for programming. They introduce the general principles of computer programming using dBASE as an example, and then they guide you through writing a complete application in the dBASE language.

In this chapter, you learn:

- The basics of using the dot prompt interface
- The use of the ? command
- How to recall commands from the history buffer
- How to use dBASE expressions, literals, and memory variables

- How to use dBASE functions with character data, dates, and numbers
- How to create an index based on several data types
- How to use operators in expressions
- How to create expressions using the dBASE IV expression builder

Why Learn Expressions and Commands

As you know, dBASE IV includes both a menu-driven user interface and a computer language that you can use either to work directly on your data from the dot prompt or to write programs. There are two reasons to learn the dBASE expressions and commands that comprise the programming language.

First, they are useful even if you are strictly a dBASE user rather than a programmer. There are places where dBASE expressions make even the menu-driven interface more powerful. They can let you create more powerful indexes and queries, for example. Working from the dot prompt using dBASE commands and expressions is sometimes more convenient than using the interface. If you are doing repetitive work, for example, it is very easy to edit and reuse the command line. Commands also give you more power than the interface For example, commands with WHILE clauses can speed up searches substantially, when compared with Query by Example.

Second, learning expressions and commands is indispensable if you go on and learn programming. Programs are simply lists of commands, many of which include expressions. Virtually all programming languages include expressions and commands, and studying how they are used in dBASE is a good introduction to programming in general.

Using the Dot Prompt

You learned in Chapter 1 that dBASE II could only be used by entering commands at the dot prompt, and that dBASE IV still lets you exit to the dot prompt and do your work by entering commands there, ignoring the user interface that you have used up to this point. You should exit to the dot prompt to learn about expressions and commands, but there are a few features of the dot prompt that you should know about first.

Before exiting to the dot prompt, you will use a file from the Control Center. This file remains in use at the dot prompt, unless you enter a command to close it. When you work from the dot prompt, the status line lets you know what file is in use and what record the pointer is on.

While the file is in use, you can use expressions that include data in the fields of its current record, and this will be very handy as you are learning about expressions in this chapter. Later, you will learn to move around the file and use the data in all of its records.

One feature of the dot prompt, which may puzzle you if you were not forewarned, is the dBASE *talk*. For example, if you enter a command at the dot prompt to index a file, the number of records that have been indexed is displayed on the screen; if you move through the database file, the number of the current record is displayed on the screen. If you assign a value to a memory variable, that value is displayed on the screen. Later in this chapter, you will learn what a memory variable is. The point now is that you should not be surprised at the messages or values that are displayed on the screen as you work from the dot prompt. These are referred to collectively as "talk," and they make the world of the dot prompt a bit easier to understand.

There are a couple of commands that you should learn at this point, so you can use them to experiment with expressions.

The command ? <expr> displays the content of an expression on a new line on your screen. This example, like all of the examples that follow, uses the convention of enclosing a word in angle brackets to indicate that you must actually substitute some valid data for it. Thus, ? <expr> stands for the character ? followed by some valid dBASE expression. If you entered ? FNAME, for example, dBASE would display the first name from the current record of the database file at the left margin of your screen, on a new line. Then, if you entered ? LNAME, dBASE would display the last name from the current record on a new line, one line below the first name.

You can also use ? by itself, without any expression following it, to print a blank line—that is, to skip a line. You can use ??<expr> to display an expression at the current location of the cursor (rather than on a new line).

Apart from ? and ??, which give you a quick way of seeing what the value of an expression is, there is just one other command that you should learn before you play with expressions. CLEAR is useful to clear the screen, which tends to get cluttered with expressions and talk.

SHORTCUT

Finally, you should know that dBASE stores the commands you enter in a memory buffer called the *history buffer*. For convenience, you can use the Up and Down Arrow keys to recall the last twenty commands that you entered. Press the up arrow to call back an earlier command, and you can reenter it as is, or you can edit it using the conventional editing keys. Use the Right and Left Arrow keys to move through the command or Home and End to move to the beginning or end of the command or click any location in the command line to move the mouse there. Press **Ins** to toggle between insert and typeover mode, **Del** to delete the character that the cursor is on and **Backspace** to delete the character to the left of the cursor.

NOTE

The number of commands stored in the history buffer can be changed from twenty, the default, using the SET HISTORY command, or by modifying your *Config.db* file.

You can see why it is best to learn about expressions from the dot prompt. You can use the command ? to try an expression out. Then you can go back and edit that expression and reenter it in a slightly different form with virtually no effort. When you get up to more complex expressions, you will find that you have to do this frequently just to correct typographical errors. You also might want to do it just to experiment. You can try altering the expressions used in the exercises to see how the results change.

As you read this chapter, you should experiment with the expressions that are discussed by using these commands to display them on the screen. Alter them slightly. The worst that dBASE will do is display an error message, and when you are experimenting you can learn from your errors.

If you are ready to go on and learn about expressions now, first use a database file, so you can include fields in the expressions you use, and then exit to the dot prompt .

1. Select **MEMBERS** from the data panel and select **Display data** from the prompt box. Just look at the Browse or Edit screen to see which is the current record. Then press **Esc** to return to the Control Center. (You may need to change the current catalog to SAMPLE before beginning this exercise.)

2. Select **Exit to the dot prompt** from the Exit menu.

3. To test the dot prompt, enter *? LNAME + FNAME*. dBASE displays the last and first name of the current record, including all of the trailing blank spaces of the last name, as shown in Figure 11.1.

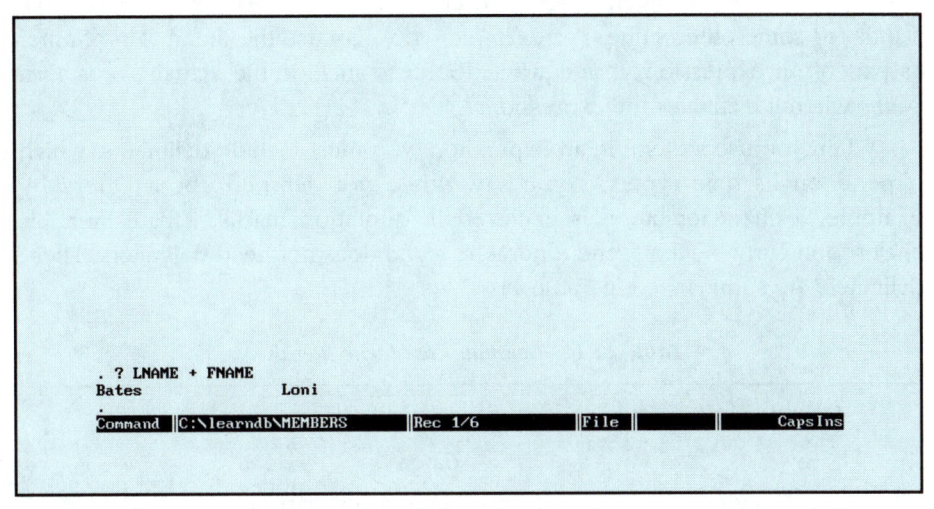

```
. ? LNAME + FNAME
Bates              Loni
```
```
Command  C:\learndb\MEMBERS    Rec 1/6      File              CapsIns
```

Figure 11.1   *Working from the dot prompt.*

Expressions

When you use an expression, dBASE IV evaluates it. For example, when you used the expression LNAME + FNAME to create an index, dBASE IV evaluated that expression for each record. It looked at the actual contents of the record's LNAME field plus the actual contents of the record's FNAME field. You just saw that, when you printed this expression from the dot prompt, dBASE IV evaluated it and printed the result for the current record.

LNAME and FNAME are field *variables*. They are called variables because their value can vary as you go from record to record. The + sign, as you know, is called an *operator*. It performs an operation on the two variables in the expression, the operation of *concatenating* (that is, combining) them.

In addition to field variables and operators, dBASE IV expressions may be made of literals, functions, and memory variables. An expression may consist of one or more of these elements.

Literals

Literals are also called *constants*—the opposite of variables—because their value does not change. The literal itself is used by an expression, while a variable stands for some other value. For example, you may use the literal "First Name" as part of an expression, if you want dBASE to include the actual words *First Name* when it evaluates the expression.

When you use a literal in an expression, you must include delimiters, which depend on its data type. As you saw when you learned about Query by Example, a character literal is enclosed in quotation marks, a date literal is enclosed in curly brackets, and a numeric literal does not need delimiters. These delimiters are summarized in Table 11.1.

Table 11.1   *Delimiters used with literals.*

" " or ' ' or [ ]	character
{ }	date
(no delimiter)	numeric or float

When dBASE IV evaluates the expression, it does not include the delimiters in the final result—the delimiters merely indicate the data type. This is easy to see when you try using some literals.

1. Enter *? "Hello"*. dBASE simply displays this word, without the quotation marks surrounding it.

2. Enter *? {10/10/91}*. Then enter *? 10*. The date literal is displayed, as the character literal was, at the left edge of the screen, without delimiters. The numeric literal, though, seems to be indented. This is because dBASE automatically gives numbers a width of ten characters and pads them out with leading blanks if they do not fill this whole width. Soon, when you learn functions, you will see how to control the width of a number.

3. Enter *?* to skip a line. Then enter *? "The last name is " + LNAME*. Be sure to include a space between the word is and the quotation mark that follows it. As you can see in Figure 11.2, dBASE displays the literal (without the quotation marks) followed by the actual last name of the current record. Because the delimiters are not included when dBASE evaluates an expression, it is easy to combine literals and variables in this way.

```
. ? LNAME + FNAME
Bates              Loni
. ? "Hello"
Hello
. ? {10/10/91}
10/10/91
. ? 10
        10
. ?

. ? "The last name is " + LNAME
The last name is Bates
.
Command  C:\learndb\MEMBERS    Rec 1/6     File              Ins
```

Figure 11.2   Displaying expressions on the screen.

4. Now try making a common error. Enter *? Hello* without including the quotation marks around the literal. Because there are no delimiters around this character string, dBASE thinks it is the name of a variable and displays the error message shown in Figure 11.3. Press **Enter** to cancel the command and return to the dot prompt.

```
. ? LNAME + FNAME
Bates              Loni
. ? "Hello"                 Variable not found: HELLO
Hello
. ? {10/10/91}              ? Hello
10/10/91
. ? 10                        Cancel   Edit    Help
        10
. ?

. ? "The last name is " + LNAME
The last name is Bates
. ? Hello
Command  C:\learndb\MEMBERS    Rec 1/6     File              Ins
```

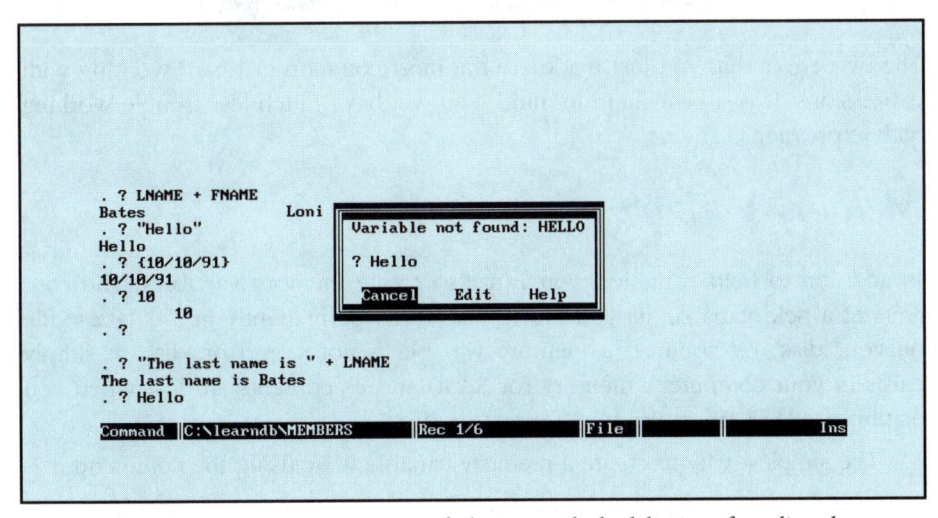

Figure 11.3   A common error: failure to include delimiters for a literal.

5. Try another common error. *Enter ? "Member until " + MEM_EXPIRS.* dBASE displays the error message shown in Figure 11.4 because you tried to create an expression using a character literal plus a date field variable. Although this appears to be similar to the exercise in Step 3, the elements of an expression must be the same data type. Press **Enter** to cancel the command.

```
. ? LNAME + FNAME
Bates              Loni
. ? "Hello"
Hello
. ? {10/10/91}      ┌─ Data type mismatch ──────┐
10/10/91            │                           │
. ? 10              │ ? "Member until " + MEM_EXPIRS │
       10           │                           │
. ?                 │  [Cancel]   Edit   Help   │
                    └───────────────────────────┘
. ? "The last name is " + LNAME
The last name is Bates
. ? Hello

. ? "Member until " + MEM_EXPIRS

Command  C:\learndb\MEMBERS      Rec 1/6       File              CapsIns
```

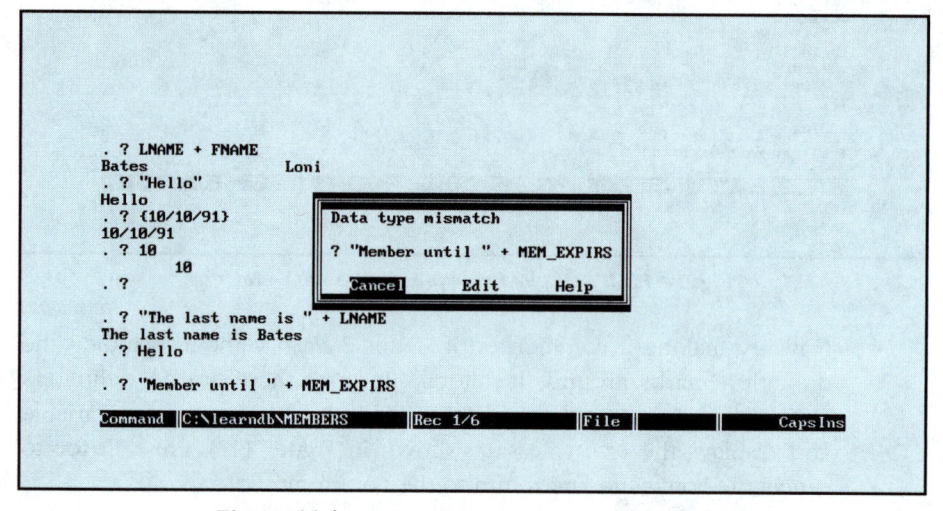

Figure 11.4   A common error: mixing data types.

The two errors that you just made are the most common errors in working with expressions. If you bear them in mind, you will have much less trouble working with expressions.

Memory Variables

In addition to field variables, you can also create memory variables. The contents of a field variable, as you know, are stored permanently in a database file on your disk. By contrast, a memory variable is not stored on disk. It simply exists in your computer's memory (or RAM) and its contents are lost when you exit from dBASE IV or turn your computer off.

The simplest way to create a memory variable is by using the command:

<mem var> = <value>

This command creates a memory variable with the name that is to the left of the equal sign and assigns it the value that is to the right of the equal sign. The data type of the memory variable depends on the data type of the value you assign to it. For example, the command mvar = 10 would create a numeric memory variable, and mvar = "Hello" would create a character memory variable.

The names of memory variables, like field names, may be up to ten characters long, they must begin with a letter, and they may contain letters, numbers, or the underscore character. Though it is not required, programmers often begin the names of memory variables with the letter *m* to identify them.

Memory variables are indispensable in programming, as you will see in Chapter 13. For now, create and display a couple for practice.

1. Enter *CLEAR* to clear the screen.
2. Enter *MNAME = "Sam"*.
3. Enter *? "The name is " + MNAME + "."*. Do not forget the space between the word *is* and the quotation mark. The expression you are printing consists of a character literal, followed by a memory variable, followed by another character literal, the final period. dBASE displays the sentence *The name is Sam.*, including the final period.
4. Enter *MNAME = FNAME*. Now that the memory variable has a new value, its old value is lost.
5. Enter *? "The name is " + mname + "."*. (You can do this by pressing the **Up Arrow** twice to reuse the earlier command.) dBASE displays the sentence *The name is Loni   .* with spaces before the period. Note again that a field variable is the width that you assigned to that field when you were defining the database structure, and that any empty spaces in it are padded out with blanks.

You can see from these examples, shown in Figure 11.5, that the = sign assigns a value to the variable. It should not be confused with the = sign that you use in arithmetic, which means that two values *are* equal. Instead, it *makes* the variable equal to some value.

To avoid confusion, it is best to read the command *mname = FNAME* as "Let MNAME equal FNAME".

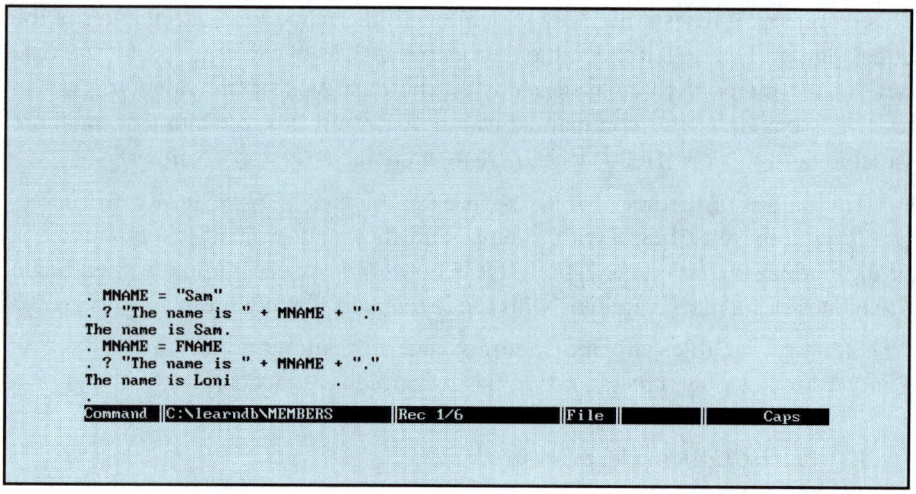

```
. MNAME = "Sam"
. ? "The name is " + MNAME + "."
The name is Sam.
. MNAME = FNAME
. ? "The name is " + MNAME + "."
The name is Loni
```

Figure 11.5   Using memory variables in expressions.

Functions

Functions are one of the most powerful features of dBASE. A large number of functions are available, but this section discusses only a few that are most useful. Once you have learned how functions work in this book, you can simply browse through your *dBASE IV Language Reference* or through any similar reference book to look at all the functions that are available in dBASE IV and see which others might be useful in your work.

A function returns a value. You can understand what this means if you consider two examples.

1. Enter *CLEAR* to clear the screen.

2. Enter *? DATE( )*. dBASE IV displays the system date (that is, the date on your computer's clock/calendar or the date that you entered when you started the computer).

3. Enter *? LOWER(FNAME)*. dBASE IV prints the first name of the current record in lowercase characters, as you can see in Figure 11.6. (Of course, the date on your computer is different from the date in this illustration.)

```
. ? DATE()
12/08/92
. ? LOWER(FNAME)
loni
```

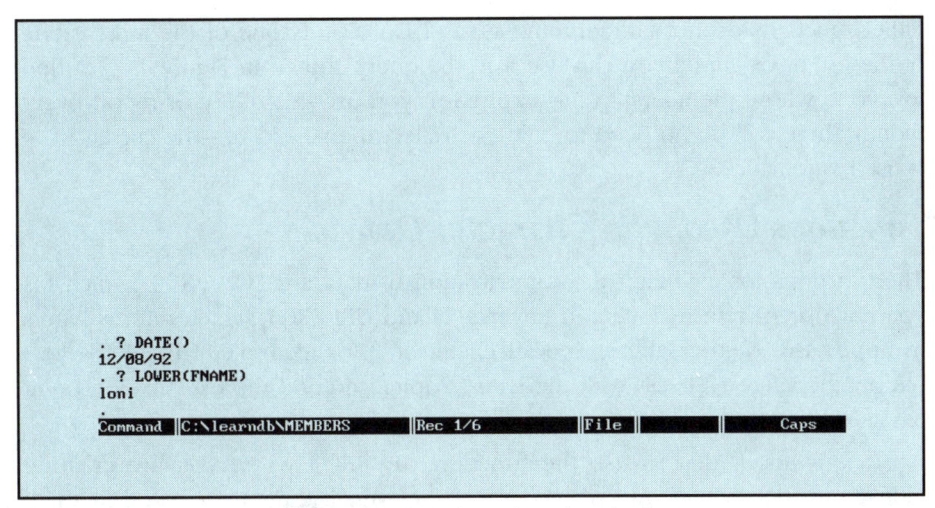

Figure 11.6 dBASE displays the values that the functions return.

Functions always are followed by parentheses. Some functions, such as LOWER ( ), require what is called an *argument* in the parentheses—a value that they return in an altered form. Note that they do not permanently alter these values. They just let you use them in a different form within the expression. For example, using LOWER( ) did not change the capitalization of the data in your database file. It just displayed it this once in lowercase.

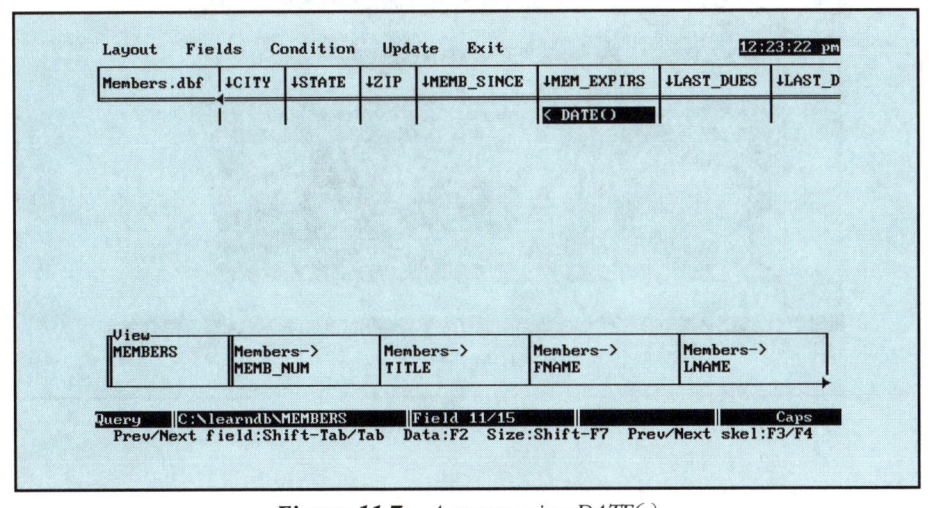

Figure 11.7 A query using DATE( ).

Other functions do not take arguments, and DATE( ) is one of the most useful of these. For example, you can use it in the query shown in Figure 11.7 to find everyone whose membership has expired. If you use this query or report every month, there will be no need to edit it to reflect the new date—the current date is used automatically.

Functions Used with Character Data

The functions for changing the capitalization of data are LOWER( ), which (as you have seen) returns letters in lowercase, and UPPER( ), which returns letters in uppercase. Neither affects special characters. For example, UPPER("Hello!") returns the value HELLO!, with the letters capitalized and the exclamation point left as is.

It is a good idea to use the function UPPER( ) when you are creating indexes, so that names are in the right order even if they are entered in small letters by mistake. Remember that the ability to use alphabetical order as well as ASCII order was the one advantage of sorting over indexing, but you can get names in ASCII order if you index on the expression UPPER(LNAME+FNAME) or on the equivalent expression UPPER(LNAME) + UPPER(FNAME), as shown in Figure 11.8.

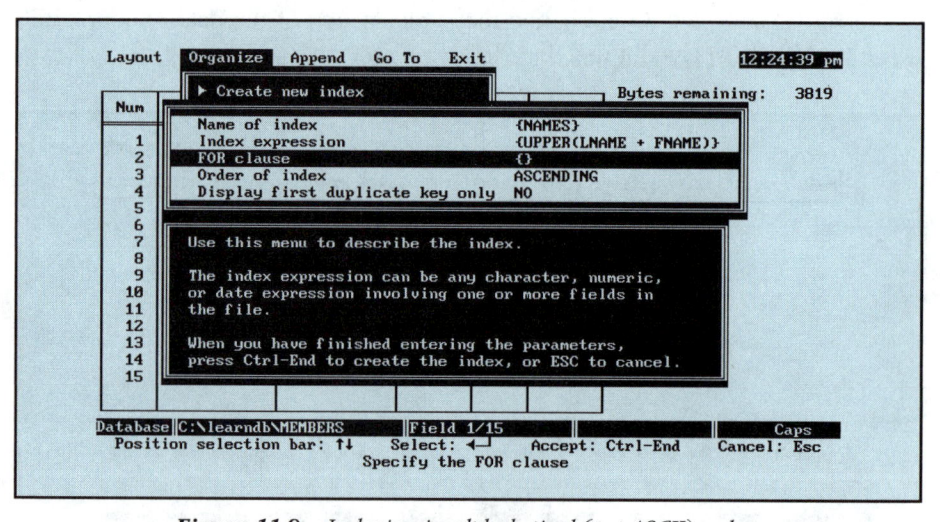

Figure 11.8 *Indexing in alphabetical (not ASCII) order.*

Other functions that are invaluable when you are working with text are TRIM( ), which trims trailing blanks, and LTRIM( ), which trims leading blanks.

A moment ago, you had trouble printing a sentence that used a name from the database file, because there were blanks between the name and the period that you wanted to put after it. Because they come after the name, these are called *trailing blanks*, and you can use TRIM( ) to get rid of them.

1. Enter *CLEAR* to clear the screen.
2. Enter *? "The name is " + TRIM(FNAME) + "."*. Now, you have put the period right after the name, without any spaces between them.

LTRIM( ), as you will see soon, is useful primarily when you have converted numbers to the character type, to trim the leading blanks that dBASE ordinarily adds to numbers.

Functions for Working with Dates

As you have seen, all of the elements of an expression must be the same data type. dBASE IV displayed an error message when you entered the command *? "Member until " + MEM_EXPIRS*.

To create expressions out of data of more than one type, you can use functions to convert all of the elements to the character type.

There are two functions to convert dates to the character type. DTOC( ) (which stands for Date TO Character) converts dates to characters in their ordinary format, mm/dd/yy. DTOS( ) (which stands for Date TO String) converts dates to character strings in ASCII format, yyyy/mm/dd. Try them both.

1. Enter *? "Member until " + DTOC(MEM_EXPIRS)*. dBASE IV displays *Member until 06/14/92*, the expiration date of the current record.
2. Enter *? "Member until " + DTOS(MEM_EXPIRS)*. dBASE IV displays *Member until 19920614*, the expiration date of current record in ASCII, as in Figure 11.9.

Of course, you should generally use DTOC( ) for text of this sort. DTOS( ) was added to the dBASE language specifically for indexing.

Imagine, for example, that you want to create an index that lists members by state but within each state, lists them in order of expiration date. If you created an index on the expression STATE + DTOC(MEM_EXPIRS), a member from California whose membership expired in January 1, 1993 would be listed before one whose membership expired in February 1, 1992. The expression would be evaluated as CA01/01/93 in the first case and as CA02/01/92 in the second case.

dBASE compares strings from left to right, and a character string beginning with CA01 comes before a string beginning with CA02, no matter what comes afterwards—just as a name beginning with SMID comes before a name beginning with SMIT, no matter what letters follow.

```
. ? "The name is " + TRIM(FNAME) + "."
The name is Loni.
. ? "Member until " + DTOC(MEM_EXPIRS)
Member until 06/14/92
. ? "Member until " + DTOS(MEM_EXPIRS)
Member until 19920614
.
Command  C:\learndb\MEMBERS    Rec 1/6    File              CapsIns
```

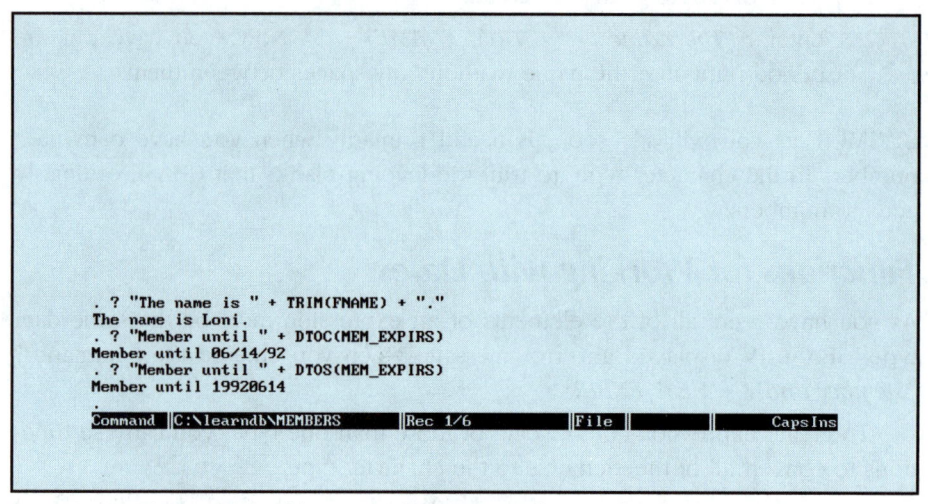

Figure 11.9   *Two ways of converting dates to the character type.*

When you use DTOC( ), then, dBASE uses first the month and then the day of the month as tie-breaker, rather than using the year.

On the other hand, if you index on the expression STATE + DTOS (MEM_EXPIRS), then the expression would be evaluated as CA19930101 in the first case and CA19920201 in the second. If the states are the same, the index uses first the year, then the month, then the day of the month as tie-breakers. The records are in the actual chronological order that you want.

Note that this expression is not needed if you are simply indexing on a date field. In this case there is no need to convert the date to a character type, and you can just use the name of the date field without any function. DTOS( ) is only needed to create a complex index that combines a date with character strings.

(dBASE IV also includes the function CTOD( ), which translates a character string to the date type. For example, CTOD("10/10/91") is equivalent to {10/10/91}. This function was needed to create dates in earlier versions of dBASE that did not include the curly bracket delimiters. It is retained in dBASE IV for compatibility, and you sometimes still see it in code written by long-time dBASE programmers.)

You can also use the following functions to isolate the day, month or year of a date.

Table 11.1   Functions to isolate the day, month, or year of a date.

DOW(<date exp>)	returns a number that represents the day of the week of the date, 1 for Sunday, 2 for Monday, and so on.
MONTH(<date exp>)	returns a number of the month of the date.
YEAR(<date exp>)	returns the year of the date as a four-digit number.
CDOW(<date exp>)	returns the day of the week written out in characters.
CMONTH(<date exp>)	returns the month written out in characters.

To test these functions, try printing out the current day:

1. Enter *CLEAR*.
2. Enter *? "Today is " + CDOW(DATE( )) + "."*.

Note, though, that you cannot yet print out: *Today is Thursday, February 20, 1992*, because that involves combining character and numeric data, something that you will learn to do in a moment.

Functions for Working with Numbers

You can use the function STR( ) to convert numeric to string data, but it is a bit more complex than the functions for converting dates to strings.

In addition to the number it is converting, it can include two numbers (or numeric expressions) to indicate the total width of the string and the number of decimal places that are included. If these are not included, then dBASE uses a width of ten and no decimal places by default.

The full function, is STR(<num exp> [, <num exp>] [, <num exp>]). The second and third numeric expressions are in square brackets preceded by commas to indicate that they are optional but that, if they are used, the comma must be included. The first numeric expression is the number that you are converting to character data, the second numeric expression represents the width of the string that the expression returns, and the third represents the number of decimal points that it has.

Try using this function:

1. Enter *CLEAR*. Then enter *? "The dues are " + STR(LAST_DUES)*. Notice that the amount is preceded by enough blanks to make it ten characters wide and that it has no decimal points.
2. Enter *? "The dues are " + STR(LAST_DUES,6,2)*. The amount includes two decimal places and is narrowed to six characters wide.

The opposite of STR( ) is the function VAL(<char exp>), which converts character data (that is made up of numbers) to numeric data. For example, if you wanted for some bizarre reason to multiply the zip code of the current record by 2, you could use the expression 2 * VAL(ZIP).

Combining Numbers and Text

Notice that, in the example above, you had to use the function STR(LAST_DUES,6,2) to allow for up to six characters in width. This is the minimum needed to hold the largest dues that may be paid, but is too large for most amounts, so that it usually is preceded by a leading zero. Thus, if you use the expression including a dollar sign, "The dues are $" + STR (LAST_DUES,6,2), there usually is an unnecessary space between the dollar sign and the amount.

To get rid of this unnecessary space, you must "nest" the STR( ) function within the LTRIM( ) function, which you learned earlier. Instead of STR(LAST_DUES,6,2), you must use LTRIM (STR(LAST_DUES,6,2)).

It is common to use this sort of "nested" function in dBASE—that is, to use one function inside of another, combining functions in complex ways. If you find this sort of function confusing, just remember to evaluate it from the inside out. First evaluate the function that is inside all of the parentheses and see what value it returns. Then substitute that value for it and evaluate the function around it.

In the example, you would first figure out what value STR(LAST_DUES,6,2) returns, and then you would figure out how LTRIM( ) affects this value.

NOTE Notice that the number of right parentheses must equal the number of left parentheses in a nested function. Often, the function ends with several right parentheses, one after another.

Now, you have learned enough to print out a date in its most complete form, for example, to print out something like: *Today is Thursday, February 20, 1992.* Look at the function to print out the current date in this way. Here, it is listed on several lines to make it easier to read, but in practice, you must enter it on a single line.

```
? "Today is "
    + CDOW(DATE( )) + ", "
    + CMONTH(DATE( )) + " "
    + LTRIM(STR(DAY(DATE( )))) + ", "
    + STR(YEAR(DATE( )),4)
```

CDOW(DATE( )) and CMONTH(DATE( )) return the name of the day of the week and of the month of the current date written out in character form. Because these are already character data, there is no need to convert them to combine them with the rest of the expression.

DAY(DATE( )) returns a number that is the day of the month of the current date. You must nest it within the STR( ) function to convert the number so that it returns to character data, which can be combined with the rest of the expression, but using STR( ) alone would pad it out with leading zeroes to make its total width ten. Since the number of digits in the day of the month can be either one or two, you cannot fix this problem by specifying the width of the string within the STR( ) function. Instead, you can nest the STR( ) function within LTRIM( ).

YEAR(DATE( )) returns the year of the current date as a four-digit number. You must use STR( ) to convert this to character data, and because it is always the same width, you can include the number 4 to specify the width of the character string that is returned, in order to make sure there are no leading zeroes. You could also have nested STR( ) within LTRIM( ), but that is a bit more difficult.

Try printing out this expression: use ? followed by the entire expression, all on a single line. The result is shown in Figure 11.10. (Note that, although you type the expression in a single line, dBASE wraps it after you enter it, to make it easier to read.)

```
. ? "Today is " + CDOW(DATE()) + ", " + CMONTH(DATE()) + " " + LTRIM(STR(DAY(DAT
E())) + ", " + STR(YEAR(DATE()),4)
Today is Tuesday, December 8, 1992
```

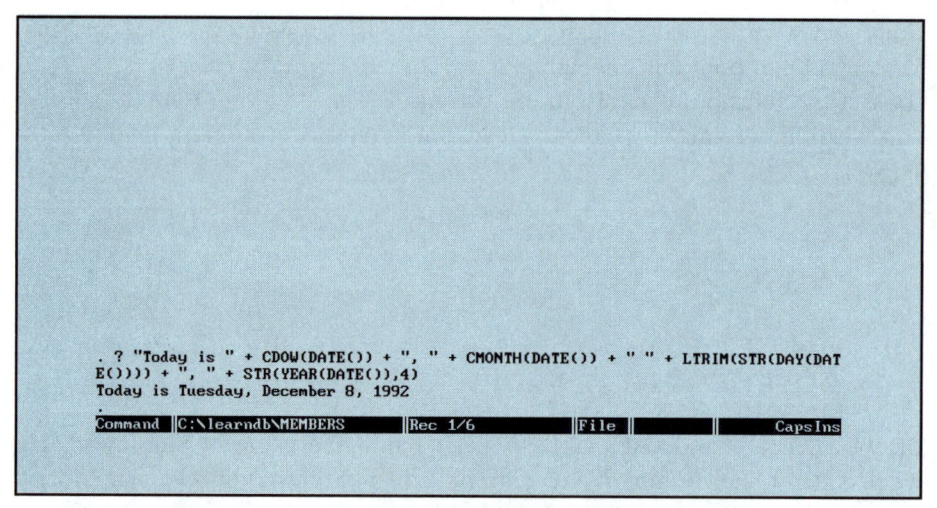

Figure 11.10   Using a complex function to display the date.

Indexes Based on Expressions

Remember that, in Chapter 4, you created an index based on LNAME + FNAME, but you were not able to create indexes based on several fields with different data types. The advantage of sorting was that it allowed you to sort on fields of more than one data type.

Now that you have learned functions, you can create indexes based on different data types. Just convert all of the data types to the character type before indexing.

NOTE If you are combining a date field with other fields, remember to use DTOS( ) rather than DTOC( ) to convert it, for the reasons discussed above.

If you are combining a numeric or float field with other fields, do not use the TRIM( ) function to trim leading blanks, as they are needed to keep the fields in proper order. For example, if they were both character fields and you used LTRIM( ), the number 100 would come before the number 22. (Remember that dBASE orders character fields by comparing the leftmost character.)

The blank character, though, comes before any number (or letter) in ASCII order, so that the number 22 with two leading blanks would come before 100 with one leading blank. Since the numbers in indexes come from the same fields and have the same widths, they are padded out with enough leading blanks to make sure they come out in the correct numeric order after they are converted to character data.

In Chapter 4, you needed to sort a database file based on fields of different data types. Now, you can use indexes. For example, imagine that you want to index a database file using a combination of the LAST_DUES, LNAME, and FNAME fields.

First, look at how to do it in a simpler way. If you use the index expression STR(LAST_DUES) + UPPER(LNAME) + UPPER(FNAME), you index on dues, so members who pay $15 are listed first and members who pay $100 are listed last. Since the name is used as a tie breaker, members with the same dues are listed in alphabetical order by name. Because you used UPPER( ), they are listed alphabetically even if capitalization is incorrect. Indexing on UPPER( ) of a character field is equivalent to sorting in dictionary (rather than ASCII) order.

Now, consider an even more complex problem. How do you index on dues in descending order and, among those with the same dues, list names alphabetically in ascending order? All you have to do is to subtract the amount of the dues from some large number—use the number 200 - LAST_DUES, for example. The larger LAST_DUES is, the smaller 200 - LAST_DUES is, so you can index on dues in descending order by using this as part of the expression.

The index expression STR(200 - LAST_DUES) + UPPER(LNAME) + UPPER(FNAME) organizes the file in descending order by dues, so that those who paid the highest dues come first and those who paid the lowest come last. Among those who paid the same dues, names are listed alphabetically.

Using the methods you have learned, you can now index in alphabetical or ASCII order and in ascending or descending order, and create indexes that combine different fields in different orders. You can now do everything with indexes that you can with the sort screen.

Other Complex Functions

A complex dBASE function that is useful in manipulating character data is SUBSTR(<char_exp>,<num_exp>[,<num_exp>]). It contains a character expression and two numeric expressions, separated by commas. Note that the square brackets around the second num_exp indicate that it is optional.

SUBSTR( ) returns a substring of the character expression that begins on the character specified by the first number. If a second number is included, it specifies the number of characters included in the substring. If the second number is omitted, the substring continues to the end of a string.

For example, the expression SUBSTR("This is a test",1,1) returns a substring that begins with the first letter of the character expression and includes just one letter in all: that is, it returns just the letter T. The expression SUBSTR("This is a test",2,3) returns a substring that begins with the second letter and includes three letters: that is, *his*. Finally, the expression SUBSTR("This is a test",2) returns a substring that begins with the second letter and continues to the end of the word.

SUBSTR( ) is sometimes used to capitalize a name properly. For example, UPPER(SUBSTR(LNAME,1,1)) + LOWER(SUBSTR (LNAME,2)) returns the first letter of LNAME in upper case and the rest of the letters in the name in lower case. Note, though, that this does not work with names such as DeLeon or Smyth-Burnes. In addition, the middle initial is not capitalized if it is used to capitalize a first name field that includes middle initials.

Operators

Many of dBASE's operators will look familiar to you. You have already used the arithmetic operators in calculated fields and the relational operators in the Query screen. This section looks at dBASE operators systematically, summarizing and expanding on what you already know.

The Arithmetic Operators

The arithmetic operators are summarized for review purposes in Table 11.2. They were discussed thoroughly in the section in Chapter 6 on calculated fields of queries, and you can go back to that section for a more extensive review.

Table 11.2 *The arithmetic operators.*

+	addition
–	subtraction
*	multiplication
/	division
^ or **	exponentiation
( )	grouping

The operators in this table can all be used with numeric or float fields in expressions. For example, if you want an expression to include a member's monthly dues payment, you can use the expression LAST_DUES/12. Try using this in a larger expression.

1. Enter *CLEAR*.
2. Enter *? "Monthly dues = $" +LTRIM(STR (LAST_ DUES/12,10,2))* to print the monthly dues of the current record.

You must use LTRIM( ) and STR( ) to combine this numeric expression with character data, just as you did earlier.

Date Arithmetic and String Concatenation

The operators + and - can also be used with date and character data.

You have seen how date arithmetic works. You can add or subtract a number of days from any date; for example, MEM_EXPIRS - 30 gives a date thirty days before membership expires. You can also subtract one date from another to find the number of days between the two, for example, MEM_EXPIRS - DATE( ) gives the number of days between the current date and the date when membership expires.

Arithmetic expressions using the DATE( ) function are often useful in queries. The query shown in Figure 11.11, for example, finds all members whose membership has not yet expired but will expire within the next thirty days. You can save this query and use it at any time without editing it. As long as your computer's system date is accurate, it will always be based on the current date.

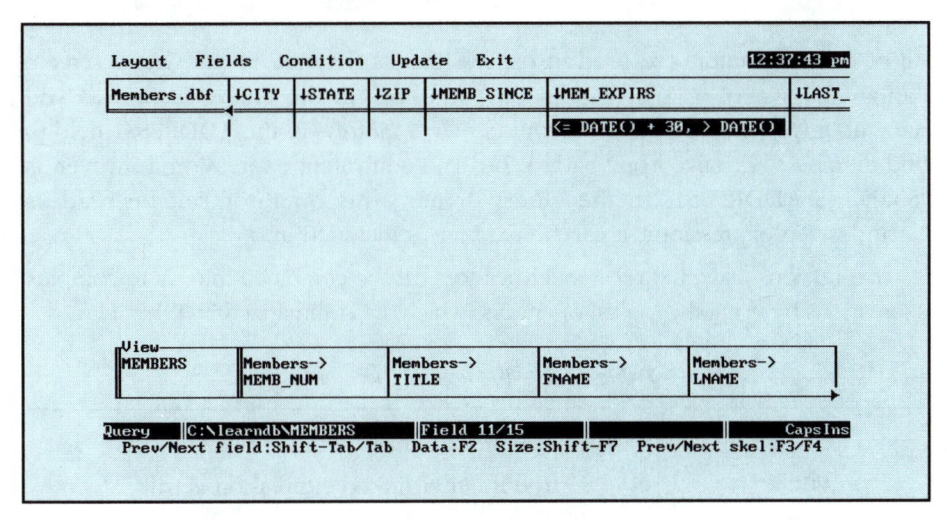

Figure 11.11 *A query using date arithmetic.*

The operators + and - are used with character data for concatenation. You have seen that LNAME + FNAME simply combines the contents of the LNAME and FNAME fields in a single string. LNAME - FNAME also combines the contents of the two fields, but it trims blanks from the fields and instead adds them at the end of the combined strings.

Relational and Logical Operators

Expressions use relational operators that are like the ones used in the query screen. These operators are summarized in Table 11.3 and may all be used with character, date, numeric, and float data, except for $, which may be used with character data and with memo fields.

Table 11.3   The relational operators.

=	equals
>	greater than
<	less than
>=	greater than or equal to
<=	less than or equal to
<> or #	not equal to
$	is included in

All of these operators are used in expressions as they are in the Query screen, though the syntax of $ may be a bit confusing. In the Query screen, as you remember, you learned that you could enter *$ "Shady"* in the ADDRESS1 field to find members who lived on Shady Lane. The equivalent expression, however, is "Shady" $ ADDRESS1. In the Query screen, this operator can be read as "includes." In expressions, it can be read as "is included in."

Expressions using the relational operators can be combined into more complex expressions by using the logical operators, which are summarized in Table 11.4.

Table 11.4   The logical operators.

.AND.	true if both linked expressions are true
.OR.	true if either linked expression is true
.NOT.	true if the following expression is not true
( )	grouping

Examples of the relational and logical operators are included in the next section.

Logical Expressions

Expressions using the relational and logical operators evaluate to either .T. or .F., indicating whether they are true or false.

If you enter *? STATE = "CA"*, dBASE evaluates this expression and display either .T. or .F., depending on whether or not the contents of the STATE field of the current record is equal to the string CA.

The relational and logical operators can be used with date and numeric (and float) functions without any problem. For example, the expression MEM_EXPIRS <= {12/31/91} .AND. LAST_DUES >= 50 returns .T. if the MEM_EXPIRS field of the current record has a date before the end of 1991 and the LAST_DUES field of that record has an amount of $50 or more.

NOTE There is one other feature you must consider if you use the = operator with character fields. Remember you learned in Chapter 9 that, if you select **Settings** from the Tools menu of the Control Center, you can use the Options menu to toggle Exact from ON to OFF; this setting determines how strings are matched. By default, Exact is OFF, and there is a match as long as the contents of the string is the same, even if the string being compared has more characters than the string it is being compared to. For example, the expression LNAME = "Sm" would be true if the LNAME field contained Smith. LNAME matches all of the characters of Sm, even though it contains additional characters. On the other hand, if Exact is ON, this expression would be false. Even the expression LNAME = "Smith" would be false, since Smith does not include the trailing blanks that are in the field. With Exact ON, you would have to use the expression TRIM(LNAME) = "Smith" to get a match.

In addition to logical expressions, there are also certain functions that return .T. or .F.. For example, the function DELETED( ) returns .T. if the current record is marked for deletion and .F. if it is not.

As you know, logical fields also contain either .T. or .F..

Any expression that returns a .T. or .F. is called a *logical expression*.

Adding a Condition Box to the Query Screen

One use of logical expressions when you are working with the dBASE IV user interface is in the condition boxes of Query screens.

If you select **Add condition box** from the Condition menu of the queries design screen, dBASE IV adds a condition box to the query. You can enter any logical expression in the condition box, and it is considered an additional condition of the query. (Select **Delete condition box** from this menu to remove the condition box. Select the toggle **Show condition box** to specify whether or not the condition box is displayed.)

For example, the query shown in Figure 11.12 finds records of members from California that are marked for deletion. "CA" is entered under the STATE field, as usual. And the logical expression DELETED( ) is entered in the condition box. The query only matches records if both of these conditions are satisfied. If CA is in the STATE field and DELETED( ) returns a .T..

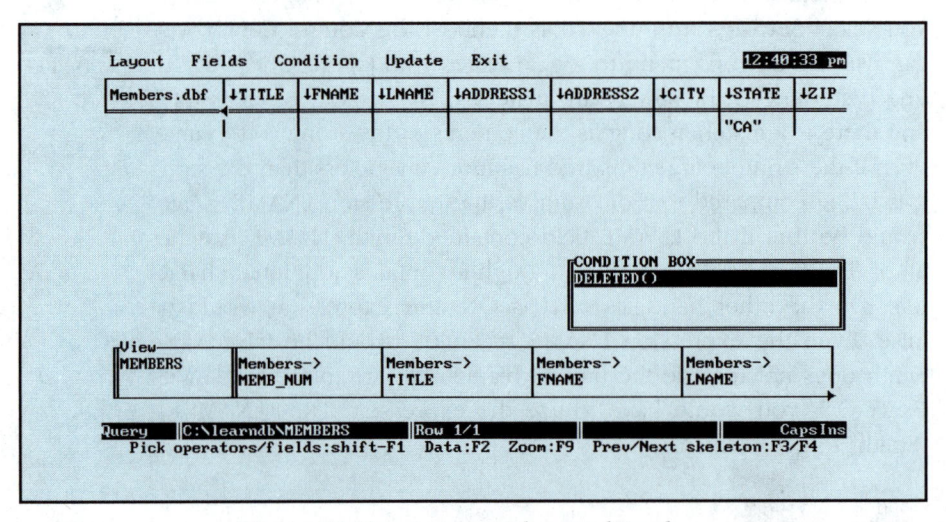

Figure 11.12   *A query with a condition box.*

If you want use the Query screen to find some value in a memo field, you must add a condition box with an expression that uses the $ operator. For example, Figure 11.13 shows a query that you could use to find which members volunteered to help with grants. Remember that the word "grant" was included in the NOTES field of many records, and the expression "grant" $ NOTES isolates these records.

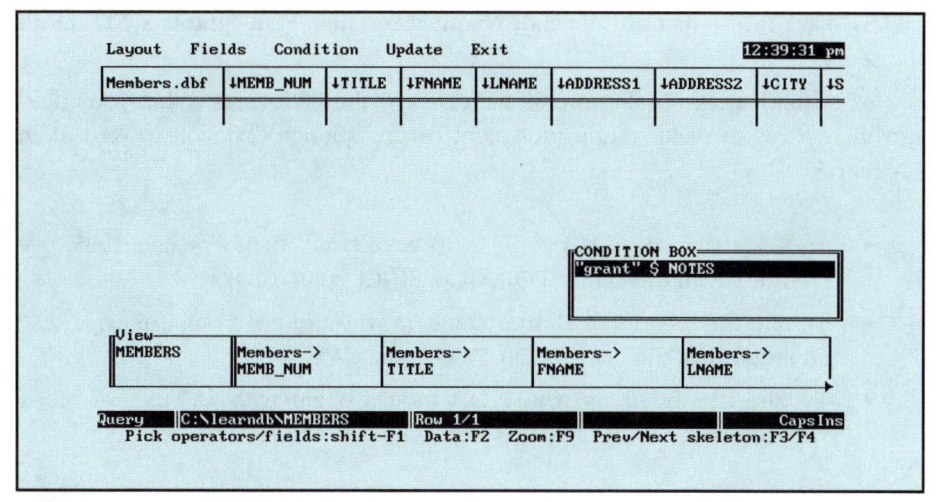

Figure 11.13 *Querying for a value in a memo field.*

Indexes with FOR Clauses

Complex logical expressions let you use indexes with FOR clauses instead of queries. The FOR clause allows you to build any query into an index to get faster performance than you could with the Query screen.

As you learned in Chapter 4, you can add a FOR clause to an index by selecting **FOR clause** from the Create new index submenu. Then, enter any logical expression as the FOR clause, and the index includes only records for which that logical expression is evaluated as .T..

For example, if you enter *STATE = "CA"* as the FOR clause, the index includes only records whose STATE fields have the string CA in them. For these records, the expression evaluates as .T..

You can enter *VOLUNTEER* as the FOR clause and the index includes only the records with .T. in the VOLUNTEER field. Notice that you do not use the expression VOLUNTEER = .T.. You do not use the relational operator because the VOLUNTEER field itself evaluates as either .T. or .F..

To find the records with .F. in the VOLUNTEER field, use the expression .NOT. VOLUNTEER. Remember that .NOT. VOLUNTEER evaluates as .T. whenever VOLUNTEER evaluates as .F..

To duplicate the queries with condition boxes that you looked at a moment ago, you could use an index with the clause FOR STATE = "CA" .AND.

DELETED( ) in the first and an index with the clause FOR "grant" $ NOTES in the second.

As examples of logical expressions, consider the FOR clauses that you could use in indexes to make them equivalent to the queries that you looked at in Chapter 5.

- To find the records of people who have been members since1985, use an index with the clause FOR MEM_SINCE < {01/01/86}.
- To find the records of all the members who are not from California, use an index with the clause FOR STATE <> "CA".
- To find the members whose last names begin with "A" use an index with the clause FOR LNAME < "B".

NOTE Note that logical expressions can not use the operators LIKE or SOUNDS LIKE, which you can use in queries.

As examples of more complex logical expressions, consider the indexes with FOR clauses that would be equivalent to the queries in Chapter 5 that used the logical AND or logical OR.

- To find members who are from California AND who have become members since 1986, use an index with the clause FOR STATE = "CA" .AND. MEMB_SINCE >= {01/01/86}.
- To find members who pay between $25 and $75 in dues use an index with the clause FOR LAST_DUES >= 25 .AND. LAST_DUES <= 75.
- To find members who are from New York OR from New Jersey OR from Connecticut, use an index with the clause FOR STATE = "NY" .OR. STATE = "NJ" .OR. STATE = "CT".
- To find members who are volunteers or who pay more than $50 in dues, or who have been members since 1985, use an index with the clause FOR VOLUNTEER .OR. LAST_DUES >= 50 OR. MEMB_SINCE <= {01/01/85}.
- To find members who are from California AND have been members since 1986 OR are from New York AND have been member since 1986, use an index with the clause FOR (MEMB_SINCE <= {01/01/86} .AND. STATE = "CA") .OR. (MEMB_SINCE <= {01/01/86} .AND. STATE = "NY").

- To find members who are volunteers OR have been members since 1986 AND pay dues of $50 or more, use an index with the clause FOR VOLUNTEER .OR. (MEMB_SINCE <= {01/01/86} .AND. LAST_DUES >= 50).

Notice that the final two examples are complex enough that parentheses are used for grouping. The meaning of the expression would be different if the parentheses were placed differently. For example, FOR (VOLUNTEER .OR. MEMB_SINCE <= {01/01/86}) .AND. LAST_DUES >= 50 would only be true for people who paid over $50 in dues and who also were either volunteers or long-term members—unlike the example above it, which is true for anyone who either is a volunteer or who is a long-term member who pays over $50 in dues.

NOTE If you have a large database and you need to find the same records repeatedly, using an index with a FOR clause can give you a significant improvement in performance over using a query. A query reads through the entire database file to find the matching records, and this can take a long time with a large file. The index takes a bit of time to maintain when you are entering data, but this usually is not noticeable. Then, when you need to find certain records, the index is ready, and making it the controlling index lets you use only those records.

Remember that the FOR clause of any index has nothing to do with the order of the records—it merely determines which records are displayed. For example, you can create an index based on the index expression LNAME + FNAME and add a FOR clause with the expression STATE = "CA". This index would list members alphabetically but include only the members from California. The index expression determines the order of the records and the FOR clause acts like a query that filters out certain records.

Remember also the main pitfall of using indexes with FOR clauses from the Control Center. Sometimes—for example, when you are including an index in a query—dBASE has you choose among indexes just on the basis of the index expression, without including the name of the index. In this situation, dBASE IV could display two indexes with the key expression LNAME + FNAME, without giving you any way to tell which included all the records and which included only records from California. You might have to see if the proper data is used to know if you used the right index.

The Expression Builder

dBASE IV includes an expression builder that lets you create expressions by choosing from picklists, rather than typing them in by hand.

If you are creating an index, after you select **Index expression** or **FOR clause**, you can press **Pick:Shift-F1** to use the expression builder shown in Figure 11.14. The expression builder is also available at other times—for example, when you are adding a condition box to a query.

To use the expression builder, simply move the highlight among the lists of field names, operators, and functions. Each time you select one of these, it is added to the expression that you are building. You return to the submenu and have to press **Pick:Shift-F1** again to use the expression builder to add another element to the expression.

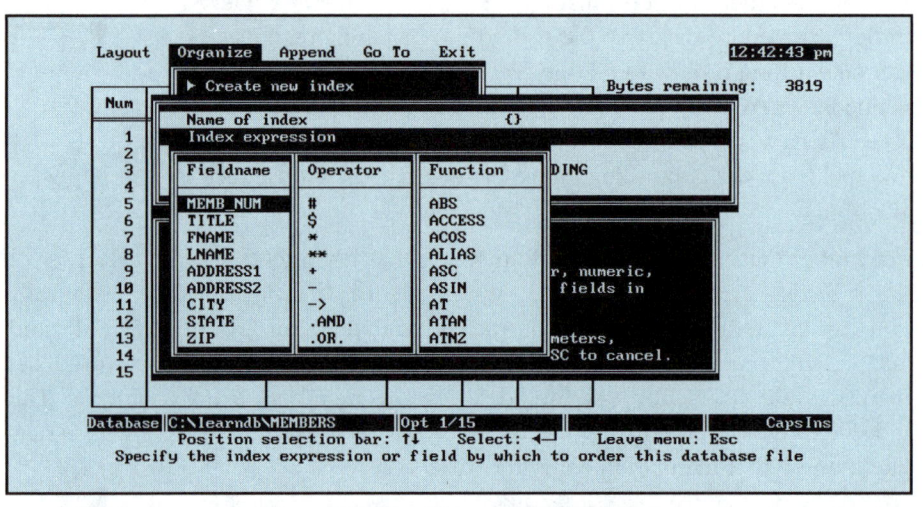

Figure 11.14   *The expression builder.*

Needless to say, you have to know what the functions and operators mean before you can select them from the expression builder. The expression builder can be useful to jog your memory when you are first learning operators and functions. For most people, once they have learned the dBASE expressions it is faster to type in expressions than to use the expression builder.

Summary

In this chapter, you learned about dBASE expressions that can be used either with the menu-driven interface to increase its power and versatility or used at the dot prompt. In the next chapter, you will see how to use dBASE commands at the dot prompt to do some of the same things you have already learned how to do using options from the menu system.

Chapter 12

dBASE Commands

The dBASE programming language has an extensive set of commands. The aim of this chapter is to teach you the basic features of the commands that are essential for using dBASE IV from the dot prompt. This chapter does not discuss all of the dBASE commands and does not cover every feature of the commands that it does discuss. In this chapter, you learn how to do with commands many of the many things you have already learned to do from the Control Center.

From the dot prompt, you learn how to:

- ◆ Create, use, and modify a database and display its structure
- ◆ Add, edit, and view data
- ◆ Delete records
- ◆ Move the pointer
- ◆ Create index tags
- ◆ Perform indexed and unindexed searches
- ◆ Use labels, reports, queries, and data entry forms

- Create and edit programs
- Set the dBASE IV working environment
- Send output to a printer or to a file
- Add optional clauses to a dBASE command
- Work with more than one database file at the same time

About Commands

As the name implies, a *command* directs dBASE to perform a certain action. These commands should be easy for you to understand, since they are doing things that you have already have done from the Control Center, so this chapter does not include formal exercises. Unlike expressions, which can be very complex and which need to be illustrated with examples, these commands are usually straightforward. For example, there is no need to tell you that you use a database with the command USE *<file name>* and then to give you an exercise with the example USE MEMBERS.

The structure of a command is called its *syntax*. Each command line begins with a verb and may contain one or more clauses that use other key words, words that are part of the dBASE language. In dBASE, a command or other key word is generally entered in uppercase. Although dBASE itself is not case-sensitive, it is considered good programming practice to distinguish key words in this way.

In addition, the following conventions for clauses in commands are used throughout this book:

Table 12.1 *Conventions for clauses in commands.*

< >	(angle brackets)	Indicates you must supply a specific value of the type required.
[ ]	(square brackets)	Indicates the item is optional.
|	(vertical line)	Indicates an either/or choice; you may use one but not both.

As you read the chapter, you should go ahead and enter examples of the commands that are discussed at the dot prompt, even though there are not specific instructions telling you to. You cannot learn these commands without practice.

To save time, you can type only the first four letters of the keywords of any dBASE command. Of course, this does not apply to the names of files, fields, or memory variables—only to the keywords that are part of the dBASE language. The language is designed so that the first four letters of the key words of any command are unique to that command. Many dBASE commands are almost always used only in the form of four-letter abbreviations.

SHORTCUT

The Database File

To create a database file from the dot prompt, enter the command CREATE <*file name*>. dBASE displays the Database Design screen with which you are already familiar, and you can define the structure of the database just as you did when you first created a file from the Control Center. When you are done, of course, you return to the dot prompt rather than to the Control Center.

To use a database file, simply enter the command USE <*file name*>. The name of the file that is in use is displayed on the status bar, along with the current record and the total number of records in the file. In Figure 12.1, the status bar shows that the MEMBERS database file is in use, and the pointer is on the first of six records (Rec1/6).

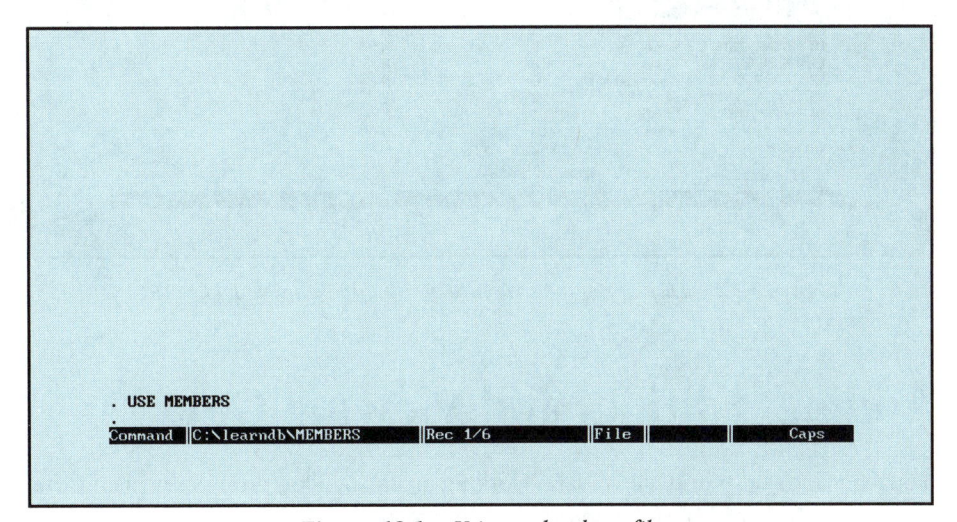

```
. USE MEMBERS
.
Command  C:\learndb\MEMBERS    Rec 1/6      File         Caps
```

Figure 12.1   *Using a database file.*

If you use a new file, the current file automatically closes. If you enter only the command USE without a file name, the current file is closed without a new file being opened.

Once a database file is in use, you can modify its structure by entering the command MODIFY STRUCTURE. This is one of those commands that is virtually always abbreviated. You need only to enter MODI STRU, the first four letters of the keywords.

You can also look at the structure of the database that is currently in use by entering the command DISPLAY STRUCTURE (or DISP STRU). This command displays information on the database's file structure, as shown in Figure 12.2. If you want to print the structure of the active file, use the command DISP STRU TO PRINT. If you want to save the file's structure in a text file, use the command DISP STRU TO FILE <*file name*>. As you will see, an optional TO PRINT or TO FILE clause can be added to many dBASE commands.

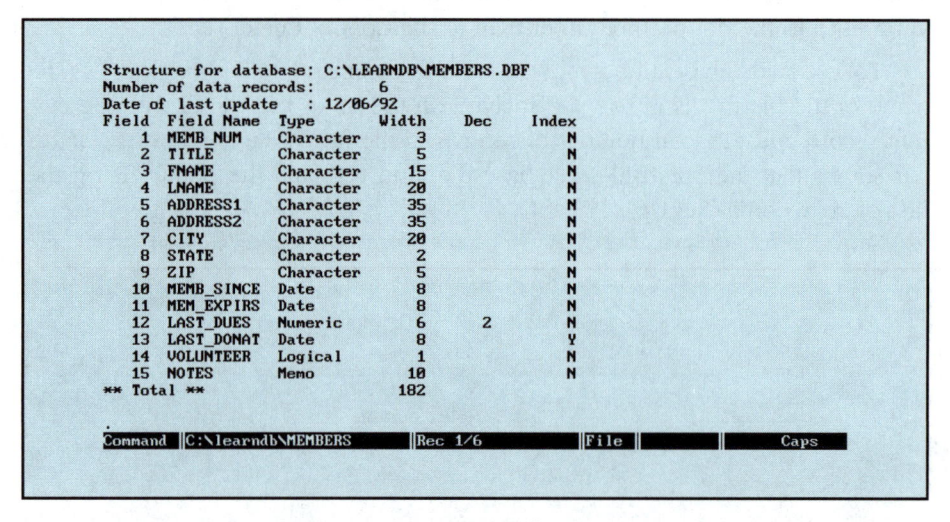

```
Structure for database: C:\LEARNDB\MEMBERS.DBF
Number of data records:       6
Date of last update  : 12/06/92
Field  Field Name  Type        Width   Dec   Index
    1  MEMB_NUM    Character       3               N
    2  TITLE       Character       5               N
    3  FNAME       Character      15               N
    4  LNAME       Character      20               N
    5  ADDRESS1    Character      35               N
    6  ADDRESS2    Character      35               N
    7  CITY        Character      20               N
    8  STATE       Character       2               N
    9  ZIP         Character       5               N
   10  MEMB_SINCE  Date            8               N
   11  MEM_EXPIRS  Date            8               N
   12  LAST_DUES   Numeric         6     2         N
   13  LAST_DONAT  Date            8               Y
   14  VOLUNTEER   Logical         1               N
   15  NOTES       Memo           10               N
** Total **                      182
```

Figure 12.2 *Displaying the structure of a database using DISP STRU.*

Adding, Editing, and Viewing Data

You can add, edit, and view data working from the dot prompt by using the Browse or Edit screen, just as you do when you are working from the Control Center.

Using the Browse and Edit Screens

To use the Browse or Edit screen to view or edit the current record, just make sure the database file you want is in use and enter either BROWSE or EDIT at the dot prompt. Then use the Browse or Edit screens just as you have in the past.

To add a new record, use the APPEND command. This command adds a blank record to the end of the database, makes the blank record the current record, and displays the Edit screen so you can edit the record. As always, you can toggle between the Edit and Browse screens by pressing **Data:F2**.

Other Commands for Editing and Viewing Data

You can view the data without using the Browse or Edit screen, by using one of the twin commands, DISPLAY and LIST.

DISPLAY [OFF] displays the data in the current record on the screen, as shown in Figure 12.3. LIST [OFF] works like DISPLAY except that it displays the contents of all of the records in the file, as shown in Figure 12.4. The optional word OFF suppresses the display of the record number. Typing DISPLAY or LIST without the optional clause OFF will cause record numbers to be displayed before the first field, as shown in the illustrations.

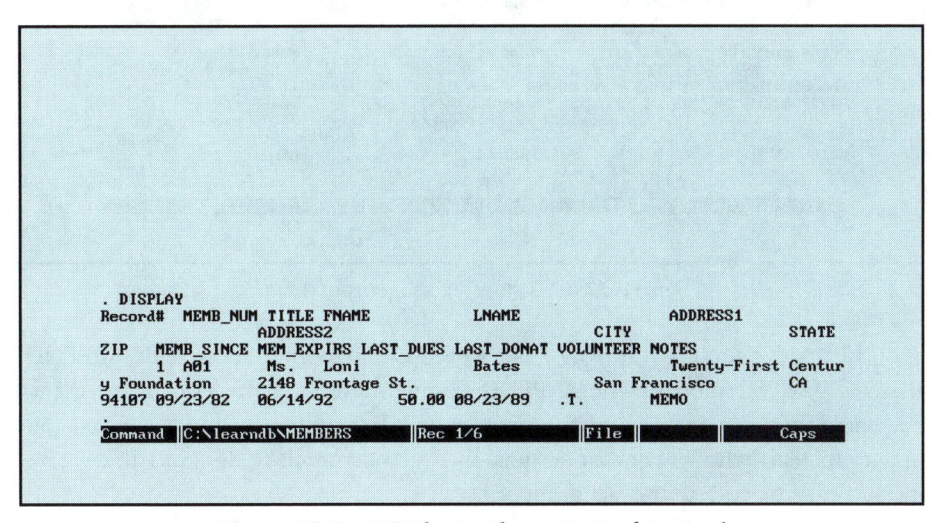

Figure 12.3   DIisplaying the contents of a record.

As you can see, the field names and data are simply wrapped to the next line if they are too long to fit in the width of the screen, which makes the display hard to read. In the example, the heading and each record's data are wrapped to three lines. In addition, the records just scroll by rapidly when you enter the LIST command. Yet these commands can be very powerful if they are used with additional options, which are covered later in this chapter.

When you are programming, you often want more control over the data than you can get by letting the user access the Browse and Edit screens directly. For this reason, it is common to use the command REPLACE <*field name*> WITH <*value*> in programming. This command replaces the contents of the field specified with a new value. By default, REPLACE affects only the current record. To use this command for editing in a program, first you move the pointer to the record that you want to edit, you write program code to get the new contents, then the REPLACE command to place those new contents into the record.

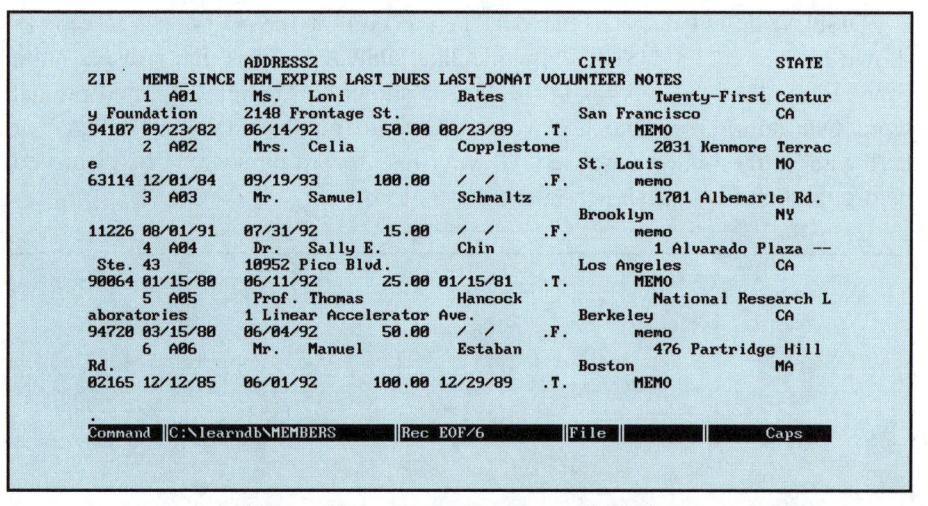

```
                    ADDRESS2                           CITY               STATE
        ZIP  MEMB_SINCE MEM_EXPIRS LAST_DUES LAST_DONAT VOLUNTEER NOTES
              1  A01    Ms.   Loni         Bates              Twenty-First Centur
     y Foundation     2148 Frontage St.               San Francisco        CA
     94107 09/23/82   06/14/92      50.00 08/23/89    .T.       MEMO
              2  A02    Mrs.  Celia        Copplestone         2031 Kenmore Terrac
     e                                                St. Louis            MO
     63114 12/01/84   09/19/93     100.00   /  /      .F.       memo
              3  A03    Mr.   Samuel       Schmaltz           1701 Albemarle Rd.
                                                      Brooklyn             NY
     11226 08/01/91   07/31/92      15.00   /  /      .F.       memo
              4  A04    Dr.   Sally  E.    Chin               1 Alvarado Plaza --
     Ste. 43          10952 Pico Blvd.                Los Angeles          CA
     90064 01/15/80   06/11/92      25.00 01/15/81    .T.       MEMO
              5  A05    Prof. Thomas       Hancock            National Research L
     aboratories      1 Linear Accelerator Ave.       Berkeley             CA
     94720 03/15/80   06/04/92      50.00   /  /      .F.       memo
              6  A06    Mr.   Manuel       Estaban             476 Partridge Hill
     Rd.                                              Boston               MA
     02165 12/12/85   06/01/92     100.00 12/29/89    .T.       MEMO
     .
     Command   C:\learndb\MEMBERS       Rec EOF/6      File                Caps
```

Figure 12.4   *Listing the contents of a file.*

To add a new record this way, use REPLACE in conjunction with APPEND BLANK. This variation on the APPEND command adds a new blank record to the end of the file and moves the pointer to it but prevents the user from editing it. Instead, the programmer gets the data from the user and then uses REPLACE to place it in the blank record.

REPLACE with APPEND BLANK can be used from the dot prompt, but they usually are not because it is easier to use EDIT, BROWSE, or APPEND.

However, REPLACE is often used from the dot prompt with other optional clauses discussed later in this chapter.

Deleting Records

To mark a record for deletion, enter the command DELETE. To unmark the record, enter the command RECALL. As you will learn later, you can also use the commands to mark and unmark groups of records.

To finalize deletions, enter the command PACK.

There is another command for deleting records, but it can be dangerous to use. The command ZAP empties the database file completely. It is equivalent to marking all of the records for deletion and then packing the database, except that it works more quickly. If you use the ZAP command, all of the records in the database are lost permanently.

This command is often used in programs that use a temporary database file to store data that they later will add to a master file. Once the data is safely in the master file, ZAP can be used to empty out the temporary file very quickly, leaving it ready to hold new data. If the program is written correctly, no data will be lost, but this command is so dangerous that you should not use it from the dot prompt.

Moving the Pointer

The commands for moving through the database file are very similar to the corresponding menu choices.

Use the command GO[TO] <*num exp*> to move the pointer to the record whose number is specified in the expression. Use the commands GO[TO] TOP and GO[TO] BOTTOM to move the pointer to the first or last record of the file.

Note that in all of these, TO is placed in brackets to indicate that it is optional. For example, you can enter either GOTO TOP or just GO TOP. GO TOP and GO BOTT are almost always used in practice.

To move the pointer a certain number of records, use the command SKIP [<*num exp*>]. The brackets indicate that the numeric expression is optional. If it is left out, the default value is 1, so that the pointer moves to the next record. If a positive or negative number is entered, the pointer moves that number of records forward or backward in the file, as it does when you use the same command from the menu system.

Indexed and Unindexed Searches

You can also move the pointer to a record that meets a specific criterion by using either an unindexed or an indexed search.

To do an *unindexed* search, use the command LOCATE FOR <*log exp*>. The FOR clause here is the same as the FOR clause that you learned to use with indexes in Chapter 11, and the same logical expressions can be used with it. A typical example is LOCATE FOR LNAME = "Copplestone", though more complex logical expressions may be used—as complex as any that you used with indexes.

LOCATE FOR reads through the entire database from the beginning, until it either finds the record that matches the condition or reaches the end of the file. To find the next record that meets the same condition, enter the command CONTINUE.

An *indexed* search uses the command SEEK <*exp*>. The expression in the command must match the key expression of the controlling index that sets the order of the records in the database file. Because it must match the key expression of the controlling index, there is no need to use a logical expression that specifies the field that the criterion matches. Instead, you simply use an expression of the same data type as the index key. For example, if the MEMBERS database is in use with the NAMES index as the controlling index, so records are listed in alphabetical order, you can use the command SEEK "Copplestone" to move the pointer to that member's record. This command has the same effect as LOCATE FOR LNAME = "Copplestone", but it works much more quickly if you are using a large database.

If you want to find the next record that matches the criterion of the SEEK command, you do not need to use any variation of CONTINUE. Because the file is in index order, the next matching record, if one exists, would be the next index in the file. You can just use the command BROWSE or SKIP and see if the next record matches.

Indexes

To create an index tag of the production .MDX file, first you must use the database file, and then enter the command INDEX ON <*key*> TAG <*tag name*> [DESCENDING]. The key here is the key expression that is the basis of the index. For example, to index alphabetically by name, use the command INDEX

ON LNAME + FNAME TAG NAMES. If the optional DESCENDING is included, the index is in descending order, by default, the index is in ascending order.

You can use an index tag to set the order of the records by opening the file with the command USE <*file name*> ORDER <*tag name*>. If the file is already open, you can enter the command SET ORDER TO TAG <*tag name*> to make the tag that is named the controlling index that determines the order of the records.

The command SET ORDER TO without any tag or index name makes dBASE process records in natural order, without a controlling index.

dBASE also has similar commands that let you create and use .NDX index files, but they are not covered here, as it would be confusing to learn two similar sets of commands at the same time.

Using Other Objects

The commands used to create or modify virtually all of the other objects about which you have learned are all very similar to each other.

For example, the command CREATE|MODIFY LABEL <*label form name*> lets you create a new label form, if the name specified is not the name of an existing form, or lets you modify a label form if the name specified is the name of an existing form. The CREATE|MODIFY LABEL command lets you use the label generator, which you learned about in Chapter 6.

In this command, the two have exactly the same effect. Though you might not expect it, both CREATE and MODIFY let you create a new label form or modify an existing one, depending entirely on whether or not the label form name that is specified already belongs to an existing form.

Similar commands are used to create or modify reports, queries, data entry forms, and applications:

```
CREATE|MODIFY REPORT <report form name>
CREATE|MODIFY QUERY|VIEW <query file name>
CREATE|MODIFY SCREEN <form file name>
CREATE|MODIFY APPLICATION <application name>
```

In all of these cases, CREATE and MODIFY are identical: either one lets you create a new object or modify an existing one, depending on the name that is specified. Note that you can use either the word QUERY or the word VIEW in the command to affect query files.

Using Label and Report Forms

The commands for producing labels and reports (using existing forms) are similar: LABEL FORM <*label form name*> [TO PRINT] and REPORT FORM <*report form name*> [TO PRINT].

By default, the labels or report are displayed on the screen. The optional TO PRINT clause sends them to the printer.

These commands can also be used with other options that are discussed later.

Using Queries and Data Entry Forms

The commands for using data entry forms and queries are also similar to each other: SET FORMAT TO <*form file name*> and SET VIEW TO <*query file name*>.

The reasons these commands begin with SET is that they are *environment commands*. When either one is used, that form or view becomes part of the permanent dBASE IV environment in which you work. After you have used SET FORMAT TO, whenever you enter EDIT or APPEND, the form you specified is used. Likewise, after you have used SET VIEW TO, the view you specified is used for many functions, such as creating reports.

Remember that data entry forms, label forms, and report forms are sometimes called *formats*.

You looked at other environment settings, used through the Settings option of the Tools menu, in Chapter 9. You will look at more SET commands in a moment.

Creating and Using Applications and Programs

As you have seen, the command for creating or modifying applications, like those for other objects, uses CREATE or MODIFY interchangeably.

To edit a program, though, you must use the command MODIFY COMMAND <*program name*>, whether it is a new or an existing program. Perhaps dBASE IV should have added an alternative using CREATE, for the sake of consistency, but old dBASE programmers are so familiar with MODI COMM that we are glad it has not been changed.

To run a program or an application, use the command DO <*program name*>.

SET Commands

The dBASE programming language includes a large number of additional SET commands that determine the working environment.

In Chapter 9, you looked at the Settings submenu of the Tools menu. All of these settings are equivalent to SET commands that you can use from the dot prompt.

This section covers only a few of the most important SET commands. For a complete listing of environment commands, see the listings beginning with the word SET in any reference book covering dBASE IV commands.

Settings that Toggle ON and OFF

The settings that toggle ON and OFF in the menu use syntax such as SET BELL ON|off to determine whether there is a warning beep, SET CARRY on|OFF to determine whether data entered in one record is carried into the next record, SET CENTURY on|OFF to determine whether the year of dates is displayed with all four digits, and so on.

It is conventional to write the default setting in capital letters and the other setting in small letters. For example, SET CENTURY on|OFF indicates that this setting is OFF by default.

There are other commands of this sort that are not included in the dBASE IV menu system, but which are very useful in programming. For example, SET CONSOLE ON|off can be used to disable the screen display. After you enter SET CONSOLE OFF, the screen display remains the same until you enter SET CONSOLE ON. These commands are not used interactively, for the obvious reason that they would freeze the screen and prevent you from doing anything else, but they are sometimes useful in programs, to hide from the user things that are being done behind the scenes.

NOTE: Another very useful SET command is SET NEAR on|OFF, which determines where the pointer is placed if an indexed search fails. By default, since this setting is OFF, the pointer is placed at the end of the database file if the search fails. If you enter SET NEAR ON, however, the pointer is placed at the record that is nearest to what you were searching for. If you mistakenly misspell a name and enter the command SEEK "Copplestne", for example, the pointer is placed at the end of the database file by default, and you will never be able to find the name you want in a long file. If you entered SET NEAR ON previously, however, the pointer is placed on the record that is nearest in spelling to "Copplestne." You can BROWSE the file and easily find the record you want, since it is near the pointer. Needless to say, this setting can be extremely useful if you do not know the exact value you are searching for.

Settings Using TO

Another group of SET commands takes the form of SET ... TO ... instead of SET ... ON|OFF.

For example, SET DISPLAY TO MONO|COLOR|EGA25|EGA43|MONO43, like the Display mode menu option, lets you set the display mode if your system supports more than one type of display. SET DECIMALS TO <num exp> lets you determine the number of decimal places that numbers use by default, like the Decimal places menu option.

Sending Output to the Printer or a File

There are two useful environment settings that let you send screen output to the printer or to a file.

You have already learned that some commands have a TO PRINT and TO FILE <file name> option to send their output to the printer or to a file, but these SET commands are easier to use if you want to send the output of a series of commands to the printer or to a file, and they can also be used with commands that do not have a TO PRINT or TO FILE option.

SET PRINT on|OFF can be used to send output to the printer. After you enter SET PRINT ON, output that is displayed on the screen is also printed, until you enter SET PRINT OFF. (This does not apply to formatted output, which is discussed in Chapter 13.)

To send output to a file is a bit trickier, because it requires two steps.

First, you must use the command SET ALTERNATE TO <*file name*> [ADDITIVE] to specify the file where the output should go. If you use the ADDITIVE option, the output is added to any text that is already in the file. Without this option, the output overwrites and destroys any information already contained in the file.

After you have used this command to specify the name of the file, you must use the command SET ALTERNATE on|OFF to send the output to the file. Note that the default is OFF, so that you must actually use this command to begin sending output to the file. You may toggle this command OFF and ON to stop and start sending output to the same alternate file. To close the alternate file entirely, use the command SET ALTERNATE TO without a file name.

Scope, Fields, FOR, and WHILE Clauses

One very powerful feature of the dBASE language is that it lets you add certain optional clauses to many different commands—for example, the TO PRINT and TO FILE <*file name*> clauses that you have already learned about.

In this section, you look at four clauses that can be used in a wide variety of commands, the Scope, FIELDS, FOR and WHILE clauses.

Specifying the Scope of a Command

There are four possible scopes for a command:

- **ALL**: the command applies to all of the records in the current database file.
- **RECORD** <*num exp*>: the command applies only to the record whose number is specified.
- **NEXT** <*num exp*>: the command applies to the number of records specified, beginning with the current record.
- **REST**: the command applies to the records from the current record to the end of the database.

These scopes can be used with many of the commands that you have already learned.

Using DELETE, RECALL, and REPLACE with a Scope Clause

For example, you know that DELETE and RECALL are used to mark or unmark the current record for deletion. You can also use the commands DELETE ALL and RECALL ALL to mark or unmark all of the records in the database file for deletion, or use the commands DELETE NEXT 10 and RECALL NEXT 10 to mark the current record and the nine records following it for deletion or to unmark any of these records that is already marked.

Commands that can include a scope clause have a default scope if no clause is included. The default scope of DELETE and RECALL is NEXT 1, for example. If no scope is specified, they apply only to the current record.

Likewise, REPLACE has a default scope of NEXT 1, but it becomes powerful when you use it with a scope clause. If you have a database that includes wages, for example, and everyone gets a cost-of-living allowance of 10 percent, you can use the command REPLACE ALL WAGE WITH WAGE*1.1 to change all of the wage fields in the current database file with just one command. If you want to give all of your members an extra year's membership for free, you can use the command, you can use the command REPLACE ALL MEMB_EXPIRS WITH MEMB_EXPIRS + 365.

REPLACE ALL is useful if you add a new field to the database, and want to put the same initial value in all of the records. It is even more powerful if you use it in combination with a FOR or WHILE clause, discussed below.

Of course, DELETE ALL, RECALL ALL, and REPLACE ALL can be very destructive commands and they should be used with great caution.

The Scope of DISPLAY and LIST

Remember the twin commands DISPLAY and LIST. Now you can see that the main difference between the two is that DISPLAY has a default scope of NEXT 1 while LIST has a default scope of ALL.

The command LIST NEXT 1 has the same results as the command DISPLAY.

> **NOTE** LIST creates a problem for the user by scrolling the data by so quickly that it is difficult to read. DISPLAY ALL avoids this problem. When you use DISPLAY ALL, dBASE IV pauses at the end of each screen and waits for you to press a key before it continues to the next screen.

Specifying a Field List

Many commands can be used with a field list, a list of the fields to which you want the command to apply.

Some commands require that you use the key word FIELDS before the field list, and for some this key word is optional. For beginners, it is easier to use the extra word FIELDS everywhere than to try to learn which commands require it and which do not.

The field names may be listed in any order separated by commas, and most commands allow the field list to consist of expressions as well as field names.

For example, you can use the command BROWSE FIELDS LNAME, FNAME to use the Browse screen in order to view or edit just the LNAME and FNAME fields. The fields are displayed in the order that they are listed in the field list.

The commands LIST and DISPLAY can be used with expressions as well as with field names. For example, LIST OFF FIELDS LNAME, FNAME, LAST_DUES/12 produces a listing of the names and the monthly dues for each, as shown in Figure 12.5.

```
. LIST OFF FIELDS LNAME, FNAME, LAST_DUES/12
LNAME               FNAME               LAST_DUES/12
Bates               Loni                        4.17
Copplestone         Celia                       8.33
Schmaltz            Samuel                      1.25
Chin                Sally E.                    2.08
Hancock             Thomas                      4.17
Estaban             Manuel                      8.33
```

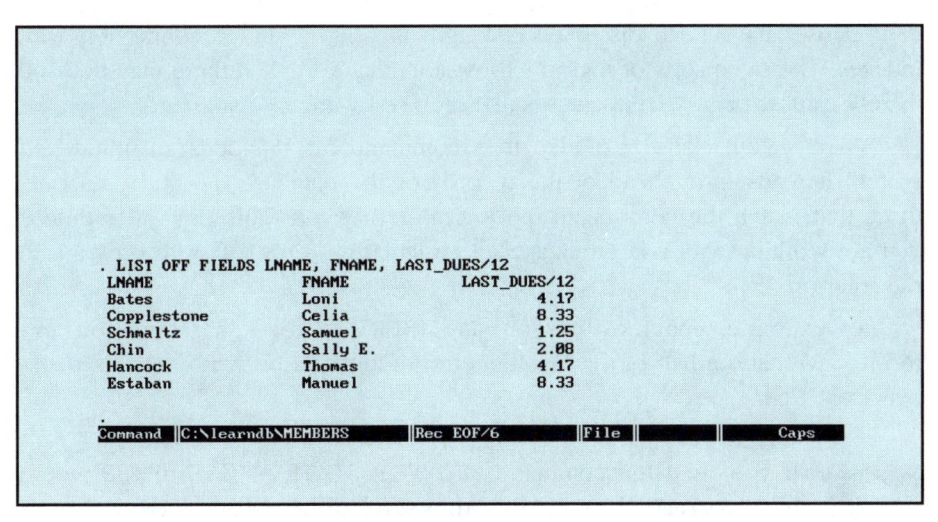

Figure 12.5 *Listing names and monthly dues.*

FOR and WHILE Clauses

Many commands can use the clause FOR <*log exp*> or WHILE <*log exp*> to restrict them to the records that meet the criteria specified in the logical expression. For example, FOR and WHILE clauses can be used with REPORT FORM or LABEL FORM to produce reports or labels that include certain records.

Often, you would use one of these clauses together with a scope clause. For example, to mark all members from California for deletion, use the command DELETE ALL FOR STATE = "CA". (If you simply used the command DELETE FOR STATE = "CA", dBASE would only look at the current record and mark it if the member were from California. If you add the ALL scope, though, dBASE looks at all of the records and marks them if the members are from California.)

Likewise, to give an extra year's membership to everyone who is a volunteer, you can use the command REPLACE ALL MEMB_EXPIRS WITH MEMB_EXPIRS + 365 FOR VOLUNTEER.

FOR Clauses

FOR clauses have been discussed at length in Chapter 11, in connection with indexes. The same sorts of logical expressions that you used there may be used in FOR clauses or in WHILE clauses that are used with any command.

When a FOR clause is added to a command, dBASE does an unindexed search. It reads through all of the records of the database file and uses only those that match the criterion in the logical expression. This can waste time if you are working with a large database, particularly if only a few records match the criterion.

For example, imagine that your MEMBERS database has ten thousand records, with about half of the members from California but with only six members from Utah.

NOTE If you used the command LIST FOR STATE = "CA", dBASE would have to read through five thousand unnecessary records in the process of finding the five thousand records from California. This would waste time, but a user watching the records being displayed or printed might not notice the wasted time because there would not be a long wait between records.

On the other hand, if you used the command LIST FOR STATE = "UT", dBASE would have to read through 9,994 unnecessary records in the process of finding the six records from Utah. A user waiting for each record from Utah to be displayed or printed would feel that the command was taking forever.

WHILE Clauses

The WHILE clause lets you speed up this sort of search tremendously by using an index, but you have to pay for the benefit by doing extra preparation.

When you use a command with a WHILE clause, dBASE checks to see if the current record matches the condition. If it does, dBASE executes the command, goes on to the next record, and checks to see if that record matches the condition. dBASE continues to execute the command as long as the current record matches the condition. As soon as it reaches a record that does not match, it stops executing the command.

Before you use a WHILE clause, then, you must have the records indexed or sorted so that all of the records you want to use come one after another. And you must move the pointer to the first record that you want to use.

A typical series of commands, assuming that you already have a STATES index tag with STATE as its key expression, is:

```
SET ORDER TO TAG STATES
SEEK "UT"
LIST WHILE STATE = "UT"
```

If you do not use SEEK (or some other command) to move the pointer to the first record before using the command with the WHILE clause, dBASE does not process any records (unless it happens, purely by chance to be on a record with UT as the state). If you do not use the proper index order and the pointer is on a matching record to begin with, dBASE keeps processing records as long as they match, but does not process matching records that do not come in sequence.

Despite the extra work they require, however, WHILE clauses are definitely worthwhile in many situations because of the time they save.

As you have seen, using indexes with FOR clauses can also speed up this sort of commands. The FOR clause of the index command is executed when you create or rebuild the index. When you make that index the controlling index, it already knows which records match the condition and does not have to read through the file to find the records to use.

The downside of indexes, though, is that they take a bit of time to maintain when you are doing data entry and also take time to rebuild when a file is packed to remove deleted records. This is not a problem if you have only one or two indexes. If you had to do reports for each state, for example, there would be excessive overhead maintaining fifty indexes with FOR clauses, one for each state. Data entry would slow down, and packing the database would seem to take forever.

SHORTCUT It is much more efficient to have one STATES index and to use it with WHILE clauses to produce the report.

WHILE clauses are also very handy in programming, since the program does the work for you. If you write a program that uses the right index order, moves the pointer, and uses the WHILE clause, you can get the speed without the extra work.

Setting a Filter

If you want to restrict the action of a series of commands, instead of using a FOR in each command, you can use the environment command SET FILTER TO <log exp>. All records that do not meet the condition of the logical expression are ignored. To access all of the records again, use the command SET FILTER TO without any logical expression to remove the filter.

The SET FILTER TO command works like a FOR clause, however. When each command is executed, dBASE reads through the entire database file and uses only the records that match. There is no environment command that works like a WHILE command.

When you create a query using the query screen, dBASE generates a SET FILTER TO command to filter out the records that do not match the criteria you enter. Whenever you use the query, this SET FILTER TO command goes into effect. Queries can be slow because this command works like a FOR clause, doing an unindexed search.

Quick Reports Using LIST

You have the background now to see that the quickest sort of quick report uses the LIST command with a field list and a FOR or WHILE clause.

Even if the criteria are very complex, it is faster to type a command with a FOR clause than to fill out the query form.

SHORTCUT

For a quick report like the one you created in Chapter 6, listing all members by state, you can just use the commands:

```
SET ORDER TO TAG ST_NAMES
LIST OFF STATE, LNAME, FNAME
```

The result is shown in Figure 12.6.

```
. SET ORDER TO TAG ST_NAMES
Master index: ST_NAMES
. LIST OFF STATE, LNAME, FNAME
STATE  LNAME                  FNAME
CA     Bates                  Loni
CA     Chin                   Sally E.
CA     Hancock                Thomas
MA     Estaban                Manuel
MO     Copplestone            Celia
NY     Schmaltz               Samuel

Command  C:\learndb\MEMBERS   Rec EOF/6   File          Caps
```

Figure 12.6 *A quick report using LIST.*

It is best to leave out TO PRINT the first time you use the command, to make sure it does what you want. Then press **Up Arrow** to edit the command line and add TO PRINT at the end.

Imagine a quick report with a complex criterion. Say that you have a PHONE field in your database and you want to print the names and phone numbers of people who either are volunteers or both pay high dues and are long-term members. You can use the command:

```
LIST OFF FIELDS LNAME, FNAME, PHONE FOR VOLUNTEER .OR.
(LAST_DUES >= 50 .AND. MEMB_SINCE < {01/01/86}) TO PRINT
```

(Of course, you must actually type this on one line.) If you need a report based on a criterion that you have an index for, you can use a WHILE clause for greater speed in processing large database files. For example, to create a telephone list for all of the members who live in Utah, use the commands:

```
SET ORDER TO TAG ST_NAMES
SEEK "UT"
LIST OFF FIELDS LNAME, FNAME, PHONE WHILE STATE = "UT"
```

You can see the advantages of using a programming language rather than a user interface that is designed for ease of use. First, you can sometimes get better performance. Second, even though it takes time to learn the language, once you know it well, you can save time by typing in commands rather than filling out screen forms.

Relational Databases

There are three different ways of working with relational databases using dBASE commands:

- You can use the same methods that you learned in Chapter 10. Create a query that relates the files, as you did in Chapter 10. Then use the command SET VIEW TO <*query name*> to use that query.
- dBASE IV includes an implementation of Structured Query Language (SQL), which you can use to work with relational databases. This is essentially a second language that is built into the dBASE command set in addition to the dBASE language itself.
- You can use two or more files simultaneously, and SET a RELATION between the two.

You are already familiar with the first of these ways. The second, SQL, is covered in books on advanced dBASE programming but is beyond the scope of this book. Now, you will look at the third.

Using Multiple Files at the Same Time

In the past, you have always used only one dBASE file at a time. When you use a file, any file that was previously in use ordinarily is closed automatically.

But dBASE IV's earlier versions also lets you create up to ten work areas and to use a different file in each one. Version 1.5 and later lets you create up to forty work areas.

You create a work area or move to a work area that has already been created by using the command SELECT <*work area*>. The work area can be referred to by a number from 1 to 40 or by a letter from A to J. (If you use more than ten work areas, you must use numbers to refer to the ones beyond ten.). If a file is already in use in the work area, you can also move to it by using the command SELECT <*file name*>.

For example, imagine that you use the series of commands:

```
SELECT A
USE DONATNS
SELECT B
USE MEMBERS2
```

You now have both files open, and you are in work area B, where MEMBERS2 is open, because you entered the command SELECT B last. If you now entered the command LIST, for example, dBASE would list the records in MEMBERS2.

You can return to work area A by entering any one of three commands: SELECT A, or SELECT 1, or SELECT DONATNS. If you entered any of these commands and then entered LIST, dBASE would list the records in DONATNS.

You can always refer to any field in a file in the current work area by just its field name. For example, if you are in work area A, you can enter the command ? AMOUNT to print the Amount field of the current record of the DONATNS file.

You can refer to a field in any file that is open in any work area by using the file name, followed by the arrow operator -> (which is made up of a hyphen and a greater-than sign) followed by the field name. For example, if you are still in work area A, you can enter the command ? MEMBERS2->LNAME to print the last name of the current record in the MEMBERS2 file, open in work area B.

There is a complication that you should not worry about now but that should be mentioned so that you do not get confused if you read about relational databases in reference books. dBASE lets you give a file an *alias* (different name) when you use it. For example, if you use the command USE MEMBERS2 ALIAS OLDFILE to open the file, you can refer to MEMBERS2 as OLDFILE for as long as it remains open, and you can refer to its fields as OLD-

FILE->LNAME and the like. Reference books usually talk about <*alias*>-><*field name*> rather than about <*file name*>-><*field name*>, so you should not be surprised if you see commands listed in this form. When they say <*alias*>, they actually mean either a file name or an alias.

Setting a Relation

You can use multiple work areas merely as a convenience, if you have to look up records in two separate files. It is quicker to SELECT the work area you need than to keep opening the same files again and again.

Multiple files really come into their own, though, if you relate them by using the command SET RELATION TO <*field name*> INTO <*file name*>.

Before you can understand this command, you have to realize that this relation works differently from the relation you created using the Query screen, because it is controlled by the controlling file.

When you set the relation, you must be in the work area where the controlling file is open, and you set the relation into the look-up file. Unlike the relation created using the Query screen, which has a record only if there are records in both files, the joined database here has one record for each record in the controlling file, with details filled in from the lookup file. For this reason, only the lookup file needs to be indexed.

To summarize, you can create a relational database using the MEMBERS2 and DONATNS files, which you worked with in Chapter 10, by using this sequence of commands:

```
SELECT A
USE DONATNS
SELECT B
USE MEMBERS2 ORDER MEMB_NUM
SELECT A
SET RELATION TO MEMB_NUM INTO MEMBERS2
```

Notice that the field name in MEMBERS2 that the relation is set into is not specified: it is the field on which the index order is based.

Now, after using this sequence of commands, whenever you move the pointer in the DONATNS file, the pointer moves to the corresponding record in the MEMBERS2 file.

Note that it does not work the other way around. If you were to move the pointer in the MEMBERS2 file, dBASE would not be able to move it to the corresponding record in the DONATNS file. There is no single corresponding record in that file.

When you relate files in this way, the different functions of the controlling file and lookup file become very clear.

After the relation is set, you can remain in the work area of the controlling file and access fields from both files by using the pointer operator. For example, to do a quick report on members' donations, you could use the command LIST OFF FIELDS MEMBERS2->LNAME, MEMBERS2->FNAME, DATE, AMOUNT.

The series of commands needed to set up this relational database and display this listing (and the result of the listing) are shown in Figure 12.7.

When you are working with multiple database files, you must remember that, because the command USE only applies in the current work area, USE without a file name following it cannot be used to close all open database files. A handy alternative is the command CLOSE DATABASES, which closes all database, index, and format files and automatically SELECTs work area 1.

```
. SELECT A
. USE DONATNS
. SELECT B
. USE MEMBERS2 ORDER MEMB_NUM
. SELECT A
. SET RELATION TO MEMB_NUM INTO MEMBERS2
. LIST OFF FIELDS MEMBERS2->LNAME, MEMBERS2->FNAME, DATE, AMOUNT
MEMBERS2->LNAME     MEMBERS2->FNAME  DATE       AMOUNT
Bates               Loni             01/01/88   100.00
Bates               Loni             05/15/89    50.00
Bates               Loni             02/10/90    50.00
Copplestone         Celia            08/16/91   100.00
Chin                Sally E.         12/30/89   150.00
Chin                Sally E.         12/28/91   150.00
Estaban             Manuel           01/15/91    30.00
                                     10/07/91  1000.00
```

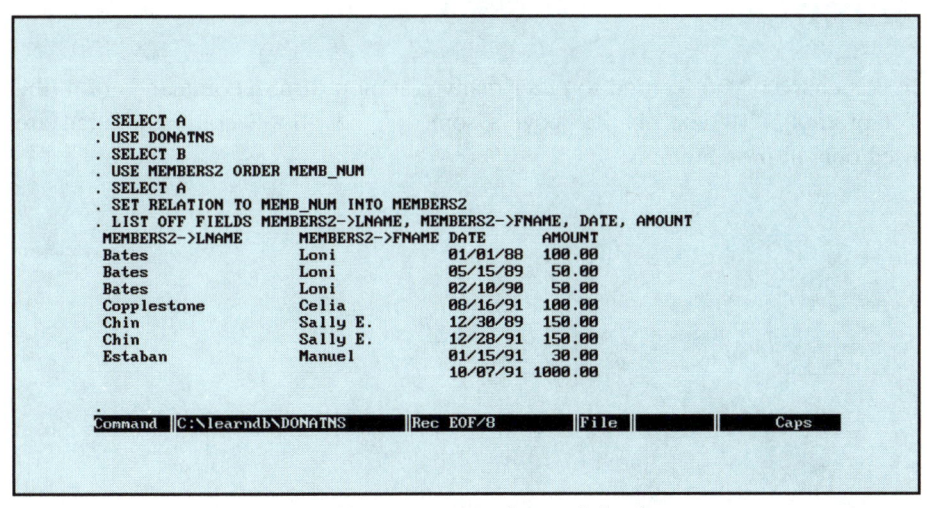

Figure 12.7   *Using a relational database.*

Indispensable Utilities

Finally, there are a few commands that are indispensable utilities.

In Chapter 11, you looked at the command ? <*expr*>, which prints the value of an expression, and the command CLEAR, which clears the screen. In Chapter 1, you learned the command ASSIST, which takes you back to the Control Center from the dot prompt.

dBASE also has a series of commands that work like DOS commands but that may have a slightly different syntax than DOS. Usually, they are longer than DOS commands. For example, dBASE uses DELETE FILE <*file name*> to delete a file rather than DOS's DEL <*file name*>.

Rather than learning a whole new set of commands to do things that you can already do in another way, you can use the dBASE utility RUN <*DOS command*> to use any DOS command from the dBASE dot prompt. For example, use RUN DEL <*file name*> to delete a file.

Last, but certainly not least, when you are done, you use the command QUIT to quit dBASE and return to DOS.

Summary

In this chapter, you learned to enter many common dBASE commands from the dot prompt. The next chapter covers some of the dBASE commands that are used only in programming.

Chapter 13

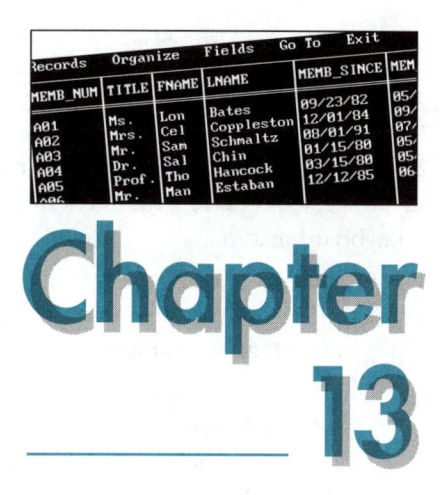

An Introduction to Programming

Now that you have learned dBASE commands and expressions and used them from the dot prompt, you are ready to go on to programming. Structured programming is essential to writing programs that are easy to debug and to maintain, and so this chapter concentrates on it.

In this chapter, you learn:

- The mechanics of creating a dBASE program
- How to identify and fix errors in dBASE programs
- Simple input/output
- Control flow, modular program design, and other basics of structured programming

Programming Basics

The simplest sort of program is just a list of commands. The program runs the commands one after another, but it does the same thing that you could do by entering them one at a time. Used in this way, a program is really no more than a keyboard macro.

Programming can have far more power than macros that just speed up what you can do from the keyboard, though, because you can also use two different types of commands, that are not available from the dot prompt:

- **Input/Output (I/O)**: lets you communicate with the user. You can tell the user what to do, and the user can make entries that are used by the program.
- **Control flow**: redirects control of the program. For example, the program can execute one block of commands if the user makes one choice, or another block of commands if the user makes a different choice.

dBASE has two different sets of input/output commands. Simple input/output works one line at a time. Formatted input/output lets you work with the entire screen. As you will see, these formatted input/output commands can be used to create data entry screens, such as the screen you created in Chapter 8 by using the forms generator.

Control flow is the heart of programming, and it has improved radically since the early days of computer programming (in the 1960s) as structured programming has developed.

The Mechanics of Creating a Program

Before you can learn these new commands, though, you must learn the basics of creating and running a program.

A dBASE program is just a plain ASCII text file with the extension .PRG. You can write it using any text editor or word processor. dBASE has no problem running programs that you create with another word processor, as long as they are saved as plain ASCII files.

Each command must be on a separate line. You can break up a single command into more than one line by adding ; (a semicolon) at the end of a line. dBASE considers the next line an extension of the line that ends with the semicolon.

dBASE ignores blank lines, so you can skip lines to make the program easier to read. It is also very important to add comments to a program. Comments are ignored by dBASE when it executes the program. They are intended to make the program easier to understand when it is modified in the future.

You can add comments in two ways.

- *|**NOTE**: If a line begins with an asterisk or with the word NOTE, dBASE ignores any text on that line: the entire line is a comment.
- **&&**: dBASE ignores any text to the right of && on a line. Unlike * or NOTE, it does not have to be used as the first word of the line. You can have a command at the left of the line, and a comment beginning with && on the same line, to its right.

You can create and run programs either from the Control Center or from the dot prompt.

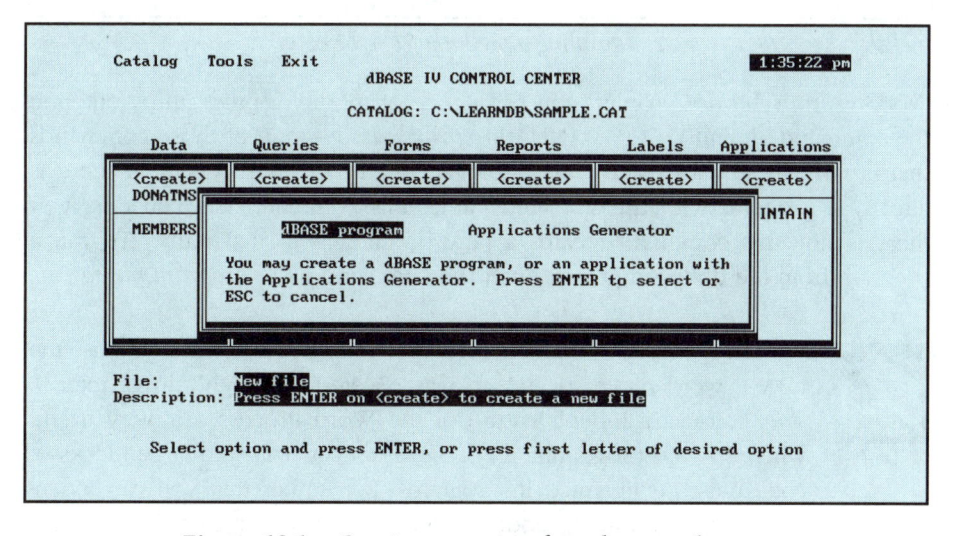

Figure 13.1 Creating a program from the control center.

To create a program from the Control Center, select **<create>** from the Applications panel and select **dBASE program** from the prompt box, shown in

Figure 13.1. To run a dBASE program from the Control Center, select its name in the Applications panel, and select **Run application** from the prompt box shown in Figure 13.2. As you know, this prompt box also has a Modify application option, which lets you edit programs. You can also edit a program by highlighting its name in the Control Center and pressing **Design:Shift-F2**.

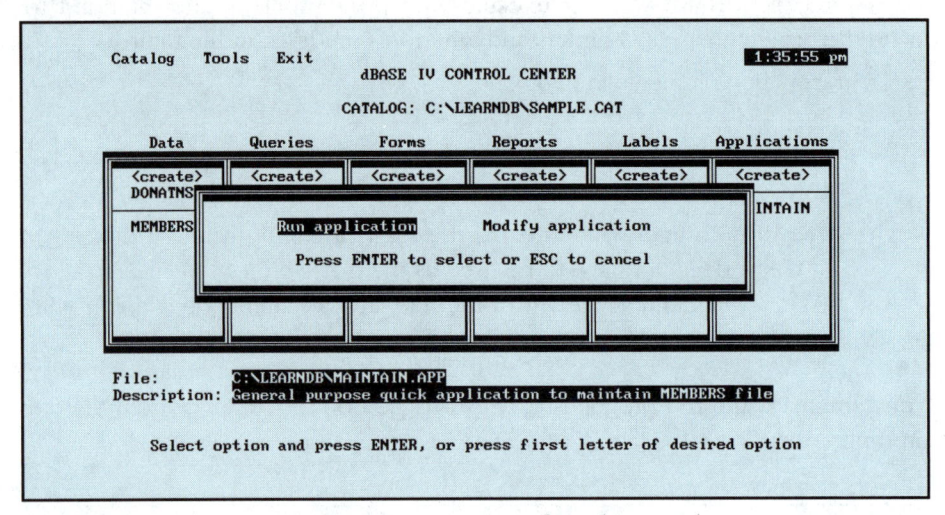

Figure 13.2   *Running a program from the control center.*

Working from the dot prompt, you can create or modify a program by entering the command MODIFY COMMAND <*program name*>—one of those commands that is virtually always used in its abbreviated form, MODI COMM. If there is already a program with the specified name, this command lets you edit it. If there is not, this command creates a new program with that name. To run a program from the dot prompt, just enter the command DO <*program name*>.

NOTE: When you create or edit a program in either of these ways, you use the dBASE word processor, which was covered thoroughly in Chapter 9. The Automatic Indent feature of the Word Processor is very useful when you are programming, because (as you will see) large blocks of code must be indented in programs. Remember that you can indent lines of programming code by pressing **Tab** and then unindent by pressing **Shift-Tab**, which moves the cursor and the margin back a tab stop. (If there is another text editor you prefer, you can also make dBASE use a different text editor by altering the Config.db file, discussed in the Appendix.)

When you run a program for the first time, dBASE automatically "compiles" it, translating the original .PRG file into a file with the extension .DBO (short for dBASE Object). Often, programmers use the word "compiling" to mean translating a program into an .EXE file, which can be run directly from DOS. dBASE does not do this, however, dBASE's compiling does make programs run more quickly.

A Sample Program

Try creating a sample program, which simply works as a macro, so you understand the mechanics of creating a program before you go on to learn new programming commands.

1. Begin from the dot prompt, and enter the command *MODI COMM SAMPLE1*.
2. When the word processor appears, type in the program exactly as shown in Table 13.1 following this exercise.
3. Press **Ctrl-End** to return to the dot prompt.
4. Enter *DO SAMPLE1*. After taking a moment to compile the program, dBASE should display the screen shown in Figure 13.3, just as if you had entered these commands by hand. If you made an error in entering the program, however, it will display an error message instead. See the next section for instructions on how to correct the error.
5. Press **Esc** to return to the dot prompt, and enter *CLOSE DATABASES*, so the open database files do not cause trouble in the future.

Table 13.1 A program to browse related files (SAMPLE1.PRG).

```
***************
*    SAMPLE1.PRG
*    a sample program to browse the fields of a
*    relational database
***************
```

```
SELECT A                                && use files in different
USE DONATNS                             && work areas
SELECT B
USE MEMBERS2 ORDER MEMB_NUM
SELECT A
SET RELATION TO MEMB_NUM INTO MEMBERS2  && relate files
BROWSE FIELDS B->LNAME,B->FNAME,DATE,AMOUNT   && browse the
                                              && desired fields
```

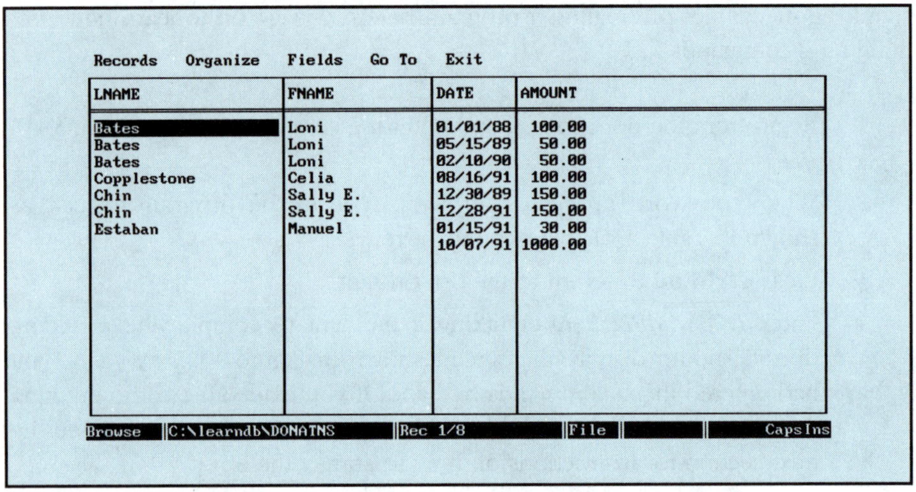

```
 Records   Organize   Fields   Go To   Exit
 LNAME                FNAME           DATE       AMOUNT

 Bates                Loni            01/01/88    100.00
 Bates                Loni            05/15/89     50.00
 Bates                Loni            02/10/90     50.00
 Copplestone          Celia           08/16/91    100.00
 Chin                 Sally E.        12/30/89    150.00
 Chin                 Sally E.        12/28/91    150.00
 Estaban              Manuel          01/15/91     30.00
                                      10/07/91   1000.00




 Browse   C:\learndb\DONATNS       Rec 1/8         File            CapsIns
```

Figure 13.3 *The result of the SAMPLE 1. program.*

Note the use of comments in this listing, particularly the heading of the program. It is generally a good idea to use a heading like this, with the name and a description of the program. The other comments, with a step-by-step description of how the program works, are not actually needed in a program as short as this one, though they are vital in longer programs. Here, they are just included as an illustration of comments using the && command.

The rest of this chapter simply has listings of sample programs, without numbered instructions telling you how to enter and run them. In each case, enter and run the program as you did above. Use a .PRG file with the name mentioned in the heading of the program and, if you want, add a description based on the heading also.

Errors

Programs can contain two types of errors: *compilation errors* and *run-time errors*.

A compilation error is an error in syntax so apparent that dBASE can find it while compiling the program—for example, an expression with unbalanced parentheses or a string with only one delimiter.

If there is a compilation error, dBASE displays the prompt box shown in Figure 13.4. You can select **Cancel** to return to the dot prompt. Select **Edit** to return to the dot prompt with the last command ready to edit. Or select **Help** to display a help screen. Notice that the line that contains the error and a brief description of the error (or at least of what dBASE thinks the error is) are displayed on the screen below the command line. In this illustration, it is described as an unterminated string, and you can see that the string is missing the final quotation mark.

Figure 13.4   *A prompt box indicating a compilation error.*

In general, the errors that you might make in these sample programs are so simple that you can identify them by looking at the program line and error description displayed on the screen or by looking at the same program line within the program. After studying the erroneous line in the prompt box, select **Cancel** or **Edit** to return to the dot prompt, press **Up Arrow** to recall the MODI COMM command that created the program, and press **Enter** to edit the program. After correcting the error, save the program and try to run it again. Keep trying to run the program until you have corrected all compilation errors, so that the program compiles and runs.

A run-time *error* cannot be detected during compilation. For example, if you type the name of a field in your database file incorrectly, dBASE has no way of knowing that this is not the name of an actual field while it is compiling the program. When it is running the program, though, and it reaches this line, it will find that there is no such field.

If your program contains a run-time error, dBASE displays a prompt box like the one shown in Figure 13.5.

```
Variable not found: MEM_NUM
SET RELATION TO MEM_NUM INTO MEMBERS2        && relate files
     Cancel              Ignore              Suspend
```

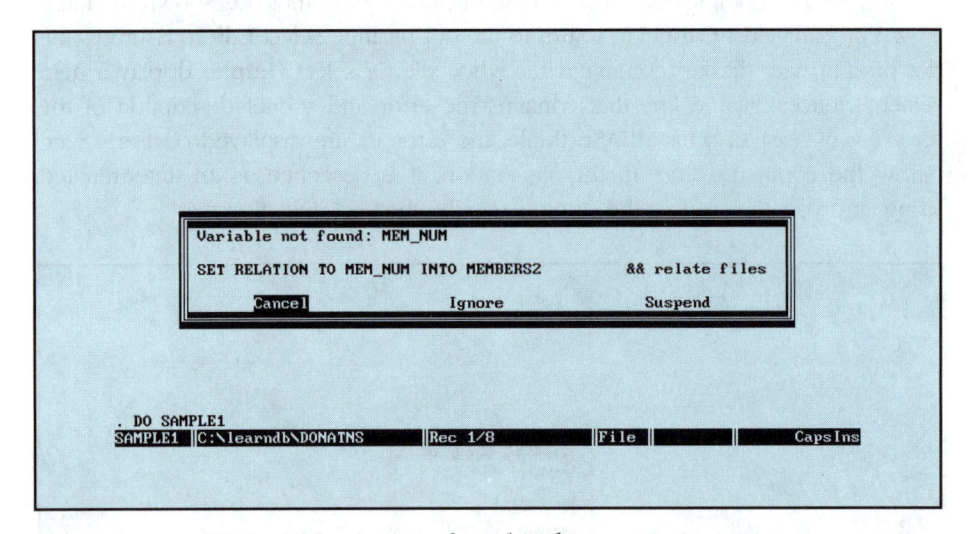

```
. DO SAMPLE1
SAMPLE1  C:\learndb\DONATNS      Rec 1/8        File           CapsIns
```

Figure 13.5 *A prompt box identifying a run-time error.*

In this illustration, the field name in the SET RELATION command was mistakenly typed as MEM_NUM instead of MEMB_NUM. Notice that the prompt box itself contains the line that has the error in it, and, at the top, includes a description of the error—in this case, Variable not found: MEM_NUM.

Since the program is running, this prompt box has three options, Cancel, Ignore, and Suspend.

The Cancel option closes the program file and returns you to the dot prompt.

The Ignore option continues executing the program despite the error. In general, an error in an early line of the program creates more errors later in the program, and you should not select Ignore from a prompt box that indicates an error unless you understand the error and know that it will not create more problems later on.

The Suspend option stops execution of the program temporarily and returns you to the dot prompt. You can then continue the program from where you left off by entering the command *RESUME*, or you can terminate the program entirely by entering *CANCEL*. You cannot use the command DO to run the program again from the beginning while it is suspended. You must CANCEL it first.

One advantage of **Suspend** over **Cancel** is that it does not close any files or release any memory variables. This can often be a help in debugging, for example, after suspending the program, you can enter the command DISPLAY MEMORY to get a list of all active memory variables, which can be useful in debugging.

For a beginner, though, it is easiest and most instructive to note carefully the line that contains the error and select **Cancel** from the prompt box. Then edit the program file, analyzing it to try to understand the error. After you have corrected the error, DO the program again, and see if it runs correctly.

When you are debugging, however, you must always bear in mind that the real error might be in an earlier line than the one that dBASE indicates. It often happens that you type in something early in the program that is syntactically correct but that is not what you intended. This can cause an error later in the program, where you that would have been correct if it weren't for the earlier error. Often, to find the source of an error, you have to look through the entire program to find the line of code that can make dBASE think that there was an error in the command that it displays as an error.

In this chapter, you learn structured programming techniques that let you break a program down into more manageable pieces (or modules), and in the next chapter, you learn to test and debug each module individually. This process can simplify debugging considerably. You should be able to find errors without any trouble simple by canceling program execution and looking carefully at the program file.

The Esc Key

You can also press **Esc** at any time while a program is running to display a prompt box with the options, Cancel, Ignore, and Suspend, which works just like the prompt box described above. Of course, you should select **Ignore** if you interrupted the program accidentally and want it to continue.

In general, you must hold down **Esc** or press it repeatedly to interrupt a program in this way. This is because, when you are using formatted input/output, described at the end of this chapter, pressing **Esc** skips the input screen and lets the program proceed to the code that follows the input/output commands. Users have a natural tendency to press **Esc** to back out of the current screen, and this feature lets you take advantage of it.

If you press **Esc** gently when you are using formatted input/output, the program usually proceeds to the code that follows the input/output command.

You must press **Esc** more persistently to interrupt the program.

Once the program is thoroughly debugged, you can use the command SET ESCAPE OFF to prevent the program from being interrupted by the **Esc** key. However, while you are writing a program, you probably want to be able to interrupt the program, and so you should not add this command until the program is thoroughly debugged and ready for the user.

Simple Input/Output

Before going on to learn the basics of structured programming, you must learn at least the simple input/output that you will need for sample programs.

You have already learned the basic output command, ? <*expr*>, which prints an expression on a new line, and the command ?? <*expr*>, which prints an expression on the current line, at the current location of the cursor. For example, the commands:

```
? "Hello, "
?? FNAME
```

do just the same thing as the command ? "Hello, " + FNAME.

Another very handy output command that can be used in programs is TEXT ... ENDTEXT. If the word TEXT appears on a line, dBASE displays all of the lines of text that follow, until it comes to a line with ENDTEXT on it. This text does not require delimiters. For example, the commands:

```
? "These are the times"
?" that try men's souls."
```

do exactly the same thing as the commands

```
TEXT
These are the times
   that try men's souls.
ENDTEXT
```

Needless to say, if you have a whole screen of text to display, using TEXT ... ENDTEXT is much easier than using ? with delimiters on each line.

Input commands generally take the data that the user enters and stores it in a memory variable. In Chapter 11, you learned how to assign a value to a memory variable by using the command *<mem var>* = *<expr>*. This command is common in programming, but it is also common to let the user assign the value to the memory variable.

There are two similar commands that you can use to get input from the user and store it in a memory variable:

```
INPUT [<char exp>] TO <mem var>
ACCEPT [<char exp>] TO <mem var>
```

Both of these commands use the optional character expression as a prompt to the user, if it is included. Both store the value that the user enters in the memory variable whose name is specified, creating that memory variable if it does not already exist.

For example, these two commands do almost the same thing:

```
INPUT "What is your name? " TO mname
ACCEPT "What is your name? " TO mname
```

Both display the prompt *What is your name?* and then wait for the user to enter something. The value that the user enters will be assigned to the variable mname.

The difference between these two commands, though, is very important.

INPUT can create memory variables of all data types. The data type of the variable depends on the data type of the user's entry. It is useful to get numeric data, since the user can just enter a number, such as 100. As you know, numeric data does not need delimiters. To create a character variable, however, the user would have to enter the characters surrounded by quotation marks (or other character delimiters): in the example above, the user would have to enter something like "Josephine". If the user's entry is not valid—for example, if the user enters letters without quotation marks—then dBASE IV displays an error message and repeats the prompt.

On the other hand, ACCEPT does not need delimiters. It always creates a character variable, whatever is entered. If the user enters Josephine, it creates a character variable with that value. If the user enters 100, it creates a character variable with the value 100. You cannot use this in calculations unless you use the function VAL( ) to convert it to numeric data.

Obviously, ACCEPT is better for most purposes, though it does create a risk that invalid data will be entered. As you will see later, it is best to use formatted input/output when there are worries about validating data.

There is one other handy command that lets you get input from the user:

```
WAIT [<char exp>] [TO <mem var>]
```

ACCEPT and INPUT both let the user enter any number of characters. Users can continue typing until they press the **Enter** key. On the other hand, WAIT just lets the user press a single key. As soon as any key is pressed, the program continues with the next line.

Notice that both the character expression and the TO *<mem var>* clause are optional. If the command WAIT is used alone, it displays the prompt: *Press any key to continue...* and does not create a memory variable when the user presses a key. In this form, it is simply used to stop the program for a moment—for example, so the user has time to read the information on a screen before the next screen is displayed.

If you include the optional character expression, that expression is used as a prompt. If you include the optional TO *<mem var>* clause, dBASE creates the specified memory variable and stores the key that is pressed in it. For example, if you use the command:

```
WAIT "Do you want to continue (Y/N) " TO mchoice
```

dBASE displays the prompt *Do you want to continue (Y/N)*. As soon as the user presses a single key, dBASE stores that key to the variable mchoice and continues to execute the program. The program can decide what to do next depending on whether the user pressed Y or N. Because it does not make the user press **Enter**, the command WAIT can make programs feel faster and more responsive.

Before going on to use these input/output commands in combination with control flow, try a couple of simple exercises to use them alone.

Enter and run the program in Table 13.2. When you run the program, you can try to run it in a different way. Instead of pressing **Ctrl-End** to save it and exit to the dot prompt, try selecting **Run program** from the Exit menu of the dBASE IV program editor. When you run the program, it asks "What is your name?" Type any name and press **Enter**. Its results are shown in Figure 13.6.

Table 13.2 *A program using simple input/output.*

```
***************
*    SAMPLE2.PRG
*    a program using simple input/output
***************

SET TALK OFF
CLEAR
?
ACCEPT "What is your name? " TO mname
?
? "Hello, " + mname
?
WAIT
```

```
What is your name? JOSEPHINE
Hello,JOSEPHINE
Press any key to continue...




                                                                    
SAMPLE2                                                      Caps Ins
```

Figure 13.6 *The result of this program.*

If you would like, you can also try running this program without the command SET TALK OFF, to see how the dBASE "talk" interferes with it. The easiest way to eliminate this command from the program is to type an asterisk in front of it, so that dBASE considers it a comment. After you have run it this way, you can just delete the asterisk, so the program runs properly again.

When you try this program, you might notice problems with capitalization. If you enter JOSEPHINE, as you can see in the figure, the program prints Hello, JOSEPHINE.

The revised version of the program in Table 13.3 remedies this problem and also illustrates the use of memory variables in expressions. The listing uses a semi-colon to break up the commands into two lines so that it fits on the page. You can enter it in this way, or you can omit the semi-colon and type the command on a single line. (Note that the program in Table 13.3 is so similar to SAMPLE2 that the easiest way of creating it is by modifying SAMPLE2 and saving the revised program under the name SAMPLE3. The same is true of many of the other programs that follow.) Its results are shown in Figure 13.7.

Table 13.3 *A program using simple input/output with expressions.*

```
***************
*    SAMPLE3.PRG
*    a program using simple input/output,
*    revised to capitalize properly
***************


    SET TALK OFF
    CLEAR
    ?
    ACCEPT "What is your name? " to mname
    ?
    ? "Hello, " + UPPER(SUBSTR(mname,1,1)); + LOWER(SUBSTR(mname,2))
    ?
    WAIT
```

In Chapter 11 you looked at this use of the UPPER( ), LOWER( ), and SUBSTR( ) functions to capitalize a name properly. The only difference here is that it is used with a memory variable entered by the user.

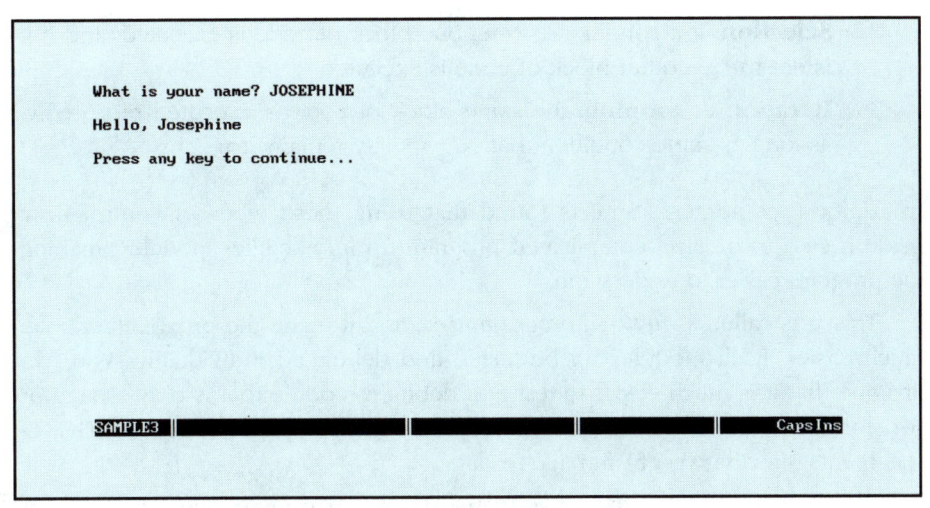

```
What is your name? JOSEPHINE
Hello, Josephine
Press any key to continue...




SAMPLE3                                                    CapsIns
```

Figure 13.7   *The result of Sample 3 program.*

Structured Programming

So far, the programs that you have looked at just run one line after another, from beginning to end. The real power of programming, though, depends on directing the flow of program control, so that you can run a block of code any time you want to.

Early programming language used the command GOTO to direct program control. This is still used in many versions of BASIC, which use a command such as GOTO 10030 to make the program continue at line 10030.

Computer scientists quickly discovered, however, that a long program filled with GOTO statements is very difficult for programmers to understand. Trying to follow this sort of program could get you so tangled up that programmers started calling it *spaghetti code*.

The difficulties of early programming languages led computer scientists to discover that GOTO statements were not needed for programming. It was proven that any program that could be written using GOTOs could also be written using only the following three types of control flow:

1. **Sequence**: one line is executed after another—the basic control flow that you have used so far.

2. **Selection**: if a condition is true, one block of code is executed, and if it is not true, another block of code is executed.
3. **Iteration** or **looping**: the same block of code is executed repeatedly, as long as some condition that you specify remains true.

In addition, computer scientists found that using these types of control flow made it easy to break a complicated program up into smaller modules, making the program easier to understand.

This was called *structured programming*, and it made the programmer's job much easier. Each module can be tested and debugged individually. You can imagine that it is much easier to test and debug a module that is only a page or two long than it is to debug an entire program—fifty pages long with GOTO statements directing you from page to page.

dBASE is a language that encourages structured programming. It does not include anything like the GOTO command. It only has structured methods of control flow, based on *selection* and *looping*, which you learn in the next two sections. As you will see in the following section, it also makes it easy to break down programs into separate modules.

Selection

dBASE has two major commands that let the program select which block of code to execute. The command IF ... ELSE ... ENDIF is best for selecting one of two blocks of code. The command DO CASE ... ENDCASE is best for selecting among many blocks of code.

IF ... ELSE ... ENDIF

The most basic form of selection in dBASE is the command:

```
IF <log exp>
...
[ELSE
...]
ENDIF
```

The ellipses (...) stand for one or more lines of code.

If the logical expression is true, only the code following IF is executed. The code following ELSE is skipped, and the program continues with the code following ENDIF. On the other hand, if the logical expression if false, only the code following ELSE is executed.

Notice that the ELSE is optional. If you leave it out, the code following IF is executed if the logical expression is true. Nothing is done if the logical expression is false. In either case (of course) the program then continues with the code following ENDIF.

A simple example should make this very clear. Imagine that you want to revise the program that says Hello, which you wrote above, so that the user has the choice of whether or not capitalization is changed. You could use the code shown in Table 13.4. Figure 13.8 shows one possible output of this program.

Table 13.4   A program using IF ... ELSE.

```
***************
*    SAMPLE4.PRG
*    a program using simple input/output,
*    revised to let the user choose whether to
*    capitalize properly
**************


SET TALK OFF
CLEAR
?
ACCEPT "What is your name? " to mname
?
WAIT "Do you want capitalization changed (Y/N) ";
      to mchoice
?
IF UPPER(mchoice) = "Y"
  ? "Hello, " +
UPPER(SUBSTR(mname,1,1));
      +LOWER(SUBSTR(mname,2))ELSE
  ? "Hello, " + mname
ENDIF
?
WAIT
```

```
What is your name? JOSEPHINE
Do you want capitalization changed (Y/N) Y
Hello, Josephine
Press any key to continue...


SAMPLE4                                                    Caps Ins
```

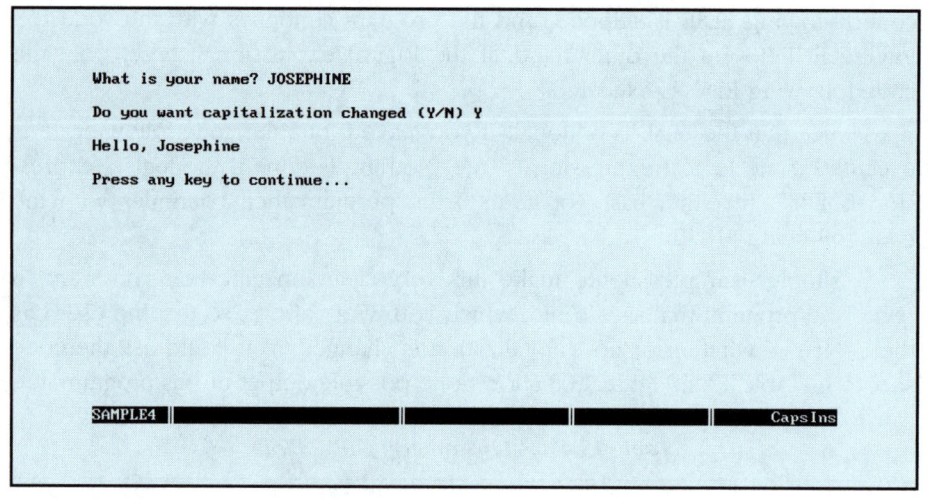

Figure 13.8   *One possible result of this program.*

NOTE As you work with more complex programs such as this one, remember that to test and debug them, you must try every possible option.

After getting the user's name, the program uses a WAIT command to ask if the user wants capitalization changed and to store the user's response in the memory variable mchoice. Apart from that, the program is identical to the earlier versions, except that it has an IF ... ELSE ... ENDIF in it that determines what is printed. If the user pressed *Y* when dBASE created mchoice, the program changes the capitalization of the name; if the user did not press *Y*, the program leaves capitalization as is.

Notice that you test what the user entered by using the expression IF UPPER(mchoice) = "Y". The function UPPER( ) is used so that the program reads the choice as yes regardless of whether the user entered a small or a capital *Y*.

NOTE Notice also that the code following IF and ELSE is indented. Indenting to show control flow makes the program much more readable. The difference is not noticeable in this program, but proper indentation is invaluable in a longer, more complex program.

The IF ... ELSE Ladder

The last version of the sample program only included two choices: the user could enter Y or not enter Y. But what if you want more than two choices—for example, one response for Y, a second response for N, and a third response for any other letter.

One way of doing this is sometimes called an IF ... ELSE ladder. It involves nesting one IF ... ELSE statement inside of another, as in Table 13.5. One result of this program is shown in Figure 13.9.

Table 13.5 A Program using an IF ... ELSE ladder (SAMPLE5.PRG).

```
***************
*    SAMPLE5.PRG
*    a program using simple input/output,
*    revised to let the user choose whether to
*    capitalize properly and
*    to accept only Y or N as valid choices
*    using an IF...ELSE ladder
**************
    SET TALK OFF
    CLEAR
    ?
    ACCEPT "What is your name? " to mname
    ?
    WAIT "Do you want capitalization changed (Y/N) ";
         to mchoice
    ?
    IF UPPER(mchoice) = "Y"
      ? "Hello, " + 
          UPPER(SUBSTR(mname,1,1));
          +LOWER(SUBSTR(mname,2))ELSE
      IF UPPER(mchoice) = "N"
          ? "Hello, " + mname
      ELSE
          ? "Invalid entry: You must enter Y or N."
      ENDIF
    ENDIF
    ?
    WAIT
```

Notice that there is a new IF ... ELSE ... ENDIF command following the ELSE of the original IF ... ELSE ... ENDIF command.

The indentation makes the logic easier to follow, by lining up the corresponding IF ... ELSE and ENDIF one under another.

If the user enters Y, the program prints the name with the capitalization changed, and then it skips everything between the next ELSE and the final ENDIF, going to the end of the program. If the user does not press Y, the program skips the code under the first IF and goes to the code under the first ELSE, where it finds the second IF ... ELSE command. Then it decides whether to execute the code following the IF or the ELSE of this second command depending on whether the user entered N. If so, it prints the name without changing capitalization, and if not, it prints an error message, since it now knows that the user entered neither Y nor N.

```
What is your name? JOSEPHINE
Do you want capitalization changed (Y/N) Q
Invalid entry: You must enter Y or N.
Press any key to continue...
```

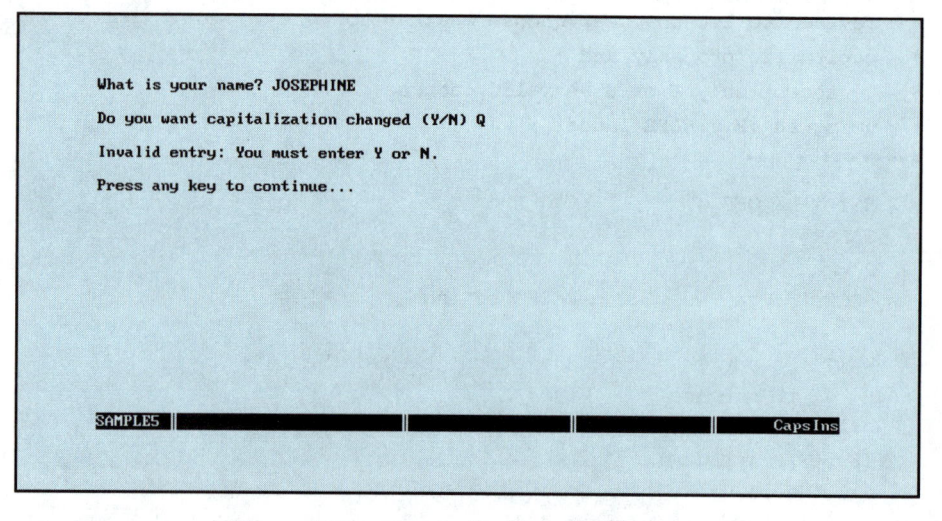

Figure 13.9   *One result of Sample 5 program.*

DO CASE ... ENDCASE

IF ... ELSE can handle multiple choices in this way, but you can see that the logic of an IF ... ELSE ladder can be hard to follow. For this reason, dBASE offers an alternative command, which works like an IF ... ELSE ladder.

You can select among multiple choices by using the command:

```
DO CASE
   CASE <log exp>
      ...
   CASE <log exp>
      ...
   ...
   [OTHERWISE
      ...]
ENDCASE
```

If the logical expression following the first CASE is true, dBASE executes the code under it and then skips the rest of the CASES and continues with the code following ENDCASE. Likewise with the code following any of the CASE statements. If no CASE is true, then dBASE executes the code following the optional OTHERWISE, if it is included, before going on to the code that follows ENDCASE.

SAMPLE6.PRG, shown in Table 13.6, works exactly like SAMPLE5.PRG. The difference is that is uses a DO CASE statement rather than an IF...ELSE ladder.

Table 13.6   *A program using DO CASE.*

```
***************
*    SAMPLE6.PRG
*    a program using simple input/output,
*    revised to let the user choose whether to
*    capitalize properly and
*    to accept only Y or N as valid choices
*    using DO CASE
**************

   SET TALK OFF
   CLEAR
   ?
   ACCEPT "What is your name? " to mname
   ?
   WAIT "Do you want capitalization changed (Y/N) ";    to
   mchoice
   ?
   DO CASE
      CASE UPPER(mchoice) = "Y"
```

```
        ? "Hello, " + UPPER(SUBSTR(mname,1,1));
            +LOWER(SUBSTR(mname,2))
    CASE UPPER(mchoice) = "N"
        ? "Hello, " + mname
    OTHERWISE
        ? "Invalid entry: You must enter Y or N."
    ENDCASE
    ?
    WAIT
```

You can see that the program is easier to follow with the options lined up one under another in a DO CASE than it was when you used an IF ... ELSE ladder even though there are just three options. The advantage of DO CASE over the IF...ELSE ladder is even greater if there are more options.

Looping

There is only one basic command that you must learn for the final form of control flow, looping. It takes the form:

```
DO WHILE <log exp>
    ...
ENDDO
```

As always, the ellipsis (...) stands for any number of lines of code.

When the program comes to the DO WHILE, if the logical expression if false, it skips all this code and continues after ENDDO.

On the other hand, if the logical expression is true, it executes all of the code following DO WHILE. Then, when it gets to ENDDO, it loops back up to DO WHILE and checks again to see if the logical expression is true. If it is not, the program executes the code following ENDDO; but if it is, the program executes the code following DO WHILE once again.

Using the DO WHILE loop

Needless to say, the code following DO WHILE should include some command that eventually makes the logical expression untrue.

Consider the simple example in Table 13.7, whose result is shown in Figure 13.10.

Table 13.7 *A simple example of a DO WHILE loop.*

```
***************
*   SAMPLE7.PRG
*   a simple example of a DO WHILE loop
***************

    SET TALK OFF
    CLEAR
    mnum = 10
    ?"countdown!"
    DO WHILE mnum >= 0
       ? mnum
       mnum = mnum - 1
    ENDDO
    ?
    WAIT
```

Figure 13.10 *The result of this program.*

First, the program creates the numeric memory variable mnum and gives it the value 10. When it gets to DO WHILE, the condition is true, because 10 is greater than 0. It prints 10, the current value of mnum, and then it subtracts one from mnum. The command mnum = mnum -1 sometimes puzzles beginning programmers, because it seems like a mathematical contradiction. You must remember that = here is the assignment operator, so that you can read this command as "let mnum equal (the current value of) mnum minus 1."

When the program gets to ENDDO, it loops back up to DO WHILE, and the condition is still true, because the new value of mnum, 9, is greater than 0. It prints this value, subtracts one from mnum again, and loops back to DO WHILE. It keeps doing this until the DO WHILE condition is no longer true—until mnum is less than 0.

Now, consider a slightly more complex example of a DO WHILE loop, shown in Table 13.8, which nests the sample program that capitalizes names within a DO WHILE loop, in order to give the user the choice of trying the program again and again. One result of this program is shown in Figure 13.11.

Table 13.8 *A more complex example of a DO WHILE loop.*

```
***************
*    SAMPLE8.PRG
*    a program using simple input/output,
*    revised to let the user choose whether to
*    capitalize properly
*    and to let the user choose to repeat the program
***************
   SET TALK OFF
   m_again = "Y"
   DO WHILE UPPER(m_again) = "Y"
     CLEAR
     ?
     ACCEPT "What is your name? " to mname
     ?
     WAIT "Do you want capitalization changed (Y/N) ";
          to mchoice
     ?
     DO CASE
        CASE UPPER(mchoice) = "Y"
           ? "Hello, " + UPPER(SUBSTR(mname,1,1));
             +LOWER(SUBSTR(mname,2))
```

```
        CASE UPPER(mchoice) = "N"
            ? "Hello, " + mname
        OTHERWISE
            ? "Invalid entry: You must enter Y or N."
    ENDCASE
    ?
    WAIT "Do you want to try again (Y/N) " to m_again
  ENDDO
  ?
  WAIT
```

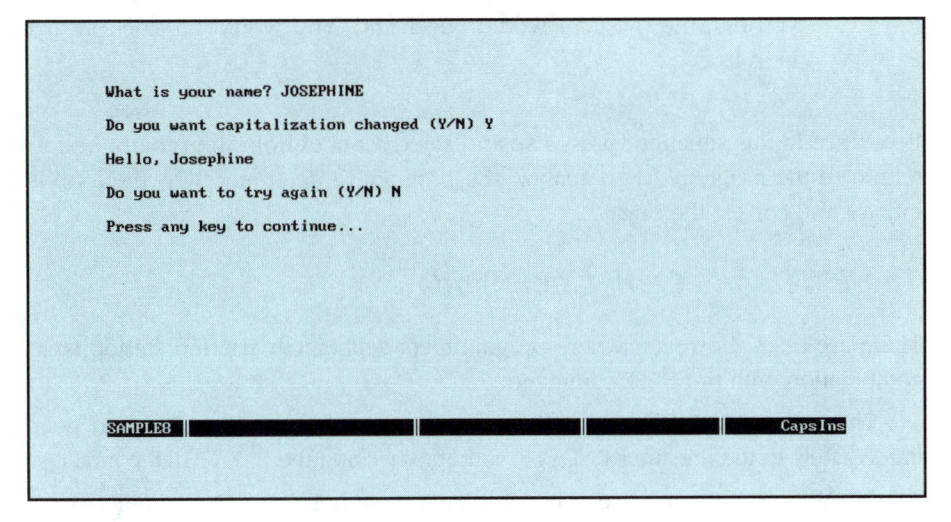

```
What is your name? JOSEPHINE

Do you want capitalization changed (Y/N) Y

Hello, Josephine

Do you want to try again (Y/N) N

Press any key to continue...




SAMPLE8                                                    Caps Ins
```

Figure 13.11 *A result of this program.*

This program is just the same as the previous version except that it is all nested within a DO WHILE loop based on the condition DO WHILE UPPER(m_again) = "Y". The program begins with the command m_again = "Y", so this condition is true the first time the program gets to it. After the main code is executed, the final command in the DO WHILE. loop is WAIT "Do you want to try again (Y/N) " to m_again, which lets the user determine the value of m_again. Then the program loops back to DO WHILE. If the user entered Y, the condition is true, and so it executes the entire loop again. If the user entered **N**, the condition is untrue, and so it skips the loop and continues with the code after ENDDO, which simply prompts the user to press any key before the program ends.

Infinite Loops

The *infinite loop* is one of the most common bugs that you will run into when you are developing programs.

> **NOTE** Imagine that you made a typographical error in the last listing, for example. Instead of typing *WAIT "Do you want to try again (Y/N) " to m_again*, you left off the final "n" and typed *WAIT "Do you want to try again (Y/N) " to m_agai*. When dBASE got to this command, it would create a new memory variable named m_agai. There would be nothing in the program to change the value of m_again, so the condition of the DO WHILE loop would always be true. No matter what you did, the program would never end. You would be stuck in that loop forever.

If you are in this situation, press **Esc** and select **Cancel** from the prompt box to terminate the program. Then analyze the program to determine why the loop is infinite and correct the bug.

The EXIT and LOOP Commands

There are cases, however, where programmers deliberately use infinite loops, in combination with the EXIT command.

The command EXIT breaks the program out of the current loop. It goes immediately to the line after ENDDO, without checking the DO WHILE condition.

LOOP is sometimes used in combination with EXIT. LOOP immediately begins the loop again, returning control to the DO WHILE condition: as always, the loop is executed if the condition is true, or it is skipped if it is false.

In the sample program you were just working with, for example, rather than the condition **DO WHILE UPPER(m_again) = "Y"**, you could deliberately use a condition that creates an infinite loop. You could use a condition such as **DO WHILE 1 = 1**, which is always true. But remember that, when dBASE sees a logical expression of this sort, it evaluates it as .T. or .F.. When programmers want to create an infinite loop, they generally save dBASE the trouble of evaluating the expression by beginning the loop **DO WHILE .T.**.

After creating an infinite loop at the beginning of the program, you could end it with the commands:

```
            ?
            WAIT "Do you want to try again (Y/N) " to m_again
            IF UPPER(m_again = "Y")
                LOOP
            ELSE
                EXIT
            ENDIF
    ENDDO
    ?
    WAIT
```

This runs just like the previous version of the program. If the user presses Y, it goes back to DO WHILE and goes through the loop again. If the user presses anything else, it breaks out of the loop and goes to the end of the program.

This method is more verbose than including the condition in the DO WHILE command itself. In fact, even if you used an infinite loop, you could rewrite the code so it is more concise, as:

```
            ?
            WAIT "Do you want to try again (Y/N) ";
                to m_again
            IF UPPER(m_again <> "Y")
                EXIT
                ENDIF
            ENDDO
            ?
    WAIT
```

If m_again were equal to Y, the program would loop automatically when it got to ENDDO.

It is sometimes worth using EXIT and LOOP, though, despite the extra lines of code, in order to make a program easier to understand. You will see an example of this in Chapter 14, when you create a simple menu system.

Modular Program Design

The final element of structured programming involves breaking a long program down into small modules, each of which can be tested, debugged, and (if it becomes necessary later) modified individually. It is much easier to work with individual modules than with a long program.

In early versions of dBASE, each module had to be a separate .PRG file, and you can still write complex dBASE programs in this way. One .PRG can run another in the same way that you run a PRG file from the dot prompt. Just include the command DO <*PRG file name*> in a program.

When the called .PRG file ends, control returns to the calling .PRG, to the line following the DO command that ran the called .PRG.

You can also use the command RETURN in a called .PRG to return control to the next line of the calling .PRG. (If the PRG is used from the dot prompt, RETURN returns to the dot prompt.)

For example, a .PRG might ask the user whether to continue and then use the commands:

```
IF m_again = "N"
   RETURN
ENDIF
```

in order to return to the calling .PRG if the user enters N.

NOTE In general, though, it is not good practice to use RETURN in the middle of a module. Studies of structured programming have shown that programs are easier to understand if control passes through the end of each module. Rather than the code above, for example, it is better to use:

```
DO WHILE .T.
   ...
   IF m_again = "N"
       EXIT
   ENDIF
   ...
ENDDO
[RETURN]
```

The EXIT command makes control pass to the line after ENDDO—that is, to the end of the module—and in complex programs, this makes control flow easier to understand.

The command RETURN is optional at the end of the module. Control automatically passes back to the next line of the calling module when you reach the end of the called module. Some programmers like to use the command RETURN at the end of each module, for the sake of clarity, but the module runs in the same way whether or not RETURN is explicit.

Early dBASE programmers found it inconvenient to include each module of a large program in a separate .PRG file, and they complained about other limitations that made structured programming difficult, and so later versions of dBASE added more features, designed specifically to encourage modular programming.

Of course, it is difficult to illustrate these features adequately with brief examples, as we have illustrated the programming commands described earlier in this chapter, because they are meant to be used to break up long programs. This section has a few illustrations, but when you read it, you should bear in mind that modular programming is illustrated more adequately in Chapter 14, where the entire chapter is spent developing a longer program.

Procedures

If you include each module of a program in a separate .PRG file, it can be hard to keep track of them all. It is more convenient to keep them all in a single .PRG file, using the command PROCEDURE *<procedure name>*, which lets you create procedures that can be used exactly as you use .PRG files.

All of the commands that follow this command are treated as if they were a separate program. A program can use the command DO *<procedure name>* to run a procedure, in precisely the same way that it uses the command DO *<PRG file name>* to run a separate .PRG file.

Procedures can be kept in the same .PRG file as the program that runs them. The main program code at the beginning of the file is executed when you run the program from the dot prompt. Whenever the program has DO *<name>* command, dBASE looks at the Procedures in that .PRG file and, if it finds a procedure with the name specified, it runs it.

Procedures can also be kept in a separate procedure file, which has contains only procedures. Before using one of these procedures, you must enter the command SET PROCEDURE TO *<procedure file name>*. Then, when a program comes to the command DO *<name>*, it looks in that procedure file as well as the .PRG file itself to find the procedure whose name is specified.

The Scope of Variables

If you want to break up programs into separate modules that you can test or modify independently, there is an advantage to creating a different set of memory variables for each module. If you add a new memory variable to a module you are modifying, for example, you do not want to affect the value of a memory variable in another module that happens to have the same name.

For this reason, you must think about the *scope* of variables—a term that refers to the parts of the program to which the variables are accessible.

Field variables are accessible to any module of the program. Once you use a database file, any part of the program can read the data in the fields of that file.

Memory variables, though, are not necessarily accessible to all of the modules of a program.

By default, a memory variable is accessible to the module where it is created and to any module called by that module. Imagine that the EDIT procedure lets the user assign a value to the variable mname. Then the EDIT procedure uses the command DO LOOKUP to run the LOOKUP procedure. The LOOKUP procedure can also use the value that the user assigned to mname.

On the other hand, if the LOOKUP procedure creates a variable named mrandom and assigns a value to it, then after the LOOKUP procedure is done and control returns to the EDIT procedure, it cannot use this variable. If the EDIT procedure had a command such as ? mrandom, dBASE would display an error message saying that no such variable exits.

You can change the default scope of variables, however, by using the commands PUBLIC <*mem var list*> and PRIVATE <*mem var list*>. In either case, the command is used with a list of memory variables that can consist of the name of a single memory variable or of names of a number of memory variables separated by commas. These commands must be used before the variables are assigned values.

The command PUBLIC makes the specified memory variables accessible to all of the modules of the program. The variable must be declared as public before it is assigned a value. It is usually better programming style to declare all of the public memory variables at the beginning of the program.

The command PRIVATE makes the specified memory variables inaccessible to the calling module. If the module that runs the module with a private variable has a variable with the same name, dBASE treats them as two separate variables—the variable of that name from the calling module is not accessible within the called module. Likewise, if the program has a public memory variable with the same name as a memory variable declared as private in a module, that public variable is not accessible in that module. It is best programming style to declare private memory variables at the beginning of the module.

For example, if you begin a module with the command PRIVATE m_choice, the variable m_choice used in that module is a separate variable from m_choice that is used in the calling module or from a PUBLIC m_choice declared in another module. Though they have the same name, the values in this module do not affect each other.

On the other hand, this PRIVATE variable is accessible to modules called by the module where they are declared.

Parameters

You can pass values between two modules by using the PARAMETERS command.

The command PARAMETERS <*mem var list*> must be in the first line of the module to which the parameters are passed.

Then you can run that module with the command DO <*name*> WITH <*expr list*>, and the expressions in that list are assigned as values to the memory variables in the PARAMETERS command.

Consider this simple example:

```
...
DO hello WITH "Sam"
...
PROCEDURE hello
PARAMETERS mname
? "Hello, " + mname
```

This example has only one line of code from the main program, which runs the HELLO procedure, passing "Sam" to it as a parameter. The HELLO procedure begins with the command PARAMETERS mname, which assigns the value passed as a parameter to the memory variable mname. In this case, the command ? "Hello, " + mname prints Hello, Sam. On the other hand, if another part of the program runs this procedure with the command DO hello WITH "Josephine", it prints Hello, Josephine.

The command DO <*name*> WITH can be used to run either procedures or .PRG files, and it can include a list of up to fifty expressions, separated by commas. The PARAMETERS command should include a corresponding list with names of up to fifty memory variables separated by commas.

dBASE also lets you pass parameters back from the called module to the calling module. The parameter that you want to pass back must be initialized in the calling module, and it must be included in the parameter list of the called module. Then the changed value is passed back to the calling module.

Consider a simple example, a procedure to cube a number, shown in Table 13.9, with its result shown in Figure 13.12.

Table 13.9   *A sample use of a procedure to cube a number.*

```
***************
*    SAMPLE9.PRG
*    a sample use of a procedure to cube a number
***************

     SET TALK OFF
     CLEAR

     tencubed = 0
     DO cube WITH 10,tencubed
     ?
     ? "Ten to the third power is "
     ?? tencubed
     ?
     WAIT
     SET TALK ON


***************
*    CUBE PROCEDURE
*    a procedure to raise a number to the third power
***************

     PROCEDURE cube
     PARAMETERS x, xcubed

     xcubed = x^3
```

This is not a procedure that you would actually want to use in a program, since it is easier just to use the operators ^3 or **3 to cube a number, but it does illustrate the principle of passing parameters to the procedure and back.

Notice that the CUBE procedure has two parameters: x is the parameter that is passed to it, and xcubed is the parameter that it passes back. The calling procedure has to initialize the parameter that is passed back before it calls the CUBE procedure. It does this with the command tencubed = 0, or it could initialize it with any numeric value. Then, the command DO cube WITH 10,tencubed calls the CUBE procedure and passes the value 10 to its parameter x and the value tencubed to its parameter xcubed. The value of xcubed changes in the CUBE procedure, because of the command xcubed = x^3. Because the parameter is passed back, tencubed also changes to that new value. And so the calling program concludes by saying that 10 to the third power is 1000.

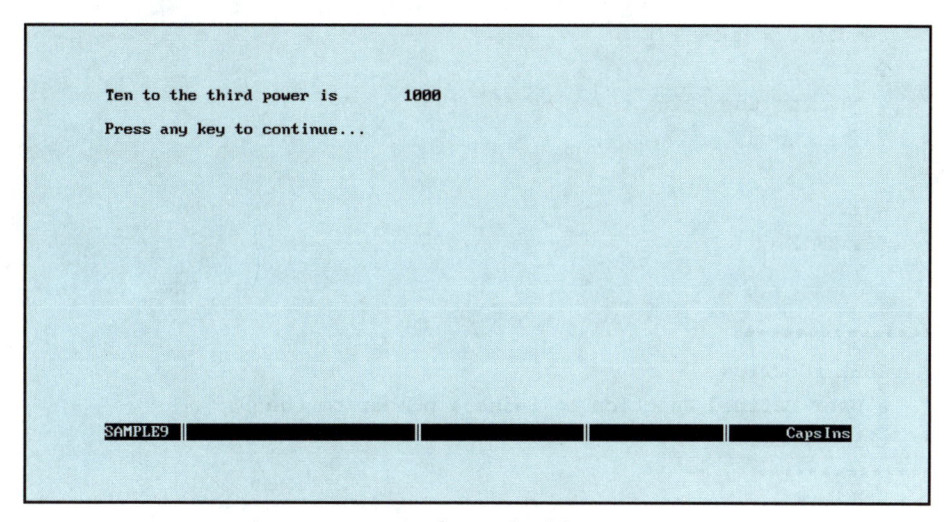

Figure 13.12 The result of this program.

User-Defined Functions

dBASE IV provides another, more elegant way of passing parameters back and forth between modules, the user-defined function (or UDF).

If you define the called module as a *function* rather than as a *procedure*, it can use the RETURN command followed by a value to pass that value back to the calling module.

The calling module can use a user-defined function just as it uses any function. The example shown in Table 13.10 should make this clear.

Table 13.10 *A sample use of a user-defined function.*

```
**************
*   SAMPLE10.PRG
*   a sample use of a User-Defined Function to cube
*   a number
**************

    SET TALK OFF
    CLEAR

    tencubed = cube(10)
    ?
    ? "Ten to the third power is "
    ?? tencubed
    ?
    WAIT
    SET TALK ON


**************
*   CUBE FUNCTION
*   a User-Defined Function to raise a number to the
*   third power
**************

    FUNCTION cube
    PARAMETER x
    RETURN x^3
```

This program has exactly the same result as the last one. The calling module passes the value 10 to the CUBE function simply by putting it in parentheses following the name of the function. (You can also call a UDF without passing a value to it by using its name followed with empty parentheses, as you do with any function.) The CUBE function uses the command RETURN x^3 to return the value passed to it raised to the third power. As with any function, the UDF itself has the value that is returned, so the calling module can assign the value to tencubed simply by using the command tencubed = cube(10).

In fact, the memory variable tencubed was used purely for instructional purposes, to make the program easier to understand. Instead, the program could simply have used the commands

```
? "Ten to the third power is "
?? cube(10)
```

You can see how much more elegant user-defined functions are than procedures in certain cases. Writing and using the CUBE function required only about half as much code as the CUBE procedure.

This sample UDF simply returned a value, but UDFs can be much more elaborate. Chapter 14 illustrates more capabilities of user-defined functions and also illustrates structured programming in general.

Formatted Input/Output

Like the simple input/output that you learned about at the beginning of this chapter, formatted input/output lets you communicate with the user. But formatted input/output has additional features that give you tremendous power to control the screen and to control what the user enters.

The basic form of the formatted input/output command is:

```
@ <row>, <col> [SAY <expr>] [GET <variable>]
...
READ
```

This command is sometimes used for printer output, but for the moment, we discuss its use only for screen input/output.

The beginning of the command @ <row>, <col>, moves the cursor to the specified row and column of the screen. The screen has twenty-five rows, designated by the numbers 0 to 24, and eighty columns, designated by the numbers 0 to 79.

The SAY <expr> clause displays the expression that is specified at the row and column where the cursor has been moved. For example, to print HELLO at the center of the screen, use the command @ 12,38 SAY "HELLO".

The GET *<variable>* clause displays the variable in reverse video. A value must be assigned to the variable before it is used in the GET clause.

Usually, a program has a number of @...SAY...GET commands followed by READ. When the program reached the READ command, it lets the user edit the variables in all of the previous GET clauses. The user begins at the first GET, and can press **Enter** to keep the value in it or can edit it first and press **Enter** to keep the new value.

The sample program that follows illustrates these points. Because formatted input/output works differently than other sorts of input/output, you cannot print it by using the SET PRINT ON command, and you cannot save it in a file by using the commands SET ALTERNATE TO and SET ALTERNATE ON. Instead, you can redirect this output by using the command SET DEVICE TO SCREEN|PRINT|FILE *<file name>*. If you SET DEVICE TO PRINT or FILE *<file name>*, dBASE ignores the GET clauses.

A Sample Program

Try a simple example of formatted input/output, shown in Table 13.11, with its output shown in Figure 13.13.

This example uses the function SPACE(*<num exp>*) to define variables. This function simply returns a character string made up of a number of blank spaces equal to the numeric expression that is specified. For example, SPACE(5) is equivalent to "   " (five blank spaces surrounded by quotation mark delimiters to indicate that they are a character expression). This function is used here only because it is difficult to read character expressions made up exclusively of blank spaces.

Table 13.11   A sample program using formatted input/output.

```
**************
*    SAMPLE11.PRG
*    a sample program using formatted input/output
**************

     SET TALK OFF
     mfname = SPACE(15)
     mlname = SPACE(20)
     DO WHILE .T.
```

```
    CLEAR
    m_again = " "
    @ 6,0 SAY "Enter your name"
    @ 8,0 SAY "First name:" GET mfname
    @ 10,0 SAY "Last name: " GET mlname
    READ
    @ 15,0 SAY "Do you want to edit your name (Y/N) ";
                         GET m_again
    READ
    IF UPPER(m_again) = "Y"
          LOOP
    ELSE
         EXIT
    ENDIF
ENDDO
mdummy = " "
@ 18,0 SAY "Press any key to continue... ";
             GET mdummy
READ
```

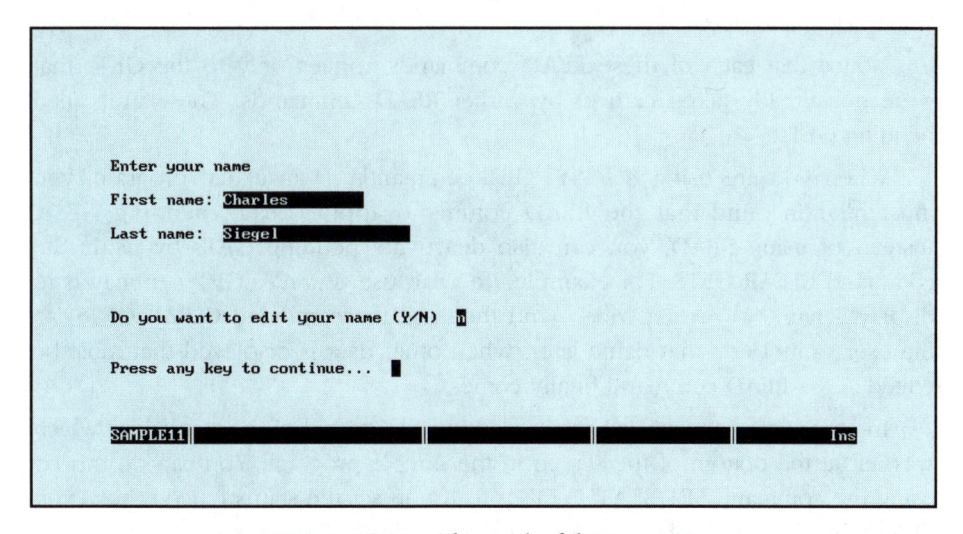

Figure 13.13   *The result of this program.*

First, a series of @...SAY...GET statements are used to prompt the user to enter his or her name and to let the user edit the mfname and mlname variables, which were defined earlier as a series of blanks. The first READ command lets the user edit both of these name fields, and the variables are assigned the new values that the user enters.

NOTE Notice that, when you use an @...SAY...GET statement, you do not have to leave a space after the word in the SAY clause: use the command @ 8,0 SAY "First name:" GET mfname, and dBASE automatically adds a space between the text and the variable. The next line has a space just so the data entry fields line up.

After the user is done entering the names, another @...SAY...GET statement asks the user whether to edit the names again. The second READ lets the user type a single character here. Because the entry field is just one space wide, the program beeps and continues as soon as the user presses Y or N, just as it does when it fills a data entry field in the Edit screen. Since the program so far was nested in a DO WHILE loop, it can let the user loop back DO WHILE and edit the name again or EXIT and continue after the loop, depending on whether of not Y was entered.

Finally, after exiting from the loop, another @...SAY...GET and a third READ command are used to wait for a keystroke before continuing, very much as the WAIT command does.

Notice that each of these READ commands applies only to the GETs that were not already taken care of by earlier READ commands. These are called pending GETs.

When you are using @...SAY...GET commands in an actual program, you must bear in mind that the READ command applies to all pending GETs. Instead of using READ, you can also deactivate pending GETs by using the command CLEAR GETS. For example, you can use @...SAY...GET commands to display a name in reverse video, and then use the command CLEAR GETS, so the user cannot edit that name later, when other data is displayed that must be edited and a READ command finally comes.

In an actual program, you might also want to get rid of the status bar, which was left at the bottom of the screen in the sample program. You can do this by using the command SET STATUS ON|off. If you set the status bar off, however, dBASE by default displays words on the top line of the screen to indicate if CapsLock and Ins mode is on, if the current record is deleted, and the like: this information is sometimes called the *Scoreboard*, and it can be controlled with the command SET SCOREBOARD ON|off. The scoreboard was used in dBASE III. If you want the dot prompt to look like it did in dBASE III, you can use SET STATUS OFF by itself. On the other hand, if you are writing a program and want to eliminate both of these, you should also use SET SCOREBOARD OFF.

Like SET TALK ON|off, these commands can be used at the beginning of the program to change the default setting and then be used at the end to return to the default, so the environment is what you expect when you return to the dot prompt.

Finally, when you are using formatted input/output in an actual program, you should remember that (as mentioned early in this chapter), if the user presses Esc the program skips the input screen and lets the program proceed to the code that follows. Users tend to press Esc whether you want them to or not, and so you must think about the effect it will have.

Format Files

No doubt, the screen produced by SAMPLE11.PRG seems familiar to you. It looks something like the data-entry form that you created in Chapter 8.

In fact, the FMT format file that is generated when you create a data entry form consists primarily of @...SAY...GET commands—though the GET clause uses field names instead of the names of memory variables. If the MEMBERS database file is in use, for example, you can use the command, @ 8,0 SAY "First name: " GET FNAME (instead of the command @ 8,0 SAY "First name: " GET mfname that you used in the sample program) to display the value of FNAME in the current record of the database and let the user enter it, and an FMT file is just a series of commands of this sort.

Thus, you can use a SET FORMAT command followed by READ as well as by APPEND or EDIT. If you use READ, dBASE only executes the @...SAY...GET statements in the FMT file once, just as if you had them in the program itself followed by READ.

For this reason, you must be careful about using READ following other @...SAY statements at a time when you have already SET FORMAT TO a FMT file. The easiest way to avoid bugs is to use the command SET FORMAT TO *<file name>* immediately before APPEND or EDIT and to close the format file by using SET FORMAT TO immediately afterwards, as you will do in the program in Chapter 14.

Before forms generators were invented, dBASE programmers used to create FMT file by hand, by figuring out the rows and columns where text and data entry fields should go, typing a series of @...SAY...GET commands into a program file, and saving it with the extension FMT. The FMT file was simply a convenience that let programmers put all the @...SAY...GET statements in a separate file, and use them all at any time to let the user add or edit records simply by using the command SET FORMAT TO followed by APPEND or EDIT.

Since you have already created FMT files using the form generator, it should be easy for you to understand some of the optional clauses which you can use with @...SAY...GET commands. You can use these clauses to add templates, picture functions, and message lines to the command—as you did when you used the form generator.

To use a template, add the clause PICTURE "<*template symbols*>" to the command.

To use a Picture function, add the clause PICTURE "@<*function symbol*>" to the command. The @ before the symbol indicates that it is a Picture function and not a template symbol. Alternatively, add the clause FUNCTION "<*function symbol*>" to the command. This version does not require the @.

Notice that both the template and function symbols must be enclosed in quotation marks.

To add a message line, add the clause MESSAGE <*char exp*> to the command.

As an example of how @...SAY...GET works, look at Table 13.12, which contains most of the code that was generated when you created a data entry form in Chapter 8. Figure 13.14 shows the data entry screen that this program creates. Although you are familiar with it from Chapter 8, it is shown again here so you can compare its layout with the code that creates it. Unlike the other listings in this chapter, this one cannot be entered and run because some code have been omitted. In addition, some lines have been broken up with semicolons to fit them on the page. Apart from these changes, this listing is made up of the actual code generated by dBASE IV. If you want to compare the code shown in Table 13.12 with the original code that dBASE IV generated, you can type *MODI COMM MEMBFORM.FMT* and view the program on your screen.

Remember that dBASE IV created a window for you to edit the memo field: for this reason, the command beginning @ 11,40 has an OPEN WINDOW clause added—an advanced feature of the dBASE language, which cannot be used unless a DEFINE WINDOW statement has been executed first. Windows are not covered in this book, and so the DEFINE WINDOWS command is omitted from this listing. The generated program also has a large number of environment commands at the beginning and end which are omitted in this listing.

Table 13.12   *Code from the FMT file generated in Chapter 8.*

```
**************
*   — Name.......: MEMBFORM.FMT
*   — Date.......: 2-24-92
*   — Version....: dBASE IV, Format 1.1
*   — Notes......: Format files use "" as delimiters!
**************

    @ 0,0 TO 2,76 DOUBLE
    @ 1,24 SAY "Edit the MEMBERS database file"
    @ 3,0 SAY "MEMBER NUMBER "
    @ 3,16 GET Memb_num PICTURE "!99"
    @ 3,64 SAY "TITLE"
    @ 3,72 GET Title PICTURE "@M;    Mr.,Ms.,Mrs.,Miss,Dr.,Prof.";
      MESSAGE "Press spacebar to view choices"
    @ 5,0 SAY "FIRST NAME"
    @ 5,12 GET Fname PICTURE "XXXXXXXXXXXXXX"
    @ 5,45 SAY "LAST NAME"
    @ 5,57 GET Lname PICTURE "XXXXXXXXXXXXXXXXXX"
    @ 7,0 SAY "ADDRESS"
    @ 7,12 GET Address1;
      PICTURE "@SXXXXXXXXXXXXXXXXXXXXXXXXXXXXXX"
    @ 7,47 GET Address2;
      PICTURE "@SXXXXXXXXXXXXXXXXXXXXXXXXXXXX"
    @ 9,0 SAY "CITY"
    @ 9,12 GET City PICTURE "XXXXXXXXXXXXXXXXXXX"
    @ 9,45 SAY "STATE"
    @ 9,53 GET State PICTURE "@! XX"
    @ 9,66 SAY "ZIP"
    @ 9,72 GET Zip PICTURE "XXXXX"
    @ 11,0 SAY "MEMBER SINCE "
    @ 11,21 GET Memb_since
    @ 11,38 TO 19,76 DOUBLE
    @ 12,0 SAY "MEMBERSHIP EXPIRES "
```

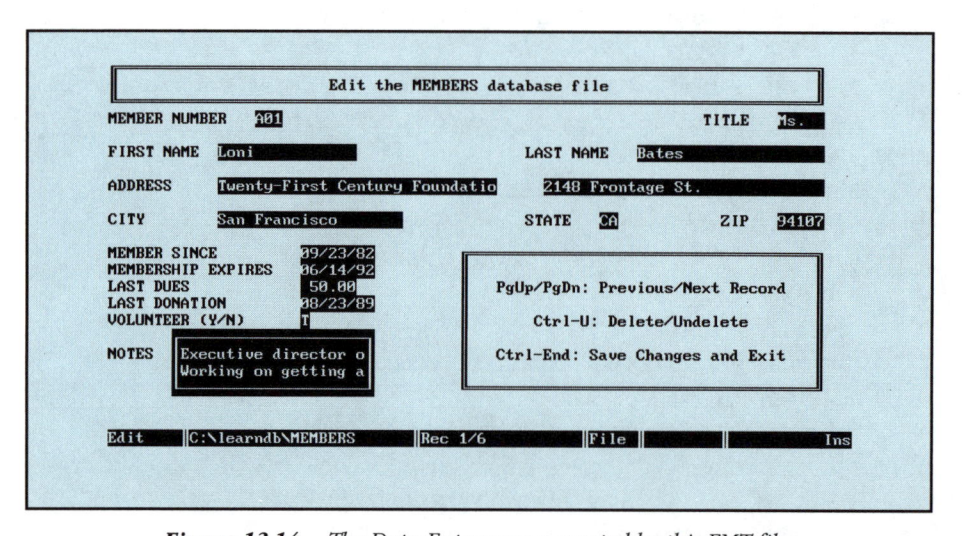

```
@ 12,21 GET Mem_expirs
@ 13,0 SAY "LAST DUES "
@ 13,21 GET Last_dues PICTURE "999.99"
@ 13,42 SAY "PgUp/PgDn: Previous/Next Record"
@ 14,0 SAY "LAST DONATION "
@ 14,21 GET Last_donat
@ 15,0 SAY "VOLUNTEER (Y/N)"
@ 15,21 GET Volunteer PICTURE "L"
@ 15,46 SAY "Ctrl-U: Delete/Undelete"
@ 16,7 GET Notes OPEN WINDOW window1 MESSAGE;
  "Press Ctrl-Home to edit, F9 to Zoom, ";
  + "and Ctrl-End when done"
@ 17,0 SAY "NOTES"
@ 17,42 SAY "Ctrl-End: Save Changes and Exit"
```

Figure 13.14 *The Data Entry screen created by this FMT file.*

You should have very little trouble understanding the code in this file. Its only peculiarity is that the generator creates a separate @...SAY command for each element of text and a separate @...GET command for each data entry field, while it is more common to combine the two. For example, near the beginning of the program, you can see the following commands:

```
@ 3,0 SAY "MEMBER NUMBER "
@ 3,16 GET Memb_num PICTURE "!99"
```

If this program had been written by hand, it could use the following command, which could be written on a single line, instead:

```
@ 3,0 SAY "MEMBER NUMBER " GET Memb_num;      PICTURE "!99"
```

The two sets of commands have the same effect.

The first is easier for the code generator to create, and the second is easier to write by hand.

The first line of this listing is a variation of the @...SAY command: @ 0,0 TO 2,76 DOUBLE. The command @ <row>,<col> TO <row>,<col> draws a box between the locations indicated by the two sets of row and column coordinates, and the option DOUBLE makes this box a double line.

Notice how templates are used in the listing: for example, PICTURE "!99" for the MEMB_NUM field, near the beginning of the listing. They use exactly the same symbols that you already learned in Chapter 8 enclosed in quotation marks.

Picture functions also use the all symbols that you learned in Chapter 8, though the menu there included a description of the function as well as the symbol. For example, to capitalize, add the clause PICTURE "@!" or the clause FUNCTION "!".

You can use multiple functions or a template with functions, as in the command @ 9,53 GET State PICTURE "@! XX" In some cases, you must add other options in addition to the function symbol. The command that allows a multiple choice, for example, uses the clause PICTURE "@M Mr.,Ms.,Mrs.,Miss,Dr.,Prof.". You can also see an example of a MESSAGE clause in this command and in the command that uses the memo window.

This discussion does not exhaust the possibilities of the @...SAY...GET command, one of the most powerful commands in the dBASE language, but it has covered its basic features. For a thorough discussion of this command, and the variations on it, look under @ in any dBASE IV language reference.

Summary

In this chapter, you learned basic techniques of structured programming. In the next chapter, you put what you have learned so far into practice when you actually create a dBASE program much like the one you would create for a user.

# Chapter 14

Programming an Application

Now that you have learned the principles of programming, you can apply them by programming an application that you might actually create for a user.

In this chapter, you apply what you have learned so far to create a program using the dBASE IV program editor, including:

- How to analyze the tasks the program performs and decide basic programming issues
- How to structure the program
- Setting the working environment in which the program operates
- Writing, testing, and debugging the program's modules

Analysis

Much of the work that dBASE programmers do is simply a matter of creating the database files, report forms, labels, and data entry screens that users need and then programming a menu system to tie them together. The user does not have to know anything about dBASE and never even sees the database or the labels, reports, or forms design screens. The programmer does the thinking and the user has only to make menu choices to run the application.

Since this is your first program, it is relatively simple. For example, it does not include a relational database. This chapter also uses old-fashioned menus, which illustrate basic principles of programming, such as selection and looping. dBASE IV also has a set of commands that can be used to create pop-up menus, which are covered in advanced books on dBASE programming. For your first major program, however, it is best to use simple menus that illustrate basic structured programming principles.

If you were creating this application for an actual client, you would spend a long time examining the system that you are replacing—whether it is on paper or computerized—and interviewing the client, in order to determine what the user's needs are.

For the sake of this sample program, let us assume that you have found that the user needs a program to do the following:

- Browse through the database to see certain fields with a variety of different filters—for example, to see the names of members who are volunteers, and of members who have given donations. The user also needs to be able to print a listing of these members.

- Modify and update the file in the usual ways: to add, edit, look up, and delete individual records, and also to delete records of all members who are more than four months overdue for renewal.

- Produce labels for mailings to volunteers, donors, recent donors, members who should renew, and to the general membership.

- Produce the BY_STATE report created in Chapter 8 and other reports listing general membership data on volunteers, donors, members from California, and members from all other states.

This list simplifies the requirements of an actual organization.

In practice, a real organization would probably want to print form letters to go along with all or some of the sets of labels. It may also want to produce labels and form letters for three or four different mailings asking for membership renewal—starting with a very appreciative letter a month or two in advance, and ending with a warning letter several months after the deadline—before deleting the member from the database.

However, the simplified example of an application that you program in this chapter is enough to teach you the principles of programming. For educational purposes, there is no need to take the extra time to prepare form letters or to add other options to the menu system. If you program an actual application, though, you should bear in mind that it will probably be more complex than this one.

Structuring the Program

In an actual application, you would also think carefully about how to organize the program into separate modules before you did any actual programming.

In general, the major modules of this sort of application are easy to sketch out. There is a submenu for each of the main functions of the program—browse the database, modify records, produce labels, and reports—and a main menu to tie them all together. If you use the old-fashioned kind of menus that we are using in this chapter, each of these menus will be in a separate module.

Before programming, you should try to identify repetitive parts of the code and to put them in separate modules also. Even if you do not identify them in advance, if you find, as you are writing one module, that you are repeating code that you have already written elsewhere, you should put the repetitive code in a separate procedure, and DO that procedure wherever the code is needed.

This is not only training in good programming practice. It also saves you time and effort if you ever have to modify the program. There are few things that are more frustrating than modifying code that is repeated in several modules. You have to make the same change several times, and then, when you test the program, you generally find that you made a typographical error someplace, and the program's interface no longer looks consistent to the user, and so you have to go back and correct your previous correction.

You can avoid this sort of problem if you examine your code and constantly try to make it more modular and more compact. If you do this when you are a beginner, you will find that before you know it, you will be writing modular code almost automatically.

There are two examples of repetitive code in this sample program.

The same header is used for all of the menu screens—each screen has the name of the menu and the date underlined at the top. Though the program names are different, you will see that you can use a single header module and pass the different names to it as parameters.

Many options involve printing. Before each of these, you should tell the user to make sure that the printer is on before doing any of them. You should also let the user cancel, in case the option was chosen by mistake.

The program will pass the parameter to the header using a DO...WITH command. Since the printer warning must pass a value back to the calling program, to indicate if the user canceled, it is more elegant to place it in a user-defined function. Thus, these two simple modules give you a good introduction to the two methods of passing parameters.

Other Basic Issues

During the analysis, you should also make some basic decisions about how much access to give the user to the database file. For example, when the user asks to edit a record, should you SET NEAR ON so that the user can browse through nearby records if there is not an exact match?

There are some applications where you should never give the user this sort of direct access to the database. For example, in accounting programs, you would want the program to check to make sure that credits and debits balance when the user makes each entry, and you would not want to let the user access the files directly because a mistake could possibly unbalance the accounts. In some kinds of programs, letting the user access the records directly can also create the possibility of fraud and so should be avoided.

Some dBASE programmers are very reluctant to use the SET FORMAT TO and EDIT or APPEND commands, because they lose control of what the user does. They may prefer to use the method mentioned briefly in Chapter 12—to read all of the user's entries into memory variables and to use the REPLACE command to put these entries into the database file, so the user never has direct access to the file.

Let's assume that in this case, though, there is no objection to giving the user direct access to the database file. Since this is your first program, you should make it easier for yourself by using this "quick and dirty" method of data entry. Let's also assume that you want to SET NEAR ON, so that, if the program cannot find a record that the user asks for, the user can page through nearby records.

Another basic issue that you should consider before you begin programming is how to handle deleted records. Do you want to SET DELETED ON, so the user no longer has access to records marked for deletion. This has the advantage of making sure that reports and labels do not inadvertently include records that are marked for deletion, in case the user forgets to erase marked records (PACK) before creating the labels or reports. But it has the disadvantage of not letting the user view and possibly recall records marked for deletion.

This program will try to combine the best of both worlds. It will SET DELETED OFF during most of the program, so that records marked for deletion are not included when the user views the file or prints reports or labels. But it will SET DELETED ON when the file is being modified, so the user has the option of searching for records that have been marked for deletion and undelete them.

In addition, this program uses SET commands to get rid of the status bar during most of the program. You do not want the status bar on when the menus are displayed, for example. When the file is being modified, though, it will SET STATUS ON to bring back the status bar, so the user can know whether the current record is marked for deletion. The other features of the status bar are also useful when the user is editing records—to show where the current record is in the file and whether Ins and Caps Lock are toggled on or off.

The Main Menu

The main menu program is shown in Table 14.1, and the menu displayed by this program is shown in Figure 14.1. After you have looked at and read about this listing, create a program file named MEMBLIST.PRG and type in the program exactly as it is displayed in the table. Do not try to run the program yet, though. The next section explains what you have to add before you can run and test this first module.

Table 14.1   *The Main Menu program.*

```
**************
*   MEMBLIST.PRG
*   menu driven membership application
**************


   ***set environment variables
   *SET ESCAPE OFF           && add after program is debugged
   SET TALK OFF
   SET STATUS OFF
   SET SCOREBOARD OFF
   SET DELETED ON
   SET BELL OFF
   SET NEAR ON
   USE MEMBERS ORDER NAMES   && open database file
   mchoice = " "             && memory variable to
      && hold user's choice
   ***loop to repeat main menu until user selects quit
   DO WHILE .T.
     CLEAR
     DO HEADER WITH "Main Menu"
     @ 8,28 SAY "V - View Data"         && list options
     @ 10,28 SAY "M - Modify Data"
     @ 12,28 SAY "R - Reports"
     @ 14,28 SAY "L - Labels"
     @ 16,28 SAY "Q - Quit"
     @ 20,26 SAY "Enter your choice> " GET mchoice;
             PICT "!"
     READ
   ***display submenu depending on user's choice
     DO CASE
     CASE mchoice = "V"
          DO viewmenu
     CASE mchoice = "M"
          DO modimenu
     CASE mchoice = "R"
```

```
            DO repmenu
   CASE mchoice = "L"
            DO labmenu
   CASE mchoice = "Q"
       EXIT
   OTHERWISE
         ? CHR(7)
   ENDCASE
ENDDO
***return to default settings before returning to dBASE
SET TALK ON
SET STATUS ON
SET SCOREBOARD ON
SET DELETED OFF
SET NEAR OFF
SET BELL ON
USE



**************
*   **HEADER PROCEDURE**
*   **display the header for the menu screen**
*   **called by the MAIN module**
*   **and by VIEWMENU, MODIMENU, REPMENU,**
*   **LABMENU**
**************


    PROCEDURE header
    PARAMETERS menuname
    @ 1, 0 SAY "Membership Application: " + menuname
    @ 1,70 SAY DATE( )
    @ 2, 0 SAY "─────────────────────";
             + "─────────────────────"
```

```
Membership Application: Main Menu                          12/08/92
_____


                         V - View Data

                         M - Modify Data

                         R - Reports

                         L - Labels

                         Q - Quit


                         Enter your choice> ▉
```

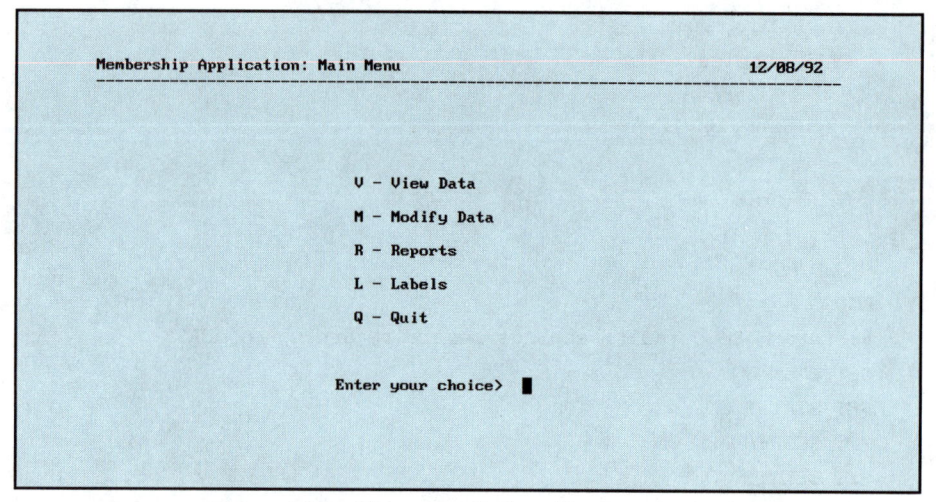

Figure 14.1   *The menu displayed by this program.*

Setting Environment Variables

The program begins with environment settings. SET TALK OFF, SET STATUS OFF, and SET SCOREBOARD OFF are needed to avoid confusing the user with dBASE "talk," the status bar, or the "scoreboard" that ordinarily takes the place of the status bar when it is turned off. As mentioned, SET DELETED OFF is used in this program, except when the user is actually editing records.

SET BELL OFF is used to prevent the program from beeping whenever you fill a data-entry field. As you will see, the program gets the user's choices by using an @...SAY...GET command to GET a variable that is only one character long. This lets the user enter a choice by pressing a single key. The single character fills the data entry field, so the program would normally do what it always does when a data entry field is full—beeps and continues without waiting for the user to press **Enter**.

Of course, it is good to let the user make menu choices with a single keystroke, but the beep is confusing. You want the menu system to beep only when the user makes an error, and so you SET BELL OFF to avoid this routine beeping. During data entry, you SET BELL ON again, so the user does not inadvertently keep typing after an actual data entry field is full.

To make the bell beep when there is an error, you use a new function, which is useful primarily in programming. The function CHR(*<num exp>*)

returns the value of any ASCII character. For example, a capital A is ASCII character 65, so the dBASE command ? CHR(65) prints a capital A, just as ? "A" does. Now, it happens the beep is also an ASCII character, character number 7, so that the command ? CHR(7) makes the computer beep. You will see this when you run the program, and you can also try it from the dot prompt if you want.

The next environment setting, SET NEAR ON, is useful when the user looks up a record—to edit it or just to view it. If there is not an exact match, you can let the user page through the nearest records.

After setting the environment, the program uses the MEMBERS file with the NAMES tag as the controlling index that sets the order of the records. The user probably wants the records in alphabetical order—for example, to print most reports or to look up a record using SET NEAR ON.

Adding the Main Loop

After these preliminaries, which have to be done only once, when the program begins, the program gets to the main loop, which repeatedly displays the menu and uses another module that depends on the user's choice.

The variable mchoice, which holds the user's choice, is initialized before the loop begins. You can put the command mchoice = " ", which initializes the variable, either before or after DO WHILE .T., but the program works differently depending on where it is. If it were inside the loop, after DO WHILE .T., its value would be made equal to a blank again each time the program looped, before it displayed the menu again. When it got up to GET mchoice, the value of mchoice would always be a blank. As it is, however, the value is only initialized as a blank once. Then, each time through the loop, it keeps the value it had last time. If you chose V last time through, mchoice would still have the value V, which would be displayed as the default option by the command GET mchoice, so you could choose it again simply by pressing **Enter**. Which of these you want to do depends on your preference and the user's preference.

Note that the list of options is preceded by the command DO header WITH "Main Menu". Remember that the header is kept in a separate procedure, because it is used by all the menus. Look at the HEADER PROCEDURE, which is at the bottom of the listing, and notice that it begins with the command PROCEDURE header and PARAMETERS menuname. When the program reaches the command DO header WITH "Main Menu", it executes the HEADER procedure and passes the value Main Menu to the variable menuname in that procedure. Thus, its next command, @ 1, 0 SAY "Membership Application: " + menuname, makes it display Membership Application: Main Menu as the beginning of the heading. It also displays the current date, and it underlines all of this by printing eighty hyphens on the next line. When it is done, the program control returns to the line following the command that called this procedure and continues printing the main menu.

The basics of the main loop are easy to understand. First, it uses a series of @...SAY commands to display the options that are available, such as V to view the data and M to modify the data, and an @...SAY...GET statement to get the user's choice. Then it uses a DO CASE statement to display a submenu that depends on the user's choice, for example, to DO the VIEWMENU module if the user pressed V. The OTHERWISE of the DO CASE beeps if the user's choice is not one of the available options. Since the menu and execution of options are in a DO WHILE .T. loop, they are repeated indefinitely, until the user presses "Q" to EXIT from the loop.

Because the program uses an @...SAY...GET statement to get the user's choice, there is no need to worry about whether the user enters uppercase or whether you need to use the UPPER( ) function. Instead, you simply use the PICT "!" clause to convert the entry to uppercase.

Restoring the Environment

After the user exits from the loop, the program has a number of environment commands that return the settings that were changed at the beginning back to their default value, and the command USE, which closes the database file before returning to the dot prompt.

Stub Testing

As you learned earlier, it is much easier to test and debug a program one module at a time than it is to test the entire program all at once. Yet the main menu module that you just wrote calls all the other modules of the program.

Stub testing lets you test one module (such as the main menu) without first writing all of the other modules that it calls. Instead of writing the modules that are called, you just write stubs with their names.

If the module that is called, when it is finally written, actually returns one of ten possible values for a variable to the calling module, depending on what the user enters, you can just write a stub with a simple assignment command to give that variable one valid value. That is enough to let you test the calling module.

Once the calling module is debugged, replace the stub with the program that is needed to let the user make the entry that gives that variable a value.

In this program, the stubs are not complex. They "kill time" and then return to the calling module, as shown in Table 14.2.

> **NOTE** Of course, it would be easiest to write only one stub for the VIEW-MENU procedure and then copy it three more times, making the necessary modifications to each copy made. To do this, you would first select the block of programming code that you wished to copy using **Select:F6**. Then move the cursor to the location where you want to place the copy of the code and press **Copy:F8**. Then use the standard dBASE IV editing keys to make any changes needed. Copying can be a useful shortcut that saves time and helps reduce the chance of typing errors when you write programs that contain repetitive code.

The screen displayed by one of these stubs is shown in Figure 14.2.

Add these stubs to the end of Table 14.1.

Table 14.2 *Stubs for testing (to be added to end of Table 14.1)*

```
**************
*
*    stubs of VIEWMENU, MODIMENU, REPMENU,
*    LABMENU for testing only
*
**************


      PROCEDURE viewmenu
      CLEAR
      ? "This stub replaces the View Menu for testing."
      WAIT
      PROCEDURE modimenu
      CLEAR
      ? "This stub replaces the Modify Menu for testing."
```

```
WAIT
PROCEDURE repmenu
CLEAR
? "This stub replaces the Reports Menu for testing."
WAIT
PROCEDURE labmenu
CLEAR
?
"This stub replaces the Labels Menu for testing."
WAIT
```

Figure 14.2 The screen displayed by one of these stubs.

Notice that each of these stubs is a separate procedure, because each begins with the PROCEDURE command, even though they display only a single note identifying them all as stubs for testing.

1. When you are finished entering the code, compare it to Tables 14.1 and 14.2 and correct any errors.
2. Now run the program by entering *DO MEMBLIST.*
3. Test the program thoroughly. Try each of the valid selections from the main menu, using both a capital and a small letter to make the selec-

tion, and try entering an invalid letter, to make sure the program beeps. Be sure, that the previous selection is there as the default selection when you return to the main menu from one of the stubs.

In case you press a function key as one of the invalid menu selections, you should be aware that, when you are working from the dot prompt, these keys are assigned values that are passed to the program if you press one. For example, the F2 key has the value ASSIST, and if you press it, the main menu loops six times, reading each of the letters in the word ASSIST and deciding that each is an error. You can change the value of the function keys by using the command SET FUNCTION *<key>* TO *<char exp>*. Here, for example, you could make them into valid, single-letter menu choices. For more information, see any reference manual on dBASE commands.

If you make an error in programming, you may have to press **Esc** and select **Cancel** to cancel execution of the program and return to the dot prompt. (You generally must press **Esc** several times before dBASE interrupts the program.) If you do this, remember that the program has not gotten to the SET commands following ENDDO, which return the environment to its default settings. Thus, you will probably find that the status bar has disappeared when you return to the dot prompt. You can return to the usual environment settings by entering any of these commands at the dot prompt. Leaving the settings does not get in the way of running the program again, though, and once you have corrected any errors and run the entire program, it executes all of the commands that return the settings to their default values.

One common programming error is forgetting to enter READ after the @...SAY...GET command that gets the menu choice. If you made this error, the program continues to loop and display the menu endlessly, without getting input from the user.

Another common error is misspelling the name of the memory variable in one of the CASE statements, so that dBASE considers it an error if you enter that menu option and beeps rather than executing the appropriate stub.

In a short program such as this one, it is easy to isolate and identify errors. Make sure you have tested the program thoroughly and corrected them all before going on to enter another module in the next section.

The View Submenu

Now that you have tested the main menu, you can write the first submenu module, the View submenu, which lets the user print out a listing or browse through the database to see the name, and state fields of members who are volunteers and of members who have given donations. In an actual application, these lists might be used for telephoning members to appeal for more donations or for volunteer help, and they would include the PHONE field which was left out of this sample database. The list may be printed if a large number of members are to be telephoned, but it may just be displayed on the screen when a smaller number are to be telephoned.

This menu is so similar to the program's main menu that it is probably easiest to copy the main loop of the main menu module and alter it to use in this procedure. Remember that, when you enter the procedure in Table 14.3, you must delete the stub of the View procedure that you created earlier for testing. Remember also to enter the stub of PRNTCHK( ), so you can test this menu. Figure 14.3 shows the menu displayed by this procedure.

Table 14.3   *The View menu and stub of PRNTCHK( ).*

```
**************
*    VIEWMENU PROCEDURE
*    display the View menu and execute the user's
*    choice
*    called by the MAIN module
**************

     PROCEDURE viewmenu
     PRIVATE mchoice              && private memory variable to
     mchoice = " "                && hold user's choice
     SET ORDER TO ST_NAMES
     ***loop to repeat view menu until user selects quit
     DO WHILE .T
```

```
    CLEAR
    DO HEADER WITH "View Menu"
    @ 8,28 SAY "V - Display Volunteers"
    @ 10,28 SAY "D - Display Donors"
    @ 12,28 SAY "Y - Print Volunteers"
    @ 14,28 SAY "Z - Print Donors"
    @ 16,28 SAY "R - Return to Main Menu"
@ 20,26 SAY "Enter your choice> " GET mchoice PICT "!"
READ
***execute user's choice
DO CASE
  CASE mchoice = "V"
       SET FILTER TO volunteer
       BROWSE FIELDS state, fname, lname, volunteer;
            NOEDIT NODELETE NOAPPEND NOMENU
       SET FILTER TO
  CASE mchoice = "D"
       SET FILTER TO last_donat > {01/01/01}
       BROWSE FIELDS state, fname, lname, last_donat;
            NOEDIT NODELETE NOAPPEND NOMENU
       SET FILTER TO
  CASE mchoice = "Y"
  IF prntchk( )
         CLEAR
         LIST OFF FIELDS state,fname,lname,volunteer;
            FOR VOLUNTEER   && TO PRINT
         WAIT
      ENDIF
  CASE mchoice = "Z"
      IF prntchk( )
         CLEAR
         LIST OFF FIELDS state,fname,lname,last_donat;
      FOR last_donat > {01/01/01}&& TO PRINT
         WAIT
      ENDIF
  CASE mchoice = "R"
      EXIT
  OTHERWISE
```

```
            ? CHR(7)
         ENDCASE
      ENDDO
      SET ORDER TO NAMES


***************
*
*    PRNTCHK FUNCTION: stub for testing only
*    called by VIEWMENU
*
***************


      FUNCTION prntchk
         RETURN .T.
```

The View menu procedure is very much like the main menu. A series @...SAY statements are used to display the valid choices, an @...SAY...GET statement is used to get the user's choice, and a DO CASE statement is used to do what the user wants. Notice that the HEADER procedure is called using the parameter "View Menu." Once again, the menu is nested in a DO WHILE loop, so it is repeated until the user makes the selection needed to return to the calling menu.

Notice that, because all of the menu choices use the ST_NAMES index to control the order of the record, the command SET ORDER TO ST_NAMES is used once before the loop begins, and the command SET ORDER TO NAMES is used after ENDDO to restore the default index order before returning to the main menu.

Notice, also, that mchoice is declared as a PRIVATE variable in the second line of this module, before it is initialized. Because of this, the mchoice variable used in this module is distinct from the mchoice used in the main menu module. The value of mchoice in the main menu (which became V when you chose to use this submenu) will not be changed by the selection that the user makes for mchoice in this module. V will still be there as the default option when you return to the main menu.

You could get the same effect by using different names for the variables in the different menus, but that would make the program a bit less modular. Changing the name of the variable in the main menu could cause unexpected results, unless you kept in mind the names of the variables in all the other modules. In a more complex program, there is a real advantage to using PRIVATE variables to make the program more structured.

To display the necessary fields on the screen, use the BROWSE command with a fields list. To make sure that the database is not altered inadvertently during telephoning, you can add some other special clauses to the BROWSE command. NOEDIT prevents the user from changing a record, NODELETE prevents the user from deleting a record, and NOAPPEND prevents the user from adding new records. In addition, use the clause NOMENU, which removes the menu from the Browse screen. The only submenu that might be relevant here is Go To, but (as you will see in the next section) the Modify submenu lets the user move the pointer to search for records, and there is no need to do it here. The user has to be trained to search for a record using the Modify submenu, to return to the main menu, and then to use the View submenu to browse the database with the pointer on that record.

The basic form of the command to view the records on screen, then, will be:

```
BROWSE FIELDS STATE, FNAME, LNAME NOEDIT NODELETE NOAPPEND NOMENU
```

The command also includes the VOLUNTEER or LAST_DONAT field, depending on which is relevant. Notice that commas are used only between the names in the field list. The other optional clauses of the command are not separated by commas.

NOTE In an actual application, the user might want the telephone workers to make an entry indicating whether the user was willing to help or not. In this case, you could modify the database structure to add a logical field called WILL_HELP. Then, you could use another feature of the BROWSE command to let the user edit this field without being able to edit the other fields. If you include the option /R after the name of a field in a field list, it makes that field read-only. Instead of NOEDIT, you could use this option for all of the fields except WILL_HELP. Of course, you would also need a separate menu option to make WILL_HELP read false per all records before a new phone campaign begins. If the user selected it, it would ask for confirmation and then execute the command REPLACE ALL will_help WITH .F..

With all of its other features, though, the BROWSE command does not let you use a FOR or WHILE clause. Instead, you must use SET FILTER TO to use the filter before the command is executed and use SET FILTER TO again to remove the filter afterwards.

To print the listing, you can simply use the command LIST with a fields list, a FOR clause, and a TO PRINT clause. You should remind the user to turn the printer on before executing this command, and you should also give the user a chance to cancel the command.

You can save paper while testing this program by commenting out the TO PRINT clauses. To do this, put && before them so dBASE does not execute them and instead just lists records to the screen. Once the program is thoroughly debugged, you can delete the ampersands to actually print the listings if you wish.

To find the members who gave donations, you can use the condition FOR last_donat > {01/01/01}; if the member ever gave a donation, the date is more recent than the one used, January 1, 1901, and if the member never gave a donation and the field is blank, this condition is not satisfied.

As mentioned above, you are going to create a user-defined function to remind the user to turn on the printer and give the opportunity to cancel before printing begins. In the next section, you write a UDF called PRNTCHK( ) that does this. It returns .F. if the user chooses to cancel. Otherwise, it returns .T.. For now, you can create a stub of this function for testing: the stub just consists of the command RETURN .T., the minimum you need to test the program. Because the function returns the value .T., the program continues.

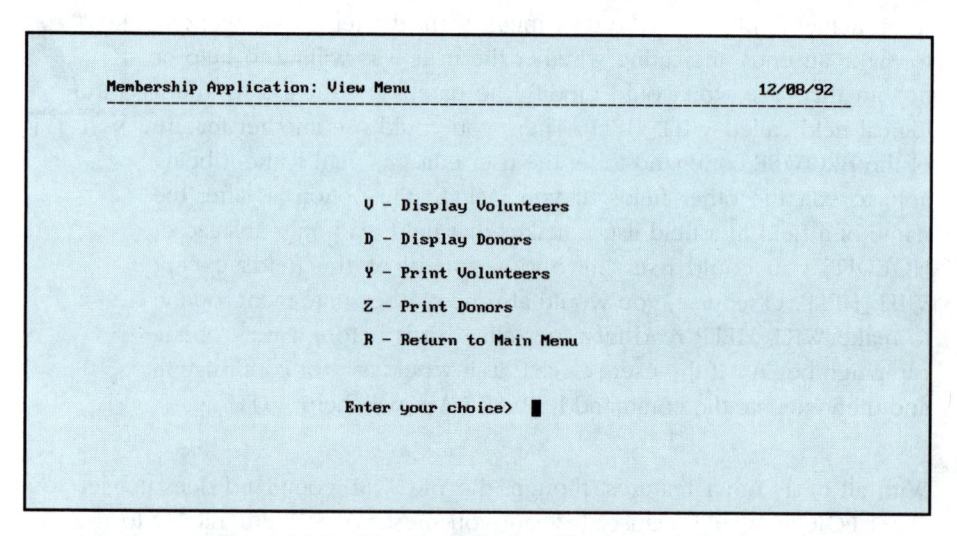

```
Membership Application: View Menu                              12/08/92
───────────────────────────────────────────────────────────────────────



                         V - Display Volunteers

                         D - Display Donors

                         Y - Print Volunteers

                         Z - Print Donors

                         R - Return to Main Menu


                       Enter your choice> █
```

Figure 14.3   *The menu displayed by this procedure.*

Notice in Table 14.3, in the PRNTCHK stub at the end of the listing, the two commands that are supposed to print listings depend on the condition IF prntchk( ). Since prntchk( ) always returns .T., the commands to print should always be executed when you test the program. In the test version of the program, of course, they just display the listing on the screen, since the TO PRINT clause is commented out.

After you are finished testing the VIEWMENU module, you can add a working PRNTCHK function.

The PRNTCHK Module

The actual PRNTCHK function, shown in Table 14.4, is fairly simple. Delete the stub of the PRNTCHK function that you used for testing VIEWMENU, and enter and test the full PRNTCHK function. The screen displayed by this function is shown in Figure 14.4.

Table 14.4   *The PRNTCHK function.*

```
****
*    PRNTCHK FUNCTION
*    tell the user to get printer ready and allow
*    to cancel
*    called by VIEWMENU, REPMENU, and LABMENU
**************

     FUNCTION prntchk
     PRIVATE mconfirm
     mconfirm = " "
     CLEAR
     @ 10,10 SAY "Press X to cancel printing"
     @ 12,10 SAY "or make sure your printer is ready"
     @ 14,10 SAY "and press any key to proceed . . .";
       GET mconfirm
     READ
     IF UPPER(mconfirm) = "X"
       RETURN .F.
     ELSE
       RETURN .T.
     ENDIF
```

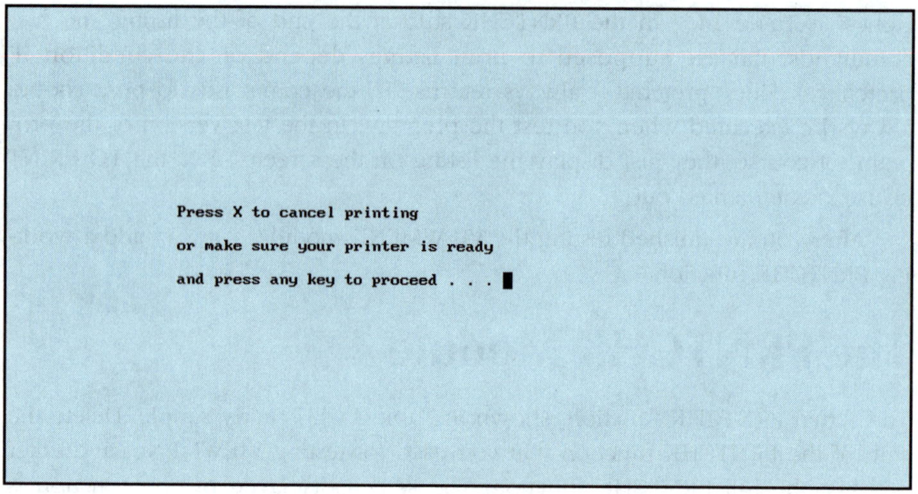

```
Press X to cancel printing
or make sure your printer is ready
and press any key to proceed . . . ■
```

Figure 14.4 *The screen displayed by this function.*

It begins by declaring mconfirm as a PRIVATE variable, so that you do not have to worry about whether there are variables of the same name in the calling program, and initializing it as a blank space. Then it uses an @...SAY...GET commands to display a message telling the user to press X to cancel or to get the printer ready and press any key to continue, and to read the user's response into mconfirm. Finally, it returns .F. if the user entered X, or .T. if the user pressed any other key.

Thus, if the user presses X, the condition IF prntchk( ) in the calling module is false, and the program skips the commands that do the printing. Otherwise, the condition is true, so the program executes those commands.

Delete the stub of this function that you used for testing VIEWMENU, and enter and test the full PRNTCHK function.

The Modify Submenu

As you learned earlier, a programmer can give the user more or less access to the database, depending on what the application needs. At one extreme, you can keep the user out of the database entirely by reading all entries into memory variables. At the other extreme, you can simply use SET FORMAT TO and EDIT, to allow the user to page through the database file, press **Ctrl-U** to delete and recall records, and so on.

Since this is your first program, it uses the simplest method, with the least control over the user. There is just one menu choice to view and look up and edit a record. The user also selects this option and press **Ctrl-U** to delete or undelete the record.

It does add one extra option, however—if there is not an exact match, it asks the user whether to display the nearest record.

It does this by using SET NEAR ON and SEEK. In order to let the user enter the name to search for in either upper or lower case, it uses the command SEEK UPPER(mname) to look for the user's entry.

As you remember, though, you created the NAMES index tag before you had learned the UPPER( ) function. Apart from its use in this program, it is generally best to use this function in an alphabetical index to avoid problems with capitalization and make sure the names are in dictionary (not ASCII) order.

Before entering the program, then, you should change the existing index key:

1. At the dot prompt, enter *USE MEMBERS*.
2. Enter *INDEX ON UPPER(LNAME+FNAME) TAG NAMES*.
3. When dBASE displays a prompt box indicating that this tag already exists, select **Overwrite**.

dBASE builds the new index tag to replace the old NAMES tag.

Now, look at the MODIMENU module of the program, shown in Table 14.5. Enter and test this module, being sure to delete the stub of the MODIMENU PROCEDURE. The menu displayed by this procedure is shown in Figure 14.5.

Table 14.5 *The Modimenu module.*

```
***************
*   MODIMENU PROCEDURE
*   submenu to modify the database file
***************

    PROCEDURE modimenu
    PRIVATE mchoice
    mchoice = " "
    SET DELETED OFF          && set environment for editing
```

```
***loop to repeat modify menu until user selects quit
DO WHILE .T.
  CLEAR
  DO HEADER WITH "Modify menu"
  @ 8,28 SAY "A - Add New Records"        && list options
  @ 10,28 SAY "E - Edit Records"
  @ 12,28 SAY "D - Delete Expired Members"
  @ 14,28 SAY "F - Finalize All Deletions"
  @ 16,28 SAY "R - Return"
  @ 20,26 SAY "Enter your choice> " GET mchoice PICT "!"
  READ
  ***display submenu depending on user's choice
  DO CASE
  CASE mchoice = "A"
        SET STATUS ON
        SET BELL ON
        SET FORMAT TO MEMBFORM
        APPEND
        SET FORMAT TO
        SET BELL OFF
        SET STATUS OFF
  CASE mchoice = "E"
      CLEAR
      mname = SPACE(20)
      @ 10,0 SAY "Enter the last name to be edited";
          GET MNAME
      @ 12,10 SAY "(or press Enter to return to menu)"
      READ
      IF mname <> SPACE(20)
      SEEK UPPER(mname)
      IF .NOT. FOUND( )
          mbrowse = " "
          @ 14,20 SAY "That name was not found."
          @ 15,20 SAY "Do you want to see the ";
                  + "nearest match (Y/N)";
                  GET mbrowse PICT "!"
          READ
          IF mbrowse <> "Y"
```

```
            LOOP
         ENDIF
      ENDIF
      SET STATUS ON
      SET BELL ON
      SET FORMAT TO MEMBFORM
         EDIT NOAPPEND
      SET FORMAT TO
      SET BELL OFF
      SET STATUS OFF
   ENDIF
CASE mchoice = "D"
   CLEAR
   mconfirm = " "
   @ 10,0 SAY "This option deletes all members ";
      + "whose dues are over 120 days overdue."
   @ 12,10 SAY "Press Y to continue or any key to ";
      + "return to the menu. " GET mconfirm PICT "!"
   READ
   IF mconfirm = "Y"
      @ 14,20 SAY "Deleting records. ";
         + "One moment please..."
      DELETE ALL FOR mem_expirs < DATE( ) - 120
      mconfirm = " "
      @ 16,20 SAY "Records deleted. Press any ";
         + "key to continue..." GET mconfirm
      READ
   ENDIF
CASE mchoice = "F"
   CLEAR
   mconfirm = " "
   @ 10, 0 SAY "This option finalizes deletions ";
      + "so that data can never be recovered."
   @ 12,10 SAY "Press Y to continue or any key to ";
      + "return to the menu. " GET mconfirm PICT "!"
   READ
   IF mconfirm = "Y"
      @ 14,20 SAY "Finalizing deletions. ";
```

```
                + "One moment please..."
            PACK
            mconfirm = " "
            @ 16,20 SAY "Deletions Finalized. Press ";
                + "any key to continue... ";
                GET mconfirm
                   READ
                ENDIF
            CASE mchoice = "R"
                EXIT
            OTHERWISE
                ? CHR(7)
        ENDCASE
    ENDDO
    SET DELETED ON
```

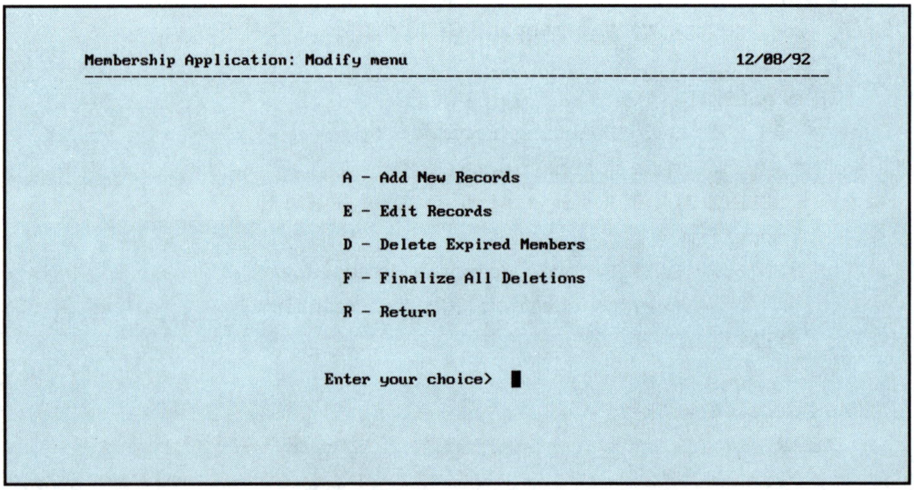

```
Membership Application: Modify menu                           12/08/92
----------------------------------------------------------------------




                        A - Add New Records

                        E - Edit Records

                        D - Delete Expired Members

                        F - Finalize All Deletions

                        R - Return


                      Enter your choice> █
```

***Figure 14.5**   The menu displayed by this procedure.*

This procedure begins in the usual way, by creating and initializing a PRIVATE variable to hold the menu choice.

Before the DO WHILE .T. command that begins the main loop, it also changes one of the environment settings to what is needed for editing, the command SET DELETED OFF lets the user look up and undelete records that are marked for deletion. Other environment settings are changed only immediately before the EDIT and APPEND command and are changed back to the default value immediately afterwards. SET STATUS ON is used only there because you do not want the status bar under the menu or other screens, SET BELL ON is used only there because you do not want the program beeping when the user makes menu choices or enters other keystrokes, and SET FORMAT TO MEMB-FORM is used only there because the @...GET commands in a data entry form can interfere with other @...SAY...GET commands if the data entry form is left in effect. On the other hand, SET DELETED OFF cannot cause problems during any other parts of this module, so it is easier to use it here once.

The first CASE, A to add new records, is simple. You simply SET STATUS ON, so the status bar is available to let users know whether the record has been marked for deletion when they use the Ctrl-U toggle. You SET BELL ON so the program beeps when it comes to the end of a data entry field, and you SET FORMAT TO MEMBFORM to use the data entry form. Then you use the APPEND command, which takes care of the actual work of adding records, as shown in Figure 14.6. After the user presses Ctrl-End to finish appending, the program continues with the next lines, which return the STATUS, BELL, and FORMAT settings to the default for this program.

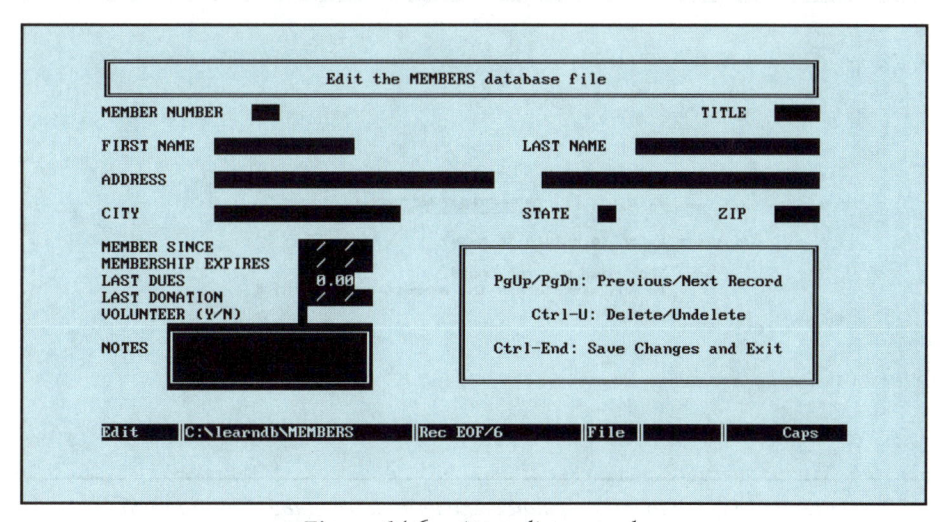

Figure 14.6   *Appending records.*

The second CASE, E to edit existing records, is more complex. First, it must let the user enter the name to edit so it can move the pointer to it. Notice that it gets just the last name. Because you are letting the user page through records, you do not have to worry about the possibility that there is more than one person with the same last name. The pointer would be moved to the first one, and the user can press PgDn to reach the one that is needed. (A program with stricter control over the data, which did not let the user page through the records, might display all the records with the name and ask the user which to edit.)

Instead of entering the name, the user also has the option of just pressing Enter to cancel, so the user can avoid the trouble of using the edit screen if this menu choice was made by mistake. Thus, the rest of the commands in this CASE are nested within an IF mname <> SPACE(20). If the user pressed Enter without typing a name, mname would still have its initial value of twenty blank spaces, and it would skip all of these commands.

If the user does enter anything here, though, the program uses the command SEEK UPPER(mname) to see if there is a record with that name in the file. It uses a function, which you have not learned yet, to test if there was a match. FOUND( ) returns .T. if there was a match and .F. if there was not.

If a match was found, the program skips all the commands in the IF .NOT. FOUND( ) statement, and goes right to the commands that let the user edit the file.

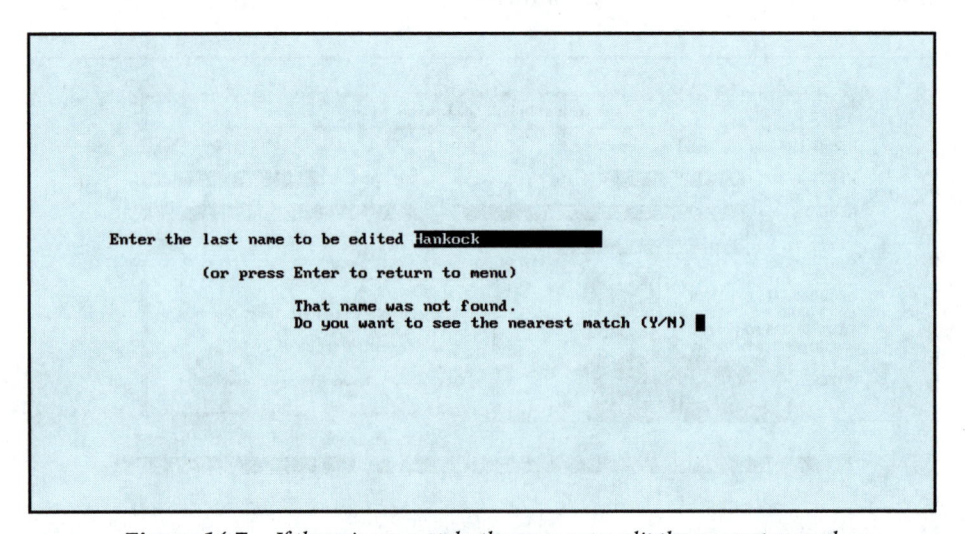

```
Enter the last name to be edited Hankock
        (or press Enter to return to menu)
                That name was not found.
                Do you want to see the nearest match (Y/N) ▮
```

Figure 14.7   *If there is no match, the user may edit the nearest record.*

If a match was not found, though, it uses these commands to give the user the option of editing the nearest record, as in Figure 14.7. It tells the user the record was not found and asks whether the user wants to see the nearest match. If the user does not enter Y, the LOOP command makes control flow back to DO WHILE .T., without getting to the EDIT command. If the user enters Y, it proceeds to the commands SET STATUS ON, SET BELL ON, SET FORMAT TO MEMBFORM, and EDIT NOAPPEND. This EDIT command handles the actual editing, and when the user presses Ctrl-End, control returns to the next line, which return the STATUS, BELL, and FORMAT to normal before getting to the end of this CASE.

This CASE is fairly complex, and you should study it carefully to make sure you understand how it works. Notice how much easier it is to understand the program when you use proper indentation.

The next two options are much simpler.

If the user selects D, the program uses @...SAY...GET statements to warn the user about what this module does and get confirmation before continuing. If the user presses Y, it displays a message saying that the user should wait, and it uses the command DELETE ALL FOR mem_expirs < DATE( ) - 120 to mark the records for deletion. Then it tells the user the records have been deleted and to press any key to continue, as in Figure 14.8.

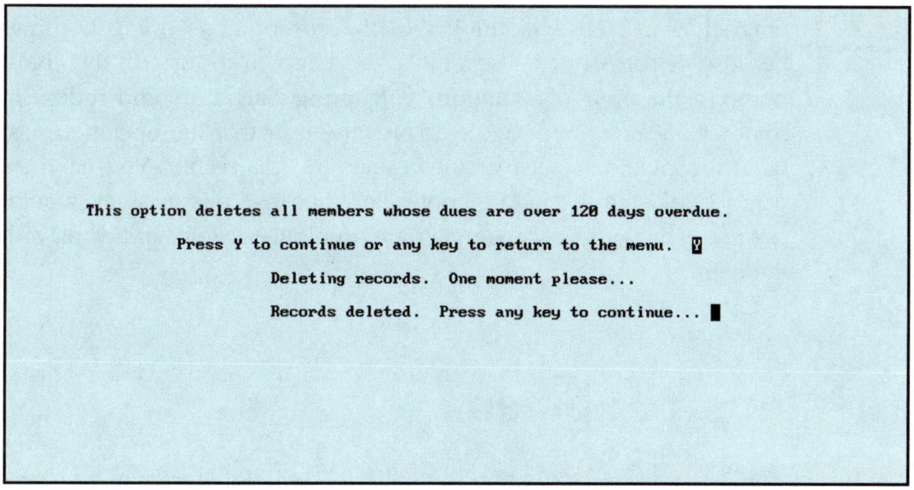

```
        This option deletes all members whose dues are over 120 days overdue.
            Press Y to continue or any key to return to the menu.  Y
                       Deleting records.  One moment please...
                       Records deleted.  Press any key to continue... ▌
```

Figure 14.8 *Deleting records with expired membership.*

Likewise, if the user selects F, the program warns the user what the module does. If the user presses Y it tells the user to wait, uses PACK to finalize deletions, and tells the user that deletions are finalized and to press any key to continue, as in Figure 14.9.

```
This option finalizes deletions so that data can never be recovered.
    Press Y to continue or any key to return to the menu.  Y
              Finalizing deletions. One moment please...
              Deletions Finalized.  Press any key to continue... ▊
```

Figure 14.9   Finalizing deletions.

NOTE It is always a good idea to display messages telling the user to wait when a program performs operations such as these, which can take time. If not, users will think that the computer is doing nothing because of some error. Users have been known to turn off the computer in this sort of situation, corrupting data files and indexes. Another on-screen message reassures the user that the operation has been completed, whenever the results are not visible. You have to wait for a keystroke before continuing, because this message would not be readable if the program continued immediately, and displayed the menu.

The Report Submenu

The program must print reports with all members listed alphabetically by state, using the BY_STATE form you created in Chapter 7. There should also be two special reports, one listing only volunteers and one only donors, which can also be listed alphabetically by state. Finally, assume that, because most members live in California, the user wants one report with just members from California and one with members from all other states. These can use the STANDARD form.

You need to customize the BY_STATE report form you created earlier to accommodate the two new reports. In an actual application, you might want to modify them in a more elaborate way, but as an exercise, you can just add a new page heading:

1. At the dot prompt, enter *USE MEMBERS*. Then enter *MODI REPORT BY_STATE*.
2. When the report form appears, press the **Down Arrow** key twice and then press **End**, to move the cursor to the right of the page number.
3. Press the **Tab** key four times.
4. Then type *Report on Volunteers*.
5. Select **Save this report** from the Layout menu. When dBASE IV prompts you to enter the report name, edit the name so that, instead of C:\LEARNDB\BY_STATE.FRM, it reads C:\LEARNDB\VOLSBYST. (Of course, if you are using a different disk or directory to work in, leave those names. Just change the report name.) Then press **Enter**, and wait for a moment while dBASE generates the report.
6. Now, press **Backspace** to delete the word *Volunteers*, and type *Donors* to replace it. Again select **Save this report** from the Layout menu, and when dBASE prompts you to enter the name, edit it so it reads *C:\LEARNDB\DONSBYST*, and wait for a moment while dBASE generates the report.
7. Press **Esc** and *Y* to return to the dot prompt. In an actual application, you might want to modify the STANDARD form also, for the special reports produced using it, and you might want to make more elaborate modifications than this, but what you have done is enough for purposes of illustration.

Now, you can go on to add the report module, shown in Table 14.6 to the program. (It is probably easiest to create this module by copying and modifying the VIEWMENU module.) Do not forget to delete the stub of the REPMENU procedure before testing this module. The menu displayed by this procedure is shown in Figure 14.10.

Table 14.6 *The report module*

```
**************
*    REPMENU PROCEDURE
*    display the Report menu and execute the
*    user's choice
*    called by the MAIN module
**************


     PROCEDURE repmenu
     PRIVATE mchoice              && private memory variable to
     mchoice = " "                && hold user's choice
     SET ORDER TO ST_NAMES        && needed for most reports
     ***loop to repeat view menu until user selects quit
     DO WHILE .T.
     CLEAR
     DO HEADER WITH "Report Menu"
     @ 6,28 SAY "G - General Membership"
     @ 8,28 SAY "V - Volunteers"
     @ 10,28 SAY "D - Donors"
     @ 12,28 SAY "C - California Members"
     @ 14,28 SAY "O - Members From Other States"
     @ 16,28 SAY "R - Return to Main Menu"
     @ 20,26 SAY "Enter your choice> " GET mchoice PICT "!"
     READ
     ***execute user's choice
     DO CASE
       CASE mchoice = "G"
           IF prntchk( )
              CLEAR
              REPORT FORM st_names                  &&TO PRINT
                 WAIT
           ENDIF
       CASE mchoice = "V"
           IF prntchk( )
              CLEAR
              REPORT FORM volsbyst;
```

```
                          FOR volunteer     &&TO PRINT
                WAIT
            ENDIF
    CASE mchoice = "D"
        IF prntchk( )
            CLEAR
            REPORT FORM donsbyst FOR last_donat;
                > {01/01/01}     && TO PRINT
            WAIT
        ENDIF
    CASE mchoice = "C"
        IF prntchk( )
            CLEAR
            REPORT FORM standard FOR state;
                           = "CA"            && TO PRINT
            WAIT
        ENDIF
    CASE mchoice = "O"
        IF prntchk( )
            CLEAR
            SET ORDER TO NAMES
            REPORT FORM standard FOR state;
                <> "CA"         && TO PRINT
            SET ORDER TO ST_NAMES
            WAIT
        ENDIF
    CASE mchoice = "R"
        EXIT
    OTHERWISE
        ? CHR(7)
    ENDCASE
ENDDO
SET ORDER TO NAMES
```

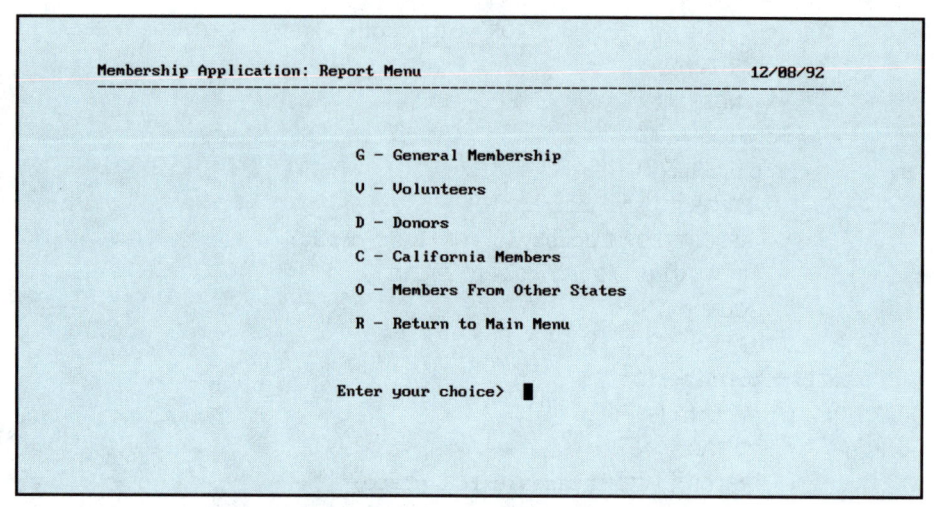

```
Membership Application: Report Menu                        12/08/92
------------------------------------------------------------------

                    G - General Membership
                    V - Volunteers
                    D - Donors
                    C - California Members
                    O - Members From Other States
                    R - Return to Main Menu


                    Enter your choice> ▮
```

Figure 14.10   *The menu displayed by this module.*

This module should be very easy for you to understand. It contains the usual DO WHILE loop with @...SAY...GET statements to display the menu and get the user's choice, and a DO CASE statement to execute the user's choice.

The commands in each CASE are very simple. Notice how easily you can use the existing PRNTCHK module to get confirmation from each user before printing each report. The report is printed using the command REPORT FORM <report name> with the appropriate report and (usually) with a FOR clause so only the records that are desired are printed. As usual, the TO PRINT clause is commented out using ampersands for purposes of testing.

Since most of the reports use order of the ST_NAMES index tag, the command SET ORDER TO ST_NAMES is placed before the DO WHILE loop, so it is executed once, before the module begins.

Notice that for only one report, the report on members from all states except California, the program has to SET ORDER TO NAMES before beginning and to SET ORDER TO ST_NAMES again after it is done. Both this report and the report on members from California are supposed to be in alphabetical order by name. But members from California are already in alphabetical order by name when you use the ST_NAMES index, so there is no need to change it.

The Label Submenu

The Label module, shown in Table 14.7 is also very simple. The menu displayed by this procedure is shown in Figure 14.11.

Enter the programming code shown in Table 14.7.

Table 14.7   *The label module.*

```
**************
*    LABMENU PROCEDURE
*    display the Labels menu and execute the
*    user's choice
*    called by the MAIN module
**************


PROCEDURE labmenu
PRIVATE mchoice              && private memory variable to
mchoice = " "                && hold user's choice
SET ORDER TO ZIPS            && order needed for labels
***loop to repeat view menu until user selects quit
DO WHILE .T.
  CLEAR
  DO HEADER WITH "Label Menu"
  @ 6,28 SAY "G - General Membership"
  @ 8,28 SAY "V - Volunteers"
  @ 10,28 SAY "D - Donors"
  @ 12,28 SAY "T - Recent Donors"
  @ 14,28 SAY "X - Expired Members"
  @ 16,28 SAY "R - Return to Main Menu"
  @ 20,26 SAY "Enter your choice> " GET mchoice PICT "!"
  READ
  ***execute user's choice
  DO CASE
      CASE mchoice = "G"
          IF prntchk( )
              CLEAR
```

```
            LABEL FORM standard               &&TO PRINT
            WAIT
         ENDIF
      CASE mchoice = "V"
         IF prntchk( )
            CLEAR
            LABEL FORM standard;
                     FOR volunteer          &&TO PRINT
            WAIT
         ENDIF
      CASE mchoice = "D"
         IF prntchk( )
            CLEAR
            LABEL FORM standard FOR last_donat;
                     > {01/01/01}           && TO PRINT
            WAIT
         ENDIF
      CASE mchoice = "T"
         IF prntchk( )
            CLEAR
            LABEL FORM standard FOR last_donat;
                     >DATE( ) - 730         && TO PRINT
            WAIT
         ENDIF
      CASE mchoice = "X"
         IF prntchk( )
            CLEAR
            LABEL FORM standard FOR mem_expirs;
                     > DATE( )              && TO PRINT
            WAIT
         ENDIF
      CASE mchoice = "R"
         EXIT
      OTHERWISE
         ? CHR(7)
   ENDCASE
ENDDO
SET ORDER TO NAMES
```

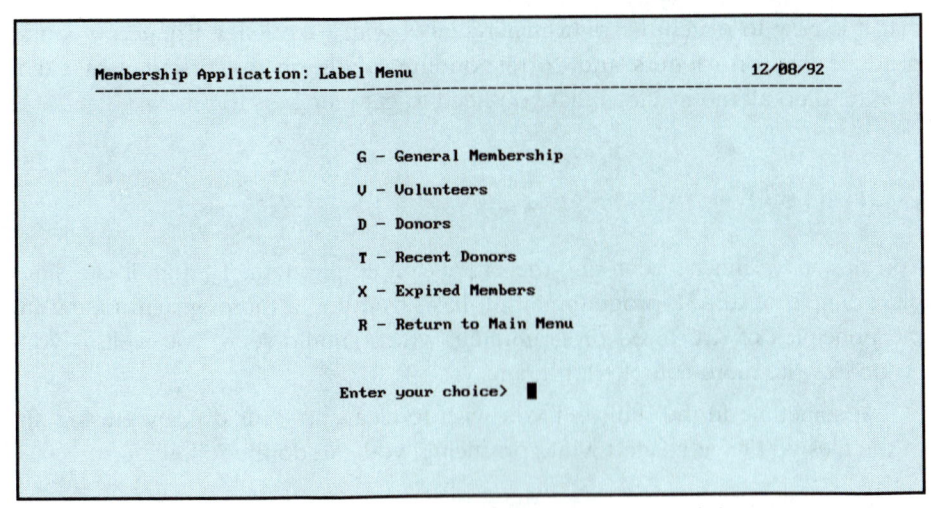

```
Membership Application: Label Menu                        12/08/92
------------------------------------------------------------------

                    G - General Membership
                    V - Volunteers
                    D - Donors
                    T - Recent Donors
                    X - Expired Members
                    R - Return to Main Menu


                  Enter your choice>  ▊
```

Figure 14.11 *The menu displayed by this module.*

Since labels are all produced in zip code order, the procedure begins by making the ZIPS index determine the order. Its main loop, as always, displays the options and gets the user's input, and then uses the DO CASE statement to execute the option the user chose. The options use the command LABEL FORM standard with various FOR clauses to print what the user wants. As usual, the TO PRINT is commented out during testing.

Notice that, if the user wants labels for recent donations, the command adds the clause FOR last_donat > DATE( ) - 730. This prints labels for members who have given donations in the last two years, (730 days is two years).

To send notices to expired members, the clause FOR mem_expirs < DATE( ) is added to print labels for members whose membership has already expired. In an actual application, you might replace this with three sets of labels—one with the clause FOR mem_expirs > DATE( ) + 30 to send a renewal notice saying that membership expires in the coming month, a second with the clause FOR mem_expirs > DATE( ) .AND. mem_expirs < DATE( ) - 30 to send a notice that membership has expired in the last month, and a third with FOR mem_expirs > DATE( ) - 30 to send a notice that membership expired more than a month ago and that this is the last chance to renew.

You probably would also create a form letter to go with each of these sets of labels, including the member's name, the exact expiration date, and whatever incentives or threats you think will get the member to renew. And you would add a LETTERS menu to produce these letters (and others) in zip code order, so that it is easy to match the right mailing label with each letter. Then you could produce the form letters and corresponding labels on the first day of each month, to do all the mailings that you need to get members to renew.

Summary

You now have finished entering the entire sample program. Though it is a simple example of dBASE programming, it has given you a thorough grounding in the principles of structured programming, which should serve you well as you go on to write more complex programs.

At sometime in the future, if you wish to clean up your disk by erasing all of the files you have created while practicing, you can do the following:

1. Use the Exit menu to quit dBASE IV and return to your computer's operating system prompt.

2. At the prompt, type *del \learndb*.** to delete all these files, and press *Y* confirm when DOS asks you if you are sure.

3. Then type the command *rd \learndb* to remove the subdirectory you created.

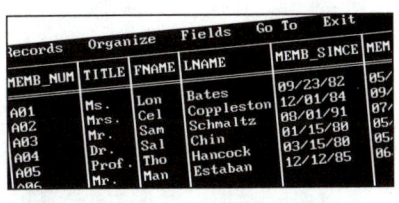

Appendix

INSTALLING dBASE IV

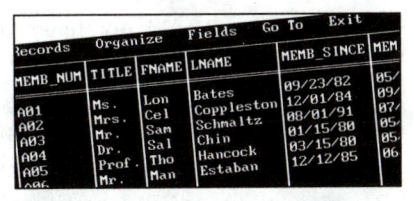

Appendix

Installing dBASE IV

The first section of this appendix covers the basics of installing dBASE IV. After following the instructions in these two sections, you can use this book. Go right to Chapter 1.

The second section of this appendix covers more advanced installation options. You might want to glance at it initially, but do not use it until after you are finished reading this book and have become more comfortable as a dBASE IV user.

Installation

To install dBASE IV 1.5, you must have 640 kilobytes of RAM and a hard disk with at least four megabytes of free space. dBASE IV version 2.0 requires four megabytes of RAM and seven megabytes of hard-disk space (ten megabytes for installation). If you have Windows, the installation program for either of these automatically alters Windows so you can start dBASE IV from it. This book assumes you are working from DOS.

NOTE You should not have any memory-resident programs active when you install dBASE IV. If you do, you must unload them or turn off and restart your computer so they are not present. You may have to alter your AUTOEXEC.BAT file so they are not started automatically when you start your computer. Use any word processor that can edit plain ASCII text files (sometimes called DOS files) to edit the AUTOEXEC.BAT file and remove the commands that start the memory resident programs.

DBASE IV 1.5 gives you three options for installation: Quick, Full, or Menu-Driven. Quick installation installs all of the files you need to run dBASE as a single user with a minimum of effort on your part. Full lets you install either the single-user or the multi-user version of dBASE and also lets you install sample and tutorial files. Menu-driven lets you use a menu to select the same options as the Full installation. If you are using version 1.5, select Quick installation, which is the easiest, and which sets up dBASE IV in a way that lets you run all of the exercises in this book.

This appendix is meant for people who are installing dBASE IV on a single personal computer, and so it does not cover installation of dBASE IV on a network. If you are working on a network and dBASE IV is not yet installed, see your network administrator for more information.

You do not need the sample and tutorial files if you are using the exercises in this book.

To do the Quick installation of dBASE IV:

1. Put the dBASE IV Install disk in the A drive of your computer. (If there is some special reason to, you may put this disk in the B drive.) Type the command *A* (or *B*) and press **Enter** to make this the current drive. Type *INSTALL* and press **Enter**. Follow the instructions on the screens, and press **F2** to accept the default choice for each.

2. Follow the instructions on each screen. Unless you have some reason to change them, press **Enter** or **F2** to accept dBASE's default suggestions.

3. When dBASE displays a registration form, fill in your name, company name, and the serial number (which is listed on the dBASE install disk). Press **Enter** to move to the next line after you have filled out each one. Use the Up and Down Arrow keys to move among lines and the other editing keys to make changes if you make any errors. When you are

done, press **Ctrl-End** if you are installing version 1.5 or **F2** if you are installing version 2.0.

4. DBASE may ask you if you want to install caching for extended/expanded memory. Unless you have some reason not to, select **Yes**, as caching speeds up performance.

5. DBASE begins copying files onto your hard disk. When it prompts you to insert new disks in the drive and press **Enter**, do so.

6. After it copies all of the disks, dBASE gives you the option of altering the PATH command of your AUTOEXEC.BAT file so it can be run from any directory. Unless you have some special reason not to, you should let it alter your AUTOEXEC.BAT file. First, it suggests the drive and directory of your AUTOEXEC.BAT. Press **Enter** to accept the suggestion unless you have a reason to change it. Likewise, when dBASE suggests altering your CONFIG.SYS file, press **Enter** to do so unless you have some reason not to.

7. The installation of dBASE IV is now complete. Press **Enter** to return to DOS. If you let dBASE make either of the changes in Step 7, you must reboot your computer. Remove the disk that you were using for installation and press **Ctrl-Alt-Del** to restart your computer.

Now dBASE IV is ready to use. If you are a beginner, you should go to Chapter 1 of this book. The next section is meant for advanced users who want to alter dBASE's configuration.

A Note on Configuring dBASE IV

Advanced users might want to change default values that the program uses by altering the CONFIG.DB file. dBASE IV reads this file whenever it starts up, and the start-up configuration depends on what is in the CONFIG.DB file.

When you installed the program, it automatically created a CONFIG.DB file, which is similar to the one listed below:

Table A.1 Sample COMFIG.DB file.

COMMAND	= ASSIST
DISPLAY	= MONO
SQLHOME	= D:\DBASE\SQLHOME
STATUS	= ON

The commands in this file are self-explanatory. The first line makes dBASE IV start in ASSIST mode (that is, to use the menu system rather than the dot prompt), and the last line makes it display the status bar. Your file differs from this one if your display is color rather than monochrome or if you changed the home directory for SQL files rather than accepting the default when you installed the program.

CONFIG.DB is a plain text file and you can alter it by using any text editor, if you know the commands that it uses.

dBASE IV also includes a program called DBSETUP, which makes it easier to alter CONFIG.DB. For example, if you have a printer with multiple fonts, you might want to use DBSETUP to install printer drivers. DBSETUP is a separate program from dBASE IV, and so it is used from DOS.

1. At the DOS prompt, enter *DBSETUP*. After displaying the dBASE IV logo, the program displays its menu system.
2. Press **Enter** to select Modify existing CONFIG.DB from the Config.db menu.
3. dBASE IV asks you to confirm the directory that contains CONFIG.DB. Make sure that the home directory in which you installed dBASE IV is displayed, and press **Enter** to use the DBSETUP menu system.

The Printer menu lets you install Drivers or Fonts and to change the default printer. The Database menu and General menu let you change environment settings, some of which are similar to the environment settings covered in Chapters 9 and 12. The Display menu lets you set display options, like the Display menu covered in Chapter 9. The Keys menu lets you set the default values of function keys. The Files and Memory menus let you set system variables.

The options on these menus are usually self-explanatory if you are familiar with dBASE IV. For more details on them, see Chapter 2 of the book *Getting Started with dBASE IV*, which comes with your dBASE IV software.

As a sample of how DBSETUP works, you might want to make changes in the CONFIG.DB file to make dBASE IV look like dBASE III when you start it. If you miss the cryptic dBASE III dot prompt, you can alter CONFIG.DB as follows:

1. Select **Status** from the General menu to toggle it OFF so the status bar is not displayed.

2. Select **Command** from the General menu. Delete ASSIST, so this command is not running when you start the program. Instead, type *CLEAR* as the initial command, and press **Enter**.

3. Select **Save and exit** from the Exit menu. Press **Enter** to confirm the directory for the CONFIG.DB file and press **Enter** again to confirm that you want to overwrite the existing CONFIG.DB file.

4. Select **Exit** from the Exit menu to return to DOS. Type *DBASE /T* to start dBASE. Nothing but the dot prompt is displayed. Test dBASE IV if you want, and, when you are done, enter *QUIT* to return to DOS.

5. Enter *DBSETUP* at the DOS prompt, and when the program begins, select **Modify existing CONFIG.DB** from the Config.db menu once again, and press **Enter** to confirm the subdirectory. Select **Command** from the General menu. Delete CLEAR and enter *ASSIST* as the initial command once again. Also select **Status** to toggle the status bar on again. Then select **Save and exit** from the Exit menu. Press **Enter** twice to confirm the subdirectory and to overwrite the existing CONFIG.DB file. Then select **Exit** to return to DOS. Now, when dBASE IV starts, it displays the familiar Control Center once again.

Now that this exercise has familiarized you with DBSETUP, you might want to experiment with its other options. Before you do, you should make a back-up copy of your CONFIG.DB file. Use the DOS command COPY CONFIG.DB CONFIG.BAK. Now, you can always restore the original configuration by using the DOS command COPY CONFIG.BAK CONFIG.DB.

Index

Symbols

? <expr> 311, 362, 372
?? <expr> 311, 372
$ operator 113, 330, 332
$ template symbol 179
$ picture function 184
+ (arithmetic operator) 145, 328
+ (date operator) 130-131, 146, 327
+ (string operator) 88-89, 329-330
- (arithmetic operator) 145, 326
- (date operator) 130-131, 146, 327
- (string operator) 329-330
-> operator 359-360
( ) (arithmetic operator) 145, 326
* (arithmetic operator) 145, 326
** (arithmetic operator) 145, 326
*| NOTE 365
/ (arithmetic operator) 145, 326
^ (arithmetic operator) 145, 326
< (relational operator) 113-115, 330
<= (relational operator) 113-115, 330
<> (relational operator) 113-115, 330
= (assignment command) 316-317
= (relational operator) 113-115, 330
> (relational operator) 113-115, 330
>= (relational operator) 113-115, 330
(relational operator) 113-115, 330
&& 365

A

Abandon changes and exit (Exit menu) 45, 66, 159, 192, 214
ACCEPT 373-376
Accept value when (Edit Options menu) 221
Activate .NDX index file (Organize menu) 84
Add a group band (Bands menu) 170, 199-201, 204
Add condition box (Condition menu) 332
Add field (Fields menu) 155, 212
Add field to view (Fields menu) 104, 125
Add file to catalog (Catalog menu) 39
Add file to query (Layout menu) 104, 132
Add line (Words menu) 170, 245
Add new records (Records menu) 58
Advanced queries 144 et seq.
Advantages of indexing 83
Aggregate operators 148, 151, 186, 187
ALL scope 354
Altering the view skeleton 106, 109

AND queries 118
APPEND 343
APPEND BLANK 344
Append menu 79
    Append records from dBASE file 79
    Copy records from non-dBASE file 79
    Enter records from Keyboard 79
Append records from dBASE file (Append menu) 79
Append to Macro (Macros submenu) 259
Application definition form 231-233
Arithmetic operators 144-145, 187, 328
Arrow operator 359
ASCII 83, 84, 87, 93, 94, 126, 142, 189, 190, 245, 246, 252, 262, 296, 320, 321, 326, 327, 364, 415, 427, 446
ASCII ORDER 83, 84, 87, 126, 320, 326, 327
ASCII text (Destination submenu) 252
ASSIST 21-22
Automatic Indent 65-66, 245, 366
AVERAGE (aggregate operator) 148
AVG (aggregate operator) 148

B

Backward search (Go To menu) 99, 102, 241, 246, 247, 296
Bands menu 170-172, 194, 195, 199-201, 204, 211, 300
    Add a group band 170, 199-201, 204
    Begin band on new page 172, 175, 176
    Group intro on each page 200
    Open all bands 171
    Modify group 200
    Page heading in report intro 173
    Remove group 200
    Word wrap band 171, 176, 194, 195
BASIC 377
Begin band on new page (Bands menu) 172, 175, 176
Begin printing (Print menu) 137, 161, 165, 204, 249
Begin recording (Macros submenu) 258
Bell (Options menu) 270
Blank delimited 79, 262

Blank field (Fields menu) 76
Blank record (Records menu) 67
BROWSE 343
Browse screen 54-56

C

Calculated fields 144-146, 148, 155, 186-188, 301, 328
Carry (Options menu) 270
Carry forward (Edit Options menu) 221
Catalog menu 12, 17-20, 36-39, 41, 44, 66, 79, 94, 257, 284-285
    Add file to catalog 39
    Change description of highlighted file 41
    Modify catalog name 39
    Remove highlighted file from catalog 41, 94
    Use a different catalog 20, 36, 38, 39, 284
Catalogs 10, 19, 20, 27, 36, 38, 41, 66, 284
CDOW( ) 323
Century (Options menu) 271
Change description of highlighted file (Catalog menu) 41
Change drive:directory (Files menu) 264
Change hidden field (Fields menu) 189
Character data type 29
CHR( ) 414
CLEAR 311
Clear deletion mark (Records menu) 60
CLEAR GETS 400
CLOSE DATABASES 361, 367
Closing and opening Bands 171
CMONTH( ) 323
CNT (aggregate operator) 148
Column layout 167, 174, 175
Compilation errors 369
Condition box 115, 129, 332, 336
Condition menu 128-129, 332
    Add condition box 332
    Delete condition box 332
    Show condition box 332
CONFIG.DB 243, 312, 366, 447-449
Constants 314
CONTINUE 345

Control flow 363, 364, 374, 377, 378, 380, 384, 391, 433
Control of printer (Print menu) 138, 252-255
    New page 138
    Quality print 253-254
Controlling file 278, 283, 289, 291, 292, 304, 360, 361
Copy (Operations menu) 267
Copy records from non-dBASE file (Append menu) 79
COUNT (aggregate operator) 148
Create calculated field (Fields menu) 144, 146
Create link by pointing (Layout menu) 286, 287
Create new index (Organize menu) 86, 88
CREATE|MODIFY APPLICATION 347
CREATE|MODIFY LABEL 347
CREATE|MODIFY QUERY|VIEW 347
CREATE|MODIFY REPORT 347
CREATE|MODIFY SCREEN 347
Creating a database file 27 et seq.
Creating a new catalog 39 et seq.
CTOD( ) 322

D

Data entry forms 210 et seq.
Data normalization 277 et seq.
Data Types 28-29
Date (data type) 29
Date arithmetic 131, 329
Date order (Options menu) 270
Date separator (Options menu) 270
dBASE Expressions 82 et seq., 309 et seq.
DBF extension 30, 49
DBSETUP 252, 448, 449
Decimal places (Options menu) 271
Default value (Edit Options menu) 221
Defining the structure of a database file 42 et seq
DELETE 345
Delete condition box (Condition menu) 332
DELETE FILE 362
Deleted (Options menu) 271
Delimiters 111, 112, 130, 314, 315, 322, 372-374, 398, 403

Destination (Print menu) 251-252
Detail file 278, 283, 285, 289, 291, 298
Dimensions menu 153, 154, 162
Disadvantages of Indexing 83
DISPLAY 343
Display as (Display Attributes menu) 214, 222
Display Attributes Menu 155, 162, 167, 177, 180, 181, 183, 184, 185, 187-189, 196, 197, 210, 214-217, 222, 225, 227, 228, 298
    Display as 214, 222
    Suppress repeated values 185, 298
Display Attributes Menu for Calculated Fields 188
Display Attributes Menu for Summary Fields 187
DISPLAY MEMORY 371
Display menu 269, 272, 448
Display only (Files menu) 264, 266
DISPLAY STRUCTURE 342
Display submenu 272
DO 349
DO CASE ... ENDCASE 378, 382
DO WHILE loop 384-388, 400, 422, 438
DOS Menu 263, 264
    GO to DOS 264
    Perform DOS command 263
    Set default drive:directory 264
DOS shell 237, 262-269
DOW( ) 323
DTOC( ) 321, 322, 326
DTOS( ) 321, 322, 326

E

Edit database description (Layout menu) 43
Edit description of form (Layout menu) 211
Edit description of label design (Layout menu) 159
Edit description of query (Layout menu) 107
Edit description of report (Layout menu) 191
Edit field name (Fields menu) 126
Edit options menu 220
    Accept value when 221
    Carry forward 221
    Default value 221
    Editing allowed 220
    Largest allowed value 221

Message 221
Permit edit if 221
Smallest allowed value 221
Unaccepted message 221
Edit screen 54-56
Editing allowed (Edit options menu) 220
Editing keys 238-240
Editing memo fields 63, 238
Eject page now (Print menu) 249
Enable automatic indent (Words menu) 65, 245
End recording (Macros submenu) 258
Enter records from Keyboard (Append menu) 79
Environment commands 348, 349, 403, 416
Erase marked records (Organize menu) 60-61
EVERY operator 290
Exact (Options menu) 271
Exclusive (Options menu) 271
EXIT (DOS command) 264
EXIT 388-389
    Abandon changes and exit 45, 66, 159, 192, 214
    Save changes and exit 45, 48, 66, 159, 192
    Transfer to query design 61
Exiting from dBASE IV 23
Exponentiation 145-146, 328
Export (Tools menu) 260-262
Exporting data 261-262
Expression builder 336

F

Field (definition) 28
Field variables 313, 316, 392
Fields menu (of the Browse and Edit screens) 72 et seq. (of the Forms screen) 212-213 (of the Label screen) 155, 158 (of the Query screen) 125-127 (of the Report screen) 176, 188-189
    Add field 155, 212
    Add field to view 104, 125
    Blank field 76
    Change hidden field 189
    Create calculated field 144, 146
    Edit field name 126
    Freeze field 76
    Insert memory variable 212
    Lock fields on left 72-75
    Modify field 176, 212
    Remove field 158, 212
    Remove field from view 125
    Size fields 72
    Sort on this field 126, 140,
File skeleton (of the Query screen) 103-107, 109, 110, 112, 119, 121, 122, 125, 126, 130, 132, 140-142, 144, 148, 151, 161, 287, 289, 291, 294, 296
File skeleton (using DOS wild card characters) 264-268
Files Menu 264, 266
    Change drive:directory 264
    Display only 264, 266
Filter 98, 105, 122, 128, 133, 144, 151, 291, 356
Float data type 29, 144
Follow record to new position (Records menu) 59, 90
FOR clause 87, 92, 105, 333, 335, 336, 345, 354-357, 424, 438
Form layout 174, 175, 192
Format files 232, 361, 401, 403
Formatted input/output 364, 372, 374, 397, 398, 401
Forms design screen 210-212, 214, 224, 226, 228, 238, 243
Forward search (Go To menu) 99-101, 241, 246, 296
FOUND( ) 428, 432
Freeze field (Fields menu) 76
FRM 168, 196, 203, 435
Functions 318 et seq.

G

Generate sample labels (Print menu) 160
GO to DOS (DOS menu) 264
Go to line number (Go To menu) 246
Go To menu 43, 61, 76, 77, 98, 99, 101, 102, 122, 133, 160, 238, 241, 246-248, 296

Backward search 99, 102, 241, 246, 247, 296
Forward search 99-101, 241, 246, 296
Go to line number 246
Last record 76
Match capitalization 248
Record number 76
Skip 77-78
Top record 76
GO[TO] 345
GO[TO] BOTTOM 345
GO[TO] TOP 345
GROUP BY operator 151
Group intro on each page (Bands menu) 200
Group summaries 150
Grouping the records in reports 198 et seq.

H

Help menu 25
Help system 24-26
Help:F1 24
Hide ruler (Words menu) 245
History buffer 312

I

IF ... ELSE ... ENDIF 378, 380, 382
Import (Tools menu) 260-262
Importing data 260-262
Include .NDX index file (Organize menu) 84
Index expression 86-89, 91, 141, 327, 335, 336
Index key search 101-102
INDEX ON 347
Indexed search 99, 101, 102, 345, 350
Indexes 81 et seq., 357
Indexes with FOR clauses 87, 333-335, 355, 356
Indexing on multiple fields 88
INPUT 373-374
Insert memory variable (Fields menu) 212
Insert page break (Words menu) 245
Insert user-input break (Macros submenu) 259

Installing dBASE 445 et seq.
Instruct (Options menu) 271
Iteration 378

K

Key field 33, 276, 278, 281-283, 286, 289, 291, 304

L

Labels 152 et seq.
Largest allowed value (Edit options menu) 221
Last record (Go To menu) 76
Layout menu (of Database Design Screen) 43-45 (of Forms Screen) 211-212 (of Label Screen) 159 (of Query Screen) 104, 124-125 (of Report Screen) 169, 173, 189, 191
    Add file to query 104, 132
    Create link by pointing 286, 287
    Edit database description 43
    Edit description of form 211
    Edit description of label design 159
    Edit description of query 107
    Edit description of report 191
    Print database structure 45
    Quick layout 173-176, 211
    Save this database file structure 44, 52
    Save this label design 159
    Use different database 211
Length of page (Page Dimensions submenu) 138, 256
LIKE operator 116
Line numbers (Print menu) 249
LIST 343, 344, 352-359
Literals 313, 314
Load library (Macros submenu) 259
LOCATE FOR 345-346
Lock fields on left (Fields menu of Browse screen) 72-75
Lock record (Records menu) 59
Logical data type 29, 34

Logical operators 330-331
Look-up file 278, 281, 289, 304, 360
LOOP 384-389
Looping 378, 384, 408
LOWER( ) 319, 320, 376
LTRIM( ) 320, 321, 324-326, 329

M

Macros submenu 257-259
    Append to Macro 259
    Begin recording 258
    End recording 258
    Insert user-input break 259
    Load library 259
    Play 260
    Save library 259
Mailing labels 152 et seq.
Mailmerge layout 174-176, 192
Many-to-many relationship 279, 282, 301
Margin (Options menu) 271
Mark (Update menu) 130 et seq.
Mark all (Mark menu) 265, 266
Mark Menu 265-266
    Mark all 265, 266
    Reverse marks 265-266
    Unmark all 265, 266
Mark record for deletion (Records menu) 58, 60
MARKER (memo field display) 222
Match capitalization (Go To menu) 248
MAX (aggregate operator) 148
Memo data type 29
Memo width (Options menu) 271
Memory variables 316-318, 341, 371, 373, 376, 392, 393, 394
Menu bar 17
Message (Edit Options menu) 221
MIN (aggregate operator) 148
Modify catalog name (Catalog menu) 39
MODIFY COMMAND 348, 366
Modify existing index (Organize menu) 92
Modify field (Fields menu) 176, 212
Modify group (Bands menu) 200
Modify ruler (Words menu) 244

MODIFY STRUCTURE 342
Modifying the structure of a file 52
Modular program design 389
MONTH( ) 323
Move (Operations menu) 267-268

N

Nested groups 204
New page (Control of Printer submenu) 138
NEXT scope 351 et seq.
Normalizing data 277 et seq.
NOTE 365

O

Offset from left (Print Dimension submenu)
    137, 191, 198, 204, 256
One-to-many relationship 33, 277-282
One-to-one relationship 32, 275-277
Open all bands (Bands menu) 171
Operations Menu 267-268
    Copy 267
    Move 267-268
    Rename 267-268
Options menu 220, 269, 270, 331
    Bell 270
    Carry 270
    Century 271
    Date order 270
    Date separator 270
    Deleted 271
    Decimal places 271
    Exact 271
    Exclusive 271
    Instruct 271
    Margin 271
    Memo width 271
    Safety 271
    Talk 271
    Trap 271
OR queries 119, 136

Order records by index (Organize menu) 85, 89, 162
Organize menu 23, 45, 51, 59-61, 85, 86, 88-90, 92-94, 101, 102, 141, 162, 164, 203, 284
    Activate .NDX index file 84
    Create new index 86, 88
    Erase marked records 60-61
    Include .NDX index file 84
    Modify existing index 92
    Order records by index 85, 89, 162
    Remove unwanted index tag 92
    Unmark all records 61
Output options (Print menu) 255
Output options 255
Page dimensions 191, 198, 204, 256
Save settings to print form 250
Use print form 251
View labels on screen 160, 161, 165
View report on screen 137, 142, 198, 203
Printing filtered labels 161
Printing mailing labels in order 162
PRIVATE 392-393
PROCEDURE 391-395
Prompt box 14-15
Protect data (Tools menu) 269
PUBLIC 392-393
Pull-down menus 14

P

PACK 345
Page dimensions (Print menu) 191, 198, 204, 256
Page heading in report intro (Bands menu) 173
PARAMETERS 393-395
Pending GETs 400
Perform DOS command (DOS menu) 263
Perform the update (Update menu) 130-132
Permit edit if (Edit Options menu) 221
Picklists 20
Picture functions 176, 180-185
Play (Macros submenu) 260
Position submenu 244
Predefined fields (label screen) 155
Predefined fields (report screen) 186
Predefined label sizes 153
Predefined Size (Dimensions menu) 153-155
Print database structure (Layout menu) 45
Print forms 250-251
Print menu 137-139, 142, 143, 160, 161, 165, 172, 191, 198, 203, 204, 205, 237, 238, 248-251, 253-256, 273, 298, 300
    Begin printing 137, 161, 165, 204, 249
    Control of printer 138, 252-255
    Destination 251-252
    Eject page now 249
    Generate sample labels 160
    Line numbers 249

Q

QBE 104, 107, 265
Quality print (Control of Printer submenu) 253-254
Queries 102 et seq., 139 et seq., 287 et seq.
Queries combining AND and OR 121
Query by example 97
Query to join related files 286
Querying for a value in a memo field 333
Quick applications 231 et seq.
Quick layout (Layout menu—Forms) 211
Quick layout (Layout menu—Reports) 173-176
Quick reports using LIST 356
QUIT 362

R

READ 398-401
RECALL 345, 352
Record (definition) 28
Record number (Go To menu) 76
Records Menu 58-60, 71, 76, 90
    Add new records 58
    Blank record 67
    Clear deletion mark 60
    Follow record to new position 59, 90

Lock record 59
Mark record for deletion 58, 60
Undo change to record 58, 76
Relational databases 32-33, 275 et seq.
Relational operators 113, 328-330
Remove field (Fields menu) 158, 212
Remove field from view (Fields menu of Query screen) 125
Remove group (Bands menu) 200
Remove highlighted file from catalog (Catalog menu) 41, 94, 284
Remove line (Words menu) 171, 245
Remove unwanted index tag (Organize menu) 92
Rename (Operations menu) 267-268
Replace (Update menu) 130-131
Report Bands 169 et seq
REST (Scope) 351
RESUME 371
RETURN 390-391, 395-396
Reverse marks (Mark menu) 265-266
Run-time errors 369

S

Safety (Options menu) 271
Save changes and exit (Exit menu) 45, 48, 66, 159, 192, 214
Save library (Macros submenu) 259
Save settings to print form (Print menu) 250
Save this database file structure (Layout menu) 44, 52
Save this label design (Layout menu) 159
Scope of variables 392
SCR 211
SEEK 345, 346, 350, 355, 427, 428, 432
SELECT 359-361
Selection 378 et seq.
Sequence 377
SET ALTERNATE 351, 398
SET BELL 349, 414
SET CARRY 349
SET CENTURY 349
SET CONSOLE 349
SET DECIMALS 350

Set default drive:directory (DOS menu) 264
SET DELETED 411, 414, 427, 430, 431
SET DEVICE 398
SET DISPLAY 350, 448
SET ESCAPE OFF 372, 412
SET FILTER 356, 421, 423
SET FORMAT 348, 401, 402, 410, 426, 428, 429, 431, 433
SET FUNCTION 419
SET ORDER TO TAG 347, 355, 357, 358
SET PRINT 350, 398
SET PROCEDURE 391
SET RELATION 360, 370
SET SCOREBOARD 400, 401, 414
SET STATUS 223, 400, 401, 411, 414, 428, 429, 431, 433
SET VIEW TO 105, 348, 358
Setting margins and tabs 244
Show condition box (Condition menu) 332
Size fields (Fields menu of Browse screen) 72
Skip (Go To menu) 77-78
Smallest allowed value (Edit Options menu) 221
Sort Menu 265
Sort on this field (Fields menu of Query screen) 126, 140, 142, 296
SPACE( ) 398
Spacing of lines 172
Spaghetti code 377
Specify update operation (Update menu) 129-132
SQL 358, 448
Status bar 22-23, 60, 158, 193, 223, 341, 400, 411, 414, 419, 431, 448, 449
String concatenation 88-89, 329
Structure of a database (definition) 28
Structured programming 377 et seq.
Structured Query Language 358
Stub testing 416
Style submenu 242-243
Submenus—how to use 19
SUBSTR( ) 327, 328, 376
SUM (aggregate operator) 148
Summary fields 186-189, 200
Summary operators 187
Summary queries 148
Suppress repeated values (Display Attributes menu) 185, 298

T

Talk (Options menu) 271
Templates (Forms) 214-216
Templates (Labels) 156-158
Templates (Reports) 177 et seq.
TEXT ... ENDTEXT 372-373
Text pitch 138, 172, 253
TO FILE clause 342
TO PRINT clause 348, 424, 425, 438
Tools menu 17, 19, 22, 61, 180, 205, 237, 243, 257, 261, 262, 269, 273, 331, 348, 349
    Export 260-262
    Import 260-262
    Protect data 269
Top record (Go To menu) 76
Transfer to query design (Exit menu) 61
Trap (Options menu) 271
TRIM( ) 320, 321, 326

U

UDFs 397
Unaccepted message (Edit Options menu) 221
Undo change to record (Records menu) 58, 76
Unindexed search 78, 99, 116, 345, 354, 356
Unmark (Update menu) 130 et seq.
Unmark all (Mark menu) 265, 266
Unmark all records (Organize menu) 61
Update menu 79, 129-132
    Mark 130 et seq.
    Perform the update 130-132
    Replace 130-131
    Specify update operation 129-132
    Unmark 130 et seq.
UPPER( ) 380, 416, 427
Use a different catalog (Catalog menu) 20, 36, 38, 39, 284
Use different database file or view (Layout menu of Report screen) 211
Use print form (Print menu) 251
User-defined functions 395, 397

V

VAL( ) 324, 374
View labels on screen (Print menu) 160, 161, 165
View report on screen (Print menu) 137, 142, 198, 203, 249, 298, 300
View skeleton 103-107, 109, 110, 125, 129-132, 140-142, 144, 146, 147, 148, 161, 287, 302

W

WAIT 374-375
WHILE clauses 351, 354-356
Wildcard characters 100, 101, 113, 116, 264
WINDOW (Memo field display) 222-223
WITH operator 130
Word processor 63-66, 238-248
Word wrap band (Bands menu) 171, 176, 194, 195
Words menu 65, 160, 170, 171, 238, 241-245
    Add line 170, 245
    Enable automatic indent 65, 245
    Hide ruler 245
    Insert page break 245
    Modify ruler 244
    Remove line 171, 245
    Write/read text file 245
Write/read text file (Words menu) 245

Y

YEAR( ) 323

Z

ZAP 345
Zoom 37, 62, 106, 223

Notes
Control Y = Delete line in quick report layout